THE LATIN AMERICA READERS
Series edited by Robin Kirk and Orin Starn

THE ARGENTINA READER
Edited by Gabriela Nouzeilles and Graciela Montaldo

THE BRAZIL READER
Edited by Robert M. Levine and John J. Crocitti

THE COSTA RICA READER
Edited by Steven Palmer and Iván Molina

THE CUBA READER
Edited by Aviva Chomsky, Barry Carr, and Pamela Maria Smorkaloff

THE ECUADOR READER
Edited by Carlos de la Torre and Steve Striffler

THE GUATEMALA READER
Edited by Greg Grandin, Deborah T. Levenson, and Elizabeth Oglesby

THE MEXICO READER
Edited by Gilbert M. Joseph and Timothy J. Henderson

THE PARAGUAY READER
Edited by Peter Lambert and Andrew Nickson

THE PERU READER, 2ND EDITION
Edited by Orin Starn, Iván Degregori, and Robin Kirk

THE WORLD READERS
Series edited by Robin Kirk and Orin Starn

THE ALASKA NATIVE READER
Edited by Maria *Shaa Tláa* Williams

THE CZECH READER
Edited by Jan Bažant, Nina Bažantová, and Frances Starn

THE INDONESIA READER
Edited by Tineke Hellwig and Eric Tagliacozzo

THE RUSSIA READER
Edited by Adele Barker and Bruce Grant

THE SRI LANKA READER
Edited by John Clifford Holt

THE

PARAGUAY

READER

HISTORY, CULTURE, POLITICS

Peter Lambert and Andrew Nickson, eds.

DUKE UNIVERSITY PRESS   *Durham and London*   2013

© 2013 Duke University Press
All rights reserved
Printed in the United States of America on acid-free paper ∞
Typeset in Monotype Dante by BW&A Books, Inc.
Library of Congress Cataloging-in-Publication Data appear
on the last printed page of this book.

Contents

VII *What Does It Mean to Be Paraguayan?* 383

Illustrations

Acknowledgments

The production of a work as complex as the *Reader* has necessarily involved the help, encouragement, and support of many people. At the end of what has been a fascinating, enjoyable, and exhausting process we find ourselves greatly indebted to friends and colleagues alike.

We would like to thank our editors, Valerie Millholland and Miriam Angress, who have been supportive of this project from the moment we first approached Duke University Press right through to completion. We would also like to thank the various interns and others at Duke who have helped us throughout the process. Our special thanks go to the extremely efficient, patient, and ever-positive Vanessa Doriott Anderson, who was tireless in her support, especially in the laborious task of contacting authors and publishing houses for permissions, and Maura High, our outstanding copy editor. We could not have hoped for a more helpful publishing team.

We were also very fortunate to be able to count on the invaluable and generous support of two dear friends who played an integral role in the production of the *Reader*. In England, Nick Regan was an extraordinary proofreader with a great eye for detail and a masterly command of English that helped turn our often stilted translations into fluent and poetic texts, always finding the *mot juste*, however long it took. His knowledge of Paraguayan culture and language as well as his advice and suggestions were invaluable. In Paraguay, the journalist Andrea Machaín carried out the painstaking work of contacting authors and publishing houses in order to obtain copyright permissions. We could not imagine completing the *Reader* without the help of these two friends.

We would also like to thank all the living contributors who were so generous in offering their work for inclusion. It is remarkable that despite the economic recession, not one author requested payment for their work, not one refused our request to include extracts from their work, and many of them went beyond the call of duty in helping with the *Reader*. It was truly a pleasure to work with such esteemed writers. We would especially like to thank Alberto Yanosky of Guyrá Paraguay and Thomas Whigham of the

University of Georgia for having responded so positively to our requests for texts specially written for *The Paraguay Reader*.

Our friend Martin Romano in Paraguay has been an inexhaustible source of information—always replying immediately to our questions about historic documents, local copyright law, and graphic images. Like Martin, Jorge Rubiani, Javier Yubi, and Milda Rivarola have opened up their personal collections of historic images and postcards for viewing, for which we are most thankful.

We would also like to thank the following people. In Asunción: Martin Burt, director of the Fundación Paraguaya, Rogelio Cadogan, Roberto Céspedes at UNDP, María del Carmen Fleytas of the Fundación Bertoni, Roberto Villalba and Clyde Soto of the Centro de Documentación y Estudios, Rosa Palau, director of the Centro de Documentación y Archivo, Museo de la Justicia, Jorge Barraza, Carlos Salcedo Centurión, Margarita Morselli, director of the Centro Cultural de la República El Cabildo, and Raquel Zalazar at the Museo Etnográfico Andrés Barbero. Thanks also go to Benno Glauser of the Iniciativa Amotocodie in Filadelfia and Margaret Hebblethwaite in Santa María. We very much valued the advice of other friends in Paraguay including Ricardo Flecha, Techi Cusmanovich, José Rivarola, Mati Da Costa, and Carlos Carvallo.

In the United Kingdom we would like to thank Pauline Thorington-Jones of the University of Birmingham, Vania Vitillo of the University of Bath, and Joseph Nickson for their great help in scanning high-resolution images for us. Thanks also go to Robert Munro, Claudia Regan, Jeremy Howat, Ricardo Medina, and Hugh O'Shaughnessy, as well as Jimmy Cadogan in Australia. We would also like to thank the historian Thomas Whigham (again), who with his vast knowledge of Paraguayan history was a constant source of help and advice, and Will Fowler at the University of St. Andrews, who generously offered to read through the entire text and offered very useful suggestions, as well as providing much-needed encouragement at a critical time.

Finally we would of course like to thank our wives Yasmina and Carolina, who have supported (as well as *soportado*) us over the time it took to write the *Reader*. Peter would also like to thank his young children, Pablo, Khalil, and Felix, for putting up with a dad who kept disappearing into his office for far too long.

Introduction

Paraguay has long been seen as one of the forgotten corners of the globe, a land falling off our conscious map of the world, a place that slips beneath the radar of most diplomats, academics, journalists, and tourists in Latin America. Even backpackers, who may spend months in neighboring countries, rarely spend more than one reluctant night in transit in Asunción.

Part of the reason for this is that Paraguay is a country defined not so much by association as by isolation. It has been variously referred to as the Tibet of Latin America (in the nineteenth century it was called the "China of the Americas"), a mysterious place cut off from the rest of the continent. The renowned Paraguayan writer Augusto Roa Bastos famously remarked that Paraguay's landlocked isolation made it like an island surrounded by land. Indeed, hemmed in by the vast, arid Chaco to the west and impenetrable jungles to the east (at least until the 1960s), Paraguay's access to the outside world was limited to the River Paraná and the cooperation (or not) of Buenos Aires, for long the administrative and commercial center of the region, and a gateway to the sea. As a result, Paraguay is exceptional in the degree to which it has been defined by isolation and difference from its neighbors, from Latin America, and from the wider world. This isolation is epitomized by the resilience of Guaraní as the preferred language of the vast majority despite repeated official efforts to impose Spanish and the fact that the indigenous population is extremely small (under 2 percent). Indeed, even in colonial times, the Spanish simply gave up trying to impose their own language beyond official arenas, and instead adopted Guaraní.

Isolation is also related to internal communications. Paraguay is almost as large as France yet it has a population of only seven million. With most people living in urban areas, it is a very sparsely populated country, and one which has only been opened up (through massive deforestation) relatively recently. Nowhere is this clearer than in the countryside, where until only a few decades ago isolated communities seemed to lie adrift in the "oceans" of surrounding cattle land and forest, cut off from modernity.

It is also a land of contrasts. The Itaipú hydroelectric plant, jointly owned by Paraguay and Brazil, is the world's largest, with an installed capacity of

Map of Paraguay. By Bill Nelson.

14,000 megawatts, generating around 90 million megawatt hours of electricity, yet Paraguay still has no heavy industry to speak of. The shopping malls and mansions of parts of Asunción would not be out of place in the richest suburbs of the developed world, but are often just a few blocks away from shacks, reflecting Paraguay's huge inequality in wealth, land, and power. Authoritarianism has been the political norm since independence, yet Paraguay has a rich history of people's struggle for social justice. It is the fourth largest exporter of soy (and home to infamous "green deserts" of agroindustrial, highly mechanized production), yet the majority of farmers use traditional subsistence techniques on tiny plots of land. In many towns gleaming four-wheel-drive vehicles still compete at the traffic lights with horses and ox-pulled carts.

Yet Paraguay is also a nation in transition. While it may be true that no other Latin American country has managed to slip under the international radar, and avoid the spotlight of media attention and planeloads of tourists quite as effectively as Paraguay, the image of a quaint country stuck in a time warp is unlikely to last for much longer. Paraguay is developing and globalizing fast. It is a major exporter of electricity, soy, and beef; its economy grew by 14 percent in 2010, the second fastest in the world; and it has one of the world's largest deposits of titanium, recently discovered in the northeast of the country. Asunción is waking up from its long siesta to the pressures of a rapidly growing population, the choking smell of fumes from seemingly unending traffic jams, and the fear of crime around every corner. In the east, new vibrant cities are emerging, buoyed by commercial agriculture, as well as drug trafficking and contraband. Over half a million Brazilians now live in Paraguay, mostly working in (and often controlling) lucrative agricultural projects, and representing a powerful political force. The deafening whine of locally produced Chinese mopeds has replaced the sound of crickets in most town squares, mobile phones exceed the number of citizens, and supermarkets are rapidly replacing tiny family *despensas*. Membership of Mercosur, a regional economic bloc set up in 1991 with Argentina, Brazil, and Uruguay, has helped drag Paraguay into the globalized world of trade and customs agreements to the disquiet of traditional *contrabandistas*. Even the military seems to have been caught a little off guard and since 1989 have largely retired from politics back to their barracks.

However, this long, historical isolation (geographical, cultural, and political) has meant that Paraguay has been largely neglected by historians, journalists, and travel writers, leading to a dearth of serious writing on its history, politics, society, and culture. This has led to considerable misunderstanding of the country based on lack of knowledge. Ignorance has allowed Paraguay to become a perfect blank space for others' writing and imaginings, where nothing seems too far-fetched, where exaggeration and imagination may go unchallenged. For centuries Paraguay has been exploited by writers of popular history, fiction, travel, and lifestyle—writers who have fallen into the trap of merely applying or repeating stereotypical images, ideas, and perceptions. Viewing Paraguay with a mix of suspicion, humor, fondness, and disdain, they have too often glided over complex issues of culture and politics, replacing them with tired references to either crazy wars, endemic corruption, Nazi war criminals, and savage natives or tin-pot dictators and brutal tyrants. In Graham Greene's *Travels with My Aunt*, Paraguay is the moral end of the line, the orange-blossom-scented paradise where the opposition is routinely "disappeared," where smuggling is a national industry, where corruption is rife, and where generals rule with an iron fist. Paul Mazorsky's film *Moon over Parador* perpetuated the myth of the nation defined by corruption and dictatorship, as did Robert Carver's recent foray into cliché and myth in *Paradise with Serpents*. Paraguay becomes a dystopia, a land corrupted by man's most base instincts.

In the midst of all this, Paraguay has become a byword for a strange, exotic land, falling off the edge of our mental maps of the world—Latin America's answer to Timbuktu. Repeatedly presented as an isolated and underdeveloped cultural backwater, a dangerous but attractive land where magical realism and reality seem to collide, it is often portrayed as the epitome of exoticism, peculiarity, and exceptionalism, in a self-perpetuating circle of myth and stereotype. Indeed, whether by ignorance or design, myth and cliché have managed to replace reality in much of the reporting and travel writing on the country. Such an image is insidious because it conveniently overlooks and ignores (and even eradicates) the less sensationalist reality of a country struggling against underdevelopment, foreign intervention, poverty, inequality, and authoritarianism, of individual and collective struggles for social justice against enormous odds, and of a nation that has developed a rich, diverse, and fascinating cultural heritage.

It is also an image that is difficult to shake off, as the national soccer team has experienced. Despite having appeared in four consecutive World Cup finals between 1998 and 2010 and being ranked among the top ten national teams in recent years by FIFA, the Fédération Internationale de Football Association, Paraguay is still seen as a surprise package, a small plucky nation somewhat out of its depth against international opposition, more akin to Jamaica, Slovakia, or Tunisia than to the "greats" alongside it in the rankings. Such invisibility is not limited to soccer, but is apparent in far more important arenas, such as trade, investment, tourism, diplomacy, and politics, with damaging results.

It is true that some of these stereotypes are rooted in history. Paraguay does have a history of authoritarian rule, from the nineteenth-century nationalist dictators to the infamous General Alfredo Stroessner, who, when he was overthrown in 1989, was the longest-ruling tyrant in Latin America (and almost the world). When Fernando Lugo won the presidential elections in 2008, it was the first time that power had peacefully changed hands between parties in Paraguayan history. Levels of corruption have indeed been significant, from the days of General Stroessner, who defined it as the "price of peace," to 2002, when Paraguay came 129th out of 132 countries in Transparency International's Corruption Perceptions Index and the then president (Luís González Macchi) was found to possess a stolen BMW. Paraguay has indeed provided refuge for an array of dictators (Nicaragua's Anastasio Somoza, for example), Nazi war criminals (Josef Mengele, the "Doctor of Death" at Auschwitz, and Eduard Roschmann, the "Butcher of Riga"), and international fraudsters. These factors are undeniable elements of Paraguayan history, but a historian could easily focus on such elements to categorize or ridicule any other country; reality is more complex and less damning.

Yet this image of Paraguay exists alongside another myth—that of the *Lost Paradise*, the *Vanished Arcadia* (to quote just two book titles on Paraguay). For centuries the country has been regarded as a potential utopia, a land where anything is possible, a land simply waiting to be turned into a tropical paradise; the "land without evil" as Guaraní mythology terms it. From the writings of the Jesuits to the epic poem *A Tale of Paraguay* published in 1825 by the English poet laureate Robert Southey, to Roland Joffe's 1986 film *The Mission*, Paraguay is portrayed as an unspoiled land, a preindustrial utopia, a blank canvas for the creation of paradise on earth.

This may not have been altogether true—the arid Chaco desert in the west provided little opportunity for settlement until the resilient Mennonites began to settle there in the 1920s—but the lure of Paraguay has remained constant. For centuries foreigners have viewed the country through their own ideological and religious gaze, often seeking to create their own utopias over existing realities. When combined with the fact that Paraguay has long been seen as an underpopulated refuge, a land for new beginnings and endless opportunity, it is easy to explain the waves of immigration over the past 150 years. Despite, or perhaps because of, its isolation, Paraguay has been a melting pot of immigrants; Spanish, Italian, German, Balkan, Middle Eastern, black African, Russian, Japanese, Korean, South African, Latin American (the list goes on) have all mixed in Paraguay, leaving a distinct impression on language, food, music, and culture in general. Some have sought to retain their identity, most notably the Mennonites, and the former escaped slaves at Cambá Cué near Asunción, but most have been assimilated into the *teko*, the Paraguayan way of life.

Isolation has also led the country to suffer a number of unique experiments throughout its history. The Spanish soon realized that Paraguay was not El Dorado, nor did it provide a viable route to the riches of the Andes; rather, it offered a relatively safe and comfortable location for settlement. The Spanish settlers took advantage of less hostile, friendly (or simply terrified) local indigenous peoples to create a colony based initially on the concept of family ties (harems in exchange for peace) rather than genocide, giving rise to an allegedly more cohesive population. The Jesuits created an empire within an empire through their *reducciones* or settlements, in which Guaraníes were organized into productive communities, indoctrinated into Catholicism, but protected from marauding Brazilian slave traders. When independence came in 1811, Dr. José Gaspar Rodríguez de Francia sought to avoid the anarchy and chaos of other newly independent Latin American states by establishing a dictatorship that destroyed the power of the Spanish elites (he forbade marriage between whites), the church, and the landowning class. This experiment was developed by his successor Carlos Antonio López (1840–62), the "Great Builder of the Nation" who oversaw Paraguay's emergence as an important regional power, complete with railway, telegraph lines, a shipyard, and an iron foundry. And throughout the late nineteenth and early twentieth century, thousands of migrants ventured into the interior of the country, seeking to create their own experiments in taming the land and establishing new communities, based on nationality, religion, ideology, or simply to begin anew.

Paraguayan history also reflects a strong element of tragedy, or idealism betrayed or at least corrupted. The Spanish conquerors soon resorted to traditional forms of repression to dominate their indigenous "family"; the Jesuits were expelled in 1767 and the "reductions" fell into ruin while their inhabitants were either enslaved by landowners who had long resented the Jesuits or fled into the forests. Francia became a feared tyrant who imprisoned his opponents (and erstwhile friends), while Francisco Solano López, the son of Carlos, led Paraguay into the catastrophe of the Triple Alliance War (1864–70) in which the destruction wrought by the allied forces of Brazil, Argentina, and Uruguay brought a dramatic end to Paraguay's state-led development.

The following eighty years were defined by political conflict, authoritarianism, and instability as Paraguay struggled to recover from defeat. Indeed, when Stroessner took power in 1954 he was the thirty-fifth president in fifty-four years. The period also contained another major international war, this time against Bolivia over the disputed Chaco region (1932–35). Paraguay gained in terms of territory (inhospitable, desolate, and arid as the "Green Hell" may have been) but lost some thirty to forty thousand lives in the process, many of them from thirst. Scarcely recovered, the country fell into a brutal civil war (1947) and then, seven years later, into the dictatorship of Alfredo Stroessner. Stroessner continued Paraguay's isolationist stance, while cashing in on U.S. support for anticommunist allies during the Cold War and crushing his "subversive" opponents in the name of the defense of

Western civilization. Together with his cronies, he ruled Paraguay harshly, thinly concealed beneath a veneer of democracy, of "peace, progress, and work," as his own propaganda maintained.

Even the transition to democracy rapidly became tainted. Led by Stroessner's former military strongman, General Andrés Rodríguez, who deposed Stroessner in a military putsch in 1989, the transition introduced a new constitution, free elections, and civil liberties, but ensured a strong dose of continuity. The Colorado Party, the mainstay of the Stroessner dictatorship, continued to win elections throughout the next two decades, despite the growth of corruption, poverty, and inequality, economic mismanagement and stagnation, crisis and political infighting. Only in 2008 did the opposition candidate, the former bishop Fernando Lugo, manage to end over sixty years of Colorado rule and usher in his aptly titled "new dawn" for Paraguay. Unfortunately, even the new dawn fell short of popular expectation because the new president, not helped by his admissions of having fathered various illegitimate children, was unable to push through much-needed reforms.

However, beyond this stereotypical image of an exotic mix of paradise lost, of tragedy and former grandeur, of a forgotten land of magical realism, where anything seems possible, Paraguay holds an unrelenting fascination for those who have the honor and pleasure of getting to know it. The rhythms of *guaranias* and polkas, the poetry of the Guaraní language, the scent of jasmine and orange blossom, the music of the crickets, the red color of the earth, the extensive unbroken landscapes, and the measured pace of life are emotional ties that continue to draw and enchant visitors. Both of the editors found their initial short visits extend into years and then into a lifetime relationship. With that relationship came the discovery, as this book aims to show, of an extraordinarily rich history and cultural heritage.

Our aim in writing *The Paraguay Reader* has been to produce an enjoyable, informative, and well-structured anthology of writings on the politics, society, and culture of the country. We have sought to include texts that will be accessible to a wide and varied readership but that are analytical and significant in their own right. Throughout we have contextualized the extracts, many of which are abridged, by using explanatory (and hopefully engaging) introductions. In the broader sense, we have striven to produce a body of work that would include the best writing on what we feel are the key issues, events, and trends in Paraguayan history. Over the course of nearly two years we consulted, debated, argued, and agonized over what texts to include and what not to include—whether we should prioritize depth or breadth of coverage, the aesthetic or the practical, complexity or simplicity of analysis. We would not claim to have always reached the right decision and accept the inevitable criticisms of aspects that we have left out or overlooked. However, we have painstakingly gone through every source that we have found or been guided toward in order to judge whether or not we should include it. The result is a final book that fulfills our initial aims and that we feel is a worthy tribute to the wealth of writing on Paraguay.

The *Reader* is divided into seven sections that cover issues of politics, society, and culture. Six sections are chronological, from the first, "The Birth of Paraguay," to the sixth, "A Transition in Search of Democracy." The sections vary in length, since we wished to give a more contemporary emphasis to the volume. Hence we have tried to create a balance, giving major historical events (such as the Triple Alliance War and the Chaco War) due attention, but at the same time expanding the more contemporary sections. The final section, "What Does It Mean to Be Paraguayan?," examines key issues surrounding identity—ranging from national identity and cultural characteristics to ethnicity, language, and gender. We felt this section was essential, in that it provides an insight into the multiple expressions and dimensions of ever-changing identities in Paraguay, which in turn are essential for a deeper understanding of the country's history, culture, and society. The special focus of this section also allowed us to group together fascinating extracts that would have been misplaced or lost in the chronological sections.

Wherever possible we have tried to include "voices from below" or at least contemporary accounts by Paraguayans, thereby giving priority to how ordinary people saw and experienced major events. This decision did, however, pose a specific problem in the case of Paraguay, primarily for reasons of language. Historically the majority of the population, and especially rural and poorer sectors, have expressed themselves in Guaraní rather than Spanish. Guaraní is an oral language (even today very few people write in Guaraní) and this fact, combined with low levels of literacy and education, has resulted in a lack of written historical testimonies and memoirs "from below" in comparison with many other Latin American countries.

Related to and partly as a consequence of the above, the most revealing, interesting, and engaging observations are often found in the writings of foreign travelers and residents. We have therefore included a number of pieces written by foreigners, but in all cases the criterion used for their selection is that they are the best piece of writing available on a specific theme.

Wherever possible we have also tried to use voices from the period under consideration. However, again, suitable extracts have often been difficult to find, and thus in some cases we have opted for more recent analyses, by outstanding historians, who we feel deserve a place in the book. Thus, we have included writings by, for example, Branislava Susnik, R. B. Cunninghame Graham, Harris Gaylord Warren, Ignacio Telesca, and Thomas Whigham because we felt they were the clearest, most analytical, and objective writings available. However, in general, we opted against most of the (dozens of) academic books that we ploughed through on the grounds that they were not sufficiently accessible, or that they lacked the concise analysis we required, or because we found an alternative piece that was more from the period itself or "from below."

Most of the texts that we selected are being published in English for the first time. We translated them ourselves but used the services of a professional proofreader who offered the advantage of having lived in Paraguay for many years and who is also very knowledgeable about Paraguayan history, politics, and culture. As a result we believe the translations are of a very high quality, not only in terms of grammatical and linguistic accuracy, but also in terms of style, fluency, and "voice." Such is the high standard of the end product that many of them sound, at least to us, not only authentic but also as if they had originally been written in English.

We are particularly proud of some of the texts that have not been previously published in any language or which carry particular significance in the *Reader*. For example "Lincolnshire Farmers," "How Beautiful Is Your Voice," and "The Psychology of López" are all published here for the first time, while "The Sufferings of a French Lady" was published just once in Buenos Aires in 1870 and is hardly known. The English translation of "The Foundation of Human Speech" was written by León Cadogan himself for a distant cousin, and we publish it here for the first time. Many other texts are simply off the radar of mainstream publishing and academic libraries.

We took the decision early on to use the introductions to each extract in order to contextualize the piece, fill in any presumed gaps in the knowledge of the reader, and highlight its importance, uniqueness, or significance. The result is that the introductions may be a little long in some cases, but this ensures that each extract stands on its own feet, allowing the reader to dip into the book as he or she pleases and to gain a more complete understanding of the text.

We have tried to be as eclectic as possible in terms of the tone, style, and nature of the extracts we have chosen. Hence we have included examples of testimonies, light-hearted journalistic pieces, academic analyses, political tracts, poetry and song, literature, and even a recipe. At the same time we have also tried to cover all major historical events, sectors, and issues—although we are painfully aware that there will be some inevitable gaps.

As we have discovered, and despite our best efforts, it is of course impossible to reflect Paraguayan history, society, and culture in a single volume. What we have therefore tried to do is to give the reader a multifaceted insight into the country through a number of different political, historical, cultural, and social lenses. By varying the kinds of texts included we believe that the *Reader* will be able to engage a very broad readership; it should prove fascinating for academics researching or writing on Paraguay (we certainly learned a huge amount ourselves about the country in the process of editing this manuscript); it serves as a very useful point of reference for students of Latin America; and it is sufficiently accessible to be of interest to those simply interested in Paraguay, whether active travelers, armchair adventurers, or prospective visitors. Hopefully, if nothing else, it will stimulate interest to find out more by following our suggestions for further reading.

As we noted at the beginning of this introduction, Paraguay has long been represented as a blank canvas or as a backdrop for the location of utopias, dreams, and even dystopias. This has necessarily led to an ignoring of Paraguayan history and the silencing of Paraguayan voices. Given this, we hope that *The Paraguay Reader* will make a small contribution to our collective knowledge and understanding of this fascinating country, its people, and culture. We hope that, in so doing, it will help dispel the many myths about the country, and that it will strike a small blow for people's history over fantasy, cliché, and stereotype.

I

The Birth of Paraguay

The first *conquistadores* to enter what is now Paraguay came in search of gold: Aleixo García traveled overland from the Atlantic coast of Brazil in 1524 en route to upper Peru in present-day Bolivia and, in 1528, Sebastian Cabot sailed up the River Paraguay as far as present-day Paraguay. False accounts of the mineral wealth of Paraguay arose because some local *caciques* possessed gold, which came from their intermittent trade with the Incas beyond the Chaco. The first expedition up the River Paraguay to establish settlements in Paraguay was consequently motivated by the mistaken belief that Paraguay was the famed El Dorado. On August 15, 1537, Asunción was founded by Juan de Salazar y Espinoza, and in 1541, when their initial settlement at Buenos Aires was abandoned in the face of attacks from hostile Pampa Indians, the Spaniards sought refuge in Asunción.

For the next fifty years the town became the headquarters of the Spanish conquest of the southern half of South America, as well as a strategic outpost for repelling Portuguese expansion westward by *bandeirantes* (marauding gangs in search of slaves) from Brazil. As the starting-off point for expeditions to create eight new settlements, Asunción became known as the *madre de ciudades* (mother of cities). When in 1549, the fruitless Chaco expedition of Domingo Martínez de Irala returned to Asunción with the news that upper Peru had been conquered from the Pacific, it became clear that Asunción would not be the gateway to the silver mines of Potosí or El Dorado. In 1617 a royal decree separated Buenos Aires from the province of Paraguay, after which Asunción declined in importance as the colonial administration was transferred to Buenos Aires. With no gold or silver mines to attract further immigration from Spain, and with no outlet to the sea, Paraguay became an economic backwater and remained isolated and weakly integrated into the world economy throughout the rest of the colonial period.

Henceforth, the indigenous peoples of Paraguay soon became the primary resource to be exploited by the relatively few conquistadores who remained in the province, especially after 1615, when growing attacks by bandeirantes forced the colonial authorities to divert human resources to the military defense of the province. From 1600 Indians were principally used for the production of yerba mate (Paraguayan tea), which soon became the major export throughout the colonial period. To this end, two radically different means of institutionalizing control over the indigenous peoples were employed, which ultimately came into conflict: that of the *encomienda* system of tribute in the form of forced labor, and that practiced by the Jesuit missions. The introduction of the encomienda system led to a radical change in the relationship between the Spanish and the indigenous people, as alliance and friendship were replaced by exploitation. The *pacto de sangre* that produced the predominantly mestizo population, which resulted from miscegenation between the Spanish and indigenous peoples, was achieved through *rancheadas*, the violent abduction of Indian women whom the conquistadores used as concubines, keeping as many as fifty each. There were eighteen major rebellions in opposition to the rancheadas and the encomienda, from the uprising of Jueves Santo in 1539 to the repression at Arecayá in 1660, generally led by spiritual leaders called the Ñande Ru, who sought a return to the precolonial integrity of Guaraní culture that had been shattered by the conquest.

In the early seventeenth century, foreign Jesuits began to evangelize the Guaranís of eastern Paraguay, many of whom had fled from the area around Asunción after the Spanish conquest. They established autocratic but self-sufficient economic units in thirty fortified settlements, called *reducciones*, which reached a population of over 200,000. Political tensions arose between the *encomenderos* (rural landowners) and the Jesuits over the appropriation of Guaraní labor for the production of yerba mate. This tension erupted in armed conflict in 1649–50 during the governorship of Bernardo de Cárdenas and more seriously, in the Comuneros rebellion (1721–35) led by the mestizo elite against what they saw as Spanish support for the privileges of the Jesuits. Although the leaders of the rebellion were executed, their objectives were eventually achieved in 1767, when the Jesuits were expelled from Paraguay and the rest of Latin America.

The seventeenth century was a period of territorial retrenchment and demographic stagnation for the province of Paraguay, and there was virtually no further European immigration during the century. Constant attacks by Chaco Indians and bandeirantes gradually whittled down the effective size of the colony, which by 1676, had been reduced to the area of the present-day metropolitan area of Asunción and the largely self-contained Jesuit missions in the southeast of the province.

The eighteenth century was a period of gradual territorial and demographic growth, assisted by the process of *mestizaje* (miscegenation) and the extinguishing of the encomienda system. With the introduction of cattle ranching, forestry and tobacco, the period also saw the gradual diversification of the provincial economy away from extreme dependence on yerba mate, and the beginnings of economic growth. In 1776, nominal control over Paraguay passed from Lima to the newly created Viceroyalty of the River Plate. The Bourbon Reforms introduced by King Carlos III had a significant impact on Paraguay, relaxing trade restrictions, and integrating Paraguay more closely into the regional economy of the River Plate. Foreign trade rose rapidly as commercial traffic on the River Paraguay increased substantially. This acceleration of economic activity encouraged the immigration of foreign merchants from the 1780s, who soon challenged the political and social hegemony of the traditional encomendero elite and gained a foothold in the Cabildo (municipal council) de Asunción, thereby contributing to the growing independence movement. After three centuries of external control and geographical isolation, a strong basis for a nationalist sentiment had been created in Paraguay, as the Spanish Empire began to collapse at the beginning of the nineteenth century.

The Foundation of Human Speech

Transcribed by León Cadogan

Language is central to the indigenous culture of the Guaraní and is reflected in the strong oral tradition of contemporary Paraguay. This is exemplified by the following opening passage of the greatest text of Guaraní literature, the classic sacred chant and creation story of the Mbya-Guaraní, Ayvu Rapyta (The foundation of human speech).[1] The story was first recorded and translated into Spanish in 1949 by Paraguay's foremost anthropologist, León Cadogan (1899–1973), the son of Australian colonists to the Nueva Australia socialist community. Cadogan grew up near Villarrica, speaking English and Guaraní, and dedicated his life to the study and defense of the rights of indigenous peoples. The text shows how the very identity of the Mbya-Guaraní depends on a shared language, a willingness to love each other, and adherence to a common religion. So important is language to identity that without a name, a human being ceases to be considered as such. We present Cadogan's own translation into English of the first two chapters of Ayvu Rapyta, which he undertook in 1966 for his cousin, Lillian Williams, in Australia. They are published here for the first time, along with the original notes.

Chapter One: The Habits of the Primeval Hummingbird

1

Our first father, the absolute one,
Emerged amidst
Primeval darkness.

2

He created the divine soles of his foot,
The little round seat[2]
In the midst of primeval darkness,
In the course of his evolution.

3

The mirror of his divine wisdom (organ of sight),
The divine hear-it-all (organ of hearing),
The divine palms of his hands and the wand (emblem of power),
The divine palms of his hands with the flowering branches,
Ñamanduï created them all in the course of his evolution,
In the midst of primeval darkness.

4

The flowers which adorned the divine feather headdress[3]
Were dewdrops.
Amidst the flowers of the divine headdress,
The primeval bird fluttered,
The hummingbird.

5

While our first father was creating, In the course of his evolution,
His divine body,
He lived amidst the primeval winds,

Before having conceived his future earthly abode,
Before having conceived his future heavens
His future earth
Which first appeared
The hummingbird refreshed his mouth:
He who sustained Ñamanduï with products of paradise,
Was the hummingbird.

6

Before our true father, the first one,
Had created his first heaven,
In the course of his evolution,
He did not know darkness;
Although the sun did not as yet exist,
The reflection of the wisdom of his own heart
Illuminated him,
He caused the wisdom contained
Within his own divinity
To serve him as a sun.

7

The true father Ñamandu, the first one,
Lived amidst the primeval winds.

Wherever he stopped to rest,
The owl produced a shadow,
And thus caused foreknowledge of night
To be perceived.

8

Before the true father Ñamandu,
The first one,
Had created his future paradise
In the course of his evolution,
Before he had created the first earth,[4]
He lived amidst the primeval winds.

The original wind amidst which
Our father first lived is reached,
Every time that the primeval time-space (winter)
Is reached

As soon as the primeval time-space ends,
Announced by the blossoming of the lapacho tree,[5]
The winds shift to the new time-space;

New winds arise, space-time is renewed,

And the resurrection of time-space
Takes place (spring arrives).

Chapter Two: The Foundation of Human Speech

1

The true father Ñamandu, the first one,
Out of a small portion of his own godliness,
And out of the wisdom contained in his
Own godliness,
Caused flames and tenuous mist to
Be begotten.

2

Having emerged in human form,
Out of the wisdom contained in his own godliness,
And by virtue of his creative wisdom
He conceived the foundation of human speech.
Out of the wisdom contained within his own godliness,

And by virtue of his creative wisdom
Our father created the foundation of human speech,
And caused it to form part of his own godliness.
Before the earth existed,
In the midst of primeval darkness,
Before there was knowledge of things,
He created the foundation of future human speech,
And the first true father Ñamandu
Caused it to form part of his own divinity.

3

Having conceived the origin of future human speech,
Out of the wisdom contained within his own godliness,
And by virtue of his creative wisdom
He conceived the foundation of love of one's fellow men.
Before the earth existed,
In the midst of primeval darkness,
Before there was knowledge of things,
And by virtue of his creative power
He conceived the foundation of love of one's fellow men.

4

Having created the foundations of human speech,
Having created a small portion of love,
Out of the wisdom contained within his own godliness
And by virtue of his creative wisdom
He created, in his solitude,
The beginning of a sacred hymn.
Before the earth existed,
In the midst of primeval darkness,
Before there was knowledge of things
He created, in his solitude,
The beginning of a sacred hymn.

5

Having created, in his solitude, the origin of human speech;
Having created, in his solitude, a small portion of love,
Having created, in his solitude, a short sacred hymn,
He pondered deeply
About sharing the origin of human speech,
About sharing the words of the sacred hymn,
About sharing the love for one's fellow men.

Having pondered deeply,
Out of the wisdom contained within his own godliness,
And by virtue of his own creative wisdom,
He created those who could share his godliness.

6

Having pondered deeply,
Out of the wisdom contained within his own divinity
And by virtue of his creative power,
He created the brave-hearted Ñamandu;[6]
He created him simultaneously with the reflection of his wisdom
   (the sun).

Before the earth existed,
In the midst of primeval darkness,
He created the brave-hearted Ñamandu.
For the father of his future numerous sons,
For the true father of the word-souls of his future numerous sons
He created the brave-hearted Ñamandu.

7

Following these things,
Out of the wisdom contained within his own divinity
And by virtue of his own creating power,
To the true father of the future Karaí,[7]
To the true father of the future Jakairá,[8]
To the true father of the future Tupá[9]
He granted knowledge of godliness.

8

Following these things,
The true father Ñamandu
To seat herself opposite his own heart,
Imparted knowledge of godliness
To the future true mother Ñamandu.

The true father Karaí
Granted knowledge of godliness
To whom would seat herself opposite his heart,
To the true future mother Karaí.

The true father Jakairá, in the same manner,
Imparted knowledge of godliness
To the true mother Jakairá.

The true father Tupá, in the same manner,
To whom would seat herself opposite his heart,
Imparted knowledge of godliness,
To the true future mother Tupá.

9

For having assimilated
Divine knowledge from their own
True father,
After having assimilated
Human speech,
After having inspired in love
Of one's fellowmen,
After having assimilated the series of
Words of the sacred hymn,
After having inspired themselves
In the foundation of creative wisdom;
We call these, also,
The sublime true fathers of
The word-soul,[10]
The sublime true mothers of
The word-soul.

Notes

1. The hummingbird named in the title of the opening section is considered a messenger of the gods by the tribal shaman.
2. Apyka (little round seat) is a symbol of the incarnation in Guaraní mythology.
3. A feather headdress is an emblem of manhood or masculinity.
4. The first earth was later destroyed by the Flood and replaced by the present world.
5. The blossoming of the lapacho announces the end of winter and coming of spring.
6. The brave-hearted Ñamandu is god of the sun.
7. Karaí is the god of fire.
8. Jakairá is the god of medical lore and sorcerers.
9. Tupá is the god of thunder, rain, and water.
10. "Word" and "soul" are synonymous in Guaraní.

Contact, Servitude, and Resistance

Branislava Susnik

Relations between the Spanish and the Guaraní evolved rapidly over the first fifty years of contact. Initially, relations were based on mutual benefit and cemented through kinship ties that for the Guaraní at least, were binding. Second came a series of Guaraní rebellions, provoked by perceptions of violation of kinship codes and the gradual demographic decline of Guaraní communities. Once these rebellions had been put down, relations based on kinship were replaced by violent coercion and owner-servant relations, leading to the great pan-Guaraní revolt of 1546, a final and unsuccessful effort to rid their lands of the Spanish. Only in 1551 was the colonial encomienda *system imposed.*

Branislava Susnik (1920–96), Paraguay's foremost anthropologist and the director of the Museo Etnográfico "Andrés Barbero," was one of the most important writers on the relationship between the Guaraní and the Spanish. Her studies dispel the myth of the peaceful encounter and coexistence of the two cultures and argue that while mutual benefit might have characterized initial relations, this state of affairs was soon replaced by the destruction of the Guaraní through both mestizaje *and violent repression and persecution.*

The First Hispano-Guaraní Contact

The Guaraní found themselves in an atmosphere of insecurity due to the permanent threat from the Guaicurú and the Payaguaes on the River Paraguay. In addition, interethnic relations were strained, with frequent struggles among the Guaraní themselves.

According to a census carried out by Irala, there were only about four hundred Spanish settlers before the arrival of Alvar Núñez de Cabeza, all of them male, with not a single female settler among them. The Guaraní witnessed the arrival of the four hundred Spanish men; they saw the horsemen, the arquebuses, and the metal, and to them everything seemed absolutely novel and magical. They accepted it because it was new but also because behind it they saw the power of magic.

The Chamacoco people of the northeastern Chaco belong to the Zamuco linguistic family. This photograph, taken in Puerto Diana in 1956, shows members of the Grupo Anabsónico "Wu'o" performing a ritual dance to exorcise demons and using rattles for music. The actors wear masks, paint their bodies according to complex symbolic codes, and don exquisite feather decorations. Photograph by Branislava Susnik. From the collection of the Museo Etnográfico Andrés Barbero, Asunción.

This conceptualization of the arrival of the Spanish as magical is important and explains why the Guaraní immediately gave the first Spanish arrivals the name of *karaí*, which is derived from the name of *karaíva*, which the ancient Guaraní had called their traveling shamans.

We should bear in mind that for the Guaraní everything of value held a magical connotation and what was not magical held little value . . . magic and not knowledge or understanding. For the Guaraní, knowledge was relative: anyone could acquire it; what was of greatest value was magic.

The Guaraní of the area north of the River Paraná heard of the arrival of the Spanish or *karaí* from the Chandules, the Guaraní of the islands along the River Paraná. The *cacique* of Arambaré (today a neighborhood of Asunción known as Lambaré) and other caciques of the area decided to block their advance.

Once they heard of the arrival of the Spanish, they held a war council and brought together warriors from across the area. However, the attempt to block the advance of the Spanish by the cacique of Arambaré was in fact a purely symbolic act, designed to await the arrival of the Spanish and see what kind of relations they would offer.

After a short and insignificant skirmish with the Spanish, the Guaraní caciques began negotiations with Ayolas, establishing what we can term a pact of interests. The Spanish needed the Guaraní; they had arrived after three months of traveling upriver from Buenos Aires to Asunción, passing through lands inhabited by nomadic hunters, with no crops of any kind, and suffering all kinds of hardship. They arrived in a region where they found crops under cultivation and immediately understood the importance of these as a secure provision of supplies. And even though the Spanish had not come to found Asunción but rather to build a settlement from whence they could continue their search for El Dorado, they immediately understood the importance of settling in a place that was populated by agrarian communities that could meet an important need for supplies.

Furthermore, the caciques offered their young warriors to accompany the Spanish on their expeditions, since they had already heard of Candiré. This explains why the Spanish were able to count on a force of about two or three thousand Guaraní warriors. Thus, they had corn, provisions, warriors to accompany them, and information from the Guaraní regarding where they had previously crossed the Chaco and the Province of Chiquitos in search of El Dorado, all of which represented the basic reason why the Spanish formalized the aforementioned pact.

For their part, the Guaraní were also interested in such a pact. Their first demand that the cacique of Arambaré put to the Spanish during the early stages of the negotiations was for an expedition to wipe out the Payaguaes, especially those who lived on the other side of the River Paraguay from the Guaraní settlements. They demanded that as soon as the first houses had been built on the shore where Asunción now stands, Ayolas should launch an expedition as proof of his friendship. Before he left on his expedition northward up the River Paraguay, Ayolas therefore did indeed take a Spanish force and attacked the Payaguaes, destroying their canoes, and complying with the demands of the Guaraní who required this proof of friendship and alliance.

The Guaraní offered the Spanish their women in order to formalize the pact because in this way they became relatives of the *karaí*. In a Neolithic society such as the Guaraní, only by way of political kinship was it possible to found a true interethnic friendship. Through kinship they could expect reciprocity, since for the Guaraní, as for all Neolithic peoples in general, to give is to receive, and to offer a favor implies the tacit security of the favor being reciprocated.

In this way we can identify a first phase of interethnic contacts between the Spanish and the Guaraní, characterized fundamentally by relations of friendship between both groups.

The Second Phase of Hispanic-Guaraní Contact: The Tapi'i

Until 1539 the relationship between Guaraní and Spanish was a peaceful one, an alliance based on family ties. Nevertheless, there followed a major change in the system of relations: in 1539 there was a major rebellion among the Guaraní of Asunción.

What is important is the motive behind the decision of the Guaraní caciques to unleash this rebellion that obviously ended in the massacre of the rebels, when the objective was to massacre the Spanish. The fundamental cause was anger due to the failure of the Spanish to treat them as relatives, but instead as *tapi'i*, or servants. The Guaraní had historically considered all those who did not speak Guaraní and were not racially or ethnically Guaraní as *tapi'i*, as slaves, and inferior beings.

When Alvar Núñez Cabeza de Vaca arrived in Paraguay, the policy toward the indigenous people did not fundamentally change. Only that Alvar Núñez, who represented central Spanish power while Irala was an exponent of the so-called *comuneros* in Spain, demanded some regulation of relations with the Indians. Alvar Núñez was the first person to question the disorder that was the result of an already weakened system based on friendship and kinship ties, a system that lacked any kind of regulation and under which each Spaniard felt free to follow his own kind of relationship with his women.

Obeying their ties of reciprocity, the Guaraní accompanied Cabeza de Vaca on his famous expedition to the Chaco and to the place termed Paradise Island in Alto Paraná, today known as the Matto Grosso. On this expedition, the Guaraní acted as vanguard troops, always first in line of attack against the other tribes.

Meanwhile, the whole system of relations was in a state of flux. The Spanish no longer limited their contacts solely to the Guaraní from the region between the rivers Manduvirá and Tebicuary, but as they explored further north into the Alto Paraná to find another route to El Dorado and Peru, they came into contact with other Guaraní, such as the Guarambarenses. These expeditions advancing up the River Paraguay with two hundred or three hundred Spanish and fifteen hundred to two thousand Guaraní warriors needed provisions and thus relations began to grow with these other Guaraní, as the Spanish sought contacts with agrarian tribes that could provide them with supplies.

When Irala was sent by Alvar Núñez to search for a new route from the River Paraguay to the Province of Chiquitos and then on to Peru, he demanded that the Guarambarenses supply his force with all the necessary provisions. He also tried to force the cacique Aracaré to organize a group of warriors to explore the Chaco around where Fuerte Olimpo is today, in search of a new route. When the Guarambarenses refused and rebelled, Alvar Núñez ordered Irala to punish them. Irala ordered the cacique Aracaré to be hanged.

However, given the Guaraní system of kinship and social relations, many caciques were bound to each other by political ties, based on reciprocal agreements. Hence, when Aracaré was hanged, his relatives found themselves obliged to seek revenge on the Spanish. Thus began one of the first great revolts of the Guaraní, led by the cacique Tavaré. The Guaraní refused to supply more provisions or more troops, and they refused to accompany the Spanish on their expeditions. This also reflected a fear among the Guaraní that the warriors that set off with the Spanish toward the Andes would not return, leading to further depopulation and weakening of their communities.

The expedition sent from Asunción to put down this rebellion did not have an easy task, since the Guarambarenses had fortified their settlements with large ditches surrounding their communal houses, which they lined with spears and covered with foliage, as a trap for the advancing Spanish. Furthermore, they erected three concentric circles of wooden barricades around their villages, from where they could fire their arrows and repel attacks.

Nevertheless, the power of firearms prevailed and the majority of the Guaraní fled to the hills. Tavaré sued for peace with the Spanish, fearing that they would take all the Guaraní women to Asunción, which would have led to a sociodemographic crisis for the Guaraní. Thus in the end the rebellion was put down with relative ease.

Meanwhile the Spanish suffered from infighting. Alvar Núñez Cabeza de Vaca was taken prisoner and sent back to Spain in chains. For the first time, the cry of "freedom" reverberated through the streets of Asunción. In fact, the cause of this revolt was the opposition to the efforts by Alvar Núñez to impose some sort of regulation on the province with regard to the treatment of Indians. The cry of freedom in reality referred to the freedom of the individual, the freedom of each conquistador to "go by his manner and in his own manner to civilize the Indians," as the documents state.

The Third Phase of Contact: The Rancheadas

In the first years of the second government of Irala, a new period of Hispano-Guaraní relations began, characterized by violent and large-scale *rancheadas*. According to the documents from the time, the term *rancheada* meant that each conquistador had the right, according to his needs for women or labor, to go into any Guaraní village, whether near the River Manduvirá or Aca-hay, Guarambaré, or Monday, and by agreement or force, take the Guaraní that he needed to his own settlements.

The rancheadas, which prevailed for almost five years, were clearly a form of violent extraction, involving disproportionate violence, through which the conquistadors, in the name of the individual freedom that they had upheld in the rebellion against Alvar Núñez de Cabeza, sought to strengthen their freedom to exploit the Indians.

The reaction of the Guaraní came in the form of a great revolt, more widespread and better organized than ever before, a revolt that was truly pan-Guaraní.

It began in 1546. By this time the great majority of children born were mestizo, while there were few pure Guaraní births. Due to relations between the Spanish and the Guaraní women, the majority of the population was already mestizo, reflecting an increasing weakening of the Guaraní communities.

A low demographic index, a notable fall in pure Guaraní birth rates and a marked resistance among the mestizos to remain in Guaraní communities, were among the causes of the revolt. The constant and growing weakening of the communities in turn led to the tendency among Guaraní women, whose importance as the procreators among the Guaraní I have already highlighted, to show a marked preference to live with the Spanish.

Furthermore, as a result of the aforementioned violent rancheadas, and as a consequence of the violent imposition of the Spanish karaí over the Guaraní, a radical change emerged in the nature of the relationship, from one based on kinship ties to one based on *yará* (owner) and *tembiguai* (servant or slave).

The rebellion began in Areguá. As a first step the cacique Mayrarú organized his defenses and troops against the advancing Spanish. When Irala saw how fired up the Guaraní warriors were, he feared ordering an attack by his "friendly Indian" troops, partly because he did not fully trust them.

Therefore in order to gain victory and definitively put down the rebellion, Irala made a pact with the Guaicurú and the Yaperú from the Chaco, who were keen on collecting Guaraní scalps, and incorporated them into his force.

When Mayrarú saw that not only the Spanish but also their feared enemies from the Chaco were approaching Areguá, he ordered a retreat toward Acahay and Quiindy, where his forces entrenched themselves in a secure place on the River Mbuyapey behind wooden barricades and surrounded by almost impenetrable forest. As he advanced, however, Irala came upon an isolated Guaraní village. When he took prisoners including the cacique, the remaining villagers showed themselves willing to betray their fellow Guaraní rather than see their community destroyed. The cacique himself led the Spanish to the Guaraní hideout. Once they had been found, what the Spanish did not do, the Guaicurú did, finding an excellent opportunity to carry out a brutal massacre.

Many of the rebels managed to flee into the forest, traveling along the River Monday and then the River Acaray, to the mountains of Caaguazú, from where they turned north along the River Ypane to the region of the Guarambaré. Irala decided to inflict a lesson on the Guaraní and to put an end once and for all to their rebellions and great gatherings. He returned to Asunción, traveled up the River Paraguay, and then followed the River Ypane into Guarambarense territory, where he unleashed a series of repressive attacks on the rebel Guaraní.

The defeated Guaraní fled into the mountains toward Amambay. The large numbers of captives brought back to Asunción further weakened the Guaraní communities and represented a further factor in the stamping out of these rebellions. The practice of personal servitude by the Indian to the Spaniard now became established.

So it was in 1500 that the true biological decline of the Indian population began and its gradual replacement with a mestizo population, the youth of which would serve the Spanish, while the Guaraní survivors fled ever further into the mountains near the River Paraná, where the Spanish could not reach them.

Spanish-Guaraní Relations in Early Colonial Paraguay

Elman R. Service

Just what makes Paraguay different from the rest of Latin America continues to provoke debate and disagreement. A pioneering attempt by the U.S. anthropologist Elman Service to answer the question has fueled much controversy. This extract forms the conclusions of his study Spanish-Guaraní Relations in Early Colonial Paraguay, *which argues that after the conquest interbreeding took place far faster and more extensively than elsewhere because of isolation, the small number of colonists, and the absence of hierarchical structures in traditional Guaraní society. As a result of this rapid process of cultural homogenization, Paraguay developed a stronger and earlier sense of national identity than elsewhere in the region. Controversially, he also contended that, as a corollary, this led to the replacement of Guaraní by Spanish culture. This was reaffirmed by his study* Tobatí: Paraguayan Town *(Chicago: University of Chicago Press, 1954), the first anthropological study of a Paraguayan community, in which he presented a revisionist interpretation of Paraguayan social history, dispelling what he termed the Guaraní myth and arguing that, apart from the Guaraní language, there is little that can still be described as indigenous in the rural culture of Paraguay.*

Conclusions

In general, the outstanding difference between the colonization of Paraguay and that of better-known regions in Spanish America was the rapidity and thoroughness with which the aborigines were adapted to Spanish culture in Paraguay and integrated into a self-sufficient colony which developed national characteristics very early in its history. The conclusion seems inescapable that Guaraní culture was so quickly altered because of the special structure of the *encomiendas*, which actually fostered, rather than retarded, the assimilation of the Indians into the dominant Spanish culture patterns. This unusual effect of the *encomiendas* in Paraguay, for its part, was a product of purely local circumstances which were quite different from the conditions in Mexico, Central America, and Peru.

The culture of the Guaraní differed considerably from the aboriginal cultures the Spaniards encountered in Mexico and Peru. The society was not politically unified nor class structured,[1] and the villages were small and only semi-permanent. This meant that the Spaniards could not simply place themselves in the position of the top-level native rulers for purposes of control and exploitation through subsidiary chiefs. The Indian *pueblos* had to be reduced to permanency and eventually to be made larger than the simple kinship units which had composed the aboriginal villages. These adjustments also necessitated personalized control by the Spaniards, which was obtained by *pobleros* who lived in the new Indian villages and enforced the fundamental changes which were to disrupt Guaraní society. Another circumstance which affected the relationship between Spaniards and Guaraní was the isolation of Paraguay from the normal currents of trade with the other colonies and with Spain. The absence of mineral resources or other important marketable wealth contributed to the commercial isolation, and the people were reduced to a barter economy. This had important consequences for the *encomienda* system, since there was no exportable product of sufficient value to be used as tribute from the *encomienda* Indians. These factors also prevented the development of a large trading class and thus inhibited the spread of middle-class attitudes, so that the gulf between the ideology of a money economy and that of the Indian production-for-use economy was never as great in Paraguay as in most of Latin America.

Even the influence of the Church was unusual in Paraguay. In most of the important areas of Spanish America the clergy usually exerted its strength against the exploitation of natives by lay Spaniards and was important in aiding the enforcement of the Crown policy of segregation of *encomienda* Indians from Spanish colonists. Clerical influence in central Paraguay, however, was relatively unimportant; there the Spaniards, and later the irreligious *mestizos*, completed the secular acculturation of the Guaraní with little opposition from the powerless clergy, the reverse of the trend observed in Mexico and Peru.

Since the country was unattractive to Spanish colonists, peninsular Spaniards were soon in such a minority that the ruling population was predominantly *mestizo*, and the remaining Indians were then subjected to a dominant culture which was somewhat different from the original Spanish.

The position of these *mestizos* in Paraguayan affairs after about 1580 is, from the standpoint of Indian acculturation, one of the most significant of the several unusual characteristics of the colony. The large population of somewhat bicultural mixed bloods succeeded true Spaniards in positions of authority as political officials and *encomenderos*. Thus, ties of kinship between *encomenderos* and Indians became stronger, linguistic barriers ceased to exist, and, in general, cultural and racial differences between the two classes of society were lessened. The Indians probably had considerably more affinity for a feudal-like non-commercial society, the members of which spoke Guaraní and possessed a comprehension of Guaraní culture.

One of the important consequences of the rather unusual form of the colonization of Paraguay was that the few Spaniards, the many *mestizos*, and the acculturated Indians came to form a true, culturally independent nation with distinctive institutions much earlier than most of the other areas of South America. Although the early Spanish rulers had added such elements of nationhood as political, economic, military, and religious institutions rather than replaced them, as in Peru and Mexico, the unusual form of the *encomienda* rapidly introduced the bulk of the aboriginal population into colonial life, with the consequent local pride in national language, territory, and customs. The *"comunero"* revolts which presaged the national wars of independence in most of Spanish America had their inception in revolts by Paraguayan *mestizos* before the colony was fifty years old,[2] and subsequent revolts against Spanish authority characterized most of the remaining colonial period in Paraguay. In other South American countries many of the important national movements did not take place until the eighteenth century.

The isolation of the early conquistadores from political and commercial ties with Spain left the colony virtually self-ruled from the beginning. The military alliance with the Guaraní and the economic dependence on the "harems" of Guaraní women gave the Indians an important role in the life of the colony, for the Spaniards desperately needed their help during the early years. The nearly continuous wars and expeditions made complete military control of the Guaraní necessary and also tended to make the tribe an integral part of the colony almost from the first year of the contact. The small number of Spaniards in the colony and its subsequent rapid diminution left *mestizos* and acculturated Guaraní Indians as the dominant groups in all classes of the society.

It would seem that the type of acculturation which occurred in Paraguay must have resulted in the replacement of much of Guaraní culture, with the exception of the language, the role of women, certain food crops and cookery, and perhaps a few miscellaneous items of folklore and superstition. As has happened with the beginnings of national consciousness in most of the countries of the world, pride of language or dialect became greatly exalted. The heavy preponderance of Guaraní-speaking *mestizos* naturally resulted in the preference for the Guaraní language over the Spanish under the circumstances of the feeling against Spain. The continuation and perhaps accentuation of the intense nationalism since the devastation caused by the War of the Triple Alliance in the 1870s has kept Guaraní in use as a national language to this day in an atmosphere similar to what has been called "revivalism" or "nativism" in more primitive societies. Probably most other elements of true Guaraní culture have long since been lost. It would seem that, although Spanish-Indian racial and cultural mixture took place to some extent in all of Spanish America, two general trends were unusual in Paraguay—the rapid loss of Indian social and cultural integrity, and the retention of the language due to the same rapid amalgamation of the Indians into a colonial society which developed national characteristics at a very early date in its history.

Notes

1. Recent studies by Kubler (1946) and Gibson (1948) give good accounts of the importance of the Inca political and class structure in determining the nature of the political controls used by the Spaniards in Peru. These provide a most effective contrast to the Paraguayan situation.

2. In a sense, the successful revolt against the Crown's governor, Cabeza de Vaca, by the followers of Irala was a "national" or "comunero" movement as early as 1545!

The Land-without-Evil:
Tupí-Guaraní Prophetism

Hélène Clastres

Despite the myth of a harmonious relationship between the Spanish colonists and placid Guaranís, in reality there were frequent rebellions against Spanish rule. In her outstanding critique of previous interpretations of Tupi-Guaraní religious movements, Hélène Clastres seeks to explain the causes behind some of these conflicts as well as the concept of the Land-without-Evil. She refutes the notion of mystical revolts led by messianic cults in resistance to colonization. Instead, she argues that the revolts and migrations were a response to internal political tensions and struggles that predated the arrival of the Spanish. The following account analyzes the revolt by Obera, a village leader and prophet, in 1579 which briefly threatened Spanish rule. This was essentially a supratribal war, rooted in political struggles, local rivalries, and loyalties, rather than a religious uprising. The account is also interesting in that it reveals the role of the supernatural in guiding the Tupí-Guaraní in political decisions and in battle. However, it also reveals the intertribal rivalries, the tensions between village chiefs and the karaí (prophets), the suspicion toward such karaí who claimed to represent the gods and thus challenged their rule, and the balance between political pragmatism and consensus, on the one hand, and the need to follow the supposed will of the gods, on the other. As Clastres makes clear, the lack of unity among the Tupí-Guaraní, which the Spanish exploited, was key to the Spaniards' survival and conquest.

The following account of the uprising led by Obera in 1579 is taken from Lozano.[1] Obera, whose name, says the author, means "splendour" in Spanish, was a magus and the chief of a village situated not far from Asunción, hence in a region under the system of *encomienda*. This new predicament had not yet affected the traditional way of life; Lozano points out that, although all Indians of the village had received Christian names, they had stayed as firmly attached to their gentility as before their baptism; magical art was flourishing, as were other "abominations." Obera proposed to free the Indians from their submission to the Spaniards; he was sure to succeed in this task because he had become master of a comet that had appeared a few days earlier, then disappeared to the west. In short, he was a *karai* and he could give a guarantee of his power as god-man. He not only convinced his own people, but also secretly concluded an alliance with three large neighbouring villages. He then left with the people from those four villages, sending part of his army in one direction and going himself toward the Paraná; it was necessary to secure as many alliances as possible in order to return in strength and attack Asunción. The results of his initiative were not long in coming: Guaraní everywhere took up arms, so that the entire province was soon in rebellion, save for the *encomendados* of Villarica. "There was not a single Indian left in the other *encomiendas* who agreed to serve the Spaniards; on the contrary, they began to strike across the entire country in surprise raids."[2]

The danger was great. In order to avert it, the governor of the province, Garay, at the head of a small troop of well-armed soldiers (a scant one hundred and thirty of them, because Asunción had to be guarded), decided to try to block Obera and prevent the Guaraní from the Paraná from joining the rebels of the region of Asunción. Arriving near the headwaters of the Ypané, Garay learned that a group of Indians was making its way in a forced march toward this point; he then hastily decided to establish a fortified camp and wait for them there. Hardly were the Spaniards barricaded before they saw two Guaraní warriors walk out of the forest. Naked and without weapons, these came forward until they were within call and challenged to single combat any two Spaniards equipped with spear and shield or sword and buckler. They had been instructed by Tapuy-Guazú, their chief, to vanquish the enemy without bows and arrows, despite the inequality of the weapons. The double combat took place, with an outcome to the disadvantage, as could have been assumed, of the Guaraní. Wounded, they went back to the Tapuy-Guazú, who, it is told, was angered by their cowardice and had them immediately put to death.

Further, the chief considered their defeat to be a bad omen and came to doubt Obera's power and promises. He found the means, under some pretext, to convene a council of warriors and, as first among them, gave a speech, the substance of which was this: public affairs, involving the interest of all, cannot be guided only by the opinion of one person, even though he may be the wisest. The relish the Guaraní always had for their freedom and their acknowledged superiority over other peoples demanded that they no longer stoop beneath the Spaniards' yoke. If it were as easy for Obera to fulfil his promises as it is for him to make them, certainly the Indians would follow him without hesitation; but already difficulties had arisen, so that the Tapuy-Guazú did not feel that he had the right to make the decision for all to start a war that did not augur very well. Everyone should voice his opinion; should the Indians follow Obera, or should they without delay be allied with the Spaniards? Having so defined the alternatives, he invited the eldest councillor to give his advice. There is no need to linger over the details of this debate: supporters of peace and partisans of war confronted one another. All, nevertheless, agreed on one point: Obera had deceived them; he was but a *pajé* [shaman] in no way superior to others, and not the god-man he pretended to be. If, consequently, the war was to be pursued, there was no reason to accept the leadership of someone who now appeared to be an imposter: and no supernatural aid should be expected. The council chose peace, and the Tapuy-Guazú immediately sent messengers to Garay to offer him his alliance. Garay accepted it with the greater eagerness as it was unexpected.

The decision of chief Tapuy-Guazú is infinitely more interesting for it is most unusual: duels were not customary among Guaraní—at least not duels between enemies. Why then did he require a preliminary fight, and why this deliberately unequal fight? The following events enable us to understand his motives. The question for the chief was not whether this war (imminent now that the enemy was present) was pleasing to the gods; only shamans could determine that, and the fact that this war was led by a *karaí* himself should sufficiently have guaranteed it—provided that he was a true *karaí*. And this is what suddenly was being questioned. The outcome of the duel was a way of verifying *the authenticity of Obera himself*; this authenticity is what the chief questioned and wanted to test before committing himself. He may have been ready to recognize Obera; but not without first putting him to a test. If Obera were a god-man, the two warriors would triumph, whatever the conditions of combat; that is what the chief wanted to see.

Why then did a Guaraní chief want a *karaí* to demonstrate his power? Perhaps because this *karaí* was at the same time the chief of another village; or more likely, it seems to me, because he had arrogated to himself a right excessive in scope: he had decided *alone* in favour of a war in which he wanted to involve *all* Guaraní tribes—thus abolishing the de jure if not de facto, intertribal political relations and situating himself above other chiefs—and he invoked his divine nature to justify his right to do so. Rallying to his war consequently signified acknowledging this right. Tapuy-Guazú may have been ready to accede, but provided only that Obera would reveal his divine nature, in other words, that he give proof of his *legitimacy*.

Portrait of a *cacique*
of the Toba tribe
of Chaco Indians.
Postcard image by
an anonymous artist.
From the collection of
Martin Romano.

Once the deception had been exposed, all means became good means with which to combat it, including alliance with the Spaniards.

Let us go back to the end of the story. Returning from the expedition against Tapuymiri, Garay learned from his new allies that Obera and his supporters had built a fort, protected on all sides by palisades and ditches. Almost three thousand warriors, led by the most renowned chiefs of the region, had drawn into the fortification and were going through martial exercises in the hope that the Spaniards would come and storm the fort. They even feverishly awaited the attack, so great was their impatience to witness the effects of the supernatural aid promised by the prophet. He had had a calf sacrificed and burned, and had dispersed its ashes on the wind, thus portraying the ease with which the enemies would be vanquished. Garay, who was kept informed of all the preparations, chose to attack. The assault was violent and the Guaraní soon realized, at dear cost, that the Spaniards were much more dangerous warriors and had much more deadly weapons than they had imagined.

At the first battle Obera ran away. As soon as the Guaraní noticed his disappearance, they stopped defending the fort and concentrated solely on withdrawing, and this in the greatest confusion. Distressed over the unexpected flight of the prophet, the chiefs were unable to control their warriors, and the Spaniards were the masters of the battlefield: numerous Guaraní had been killed, others were taken prisoner almost without resistance. Eventually, the Spaniards went back to Asunción; order was restored in the province. As for Obera, no one subsequently heard of him again.

Such is the story. Not the story of a mystical revolt engendered by a dream of a golden age or a desire to escape to the Land-without-Evil. But the story of a supertribal war incited for a political purpose by a village prophet-chief, whose motives probably were not very pure, even if he was convinced he was right. About to be questioned by all those less clever than the Tapuy-Guazú who had followed him, he chose to take to his heels, thus dropping the mask.

Notes

1. P. Lozano, *Historia de la conquista del Paraguay, Río de la Plata y Tucumán*, ed. André Lamas, vol. 3 (Buenos Aires: Casa Editora Imprenta Popular, 1873).
2. Ibid., 213.

The Republic of Plato and the Guaraní

José Manuel Peramás

By the end of the eighteenth century, political notions such as the Enlightenment were challenging the legitimacy of the monarchy and proposing ideas of a liberal state without hierarchies, in which reason is the way to understand reality and to achieve individual and social well-being. Opposition to such views was led mainly by the Catholic Church and its intellectuals, who distrusted pure reason and considered monarchy to be the best form of government.

One such intellectual, the Jesuit missionary José Manuel Peramás, chose to defuse liberal philosophical criticism of colonial evangelization by drawing on the unquestionable authority of Plato to support the church-monarchy position. Peramás's essay "The Republic of Plato and the Guaraní," published in the year of his death in 1793, draws an analogy between the organization of the Jesuit reducciones (reductions) and Plato's ideal Republic. Peramás had worked in reductions—settlements in which Guaranís were organized into productive communities, indoctrinated into Catholicism, but protected from marauding Brazilian slave traders. In this essay, he proposes that the monolithic wisdom of the Catholic Church and the Spanish monarchy had been able to make Plato's utopia a reality through the Jesuit reductions. Christian theocracy, he argues, was the true vehicle for happiness in all areas of the public and private life of the citizen. The following extracts, taken from his essay, offer fascinating and detailed descriptions of various aspects of the organization of life in the reductions.

Common Goods

45. Among the Guaraní, some goods were held in common, others not. To each was assigned a section of land for cultivation, sufficiently extensive that the head of each household might sow, for himself and his family, Indian wheat (which constitutes their principal crop; they do not hold our wheat in great esteem), various types of vegetables and edible roots: one called *mandió* [manioc] and another *mandubí* [peanuts], which on the stem next to the root, has pods containing something like nuts, similar to our almonds.

They also sowed ground potatoes, which are tubers, of soft flesh and a pleasant taste, that they call *yetí*. They also grew cotton and all the fruits of the country that each might wish. All these products were the property of the grower and were called *Abambaé*, that is, the personal property of each Indian. The commonly owned oxen were lent in turn to each head of family in order for him to plough the land which belonged to him.

47. Apart from the private plots, there were at least two other, common areas of land: in one they grew wheat and vegetables; in the other, cotton. The produce from these fields was placed into storehouses, and constituted the public fund from which were fed and dressed the orphans, the lame, boys, girls, and widows, who were attended in a house, larger than the rest, destined for them. Cooked meat, soup, and bread were sent daily to the sick.

48. In these two fields every citizen worked for the community on certain days of the year; all of them, including the mayor and the magistrates, studied agriculture according to the ancient Roman methods. The famous Thomas More, who wished all the inhabitants of his UTOPIA to be farmers, would no doubt have approved of this. In the same way, the church, the houses, and all the other buildings in the city were built and repaired by common effort.

49. Under this system all families were practically equal and owned the same goods, except when someone might cultivate his land with more diligence and so obtain a greater harvest. But this introduced insignificant inequality, and rather stood as a stimulus: anyone who saw his neighbor's land more abundant than his own felt urged to shun leisure and idleness. Among the Guaraní there was not a single beggar, because if someone was unable to work, he was fed by the community, and if he was able, he was obliged to work. There were, besides, Indians designated *ex professo*, who cared for the cattle, which were numerous in all the cities; others cared for the horses, which were public property; others watched over the sheep; others were placed in charge of various other chores.

51. If the Indians, once gathered in a community, should lack food, through their own fault or that of others, they would cast off all discipline and take refuge once more in their forests and familiar hiding places, plagued by hunger; because *the belly is*, in the words of Homer, *a great evil*. The Mocobí, once fierce and cruel Indians who later became excellent Christians, confessed openly that one of the reasons for their submission was the difficulty they had in feeding themselves during the wet season, when they could neither hunt nor fish, and the hope of finding abundant food in the city of San Francisco Xavier. And indeed they found it, thanks to the diligent labor of their first missionary, Francisco Burges (whom I knew for many years),

and his successors, who, while frugal with themselves, were generous with the neophytes.

Music

88. The Indians having such an inclination to Music—they might be compared to birds, in whom nature inspires song—they learned it to such a degree of perfection that they have caused admiration in the Europeans, and continue to do so. Cayetano Gatteneo, who traveled to those lands from Italy in 1729, wrote to his family in Modena of having met a Guaraní boy of twelve years who played on the organ the most difficult pieces by the Bolognese composers, with not a single error.

The Guaraní sang daily Mass, accompanied by the organ and other instruments. In the evening, after the Rosary, they sang a brief motet in honor of the Blessed Sacrament and Mary, the Mother of God, to which the whole of the people responded. At the end they recited the Act of Contrition. Of the music of the Guaraní it can be said that in the church it was devout and solemn and in the home and in the country it was honest and dignified, admitting of nothing that might corrupt good manners.

The Arts

126. From among the Guaraní those who appeared the most apt for the arts necessary to life in the community were chosen. Let us take, for example, Music: in each city there were some thirty musicians, between singers and instrumentalists. Since the children recited the Catechism daily, and sang some of the prayers morning and evening, it was easy to observe which of them had the clearest and pleasantest voices. These children were taught first to read and write, and they then joined the Choir, which was a great honor for their parents, whose child passed into the service of the *Tuparogmbaeupe*, that is, the House of God.

127. Almost all the useful arts were cultivated. There were carpenters, iron- and metalworkers to cast bells; there were builders, painters, and sculptors who covered the altars, church columns, and statues of the Saints with diverse colors, gold and silver; there were turners, farmers, and doctors. Among them and all other workers, each looked to his own art, without meddling in the professions of others. They were public servants, and were paid from the public fund. With a view to the future, suitable workers were apprenticed to the masters, in order that they might gradually learn the profession and succeed them in due course.

128. When I say that there were artists among the Guaraní, I would not wish any one to imagine that I refer to crude workmen, lacking in technique: these artists worked with the same skill as the most excellent European craftsmen. The magnificent organs and musical instruments of all kinds that they built; the beautiful tableware turned on the lathe; their fine textiles and other perfections of manufacture, would, I have no doubt, cause admiration in any one who saw them.

A Vanished Arcadia: Being Some Account of the Jesuits in Paraguay, 1607–1767

R. B. Cunninghame Graham

Following the proclamation in 1610 by King Felipe III of Spain that the "sword of the word" rather than the sword of steel should be used to subjugate the indigenous peoples of Paraguay, the Catholic Church granted extensive powers to the Jesuits, which they used toward their aim of creating an Indian republic in South America. Faced by resistance from Spanish settlers who saw a threat to the encomienda *system, the Jesuits focused their efforts in Guairá in the northeast of the country, far from Asunción. In a ground-breaking experiment of religious social organization, over the next century they constructed over twenty* reducciones *(reductions) in which approximately one hundred thousand Indians lived. These organized religious settlements stretched along the banks of the rivers Paraná and Uruguay, in what today includes areas of Paraguay, Argentina, Brazil, and Uruguay.*

However, the reductions, especially in Guairá, were within reach of the mamelucos *or* bandeirantes, *bandits based in São Paulo, Brazil. Beyond the effective control of the colonial governor, these mamelucos thrived on the capture and sale into slavery of Indians. As demand for slaves in Brazilian plantations increased, so the mamelucos began to make incursions into undefended Spanish territories where the reductions were established. With the Spanish crown unwilling to send troops to defend the reductions, and with little support from Spanish settlers in Asunción, the Jesuits were unable to repel the increasing number of raids by heavily armed mamelucos, who destroyed the reductions they found, burned the churches, and kidnapped the Indians in their thousands. Faced with the destruction of their reductions, the Jesuits, under the leadership of Father Antonio Ruiz de Montoya, undertook an extraordinary exodus in which approximately thirty thousand Guaranís traveled hundreds of miles south across extremely difficult terrain toward the sanctuary of the Jesuit reductions in the lower Paraná (immortalized in the 1986 film* The Mission *starring Robert de Niro). The threat from the marauding mamelucos only ended in 1639, when the viceroy of Peru agreed to allow the Indians to bear arms. This allowed the Jesuits to create well-trained and well-armed militias that successfully defeated the mamelucos and ushered in a new golden age for the reductions in Paraguay.*

The following extract is from a book published in 1901, regarding one of the most extraordinary large-scale, organized migrations of people in Latin American history. Robert Cunninghame Graham lived and traveled extensively in the region between 1869 and 1878. He became fascinated by the history of the Jesuit reductions, the legacy of which was still very apparent in the 1870s despite the expulsion of the Jesuits in 1767. His account of the reductions is noticeable for its emphasis on the communistic and utopian social and economic order and its positive interpretation of the role of the Jesuits in protecting the Indians from the excesses of both Brazilian and Spanish colonialism. A committed political activist and social reformer, who was influenced by Marxism, Christianity, and socialism, Cunninghame Graham was the Liberal member of parliament for North West Lanarkshire, Scotland, from 1886 to 1892 and a cofounder, together with Keir Hardy, of the Scottish Labour Party.

In 1631 the Mamelucos broke into the province of Guayrá. All was confusion, and Montoya sent Father Diaz Taño to Asunción to beg the Governor, Don Luis de Céspedes, to send them help. He answered that he could do nothing, and thus by leaving the whole territory of Guayrá without defense, lost a rich province to the Crown of Spain. At the time (1631) Portugal and Spain were united, yet in the Indies their subjects were at war, and though in Europe Spain was the stronger of the two, in America the Portuguese conquered about that time rich provinces, which today form part of the quondam empire of Brazil.

Whilst in Guayrá all was confusion, and the Paulistas swept through the land ruining everything, upon the Uruguay things prospered, and Padre Romero founded two new reductions, known as San Carlos and Apostoles; he also laid the foundation of that territory in which the persecuted neophytes of Guayrá were soon to find a safe retreat. Father Diaz Taño by this time had returned from Charcas with a decree of the High Court, declaring the action of Don Luis de Céspedes in failing to protect Guayrá against the Mamelucos was prejudicial to the interests of the King; but as neither he nor the High Court of Charcas possessed any power by means of which to stimulate the Governor to greater zeal, the decree was useless, and Taño and Ruiz Montoya found themselves summoned hastily to meet a new attack. Before they arrived, the missions, both of San Francisco Xavier and of San José, had been destroyed. As there were still reductions undestroyed, Montoya, as Provincial of Guayrá, called all the Jesuits of the province to deliberate as to their chance of making a defense. The debate ran high; some of the priests wished that the neophytes should fight to the end; others, more sensible, pointed out that the ill-armed and quite untrained militia of the missions could do nothing with their bows and arrows against the well-led and well-disciplined Paulistas all armed with guns.[1] Padre Truxillo gave it as his opinion that it would be more prudent to transport the Indians to a place of safety, and pointed out that near the cataract of Guayrá they would be able to cross the river and place it between themselves and the Paulistas in case of an attack. This advice seemed prudent to the rest, and Father Truxillo set out to make his preparation for the march.

[Soon after] news was brought to Montoya which made him alter all his plans. Two messengers came out to inform him that an army of Paulistas was marching on Villa Rica, and that a strong detachment of them was advancing from the south. Padre Montoya took a supreme resolve, and ordered the evacuation of the two principal reductions (San Ignacio and Loreto) which yet remained intact. They were the first which had been founded in Guayrá, and were as important as any of the Spanish towns in Paraguay. The churches, all the Jesuit writers, such as Montoya, Charlevoix, Mastrilli and Lozano, are agreed, were finer than any in the land. The Indians were, according to Montoya, far better Christians than the inhabitants of the Spanish settlements, and their faith and innocence were above all praise. They cultivated cotton and had large herds of cattle. In 1609 the Jesuits came to Guayrá, and found it absolutely untouched; and when in 1631 they left it, it was upon the road to become one of the most flourishing American provinces of the Spanish throne.

The plan by means of which the Jesuit Moses led his sheep out of the wilderness of Guayrá was most remarkable. The river Paraná forms a great artery between Brazil and Paraguay; upon each side of it a network of rivers disembogues. The Paranapané, on which most of the missions of Guayrá were situated, flows from the east and falls into the Paraná, not much more than fifty miles above the cataract. After the last of the once-flourishing Jesuit reductions had been evacuated at the orders of Montoya, he collected all the boats, rafts and canoes, and after much persuasion got all the Indians to follow him to seek for safer habitations lower down the Paraná. The population of the six reductions has been estimated at about one hundred thousand souls; but of these, during the years of 1629 and 1630, thousands had been led captive to San Paulo, and thousands had dispersed into the woods. Still, assembled on the banks of the Paranapané, there was a multitude of Indians of every sex and age. Fortunately or unfortunately, no record by an eyewitness exists, except that written by Montoya, and he is modest to a fault about all details, and absolutely silent as to the part he played himself. He tells us that at the starting-point were gathered two thousand five hundred families.

The sentinel whom they had placed to warn them of the enemy's approach gave the alarm. Montoya sent at once to Ciudad Real for help, but the Spanish settlers were too hard pressed themselves to give assistance. Nothing remained but to make a portage of all their rafts, boats and canoes, and then to re-embark and sail down the Paraná out of the reach of the Paulistas. Montoya passed in review his boats and found he had seven hundred, and that twelve thousand people had embarked with him on leaving the Paranapané. When the Paulistas found the Jesuits had evacuated all their towns, they burnt the churches, on the principle, perhaps, that the nest once pulled down, the rooks would not return.

The most difficult part of the great exodus was now to come. The rapids and the cataracts of the Paraná extend to nearly ninety miles, and the whole country is a maze of tangled forest interspersed with rocks. No paths exist, the place is desert, and over the dank mass of vegetation the moisture from the clouds of vapor thrown up by the falling water descends in never-ending rain, In order to endeavour to save the trouble of reconstructing new rafts and canoes at the bottom of the cataract, Montoya launched three hundred empty boats to see if any of them arrived safely at the bottom of the falls. Not one escaped; and so the pilgrimage began, almost without provisions and without arms, in the middle of a country quite uncultivated, and where game was scarce.

Each Indian had to take his bundle on his back; even the children carried bundles in proportion to their strength. The missionaries carried what was held most sacred, such as the alter-plate and images of saints. In front a band of men armed with machetes (cane-knives) opened the way through the dense woods and pathless jungle of the bank.

It took the fugitive Indians eight weary days of marching to reach the lower end of the cataract, where once again the Paraná was navigable. On their arrival they hoped to find provisions and more boats; but none were there, their own stores were almost done, and the people too exhausted to march on. Fever broke out, and many of them died; others, lost in the forests, without a guide, wandered till death released them from their march. A weaker man than Padre Montoya might have despaired of ever issuing from the woods. However, he set the Indians to work to make canoes, and others to cultivate patches of maize for food, working himself alternately with axe and hoe to give example to the neophytes. Others, again, cut down the enormous canes which in that region grew to fifty feet in height, to make them into rafts.

Thus after a considerable time, all was in readiness for a new start, and luckily provisions from the reductions on the Paraná arrived. So they embarked again. Many of the hastily constructed rafts and canoes sank and the mortality of the Indians was great. Eventually they found a temporary refuge in the Reduction of the Nativity upon the Acaray, and at Santa Maria la Mayor upon the Iguazú. There famine raged, and the arrival of so many people increased the scarcity so that six hundred of the new arrivals died in one reduction, and five hundred in the next. At last the scarcity became so great that the poor Indians had to roam about the forests to gather fruit, and many of them died in the recesses of the woods.

Seeing no hopes of saving the remainder, Montoya led them further on to the banks of a little river called the Jubaburrus, and there he once again founded two reductions, which he named Loreto and San Ignacio, after the two the Mamelucos had destroyed. He bought ten thousand head of cattle out of the money the King allowed to the Jesuits of Guayrá and from the sale of some few objects saved from the general destruction of the towns, and settled down his Indians, who in Guayrá had been all agriculturalists, to a pastoral life. Thus did he bring successfully nearly twelve thousand people a distance of about five hundred miles through desert country, and down a river broken in all its course by rapids, landing them far from their enemies in a safe haven at last.

Note

1. The Indians of the missions were not allowed to possess firearms at this period.

The Revolt of the Comuneros

Adalberto López

The Comuneros Revolt (1721–35) is one of the most complex and disputed periods of Paraguayan history. There were actually two separate revolts; one in 1721 and the other in 1733. The first was essentially a struggle among elites for economic domination, which led to intervention from rival factions of the colonial power, first in Lima and then in Buenos Aires. The comuneros, led by Governor José de Antequera y Castro, defeated a royalist army in 1724 before the revolt was finally suppressed by a second invasion from Buenos Aires, supported by the Jesuit missions. Antequera was executed in Lima in 1731.

With Spain unable to send a new governor until 1733, the interim governor, Martín de Barúa, oversaw a period of growing resentment against the Jesuit missions both for their perceived loyalty to Buenos Aires (and the Spanish crown) rather than to the province, as well as for their perceived protection of indigenous labor, their extensive landholdings, and their domination of the trade in yerba mate. These tensions led to a second revolt, which came to a head with the arrival of the new Spanish governor, Manuel Agustín Ruyloba, in 1733. When Ruyloba sought to dismantle alternative power structures that had arisen in Paraguay over the previous decade, he faced a revolt by the militia or comunero army, which in turn was led by some of the foremost local landowners. Ruyloba was killed in the first encounter, leading to a second army being sent from Buenos Aires to stamp out the comuneros revolt and place the province firmly under the control of the crown.

There are several radically different interpretations of the significance of the "comuneros revolts." One is that they represented the first expressions of Paraguayan independence and of the struggle for national sovereignty against the Spanish crown. Another is that they were a struggle for economic and political power between competing Paraguayan elites. A third is that they resulted from a conflict between local elites and the Jesuits (allied to the crown) over the control of land and the use of indigenous labor. What is clear is that these revolts were not uncommon in the colonies, especially in more distant and isolated parts of the Spanish Empire. In the second revolt there was a clear social dimension, with resentment over Jesuit *control of land being used as a rallying cry to unite peasants and landowners to the cause. But there is little evidence that they were a rebellion against the Spanish crown, as such.*

The following extract from one of the most detailed studies of the comuneros revolts describes the efforts of Ruyloba to restore the authority of the crown, the spread of the revolt against him, and the clear social dimension of the rebellion.

Don Manuel Agustín de Ruyloba, the man chosen by Philip V to govern Paraguay, was a native of Burgos in northern Spain and a professional soldier from an early age. As soon as he learned of his new appointment Ruyloba went to Lima to consult with the viceroy. Castelfuerte ordered him to proceed to Paraguay at once, arrest Montiel and arrange for his execution, issue a general pardon to all others, and gradually remove from their post in the militia of Paraguay those commanders who had actively supported Antequera and/or had openly refused to accept Soroeta as governor. At the time of his meetings with Ruyloba, Castelfuerte also wrote to P. Herrán instructing him to place at the new governor's disposal whatever Indian troops Ruyloba might deem necessary to make his entry into Paraguay.

Ruyloba left Lima on July 3, 1732, and arrived in Buenos Aires in December. There he was joined by Ruiz de Arellano, who described for him the situation in Paraguay. The province, he reported, was on the verge of anarchy, with the common people everywhere up in arms. There was respect for neither the king nor the Church. The news that Ruyloba had been named governor of Paraguay had not been welcomed in the province and the general sentiment was against him. He, Arellano, had done his best to convince the Paraguayans to obey the viceroy and the king. As a consequence he had been called a traitor and abused in public. Fearing that his enemies might carry out their threats to kill him he had escaped from the province.

On July 6, he wrote to P. Jaime Aguilar announcing that he was ready to enter Paraguay and instructing him to maintain on the alert the mission army which was still camped at the Aguapey. P. Aguilar replied that the army had been on the alert for more than a year and was ready to obey his every command. At the end of the month Ruyloba and his companions crossed the Alto Paraná and rode into the Jesuit mission of San Ignacio Guazú. Aguilar, Aperger, and several Indian commanders met him there and swore their allegiance to him. They also pleaded with Ruyloba not to cross the Tebicuary without a large Indian army. The governor, however, still believed in the assurances of the Paraguayans and was aware of the grave consequences of entering Paraguay with a mission army. He turned down the offer made to him by the Jesuits and the Indians, but did assure them that if anything went wrong in Paraguay he would immediately return to them for help.

Among those who met Ruyloba when the governor crossed the Tebicuary were Sebastian Fernández Montiel, who repented to the governor for his participation in the *comunero* movement and pledged his loyalty to him, and Esteban Fernández de Mora, the *alcalde* of Villa Rica, who offered him all the armed men of his city to accompany him to Asunción. Still confident that all was going well, Ruyloba turned down the offer and asked Mora and his men to return to Villa Rica. The governor then continued on his way to Asunción. On July 27, 1733, a tired but confident Ruyloba rode into the Paraguayan capital surrounded by a large and seemingly obedient crowd of several hundred.

Bishop Palos met the governor on the steps of the cathedral, welcomed him, then led him inside for a brief prayer. Before entering it he turned around and addressed the crowd which had gathered to take a look at the new governor. He promised that as governor he would listen to their grievances and would provide a just government for the province. He would not, however, tolerate any act of treason to the king. The establishment of the *Junta Gobernativa*, he went on, had just been that. As far as he was concerned, the *Junta* no longer existed; and he threatened to execute in the public plaza any one found guilty of attempting to revive it. There were neither shouts nor applause when Ruyloba finished his brief speech and entered his new home. On the following day, he was officially recognized by the *cabildo* of Asunción as the legitimate governor of Paraguay. His first official act was to turn into law the threat he had made the previous day: any person found guilty of trying to revive the *Junta Gobernativa* or even talk about it was to be executed and his family exiled from the province. To those who offered information leading to the arrests of such traitors he promised *encomiendas*.

On August 20, Ruyloba began to reorganize the provincial militia. Those in militia commands who had actively participated in the rejection of Soroeta and the expulsion of the Jesuits were removed from their posts and replaced by men on whose loyalty the governor believed he could count. On August 28, Ovelar was fired as *maestre de campo* and replaced by Sebastian Fernández Montiel, the man Ruyloba had been ordered to execute but who was now one of the governor's most loyal and staunch supporters. After his reorganization of the militia command, Ruyloba turned to the *cabildo* of Asunción. All *cabildo* elections since 1730 were declared illegal. Once the purging of the *cabildo* had been completed, the governor set out to make arrangements for the return of the Jesuits to Asunción.

Ruyloba acted too confidently and too quickly. The Paraguayans were upset by his decree sentencing to death those found guilty of trying to revive the *Junta Gobernativa*. But they had probably expected it and certainly seem to have accepted it. The purge of the militia's high command and the *cabildo*, however, had neither been expected nor accepted. Those who were removed from their posts were infuriated and so were their friends and relatives. The removal of Ovelar from his post as *maestre de campo* and from the *cabildo* was a particularly bad mistake on the part of Ruyloba, for Ovelar had a large following in the province and was close to many of the notables of Asunción. A greater mistake was to replace him as second-in-command of the militia by Montiel, who was now despised by many of his compatriots as a turncoat and a traitor to his land. But what turned the Paraguayans' resentment against the governor into a movement to overthrow him was his commitment to the return of the Jesuits to Asunción.

Troubled times did lay ahead. By early September the majority of the Paraguayans had decided that they had had enough of Ruyloba, and, despite the promise made to Arregui, former *comuneros* were making ready to depose the unsuspecting governor. In Asunción there was no inkling of what was up, but in the countryside men rode back and forth calling for the people to fight once again for the fatherland. On September 7 the governor sent Montiel to inspect the forts along the Paraguay River south of the capital. That same day some 300 men gathered in the valley of Mbocayatí, about twenty miles from the capital, and began preparations to march against the governor. Five days later they set out toward Asunción. The rebellion had begun.

The governor was dining with Arellano when he was told that the *comuneros* were up in arms again and not far from Asunción. At once Ruyloba sent orders to militia commanders to prepare their men for battle and to meet him at the farm of Alonso Pérez. At nine in the morning on the following day, the governor marched out of Asunción accompanied by Juan Báez, Arellano, Francisco Cabañas, Barreyro, Andrés Benítez, and a few troops. Behind, in charge of the city, he left Juan Caballero de Añasco.

At the farm of Alonso Pérez the governor was joined by about 250 militiamen. Some militia commanders arrived with a few men; others with none at all, explaining that their troops had refused to fight their fellow countrymen and that many had deserted to the rebels. Ruyloba stood before those who had come and spoke to them: "Gentlemen, long live the king! You are loyal vassals and the others are traitors; and each one of you is worth ten of them!" In mid-afternoon the army left the farm in the direction of the advancing rebels. By then Ruyloba had close to 300 men. After ordering the distribution of powder and bullets, he ordered his men to get a good night's rest. It was a chilly and rainy night; the governor prayed but did not sleep.

It was still raining on the morning of Tuesday the fifteenth when Ruyloba walked out of Doña Isabel's country house and discovered that of the 300 men he had commanded the night before only 150 remained. The others had deserted to the enemy during the night. By noon one hundred more had deserted. Ruyloba was shocked and disheartened by this treachery and must have certainly debated in his mind whether to obey the dictates of his honor and remain to fight, or the dictates of his reason and backtrack to Asunción or flee to the Jesuit missions where thousands of well-armed Indians were ready to fight for him. He was an honorable man, however, and decided to stay and fight.

To Ruyloba what was at stake that hot Tuesday afternoon was his honor and his king's. To retreat or to give in to the rebels' demands would have been to erase in one moment his record of over thirty-five years of loyal and honorable service to his king. The rebel army began to move forward. Ruyloba gave the order to advance. But only a handful of those with him stood by the governor. Shouting that they did not want to kill their brothers, the majority of the governor's troops broke their formation and rode to join the advancing rebel army. Only twelve men remained with Ruyloba.

There are two accounts of what happened next. According to Palos and Arellano, the governor, faced by the general desertion, decided to surrender to the rebels. He rode toward them with his hat in his hand and shouted, "Long live the king!" A few of the rebels shouted back, "Long live the king! Death to bad government!" Saavedra then approached the governor and shot him at close range. Others quickly fell upon the body and slashed it with their swords. One of them, Gabriel Delgado, split open the dead governor's head. Arregui and Fray Aranda told another story. According to them, it was Ruyloba who fired the first shot and fell dead when the rebels fired back.

Within hours after the death of Ruyloba some thirty *comuneros* rode into Asunción. There was no resistance to the rebels. By nightfall the main body of the rebel army was camped a few miles from Asunción. The *comuneros* discussed the day's events, made proposals, and voted. All the acts and orders issued by Ruyloba were declared illegal and null. All those who had supported the governor were declared traitors and were to be removed from whatever posts they held in the militia or in the *cabildo*. Those who had been fired by the governor were to return to their posts. To the *com-*

uneros, then, Ovelar was once again *maestre de campo* of the militia and *alcalde* of Asunción.

On the following day, September 16, the rebel leaders met with the members of the newly constituted *cabildo* and together they decided to petition Arregui to accept the post of governor of the province. As precedent for this they recalled the election of Bishop Cárdenas almost a century before. The rebel army approved of the decision by acclamation and a formal petition to the bishop was drafted. Signed by the members of the *cabildo* and the majority of the militia commanders present, the document urged Arregui to accept the governorship for the sake of the peace and welfare of the province. The signers assured the bishop that they were and had always been loyal to the king, their natural lord, and that they had turned against Ruyloba only to protect their land and their homes.

In the weeks that followed, Arregui declared null all acts issued by Ruyloba and approved of the decisions made by the rebels in the evening after the death of the governor. But the *comuneros* wanted more than just a return to the *status quo* of the previous July. The rebel leaders demanded that militia commanders who had held posts before the arrival of Ruyloba but had been lukewarm in their support of the rebellion against the governor be removed from their posts. They also demanded that those who had been close supporters of the governor lose their *encomiendas*, if they had any, and be refused licenses to participate in commerce or yerba mate production. To all these demands Arregui gave in.

After the establishment of the *Junta General*, the *comuneros* let loose on the province what amounted to a minor and bloodless reign of terror. The home of Añasco in Asunción was sacked and his relatives forced to leave the city. From the *estancia* of Miguel Montiel the rebels took a large quantity of cotton cloth, tobacco, and sugar, and from the ranch of his fugitive brother, 300 horses and an untold number of cattle. Merchandise and boats belonging to merchants who had supported Ruyloba were confiscated. Fernández Montiel, Barreyro and Cabanas were sentenced to death *in absentia*. Benítez was exiled from the capital and Arellano ordered to leave the province. There were by now over 1,000 rebels camped in the vicinity of Asunción. The majority of them were poor country people and, as might be expected, it was against the well-to-do of the province that they directed much of their anger. From the farms of the rich they took cattle, horses, and crops. Yerba mate on its way to the capital was often confiscated as were cattle destined for the slaughter houses of the city. Even those who had remained neutral in the conflict between Ruyloba and the rebels and even a few of those who had openly backed the rebel movement saw their properties in the countryside occupied by *comunero* bands. Slowly, the rebellion which had begun as a movement against an unpopular governor was turning into a war of the poor against the rich, of the countryside against the city.

In Lima, Castelfuerte, who had learned of the revolt against Ruyloba and the governor's death in December, met with the *audiencia* of the viceregal capital to discuss the situation in Paraguay. The decision was made to take strong military action against the rebels. On December 13, the viceroy ordered Governor Zavala in Buenos Aires to blockade all land and river routes leading into Paraguay, to invade the province with as many troops as he could muster, and to execute those who had been responsible for the death of Ruyloba. On the following day Castelfuerte sent orders to P. Aguilar, who had been recently promoted to the post of Jesuit provincial of Paraguay, to place at Zavala's disposal all Indian troops in the Jesuit missions.

During the early colonial period, and following the evacuation of Buenos Aires, Asunción became the center of Spanish conquest of the southern part of South America. The importance of Asunción, and therefore, Paraguay, was reflected in maps of the time, many of which placed Buenos Aires within the Province. Map by T. Jefferys. From the collection of Milda Rivarola.

The *reducción* (reduction) at Trinidad in the southeast of Paraguay was one of the largest missions established by the Jesuits in the Río de la Plata Basin in the sixteenth and seventeeth centuries. The ruins are now a UNESCO World Heritage Site. Photograph by Rose Stokes. Used by permission of the photographer.

On September 30, 1872, the *Kepler* sailed from Liverpool with the first of three groups of "Lincolnshire farmers" bound for Buenos Aires en route to Paraguay. This painting by an anonymous artist shows some of these 284 emigrants disembarking on November 9, 1872, from the riverboat *Cisne* at Asunción. A Brazilian gunboat is discreetly positioned in the background. From a private collection, courtesy of Christie's Images Limited.

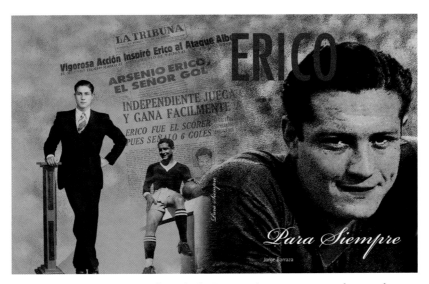

Arsenio Erico (1915–77) was without doubt Paraguay's greatest soccer player and one of the world's all-time greats. With a style often likened to that of a ballet dancer or a magician, he still holds the record for the most goals scored in the Argentinian First Division (293 in just 325 matches). Used by permission of Jorge Barraza, from the book *Erico para siempre* (Asunción: El Lector, 2010).

In the run-up to Paraguay's successful World Cup campaign of 2010, the mobile phone company Personal ran a series of advertisements supporting the national team. The ads were based on images alluding to the Triple Alliance War (1864–70), with Paraguay's star player Salvador Cabañas in the role of the "Mariscal," reflecting the striking presence of history in modern-day Paraguay. Used by permission of Personal (Núcleo) telecom company, Paraguay.

"Days of Glory." The events of March 1999 represented a high point in Paraguay's democratic aspirations, when thousands of young people demonstrated outside the National Congress in opposition to an attempted coup following the assassination of Vice President Argaña. Their bravery in refusing to budge despite the killing of eight protestors by snipers was crucial in saving democracy and is dramatically shown by the front cover from "Days of Glory," a celebratory photo album of the Marzo Paraguayo published by *Ultima Hora* newspaper. However, these high hopes would be cruelly dashed by the dismal performance of the ensuing government of national unity led by President González Macchi (1999–2003). Used by permission of *Ultima Hora*, "Días de Gloria," Asunción, April 1999.

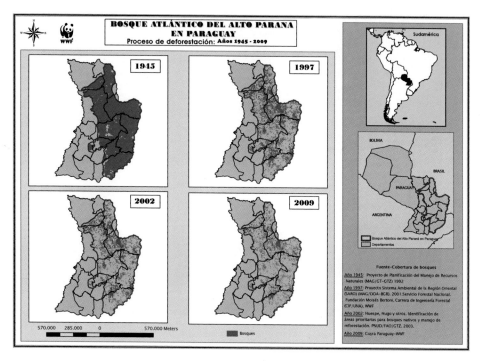

In 1945 more than half of eastern Paraguay was covered by the dense subtropical Atlantic forest. As this map shows, the rapid expansion of commercial agriculture introduced by Brazilian colonists, known as *brasiguayos*, led to its almost complete disappearance by 2009. Used by permission of World Wildlife Fund, Paraguay.

Red earth, luxuriant vegetation, and coconut palm trees are a recurrent feature of the "arcadian" rural landscape in Paraguay. Photograph by Ben Cavanna. Used by permission of the photographer.

Plata Yvyguy (hidden treasure) is a recurring theme in Paraguayan contemporary folklore. It derives from the belief that, faced with imminent defeat during the Triple Alliance War, Francisco Solano López ordered for the national treasure to be secretly buried. As portrayed in this section of a triptych by Enrique Collar, one of Paraguay's leading contemporary artists, the hallucinations experienced by searchers are regarded as indicators of the presence of the treasure. Painting by Enrique Collar. Used by permission of the artist.

II

The Nationalist Experiment

When Argentina declared its independence from Spain in May 1810, the Asunción municipal council rejected a proposal from Buenos Aires for its incorporation into an enlarged Argentinian nation. In December, a regiment was sent from Buenos Aires under General Belgrano, supposedly to liberate Paraguay from the Spanish yoke, but which was perceived by most Paraguayans as an invasion force. It was forced to retreat after two decisive defeats at the hands of the Paraguayan militia, which, in the absence of sufficient Spanish officers, was led by local mestizos. Those Paraguayans favoring independence were finally provoked into action when the governor of Paraguay attempted to strengthen the position of the royalists by requesting military assistance from Portuguese troops in Brazil, ostensibly because of the continued military threat from Buenos Aires. The Asunción barracks revolted in May 1811 and the governor was forced to capitulate. A series of congresses and *juntas* followed, and their changing composition reflected the growing ascendancy of the nationalists over those who favored some sort of union with Buenos Aires. On October 12, 1812, a general congress proclaimed Paraguay a republic, one of the first in Latin America, and one that had declared a triple independence: from Spain, Buenos Aires, and Portugal.

Dr. José Gaspar Rodríguez de Francia soon came to personify the spirit of Paraguayan nationalism. His absolute and austere rule from 1814 to 1840 was responsible for welding the nation into a viable, independent unit, and for providing a firm economic base for future development. This was against the backdrop of the constant threat of annexation by Brazil (with which there were clashes on the disputed northern borders) and Argentina, which refused to recognize Paraguayan independence and consequently pursued an economic blockade of Paraguay's foreign trade.

In the face of these external threats, Francia pursued a policy of self-sufficiency through state control of the economy, together with the ruthless suppression of political opponents suspected of spying for Argentina. Repression was directed against the urban elite, the church, and those of Spanish descent—in other words, the established power brokers of the colonial period. However, land reform, in the shape of the renting of state-owned land for an unlimited period to peasant farmers, guaranteed him widespread support among the popular classes.

The double legacy of the Francia period—widespread state control over the economic resources of the country, and the increased ethnic homogeneity of the population, which was partly the result of his ban on foreigners (including the Spanish elite) marrying among themselves—provided a firm foundation for the ambitious development strategy pursued by his successor, Carlos Antonio López (1840–62). López welcomed foreign technical expertise as long as it was under firm state control, but did not permit private foreign investment. The construction of one of the earliest railways and telegraph lines in the region, as well as the establishment of an iron foundry epitomized the economic progress and self-confidence of the López era.

Both Carlos Antonio López and his son Francisco Solano López, who succeeded him as president in 1862, regarded the independence of Uruguay as fundamental in ensuring the equilibrium of political forces in the region. Any outside intervention in Uruguayan affairs was thus interpreted as an indirect attack on the sovereignty of Paraguay herself. A Brazilian intervention to install a favorable government in Uruguay thus led to war between Paraguay and Brazil in 1864. When Argentina refused permission for Paraguayan troops to cross her territory en route to defend their allies in Uruguay, President Francisco Solano López declared war on Argentina. In May 1865, Brazil, Argentina, and the new Colorado Party government in Uruguay signed a secret pact, later known as the Treaty of the Triple Alliance, to overthrow "the barbaric dictatorship" of Francisco Solano López, as well as annex territory and gain control of Paraguayan state assets.

After five years of bitter struggle in which women and children fought alongside the Paraguayan troops, defeat finally came on March 1, 1870, when López himself was killed in battle at Cerro Corá in the far north of Paraguay. By then the country's population of around 450,000 in 1864 had been reduced to around 153,000, a catastrophic loss of 65 percent of the prewar population. The economy was prostrate, the nascent industry destroyed, Asunción had been sacked by the Brazilians, and some 55,000 square miles, equivalent to over a quarter of its prewar territory, had been lost forever to Brazil and Argentina.

The War of the Triple Alliance thus marked a turning point in the history of Paraguay. The self-reliant development strategy of the previous fifty years was cast aside by the victorious allies and replaced by a long period of economic liberalism. As Paraguay was opened up to foreign investment and speculation, state lands and industries were sold off, and the country became dependent on foreign economic and political forces.

A Report on Paraguay in the London Press of 1824

Anonymous

The first decades of the nineteenth century saw growing interest in Latin America in Great Britain. Following the collapse of the Spanish Empire, the expanding British Empire sought to spread its influence in the subcontinent. The turbulent political events in the newly independent nations were closely followed in both political and commercial circles. Paraguay was the great exception to this gradual increase in information about the region. The shortage of news about the country was so extreme that it was often referred to as the "Tibet of Latin America." The isolationist policy pursued by Dr. José Gaspar Rodríguez de Francia, in response to attempts at annexation by Argentina, greatly restricted the opportunity for interchange of information with the outside world. There were no more than forty foreigners in the whole country, all of them closely monitored by Francia. Yet in 1824, precisely during this period of total isolation, an article about Paraguay appeared in the London newspaper Morning Chronicle, *which went to great lengths to explain and justify the regime of Dr. Francia and to present Paraguay as "the Arcadia of the New World." An accompanying note from the editor confirmed the existence of a report received from Paraguay that had provided the basis for the article—in fact, the first on the country to be published in Great Britain since its independence in 1811.*

The article was forgotten for over 150 years, until Moisei Al'perovich, a Russian academic, brought it to light.[1] In search of the report that provided the basis of the article, he discovered that a few days before its publication two ships had arrived in London directly from Asunción, sent by Francia with the clear objective of opening up a trading relationship with Europe. After a detailed study of the article, Al'perovich concluded that Francia himself was probably the author of the report.

The independent State of Paraguay, situated on the river Parana, between Peru, Chile and Brazil, and comprehending all those immense and luxuriant tracts of land which stretch East and West from Brazil, nearly as far as the Andes mountains, is divided into six departments, viz. Santiago, Conception, Villareal, Curuguatia, Candelaria, and Assumption. This valuable portion of country, constituting the heart of South America, has always been represented as a perfect garden and its inhabitants as the happiest race in the whole Southern hemisphere. They are extremely fond of their own country, laborious, steady in their pursuits, mild and upright in their disposition, and particularly attached to each other.

Their productions are rich and various, and their forests abound with valuable woods, gums and rosins, entirely unknown in the markets of Europe. The country abounds in cattle, and is intersected by several of the finest rivers in America, and studded with lakes. Amidst the general waste and destruction occasioned by the wars in the herds, which formerly were so abundant in the contiguous provinces, those of the Paraguayans alone have been preserved and increased. Most of the grains known in Europe are successfully raised in Paraguay, besides a variety of native ones. Fruits of various kinds are abundant, so that the inhabitants live at ease, with few wants, surrounded by plenty, and in the possession of a country that has always been represented as the Arcadia of the New World. Peace, union and concord, reign among them, and Patriots, in the true sense of the word, have no wishes—no ambition—beyond the welfare of their beloved native land.

[In 1811], influenced by the just principle of self-preservation, and unattended by the smallest political commotion, a meeting of the principal inhabitants was convened and assembled, when their situation was fairly laid before them, and discussed, and upwards of one thousand Deputies unanimously declared in favour of a total independence, and, as it were, political seclusion, in which state they have remained ever since. They further resolved that the Government should be confided to that person among them, who, from his virtues and knowledge, should be found most deserving of the public confidence; but, in order to avoid the conflict of two parties, headed by two individuals, equally entitled to this distinction, they determined to elect Dr. Francia and M. Yegros Joint Governors. These two persons, for some time, administered the affairs of Paraguay jointly, each having a separate district, and commanding an equal force; till, in the course of time, the inconvenience of this plan was felt, and the ascendancy of Dr. Francia having, in the mean while, increased, at a second meeting of the inhabitants, he was elected sole governor—a command he has held ever since, revered and beloved by the people.

From the peculiar traits of character Dr. Francia has since evinced, it is evident he sought to exercise this supreme command from no interested or ambitious views. His country was early attacked by an enemy from Buenos

Ayres; every effort was made to induce the inhabitants to enter into the La Plata coalition, on the one hand, and that of Artigas, on the other, and had Dr. Francia been obstructed by the interference of a colleague, possibly he never would have been able to repel the aggressions of his neighbours, or so successfully shield this territory from civil commotions, and afterwards, by his foresight and perseverance, raise it to a state of prosperity and happiness it now enjoys, beyond any other portion of the same continent.

Dr. Francia is a native of Paraguay, and was bred a lawyer. Not fond of society, and rich enough to live with ease and independence, previous to the revolution, he remained retired on his own estate in the country, principally devoted to study; his pursuits gave him a reputation for learning beyond any of his countrymen, and his virtuous and moral conduct, added to his stern probity and known disinterestedness, subsequently secured their confidence. Gradually Dr. Francia has consolidated his power, and without any of the appendages or expenses of state; he exercises the duties of first magistrate, and his orders are obeyed throughout the whole territory the instant they are received. Justice is his guide, and he derives no emolument from his administration. He sees to every thing himself; purchases the clothing and arms for the militia, settles disputes, grants passports, and, in short, superintends each department of government, every thing being conducted on the most simple and economical scale. He has no favourites—no enemies—and, by a fair and impartial demeanour, he stands unimpeached in the opinions of his fellow-countrymen, after governing them for a number of years.

Strictly containing themselves to their own territorial limits, and intent only on keeping their rights and property unimpaired, for the last fourteen years the Paraguayans have had no external enemies, nor has their tranquillity been once interrupted. Thus concentrated within themselves, their country has served as an asylum for those fleeing from desolation and civil war in the surrounding provinces, by which means their numbers have been considerably increased. Emigrants have flocked thither from Corrientes, Tucuman, and Buenos Ayres; but more particularly from the eastern bank of the River Plata at the time it was desolated by Artigas, who eventually fell into the hands of the Paraguayans, by whom he is still kept a prisoner. These fugitives carried with them the property they were able to collect in their own provinces, and having thus found a secure asylum, they adopted the habits of their benefactors, and devoted themselves to the pursuits of industry. By this means, and the advantages of peace, and a regular mode of life, the population of Paraguay has increased in a manner unexampled. Numerous tribes of Indians, who formerly refused to submit to the restraints of civilised life, and wandered about without any fixed residence, have also been blended into the general mass, and become useful members of society, According to the last census, taken in the year 1822, the population of Paraguay amounted to upwards of 500,000 souls. They have 30,000 armed militia, occasionally exercised, and only called into the field in case of an external attack. Their regular armed force consists of three small vessels of war, intended for the defence of the rivers, and four legions of volunteers of 2,000 men each, paid only whilst on duty. This armed force is commanded by Dr. Francia, and the military regulations enacted by Marshal Beresford in Portugal have been adopted in Paraguay.

Old-established custom and well-authenticated precedents, such as are on record from the time of the Jesuits, together with the laws of the Indies, regulate the administration of justice, and the concerns of Government, in every thing not opposed to the Provisional Code drawn up and ordered to be observed by Dr. Francia, in which he has consulted the habits, wants, and situation of the people he governs, having their peace and prosperity at heart, and being anxious to promote their social improvement by a moral and substantial education. This Provisional Code has been drawn up so as not to clash with the customs and even the prejudices of a people, peculiar in every thing. In order to be lasting, he has been desirous that all changes and reforms should be gradual, and not adopted by the people until they could duly appreciate their value. So great is the simplicity of manners among the Paraguayans, and so prompt the administration of justice, that few or none of those crimes are to be met with which embitter corrupt and overgrown societies, where the means of existence often depend on painful toil or the abuse of ingenuity. Their Governor seems to have followed the substantial part of the old policy of the Jesuits, who, by the most wonderful address, retained, till the time of their expulsion, an absolute dominion, both in spiritual and temporal concerns, over the inhabitants of Paraguay. He foresees and provides for their wants, and by rendering them individually happy and contented at home, he binds them to the support of a Government, the practical advantages of which they have daily before their eyes. He has thus made them united, and consequently strong in case of attack. All are subject to the same laws, and no distinctions are known beyond those which superior merit bestows. Hence the public revenue is regular and secure, and having been imposed by general consent, it is easily collected, without any expense to the Government.

It has been the obvious policy of this extraordinary man to preserve his country from anarchy and civil war, and, in order to effect his purpose, he induced the principal proprietors to make a temporary sacrifice, by allowing no other intercourse with foreigners and neighbours, than what was indispensably necessary to procure arms, and such articles as the Government stood in need of, fearful that the influx of strangers might lead to confusion, and counteract his paternal plans. The Paraguayans consented to the privation of external trade, and the consequent loss of a large portion of their produce, and zealously devoted themselves to the internal improvement of their growing republic. All the surplus revenue was laid out to advantage. The idle hands were employed in opening roads, making bridges, and other useful works, and the few slaves the country possessed were gradually freed, without any loss to their owners. Public liberty is well regulated; yet the printing of political works has been discouraged until the people shall be better grounded in substantial knowledge, and more removed from the backward state in which they were when they entered on their political career. So readily did the inhabitants submit to these privations, or so efficient rather was the voluntary police, in which each co-operated for the general good, that during the first nine years not a single letter left the country without having been first inspected by the Chief Magistrate—a fact perfectly well authenticated.

With the exception of Brazil, the Paraguayans have never attempted to establish relations of amity and commerce with any independent State, not even with those situated in their own neighbourhood, their whole attention having been turned to the means by which their own liberties and tranquillity could be preserved. The frequent overtures of Buenos Ayres to enter into a general confederation of all the provinces formerly constituting the Vice-royalty of the River Plate, have uniformly been rejected, from the principle that all engagements of such a nature could not fail to embroil Paraguay in those unhappy dissensions which have so long afflicted the contiguous districts. The Emperor of Brazil lately invited the Paraguayans to form part of his dominions, but the offer was declined in a firm, although respectful manner. The Paraguayans, in short, have formed a peculiar policy of their own, and they seem resolved to continue united among themselves, prepared at the same time to make every sacrifice in order to secure their own tranquillity and independence.

Note

1. Moisei Samuilovich Al'perovich, "New World Arcadia: Unknown Materials on Paraguay in the 1820s," in *Soviet Historians on Latin America: Recent Scholarly Contributions*, Conference on Latin American History, vol. 5, ed. Russell H. Bartley (Madison: University of Wisconsin Press, 1978), 158–76 (abridged).

A Nation Held Hostage

Justo Prieto

The nature of the regime of Dr. José Gaspar Rodríguez de Francia (1811–40) has long been a highly contested issue in Paraguay. While he is seen by many across the political spectrum as having played a decisive role in defending Paraguay's independence against Argentina and Brazil, avoided the disastrous civil wars that swept much of the continent, and laid the foundations of a stable, egalitarian, and relatively prosperous nation, others have seen him primarily as a brutal tyrant who tolerated no opposition. The following excerpt falls into the latter category, arguing that Francia created a violent dictatorship under which civil rights were routinely violated, all opposition was crushed, and the nation was subjected to a regime based on isolation, violence, and fear. Justo Prieto (1897–1982) was a leading Liberal Party figure, acting at various points of his career as dean of the National University of Asunción, president of the Senate, president of the Liberal Party, minister of education and minister of foreign affairs. His interpretation is representative of that of many anti-Francistas today.

In October 1814, following a motion by Mariano A. Molas and other deputies, Francia had himself named Dictator by Congress; only one or two voices were raised in dissent. The public was unaware that dictatorship meant rule without limitation: Dr. Francia sought to emulate the example of Rome, and the new citizens [of Paraguay] foolishly believed the Roman tenet, that public threat would vanish with personal rule. Thus the government of the republic was turned into an absolute monarchy. The Dictator had his ministers, but they did not act as such, and history does not record their names or actions.

An act of protest led by military officers led to their imprisonment in remote forts along the frontier, and Dr. Francia took advantage of the situation to create a praetorian guard to replace the army. All those entering the new "Grenadier Battalion," responsible for carrying out special services such as operating as secret police, swore allegiance to the Dictator. With the machinery of despotism thus in place, Francia intensified his persecution of the Spanish, banning them from marrying white Paraguayans and from discussing politics, before finally destroying them as a group in society. He reestablished monopolies along the colonial model, and nationalized the church, laying the foundation for absolute control, closing schools, opening prison camps, and dismantling the great cultural project and organization of the nation planned and set in motion by Yegros, Cavallero, and La Mora.

In 1817, Francia's initial mandate came to an end, and Congress was convened for October 1. Even though during his first term of office an apparent honesty had cloaked his true intentions, there was clear popular opposition to his reelection, fueled by the imprisonment of several citizens and of four priests. Nevertheless, a significant number of deputies proposed Francia's reelection *ad vitam*, arguing that he had defended the independence of Paraguay against the expansionist intentions of Buenos Aires and the Portuguese, and that continued defense was necessary. Voicing wider public opinion, however, Acuña and Molas opposed a bill that they maintained went "completely against the republican-liberal system, as the proposed permanent dictatorship [was] nothing more than a monarchy behind a republican mask." These were the last throes of a thwarted revolution; the eventual triumph of the counterrevolution was plain for all to see. When Congress convened, four companies of infantry were deployed outside the building. By the time it rose, Francia had been invested as Dictator for life, his title "in perpetuity." Like all tyrants, he believed himself eternal, and claimed for himself the eternal future of the nation.

There was public dismay at the news. Many emigrated, while those who expressed their opposition were immediately imprisoned. On that day Paraguay was lost to humanity, as if some cosmic cataclysm had wiped it from the face of the earth. There is no parallel case in history of the taking hostage of an entire nation.

The special circumstances of the country made Francia's success possible, his plan of isolation a continuation of the policies of the old Jesuit reductions surrounded by their trenches and armed guards. The fiefdom of Dr. Francia was blessed with natural defenses: Paraguay was protected by deep rivers to the south and east, immense unexplored forests to the north, and the mysterious deserts of the Chaco to the west, where the indomitable Payaguaes and other nomadic tribes served as fearsome sentries, patrolling the rivers in their swift canoes. Nor were there any roads or means of transport by which to escape, and all mercy or aid for those who wished to flee this vast prison was denied by the tyrant's fearful vengeance.

It would be mistaken to claim that the people, thus imprisoned, rallied around Francia in support of his defense of independence. Civilian populations never rally to tyrants, and least of all at the cost of their own liberty. Dr. Francia was not a reflection of the Paraguayan people, but of developments at the time throughout the continent, in which brute force and aggression displaced the talent and thoughtfulness that colonial dictatorship had failed to foster. It was during this period, initiated by Francia and Rosas [in Argentina], that figures such as Páez in Venezuela, García Moreno in Ecuador, Belzú y Malgrejo in Bolivia, Castilla y Prado in Peru, and regencies, empires, and triumvirates in Mexico all the way to Porfirio Díaz, would emerge. There is no evidence that under Francia so much as a single member of the population expressed agreement with his policy of isolation even to curry favor or flatter the Dictator. He had none of the sycophants who in every age and every country seek to ingratiate themselves with those in power.

Tyranny

From that moment the distinction between public and private action was removed in the name of law and order and the personal surveillance carried out on behalf of the Dictator. When the heroes of independence, who saw the slope down which Dr. Francia was sliding, conspired to eliminate him, they were betrayed. An implacable and well-organized "gestapo" maintained surveillance in every home, on every street and in every street corner. The conspirators were discovered through the violation of the secrecy of the confession. One of them justified his actions declaring that Francia "violated every right of the community. We have tried to oppose iniquitous violence with one that was just. To defeat force with force is the natural right of men." Such was the grave rhetoric of liberation that arose from the conscience of the people in their sacred struggle to snatch the nation from the jaws of tyranny!

The years 1819–20 saw the beginning of an era of executions by firing squad, of prisoners held in dark dungeons, and of torture in the "Chamber of Justice," where savage Indians served as executioners. The rage of the tyrant fell especially on champions of independence and those who opposed his isolationist policy: Fulgencio Yegros, Pedro Juan Cavallero, Montiel, Iturbe, Acosta, Baldovinos, Noceda, Arostegui, and Galván were among the first victims in the struggle against tyranny, with dozens more following, among them several members of Congress who had lent their support to Francia's reelection and permanent dictatorship. These in turn were soon followed by Fernando de la Mora and Mariano Antonio Molas. From then on, the operation of the dictatorship became merciless and evil.

The denunciation of supposed criminals and the practice of spying—in the army, in the clergy, in homes and in the street, with fines, confiscation, and extortion—became routine. Terror gripped the people. A dark shadow fell across a nation kidnapped by a power-crazed tyrant. Dr. Francia did not seek power to liberate a nation. If he accepted the *fait accompli* of independence, it was only in order to exercise a form of despotism without limits. His system of government was one of absolute totalitarianism. Almost all land was confiscated, and the possessions of the clergy and religious communities, who suffered the same fate as that of all other real or imagined enemies of the Dictator, were turned over to the state.

The monopoly of the state was practically complete. A form of rationing was imposed in all areas of life. Commerce, cattle ranching, and industry fell under the authority or direct control of the state. Fines, expropriation, and indefinite personal service replaced taxation as sources of revenue. Francia disbanded the army and the clergy—not because they had declared their opposition to him, but because he feared and refused to allow any autonomous body. Rather than suppress them, he found it more convenient to annul them by dividing them through espionage. Educational establishments were closed as, in his opinion, "Minerva should sleep whilst Mars wakes." In his precarious military-style education system, children were taught a "reformed patriotic catechism" whose principal result was a tendency to the permanence of despotism.

Foreigners were persecuted. "The English, and Europeans in general, ruin other nations with their commerce," Dr. Francia maintained—a reaction against the failure of his own efforts to persuade England, through the intermediary of the Robertson brothers, to deliver arms and munitions in its own ships to Asunción in exchange for yerba mate and leather. The Spanish were expelled. Lack of trade undermined the price of products such as tobacco, yerba mate, and beef, ruining the incipient but promising industrial and merchant classes. The hulls of a hundred ships of various sizes split open in the ports under the burning sun. By 1831, 365,000 Paraguayans lived in slavery.

Latterly, Francia turned his attention to Brazil with a view to mitigating the effects of his disastrous policies. However, any trading licenses he granted were obtainable only through endless bureaucracy and after careful examination of the origins of income and goods, and were never awarded to the descendants of Spanish colonists, to relatives of prisoners or of those suspected of opposition, or to anyone whose surname happened to be the same as any of these. The long overland journey through the forest that covered both countries, the high prices placed by the Dictator on

Paraguayan goods—a strategy to which the Brazilians responded in kind in order to allow the establishment of a form of barter—and the high import and consumer duties he imposed meant that by the time they reached Asunción the price of goods was astronomical, and that they were often unfit for consumption.

Class struggle disappeared in Paraguay under the equality of servitude. Even in the judicial system no hierarchy remained. The only exception was the Dictator. To complete the picture one might add only arbitrariness—arbitrariness as a way of dealing with life, honor, and possessions, and a total absence of civil rights. During the first session of Congress, Francia gave a speech that conformed to the custom of the era. He spoke of the natural law which protected "a liberty proportionate to the capacity of the people, and the need to establish unbreachable defenses against the abuse of power." There has never been a contradiction as great as that between his words and deeds.

Like all despots, Francia stirred up nationalist sentiment by attacking foreigners; he painted them as contemptible, inferior beings, and Paraguay as the victim of their actions. He imprisoned the great intellectual Aimé Bonpland for many years, despite Bolívar's threats to invade Paraguay in order to liberate him.

Like all tyrants, Francia identified the state with his person. A conspiracy against the government was thus a betrayal of the nation. Just as in the times of the Jesuits, the state machinery was the product of despotism and the violent imposition of obedience. The *cabildos* (town councils) disappeared, abolished by the Dictator in 1824; with them he buried the seeds of democracy that had been both the cause of, and central to, the Revolution of the Comuneros. The judicial system also disappeared, with justice effectively administered by the Dictator in person, and the prisons became filled with political prisoners for whom there was no trial and no mercy.

And thus Paraguay lost forever its collective consciousness. A people reduced to servitude and impotence increased the power of the tyrant daily. Seven hundred prisoners languished in cells in 1839. The nation had ceased to be part of the world. All that remained of it were the borders drawn on maps.

In Defense of Doctor Francia

Richard Alan White

José Gaspar Rodríguez de Francia was the absolute ruler of Paraguay from 1814 to 1840 and the founding father of the Paraguayan nation after independence from Spain. As a historical figure, he remains something of an enigma and the subject of fierce controversy among historians—and, indeed, Paraguayans. The revisionist work entitled Paraguay's Autonomous Revolution, *by the U.S. historian Richard Alan White, remains one of the most thorough and controversial defenses of Francia's regime. According to White, Francia's austere rule was instrumental in welding Paraguay into a nation with a firm economic base for future development. Economic and diplomatic isolation and complete neutrality, in great part a consequence of foreign aggression and the annexationist desires of the Buenos Aires region, might have gained Paraguay the reputation in Europe as the "Tibet of South America," but it allowed the country to avoid the internecine conflicts that ravaged the rest of the region at that time. Furthermore, as White argues, the rule of Francia oversaw a profound and unique social revolution, which included the destruction of the power of the creole elites, of the church, and of the landed oligarchy, and the establishment of state-led development. As White points out, since Francia's policies attacked the interests of the national and international elites—precisely those who have written the history of Paraguay, he has been widely—and unjustly, in White's view—represented as a cruel, almost inhuman, tyrant.*

The continuing demands of the inhabitants of the interior provinces and Buenos Aires (*porteños*), along with the creation of the Viceroyalty of the Río de la Plata (1776), forced the reopening of the port in 1777. Instead of serving the interior, however, Buenos Aires, the imperial administrative and commercial center of the region, wielded the power of the customs house to benefit itself and its Spanish metropolis. With the introduction of Enlightenment liberal concepts and the beginning of the independence struggle in 1810, the interior provinces hoped to gain economic parity. But at the same time that the porteños promulgated revolutionary ideas and fought for American liberation from Spain, they insisted upon maintaining their traditional position as the economic center of the Río de la Plata.

In the name of the *causa común* against Spain, Buenos Aires solicited, and received, support from the interior provinces. After the Spanish had been defeated in the Río de la Plata, the porteños sought to impose a strong central government, thereby maintaining their control over the region's economy. In opposition to this centralist (*unitario*) attempt to preserve the political and economic structure of the old viceroyalty, the autonomists (*federales*) fought for a confederation of equal provinces. Although the two factions joined to oppose Portuguese intervention in the Río de la Plata, they proceeded to fight a protracted civil war among themselves. In fact, it was the struggle between the unitarios and the federales that characterized Argentina's early national history.

Paraguay constitutes the single exception to this conflict-ridden period in the region's history. Under the leadership of Dr. José Gaspar Rodríguez de Francia, this country not only maintained absolute neutrality in the bloody Río de la Plata power struggle, but, seizing political and economic independence, also enacted a radical social revolution. Although the remarkable accomplishments of the popular regime must not be considered simply another of history's "great man" stories, Francia obviously played a central role in Paraguay's profound transformation.

Born on January 6, 1766, Francia began his education at home. Later he attended the University of Córdoba, graduating in 1785 as a Master of Philosophy and Doctor of Theology. While at the university, which had been run by the more tolerant Franciscans since the expulsion of the Jesuits in 1767, he not only studied the traditional philosophers and theologians, but was also introduced to the revolutionary European and North American ideological currents of the epoch. Francia's education encompassed Saint Anselm's ontological argument and Rousseau's *Social Contract,* the moralism of Thomas Aquinas and the pragmatism of Benjamin Franklin. His years of university training and the profound influence of the Enlightenment, the North American Revolution, and the popular revolt of Túpac Amaru II in Peru all contributed to the formation of his radical philosophy. Like idealists of every epoch, Francia viewed the world around him in absolute terms, judging situations and people as either right or wrong, good or bad.

Upon his return to Paraguay shortly after graduation, the young Doctor of Theology began teaching Latin at the Seminary of San Carlos, but was forced to resign several years later when a heated dispute erupted over his radical religious and political ideas. After reading Spanish law, Francia embarked upon a legal career that won him respect throughout Asunción. He

spoke fluent Guaraní and befriended the Paraguayan peons, in whose eyes
he became a protector and hero. From the poor he asked small fees, if any,
while from his wealthy clients he demanded and received large sums. As
John Parish Robertson, a contemporary observer, remarked, "His fearless
integrity gained him the respect of all parties. He never would defend an
unjust cause; while he was ever ready to take the part of the poor and the
weak against the rich and the strong."

Although elected dictator by the enormous representative congresses of
1814 and 1816, throughout his years in office Francia avoided the personalism
which typically accompanies dictatorship. With the sole exception of Villa
Franca—founded in the mid 1820s with Francia's help after floods had forced
the inhabitants of Villa de Remolinos to abandon their homes—he did not
permit a single town, barrio, street, edifice, statue, or coin to be dedicated
in his honor. Similarly, breaking a long-standing tradition, El Dictador cate-
gorically refused to accept gifts of any kind. This policy had such a striking
impact on the people that more than twenty years after Francia's death a
number of old men recalled it vividly:

> On January 6, 1817, because of El Dictador's birthday, he was given a
> reception [which was] obviously grander than in any other year. But he
> would not accept any gifts, maintaining that it was necessary to abol-
> ish that rotten Spanish practice, which was conducive to obligating the
> poor, who oftentimes had to make a sacrifice to comply with it.

As another contemporary summarized this aspect of Francia's character,
"His private fortune has not been increased by his elevation; he has never
accepted a present, and his salary is always in arrear: his greatest enemies do
him justice upon these points."

Francia's incorruptible honesty, especially during his tenure as dictator,
became proverbial. Avoiding the accumulation of any substantial personal
wealth or property, he lived a modest, semi-secluded bachelor's life on a
fraction of the salary established for him by the popular congresses. Furthermore, as Francia left no heirs, upon his death on September 20, 1840,
all of his belongings, in accordance with the laws that he had promulgated,
were automatically confiscated by the state.

Not surprisingly, El Dictador's radical, popular, and nationalistic policies
met with growing internal and external opposition. The combined unitario
and federal attacks devastated Paraguayan commerce, serving as the catalyst for the disastrous 1820 Great Conspiracy to overthrow the popular regime by the Paraguayan elites, whose privileged position had rested upon
the nation's monocultural export economy. In fact, Paraguay's revolution

Portrait of Dr. José Gaspar Rodríguez de Francia. Photograph by Alfred Demersay, from Alfred Demersay, *Le docteur Francia, dictateur du Paraguay: Sa vie et son gouvernement* (Paris: Typo. H. Plon, 1856). Courtesy of Milda Rivarola.

denied the entire upper class, both Spanish and creole, their traditional social, political, and economic bases of power. Appointing new officials drawn directly from the common people, Francia did not allow the elites to hold government or military positions, thus prohibiting them from exercising direct power. He used a system of fines and confiscations to deny them the less direct, but equally effective, power that money commands.

Along with abolishing the elite's municipal governing council (*cabildo*), the revolutionary regime controlled the church and its auxiliary institutions. It banned the church's brotherhoods, closed its monasteries, and confiscated its landed estates. Nullifying the royal land grants and confiscating the property of the upper-class conspirators, Francia enacted a profound land reform which abolished the traditional latifundia land-tenure system. By the time of El Dictador's death in 1840, well over half of Paraguay's rich central region had been nationalized, scores of prosperous state ranches (*estancias*) had been established, and tens of thousands of people had homesteaded farms leased from the state. The private sector of the economy had to compete with the government, which, reducing taxes to a minimum, received most of its income from the sale of imported goods, livestock, and state-produced manufactured products. In addition, the state completely controlled international commerce through its own massive participation and a strictly enforced system of trade licenses.

Because Francia attacked the interests of the national and international elites—the class that has written the history of Paraguay—traditionally he has been considered the prototype of despotic tyranny. The most infamous of Latin American dictators, Francia has habitually been portrayed as a grim and somber potentate, a cruel despot with an insatiable lust for power, or simply as a vile monster; the years of his government are commonly known as Francia's "Reign of Terror." Presented as a sadistic and arbitrary despot unconcerned with the momentous liberation movements sweeping Latin America, Francia is accused of hermetically isolating Paraguay the better to impose his tyranny upon an intimidated nation.

Autonomy, Authoritarianism, and Development

Thomas Whigham

Analysis of the nationalist period (1814–70) has attracted fierce controversy and fundamental differences of opinion between advocates and detractors of the authoritarian "developmental" state model. In this unusually balanced account, written especially for The Paraguay Reader, *one of the leading historians on the period, Thomas Whigham, offers a concise overview of the rule of the three dictators, José Gaspar Rodríguez de Francia (1814–40), Carlos Antonio López (1840–62), and Francisco Solano López (1862–70) in terms of the defense of national sovereignty and the construction of a sense of national identity and nationhood, almost unique in the region at that time.*

Paraguay boasted many of the attributes of nationhood well before the other independent states of the La Plata region. It had a relatively homogeneous population with shared traditions of community and solidarity. This accorded Paraguayans their own language, Guaraní, and with it, an identity that seemed "national" even during colonial times. No other South American country could lay claim to anything similar.

The cohesion that characterized Paraguay owed a great deal to Dr. José Gaspar de Francia, who ruled as supreme dictator from 1814 to 1840. More like a Bourbon administrator than a revolutionary, Francia held the reins of power in a tight grip. Beginning in the early 1820s he imposed a near-hermetic isolation on the country by forbidding all entry and exit and operating a closed-door policy that succeeded in insulating the country from the political traumas that engulfed Argentina and Uruguay. But Paraguay paid dearly for this domestic tranquility. Its society languished under a regime that was as autarkic as it was orderly. This led to the strengthening of many earlier Hispano-Guaraní cultural traits: xenophobia, paternalism, and a narrow focus on the local community continued, unchallenged by the seductive vagaries of the Enlightenment. The economy reverted to barter, self-sufficiency, and reciprocity.

To the extent that it occurred at all, political discussion was reserved for conversations behind closed doors. The Paraguayan government was only nominally republican, and drew most of its legal practices from the Leyes de las Indias.[1] In administrative matters, Francia's officials translated his wishes into policy in the interior, while he handled all relevant matters in Asunción directly.

In general the people supported this arrangement. They saw the state as virtuous, as being legitimate because it acted responsibly. Dr. Francia's government did not clash with paternalist traditions, it embraced them. It cultivated a feeling of identity among Paraguayans, an endorsement of their status as a separate, independent people full of quiet pride, if not power. As one commentator from Asunción put it several decades later: "[Our] state or nation is a reunion of a great family that has come together to guarantee itself against the advances of other societies . . . and in guiding its common interest, it has submitted to a person chosen by society, and to the laws dictated by that submission. . . . The politics [of the chosen government] have forged the key that opens the door to happiness or unhappiness depending on how it is used." Dr. Francia could not have said it better.

When the Supreme Dictator died in 1840, his garrison commanders inherited his authority. They, in turn, relied on the secretarial skills of an obscure country lawyer, Carlos Antonio López, who soon received the rank of co-consul, and, by 1844, president. López set aside the previous interpretation of governance and statecraft, though not its spirit. He envisioned a reordering of Paraguayan administrative structures and fashioned a state apparatus to replace the colonial structures associated with Francia. These innovations included a reorganized treasury, new ministerial posts, and an officer corps for the army. He filled these positions with individuals of confidence.

López proved flexible and willing to learn from past mistakes. If his basic impulses were just as authoritarian as those of the deceased dictator, he balanced them with a "liberal" inclination. This he demonstrated by writing a new constitution for Paraguay that featured minor borrowings from the French and Spanish legal treatises that he had studied as a youth but which had little in it of an Anglo-Saxon-style democracy. Instead, it vested the executive branch with the totality of real authority.

We might wonder why Carlos Antonio López even bothered to draft such a document. Francia had ruled Paraguay by fiat, and in practice little

Portrait of Carlos Antonio López. From the collection of Milda Rivarola.

had changed since his time. However, López considered himself to be a responsible, modernizing leader. Every European state, he observed, had established a legal structure based on its needs and potential. Paraguay ought to be no different. He also wished to open the country to outside commerce, and before Europeans arrived with their radical doctrines, he wanted them to understand who ruled the country. In this sense, the constitution was directed as much to foreigners as to his own people.

One indication of this is suggested by the omission of any reference in the constitution to Paraguay's Hispano-Guaraní character. López never saw his nation in indigenous terms, nor did he need to. Since colonial times, state and community existed as parallel entities that rarely overlapped. One was Spanish-oriented and scripted toward the literate world. The other was Guaraní and directed inward as part of Paraguay's oral heritage. The modernization that López proposed had little to do with the latter, for Guaraní had no words to express key political concepts like "parliament" or "representative democracy."

Of course, the president had no reason to consult people who spoke little or no Spanish. An autocrat tends to discount the underclass, and, indeed, the *vox populi* played no role in the organization of the Paraguayan state. To López this seemed natural. To maintain and extend his power, he nonetheless needed a legal framework for Paraguay that local elites and foreigners could respect. And the chief message that he wished to convey was that the president was all-powerful and that Paraguay was his to command.

But not all outsiders accepted this interpretation. Many Argentine politicians had long regarded Paraguay as a breakaway province that sooner or later would be reunited with the motherland. Brazil, for its part, harbored no formal claims on Paraguay, although the empire's relationship with Asunción was always laced with mistrust. The frontiers between the two countries had never been properly established and no one had yet determined the status of navigation on the waterways that both countries shared. In short, Paraguayans felt their independence to be continually under threat from both neighbors, but especially from Argentina.

Carlos Antonio López is still seen today as one of the great patriots, an architect of the Paraguayan nation. He deserves such a position. During his twenty-year tenure as president he oversaw the construction of a legislative palace, an arsenal, a shipyard, a national theater, a foundry and industrial smithy, several presidential residences, and various military facilities. He also introduced the railroad to Paraguay, the first such innovation in the region. He was a builder, not a destroyer, and his authoritarianism seemed an inconsequential price to pay for modernization and economic development. The "industrial" projects demonstrated López's interest in the age of steam and iron. Yet they also revealed a strong concern that the Paraguayan state should be recognized. The new government buildings supported that effect, for they stood out like leviathans among the adobe and thatch.

While the far-sightedness of Carlos Antonio López won him praise from those who had lived as adults under Dr. Francia, for the new generation he appeared cautious. Younger eyes turned instead to his eldest son, Francisco Solano López, who far more than his lawyer father regarded modernity and national greatness as a single goal. When the thirty-seven-year-old Francisco succeeded to the presidency in 1862, he inherited his father's ambitions for a strong, modern Paraguay but little of his caution and thoughtfulness. The younger López had spent the previous decade as war minister, and had been to Europe to secure armaments and diplomatic recognition for Paraguay. Thanks to his obsessive efforts, by the 1860s, the military boasted some strikingly modern features: a flotilla of steamers converted from mercantile to naval use, several new artillery pieces, Congreve rockets, a world-class fortress, Humaitá, that European observers likened to Sebastopol, and a well-trained army of 28,000 troops.

Such militarization fed into the sense of national identity and pride, cultivated over the previous fifty years, reinforcing the dangerous idea that Paraguay was under threat of imminent invasion and would inevitably have to defend itself or be overwhelmed.

Note

1. The Leyes de las Indias were the body of legislation issued by the Spanish crown that regulated the social, political, and economic life of its American empire. [Eds.]

The Treaty of the Triple Alliance

The military treaty was signed in Buenos Aires on May 1, 1865, by representatives of the governments of Argentina, Brazil, and Uruguay, formalizing a "Triple Alliance" against Paraguay. As article 18 makes clear, it was a secret treaty, whose existence came to light only ten months later, on March 2, 1866, when it was tabled by the British government before the House of Commons. This has long given rise to speculation that Britain was instrumental in forging the alliance as part of its plans for expansion of its "informal empire" in South America. Although the stated aim of the war was to remove President López from office rather than attack the Paraguayan people, the treaty also specifically set out Paraguayan reparations (article 14). The territorial pretensions of the allies, as spelt out in article 16, also contradicted the treaty's stated commitment to maintaining the territorial integrity of Paraguay (article 8). Publication of the text of the treaty led to protest from other Latin American countries and generated considerable sympathy for the Paraguayan cause. It also stiffened Paraguayan resolve to resist the allies, as it demonstrated that the war was aimed at the dismemberment of Paraguay rather than simply the removal of López. In fact, as a result of the war, Paraguay experienced considerable territorial losses of 55,000 square miles to Argentina and Brazil, thereby reducing its area by 25 percent.

The Government of the Oriental Republic of Uruguay, the Government of His Majesty the Emperor of Brazil, the Government of the Argentine Republic:

The two last being actually at war with the Government of Paraguay, it having been declared against them by acts of hostility by that Government, and the first being in a state of hostility, and its internal safety threatened by the said Government, which calumniates the Republic, and abuses solemn treaties and the international customs of civilized nations, and which has committed unjustifiable acts after interrupting the relations with its neighbors by the most abusive and aggressive proceedings:

Being persuaded that the peace, safety, and well-being of their respective nations is impossible while the present Government of Paraguay exists, and that it is imperatively necessary for the greatest interests that that

The Triple Alliance. *Cabichui* (The wasp) was a four-page broadsheet published at army headquarters in Paso Pucú during the Triple Alliance War. Directed by Juan Crisóstomo Centurión, who had studied in England, it ridiculed the enemy by means of caricature and satire, while extolling the virtues of the Paraguayan troops. Its cartoons and graphics by Saturio Rios appear strikingly modern to the contemporary observer. In this cartoon, the three leaders of the Triple Alliance are being burnt alive in a cooking pot, with Emperor Pedro II holding a copy of the Secret Treaty. Illustration by Saturio Rios. *Cabichui*, August 22, 1867.

Government should disappear, at the same time respecting the sovereignty, independence, and territorial integrity of the Republic of Paraguay have resolved to conclude a Treaty of Alliance, offensive and defensive, with that object; and have named their Plenipotentiaries, as follows:

His Excellency the Provisional Governor of the Oriental Republic has named His Excellency Dr. Carlos Castro, Minister of Foreign Affairs; His Majesty the Emperor of Brazil, his Excellency Dr. J. Octaviano de Almeida Rosa, Counselor and deputy to the National Legislative Assembly and officer of the Imperial Order of the Rose; His Excellency the President of the Argentine Republic has named his Excellency Dr. Rufino de Elizalde, Minister of Foreign Affairs—who, having exchanged their respective credentials, which they found in good and due form, agreed to the following:

ARTICLE 1—The Oriental Republic of Uruguay, His Majesty the Emperor of Brazil, and the Argentine Republic, unite themselves in an offensive and defensive Alliance for prosecuting the war provoked by the Republic of Paraguay.

ARTICLE 2—The Allies will contribute with all the means at their disposal, by land and by water, as they may find convenient.

ARTICLE 3—The operations of the war commencing in Argentine territory, or in Paraguay bordering on Argentina, the chief command and direction of the allied armies will be confided to the President of the Argentine Republic and General-in-Chief of its Army, Brigadier-General Bartolomé Mitre. The maritime forces of the Allies will be under the immediate command of Vice-Admiral Viscount Tamandaré, Commander-in-Chief of the squadron of His Majesty the Emperor of Brazil. The land forces of the Republic of Uruguay, a division of the Argentine forces, and one of the Brazilian forces, which will be indicated by their respective commanders, will form an army under the immediate orders of the Provisional Governor of the Oriental Republic, Brigadier General Venancio Flores. The land forces of His Majesty the Emperor of Brazil will form an army under the immediate orders of its General in Chief, Brigadier Manuel Luis Osório. Although the high contracting Powers have agreed not to change the field of operations, yet, with the object of protecting the sovereign rights of the three nations, they have determined that the chief command shall be reciprocal should any operations have to be carried on in Oriental or Brazilian territory.

ARTICLE 4—The internal military order and economy of the allied troops will depend solely on their respective chiefs. The victuals, ammunition, arms, clothing, equipment, and means of transport of the allied troops will be supplied by their respective States.

ARTICLE 5—The high contracting Powers will give each other any assistance which they may require, under the forms to be stipulated on that particular.

ARTICLE 6—The Allies bind themselves solemnly not to lay down their arms, unless by mutual consent, until they have abolished the present Government of Paraguay, nor to treat separately with the enemy, nor sign any treaty of peace, truce or armistice, or any convention whatever to put an end to or to suspend the war, unless by the common consent of all.

ARTICLE 7—The war not being against the people of Paraguay, but against the Government, the Allies will admit a Paraguayan Legion, formed of the citizens of that nation, who wish to assist in deposing the said Government, and they will furnish it with all necessaries in the form and under the conditions, which shall be established.

ARTICLE 8—The Allies moreover bind themselves to respect the independence, sovereignty, and territorial integrity of the Republic of Paraguay. Consequently, the Paraguayan people may elect their own Government, and give it any institutions they deem fit; none of the Allies incorporating it, nor pretending to establish any protectorate, as a consequence of this war.

ARTICLE 9—The independence, sovereignty, and territorial integrity of the Republic of Paraguay will be guaranteed by the high contracting Powers collectively, in conformity with the foregoing article, for the term of five years.

ARTICLE 10—It is agreed by the high contracting Powers that the exemptions, privileges, or concessions which may be obtained from the Government of Paraguay, shall be gratuitous and common, and if conditional shall have the same compensation.

ARTICLE 11—When the present Government of Paraguay has disappeared, the Allies will proceed to make the necessary arrangements with the authorities which may be constituted, to insure the free navigation of the Rivers Paraná and Paraguay, so that the rules or laws of that Republic do not obstruct or prevent the transit and direct navigation of the war or merchant vessels of the allied States, on their voyages to their respective territories and dominions which do not belong to Paraguay; and to establish the necessary guarantees for the effectiveness of the arrangements, under the condition that these laws of river policy, although made for the two rivers, and also for the River Uruguay, shall be established by common accord between the Allies and other States on the boundaries, for the term which shall be stipulated by the said Allies, should those States accept the invitation.

ARTICLE 12—The Allies also reserve to themselves to concert the measures most conducive toward the guarantee of peace with the Republic of Paraguay after the fall of the present Government.

ARTICLE 13—The Allies will name Plenipotentiaries, to make arrangements, conventions, or treaties with the Government which may be established.

ARTICLE 14—The Allies will demand from this Government the payment of the expenses of the war which they have been forced to carry on, and also the payment of damages caused to public and private property, and to the persons of their citizens, without an express declaration of war— also of the damages subsequently done in violation of the laws of war. In like manner the Oriental Republic of Uruguay will demand indemnification for the damages caused by the Government of Paraguay, in the war she has been forced to take a part in, in defense of her safety, threatened by that Government.

ARTICLE 15—The manner and form of liquidation and payment, proceeding from the above-mentioned causes, will be determined in a special convention.

ARTICLE 16—With the view of avoiding discussions and wars regarding the question of boundaries, it is agreed that the Allies will demand from the Government of Paraguay, that in its treaties of limits with their respective Governments, the following basis shall be adhered to:

   i) The Argentine Republic will be divided from that of Paraguay, by the Rivers Paraná and Paraguay, as far as the boundary of Brazil, which, on the right side of the River Paraguay, is the Bahía Negra.

   ii) The Empire of Brazil will be divided from the Republic of Paraguay on the side of the Paraná, by the first river below the Seven Falls, which, according to the late map of Mouchez, is the Ygurei, following its course from its mouth to its rise.

   iii) On the left side of the Paraguay, by the Rio Apa, from its mouth to its rise.

   iv) In the interior of the tops of the mountains of Mbaracayú the streams running eastward will belong to Brazil, and those running westward to Paraguay—a straight line, as far as possible, being drawn from the tops of those mountains to the rises of the Apa and Ygurei.

ARTICLE 17—The Allies guarantee to each other, reciprocally, the faithful execution of any arrangements and treaties which may be concluded in Paraguay, in virtue of which, it is agreed that the present Treaty of Alliance shall always remain in full force and vigor, in order that these stipulations be respected and carried out by Paraguay.

    i) With the object of obtaining this result, they agree, that in case one of the high contracting parties cannot obtain from the Government of Paraguay the fulfillment of an agreement, or in case that Government should pretend to annul the stipulations agreed upon with the Allies, the other powers will employ means to make them respected.

    ii) Should these means prove useless, the Allies will concur, with all their power, to obtain the execution of the stipulations.

ARTICLE 18—This treaty will remain secret until the principal object of the Alliance has been obtained.

ARTICLE 19—Those stipulations of this treaty which do not require legislative authorization for their ratification, will come in force as soon as they are approved by the respective Governments, and the others when the ratifications are exchanged, which will be within the term of forty days from the date of said treaty, or sooner, if possible, and will take place in the city of Buenos Aires.

In faith of which, we, the undersigned Plenipotentiaries of His Excellency the Provisional Governor of the Oriental Republic of Uruguay, of His Majesty the Emperor of Brazil, and of His Excellency the President of the Argentine Republic, in virtue of our full powers, have signed this treaty, placing thereto our seals, in the city of Buenos Aires on 1st May, in the year of Our Lord 1865.

    Signed: CARLOS CASTRO, J. OCTAVIANO DE ALMEIDA ROSA,
        RUFINO DE ELIZALDE.

Protocol

Their Excellencies the Plenipotenciaries of the Argentine Republic, of the Oriental Republic, and of His Majesty the Emperor of Brazil, assembled in the Ministry of Foreign Affairs, agree:

    1. That in compliance with the Treaty of Alliance of this date, the fortifications of Humaitá shall be demolished, and that no other or others of that kind shall be permitted to be constructed, thereby interfering with the faithful execution of the treaty.

    2. That as it is a necessary measure toward guaranteeing peace with the Government which may be established in Paraguay, not to leave it

any arms or elements of war, all those found will be equally divided among the Allies.

3. That any trophies or booty which may be taken from the enemy shall be divided between the Allies by the one who makes the capture.
4. That the Generals commanding the allied armies shall concert the means of carrying these stipulations into effect.

And they sign the present in Buenos Aires, on 1st May, 1865.

Signed: CARLOS CASTRO, RUFINO DE ELIZALDE,

       J. OCTAVIANO DE ALMEIDA ROSA.

"I Die with My Country!"

Thomas Whigham

The Triple Alliance War (1864–70) between Paraguay and the combined forces of Brazil, Argentina, and Uruguay was the most destructive and costly war in post-independence Latin America and has been described as the first example of "total warfare" in the subcontinent. It was the defining event in Paraguayan history, putting an end both to its autonomous development model and also to its position as a regional power. As well as losing approximately 25 percent of its territory, an estimated 60 percent of its prewar population of 450,000 died, including a staggering 90 percent of adult males, as Paraguayans, young and old, male and female, battled desperately against both overwhelming military force and the ravages of disease and starvation. The country doggedly held off the allied invasion for nearly six years, before the allies finally caught up with Francisco Solano López and the remnants of his decimated army at Cerro Corá in the far north of the country. His famous last words "I die with my country!" were prophetic; Paraguay has never regained its former power.

The following selection, written especially for The Paraguay Reader *by one of the foremost historians of the war, is a clear, analytical summary of the course and major events of the conflict. It finishes with a concise but perceptive analysis of why Paraguayans refused to surrender when faced with overwhelming odds and when there was no hope of victory.*

The new president dreamed of transforming Paraguay into a regional power broker and, in this quest, he accelerated his father's military buildup. The future Marshal conceived of his position and that of his neighbors in geopolitical terms, like pieces on a chessboard. He consulted recent European experience and posited the existence in South America of a balance of power among the states of the La Plata region and Brazil. This dubious interpretation assigned Paraguay the role as arbiter and guarantor of continued peace in the region. However, this peace had never existed, even in colonial days, and Solano López's decision to defend it placed his country in a dangerous position that his father would surely have avoided.

Flores.   Mitre.   Pedro II.   La triple alianza.

This image shows the leaders of the Triple Alliance—Venancio Flores (Uruguay), Bartolomé Mitre (Argentina), Emperor Pedro II (Brazil)—threatening Paraguay, which is personified as Liberty and Justice. Illustration by Saturio Rios. *Cabichui*, May 13, 1867.

Things came to a head in 1864 when the Brazilian government announced its intention to intervene in the Banda Oriental (modern-day Uruguay) in support of Venancio Flores, a Colorado Party *caudillo* who also enjoyed the patronage of Bartolomé Mitre, the president of Argentina.

López felt that the threatened intervention in Uruguay would upset the regional balance of power and ultimately lead to Paraguay's annexation by one or both of her neighbors. To prevent what he felt was his country's partition between Brazil and Argentina, López issued an ultimatum demanding that Brazil refrain from invading Uruguay. When the Brazilians ignored his warning, he sent his navy to seize the Brazilian steamer *Marques de Olinda*, which at that moment was carrying the new provincial governor of Mato Grosso to his post at Cuyabá. The Paraguayans then launched a successful (though strategically unwise) incursion into the same province, occupying several towns in the process.

This bellicose Paraguayan response to Brazilian interventionism surprised the emperor's ministers and scandalized the monarch himself, who took the attack on Mato Grosso as a personal affront. A wave of patriotic indignation swept the empire. Units from the small standing army hastily embarked for the front. During the first week of January 1865, the imperial government established a new corps, the Voluntários da Patria, whose soldiers received higher pay and benefits than men in the mostly conscript army. As war fever gripped Brazil over the next few months, dozens of such battalions were raised. Enthusiasm combined with naiveté among the volunteers, who, like their counterparts in all wars, expected to be home before Christmas—with the laurels of victory in their grasp.

Only after he had completed his incursion into Mato Grosso did López try to aid the Uruguayan Blanco Party. Not surprisingly, Mitre's government in Argentina denied him permission to cross the province of Corrientes in order to march to Uruguay. López interpreted this refusal as collusion with Brazil and promptly declared war on the Buenos Aires government. Paraguayan forces landed at the river port of Corrientes in mid-April 1865 and then marched down the River Paraná toward the Argentinian capital, Buenos Aires.

On May 1, 1865, Brazilian and Argentinian diplomats met together with representatives of Flores's Uruguayan regime and signed the Triple Alliance Treaty, which committed their governments to the removal of López. Although they claimed no ill-feeling toward the Paraguayan people and made no overt demands for territorial concessions, in a secret protocol to the treaty, they did precisely that, pledging to satisfy their maximum claims against Paraguay. The Alliance marked a major shift in the historic pattern of regional relations, as the two regional powers put aside their historic rivalries in order to obliterate the Lopista state.

Historians have censured López for bringing this alliance together against him. However, he had mistakenly expected to receive support from the governor of Entre Ríos, Justo José de Urquiza, and those Argentinian Federalists who had yet to reconcile themselves to Mitre's presidency. López also assumed that an alliance between Brazil and Argentina could not survive the two states' historic rivalries. The Paraguayan occupation of Mato Grosso yielded some booty and stocks of arms but it delayed action on behalf of the Uruguayan Blancos until it was too late. Flores took Montevideo, and Paraguayan calculations were frustrated.

While Paraguay enjoyed some military advantages, the country was hardly the South American juggernaut that its enemies feared. In terms of population, resources, and access to outside supplies of materiel, it proved no match for Brazil, let alone for the Alliance countries as a whole. Paraguay's population of less than 450,000 was dwarfed by Brazil's 10 million, which when added to Argentina's and Uruguay's populations, totaled over 12 million. And each of those countries had reserves of capital and foreign sources of supply that the Paraguayans could never hope to equal.

Given such strategic disadvantages, López's only hope for a stalemate lay in quick and decisive military action, coupled with skilled diplomacy to

The portrayal of Bartolomé Mitre and Venancio Flores as subservient to the Brazilian emperor was a constant theme of *Cabichuí*, as shown in this cartoon, in which Pedro II is suffocating both of them with the cap of Liberty. Illustration by Saturio Rios. *Cabichuí*, June 3, 1867.

somehow exacerbate the divisions among his enemies. The former eluded him and he lacked the capacity for the latter. As a result, Paraguay ended up on the losing side of a bitter war of attrition.

Yet the country resisted far longer than anyone expected. The Marshal had no intention of going down easily. Soon after the treaty's signing, he sent a second Paraguayan force across the territory of Misiones toward Brazil. This army burnt isolated ranches and sacked villages before splitting into two columns that marched downriver along the Uruguay. However, the Paraguayan offensive was short-lived. On June 11, 1865, the imperial navy destroyed the greater portion of the Paraguayan fleet at the Riachuelo, just south of Corrientes, while two months later, allied forces under Venancio Flores crushed a sizable portion of the other invading force at Yataí near the right bank of the Uruguay. The remaining Paraguayan forces in

Rio Grande do Sul entered the town of Uruguayana but were soon besieged by a substantial allied army. Facing starvation, the remaining Paraguayan troops laid down their arms on September 18.

With the fall of Uruguayana, the strategic initiative passed to the allies, who spent most of the next year reforming their armies for a concerted attack on Paraguay. This was no easy task. Allied units had never worked in tandem, there were disagreements about strategy, and supply proved an ongoing problem. Finally, in mid-April 1866, allied forces surged into the southwestern corner of Paraguay, where they found themselves in difficult terrain. Their immediate objective was the fortress at Humaitá, which controlled the most direct river approach to Asunción. Hampered by swampy conditions, poor weather, and long supply lines, the allies also met stiff resistance. However, on May 24, 1866, López gambled on a frontal assault against the main allied position at Tuyutí. It was the bloodiest battle in South American history; thousands died before the allies emerged victorious.

But the war was far from over. On September 3, the allies stormed Humaitá's defensive perimeter at Curuzú. An interview between Mitre and Marshal López nine days later brought no prospect for an end to hostilities. Then, on September 22, the allies suffered a tremendous reverse when their troops failed to overrun the Paraguayan earthworks at Curupayty. Following the defeat, the allied advance stalled for two years, with the war now taking the form of a protracted siege of the Humaitá fortifications. By now, the Uruguayan role in the war had become negligible, while the Argentinian troops, who had borne the brunt of the fighting at Curupayty, saw their numbers diminish appreciably as a proportion of the allied forces. In 1867 still more Argentinians were withdrawn to suppress domestic rebellions in the west.

Expectations of a quick victory thus vanished, and disillusioned allied officers began to speak with contempt of the hollow triumphalism propagated by the Brazilian press. Brazil had to adopt desperate measures to maintain its army in Paraguay. Orders for new levies brought increasingly brutal pressganging of recruits, and the imperial government turned to freedmen to fill out the ranks. At the same time, the Marquis of Caxias, the country's most experienced general, was given command over Brazilian forces and in January 1868 he became allied commander in chief.

Caxias's appointment marked a signal difference in the organization and effectiveness of the allied army. Soon after his arrival, he started winning small engagements. The Brazilian naval squadron succeeded in forcing its way past Humaitá, a feat of limited military significance but much celebrated in Brazil as the beginning of the end for López. In July, the Marshal

In this satirical cartoon, Bartolomé Mitre asks for his watch to be repaired because it shows only the hours of defeat instead of the hours of victory. The watchmaker replies that the watch has a complex mechanism and that he should consult its manufacturer for an explanation—a veiled reference to Mitre's obsequiousness to the Brazilian emperor. Illustration by Saturio Rios. *Cabichui*, August 1, 1867.

The unequal relationship between the members of the Triple Alliance is graphically represented, with Pedro II sitting on the shoulders of Bartolomé Mitre and Venancio Flores. Illustration by Saturio Rios. *Cabichui*, September 19, 1867.

ordered the evacuation of most of Humaitá's remaining troops, all of them malnourished and in rags. Their defense had kept the allies at bay for two years, but they had reached the limits of human endurance.

Paraguay had exhausted its resources. The allies overcame a series of improvised defenses in their final march northward before outflanking the Paraguayan positions. A series of desperate battles followed in December, during which Caxias's troops destroyed the Paraguayan army. Marshal López retreated eastward to Piribebuy, where he reestablished his government and began to plan another hopeless resistance. On January 1, 1869, the allies finally landed at Asunción, which they found abandoned by the military, following the Marshal's orders. The Brazilians and Argentinians proceeded to plunder the city.

Despite having failed to capture Marshal López, the ailing Caxias unwisely declared hostilities at an end. He returned to Rio de Janeiro on health grounds and never came back. For several months, allied forces left López to lick his wounds in the hills in the east of Paraguay while they bickered among themselves. The Marshal somehow managed to cobble together an army of ten thousand boys, who attempted some modest raids, but in the main, waited and starved.

In April 1869, Pedro II named his son-in-law, the Count d'Eu, to command the allied forces. He proved to be just as much an organizer as Caxias. In August, he mounted a new offensive, over-running Piribebuy and slaughtering Paraguay's child soldiers at Acosta Ñu. Once again López eluded capture, retreating north with a shrinking band of followers. Brazilian forces took another six months before finally running him to ground at Cerro Corá on the Río Aquidabán. Like so many of his soldiers, he refused to surrender.

As Paraguay lay prostrate, the governments in Buenos Aires and Rio resumed their traditional foreign-policy stances, clashing over postwar considerations in Asunción. In 1869, the occupiers helped establish a provisional government of anti-López Paraguayans. This regime signed a peace treaty the next year, but Argentina and Brazil would continue to meddle in the country's governance until the end of the century and beyond.

The Triple Alliance War profoundly reshaped realities in Paraguay. When the struggle began, the Paraguayan people were already highly mobilized. Few doubted that Paraguay deserved a major role in the Platine region, especially in restoring the balance that had supposedly kept the peace, yet various memoirs suggest little real enthusiasm among Paraguayans in the first months of the conflict. Although it fared well in the Mato Grosso campaign, the Paraguayan military fought poorly in Argentina and Rio

Grande do Sul. Officers and men alike could not focus on an overall objective because they had no understanding of what that goal should be.

This failure not only reflected a lack of military acumen on the part of Francisco Solano López. It also revealed a basic historical pattern: when called upon to defend the homeland, Paraguayans "circled the wagons" to await the enemy assault. They did not relish moving outside their own territory to carry the attack to the enemy. This long-established defensive posture reappeared during the siege of Humaitá, where the allies encountered the obstinacy of the Paraguayans. "It would not infrequently occur," a U.S. diplomat wrote, "that one Paraguayan would be surrounded by a dozen of the enemy, all calling on him to surrender, . . . [instead, he would fight until] killed; or, if by chance he was disarmed during the unequal contest and forcibly made a prisoner, he would take the first opportunity when his hands were free to seize a musket or bludgeon . . . and kill as many as possible, until he was himself knocked senseless."

Why did the Paraguayans fight with such determination? Certainly not because they feared López. A despot can command obedience but not bravery and self-sacrifice. The Paraguayans plainly believed that their community faced imminent annihilation, and if they had to die, they intended to go down sword in hand. In this sense, the Marshal well understood his people's psychology. Paraguayan society had wrapped itself around the quest for national survival and immersed itself in the war effort. Compulsion was certainly a part of this picture but so was patriotism. Such loyalty ultimately produced an army of skeletal boys who wore false beards to fool the enemy into thinking that they were grown men still capable of fighting. And when, at the Aquidabán, a mortally wounded Marshal López exclaimed, "¡Muero con mi patria [I die with my country]!," he spoke the truth, for more than 60 percent of his people had perished.

A Chronicle of War

Leandro Pineda

The following extract provides a fascinating but haunting insight into the experience of one soldier over two years of the Triple Alliance War. It offers a firsthand account of the savagery of the conflict, the suffering of both sides, and the almost constant danger, but in a strikingly matter-of-fact tone. It is also interesting because it was written not by a high-ranking officer, nor by a member of the middle or upper classes, but by an ordinary soldier, who somehow survived the conflict to dictate his account to the justice of the peace for Guarambaré.

I enlisted at Cerro León in the Eleventh Cavalry regiment under Captain Vicente Florentín on March 31, 1864. I was soon promoted to corporal and then to sergeant, following some training at the Spanish Military School under Lieutenant (later General) Delgado. My regiment was sent to form part of the vanguard this side of the Bellaco Marsh, arriving on Wednesday, May 2, 1866. At about six or seven in the morning we received the order to cross the marshes at Paso de Cidra and attack the allied army while our troops crossed the same marshes by way of the passes at Angelito, Carrito, and Gómez, under the same order to attack. My brigade was under Colonel Bruguez.

The attack was simultaneous and quick. By the time the enemy patrols saw us, we were on them, attacking with swords, lances, and bayonets. The whole of the enemy vanguard was completely destroyed. We gathered up what loot we could, including an entire mobile artillery battery, complete with munitions. Our mission had been successful, but as we started to retreat, the main body of the allied army began to move, and a large infantry column set off to block our path to Paso de Cidra. Even though Colonel Bruguez sustained machine gun fire from his position at the pass, part of the enemy column managed to force its way through, engaging us in an intense exchange of fire. When the other part of the column was pinned down by Bruguez's machine gun fire, the colonel ordered us to draw swords and attack. We moved in quickly, forcing them back toward the narrow pass where the water was chest-deep. There they found themselves herded together, and fell into disorder, trying desperately to keep out of the reach of our swords. We lassoed some of them and pulled them out of the water. Those that escaped made their way back to their comrades on the other side. The main body of their army seemed content to bombard us from the higher ground that ran along the other side of the swamp.

My regiment continued operating in the vanguard. On Thursday, May 24, 1866, near the pass of Yataity Corá, we saddled our horses and formed up, bridles in hand, when a priest arrived. He ordered us to recite the act of contrition and gave us all absolution. Then an officer told us to take a swig of *caña* from a *guampa*.[1] All the time more of our infantry and cavalry were arriving, adding to the long line of troops. We were positioned almost opposite the pass at Yataity Corá, and the line extended almost uninterruptedly to the pass of Ybapoí. In front of us was the main body of the enemy's army. We waited for the signal to advance. When the three rockets exploded overhead we set off, trotting through Yataity Corá, Paso Ibayaí, and then the swamp, under a hail of artillery and rifle fire that opened huge gaps in our ranks.

Our orders were to attack General Mitre's headquarters, situated in an orange grove called Duré Cué or Naranhayty Rendá, directly in front of us. Although our ranks had been decimated, we managed to reach the enemy trenches and even engage with swords and bayonets. But they held us back. At sunset, the few remnants of my regiment fell back to our positions. There were so few of us that we could scarcely mount a guard. I do not know what the columns under Resquín and Barrios, which were meant to charge with us that day, from the right and left in a pincer movement, did or failed to do, but I am tempted to say that they did nothing at all. If they had, the outcome of the day would have been different.

The remains of other regiments were added to mine and from then on we became the Tenth Cavalry regiment, under Commander Gonzáles and in the vanguard, alongside two other regiments, the Twentieth under Captain Rivarola and the Second under Lieutenant Coronel. From then onward, from the pass of Yatayty to a place we called Umbú, after a tree of that name, we worked as the vanguard.

Between May 24, 1866, and October 23, 1867, we did not take part in any significant active combat, only guerrilla warfare and ambushes, some of them very bloody. But there were a few important events that deserve mention, such as the meeting between Marshal López and General Mitre in Yatayty Corá in September 1866; the launch of the aerostatic balloon in Tuyutí (I do not remember the date or month); the assault and capture of a supply convoy of mules and wagons between Tuyutí and Tuyucué, in which we gained possession of soap, biscuits, clothes, a few rolls of paper, and other items I cannot recall.

On October 2, 1867, Colonel Valois Rivarola, aide-de-camp to Marshal López, arrived at the vanguard position with two battalions of infantry and four pieces of mobile artillery. He hid his men to the right of our lines, in the bushes, scrub, and small trees, which were high enough to prevent the enemy from seeing anything in them. On the 3rd, Colonel Rivarola ordered us to advance toward the enemy and provoke them into retaliation. We advanced right up to the enemy trenches, under heavy artillery and rifle fire, suffering a number of losses. We then retreated under the same deluge of fire, but the enemy did not pursue us, seemingly content to bombard us from their positions.

Our ambush remained hidden. Colonel Rivarola ordered us to repeat the maneuver, which we did, again getting up close to their trenches, hurling insults interspersed with the piercing sound of the horns that each of us carried. Seeing that our rearguard was very thin, the enemy suddenly launched two cavalry regiments from our left, along firm ground, and from our right, which was marshy, about four battalions of infantry. The two columns converged in a pincer movement as we retreated back toward our lines. When we reached a point where we had our own hidden infantry to our left and the almost impassable boggy marshes protecting our right flank, and with the enemy columns just fifteen or twenty meters away, Colonel Rivarola gave the order to "about face." The bugle was sounded, and as one man, the hidden troops arose and fired at point-blank range on the enemy, while simultaneously the artillery opened fire. We then set upon both columns with swords, lances, and bayonets, decimating the enemy and pursuing the survivors almost to their own trenches. The butchery was horrific.

I recall that when we retreated that afternoon, each soldier carried two or three rifles that he had gathered from the battleground. The next day we buried about six hundred bodies in a mass grave, while many other bodies were lost in the swamps. Later we continued to find rifles and shotguns, which we took back to the main encampment, where we were rewarded with a jar of toasted corn mixed with coco seeds that we called *chicharró-lambaré*. This battle was known as Umbú.

On November 2, our commander, Mendoza, was summoned by Marshal López. He returned in the afternoon, gathered us together and told us to prepare to capture the forty-inch heavy cannon stationed in a fortified gun emplacement directly in front of us.[2] Before dawn on Sunday, November 3, 1867, the whole vanguard force set off at a canter, straight across the marshes, taking no detours or precautions. By dawn we were at the foot of the gun emplacement. The enemy fired from their trenches but because we had already dismounted and lay flat on the ground, the artillery shells went over our heads. The ditch around the gun emplacement was shallow, but the sides were high and sandy, making climbing them extremely difficult. However, with bayonets at the ready, we scaled the sides and entered the emplacement from several points. The enemy, a whole battalion and its officers, surrendered. A section of our forces took the prisoners back to our lines, while the rest of us tried to move the cannon. Unfortunately, it sank up to the muzzle in the swamp and we had to leave it there. We could see the enemy lines that had been attacked at the same time, still burning. From other points in their lines we managed to capture several pieces of artillery of lower caliber. I do not recall the names of the general or officers that led the operation.

At nightfall, when we had returned to our positions, Major Mendoza, our captain's brother, arrived with a small force and several teams of oxen tied together (about twenty oxen in all) and led us to where the cannon had got stuck. We got there, hooked up the cannon, and pulled it out. However, the enemy gun emplacement had been reinforced with artillery and when they saw us they opened fire. We did not return fire, as our job was just to bring back the cannon. Each time an ox was hit we untied it and carried on. In that way, we managed to get the cannon back to our lines.

Major Mendoza was injured in the operation by artillery fire and died a few days later. But that night the forty-inch cannon, which we called "Fiu" because of the noise its projectiles made, was presented to Marshal López. The battle was called Tuyutí and all of us who took part were decorated with a medal of honor. I still have it.

We continued our work as a vanguard force mainly in guerrilla operations and ambushes. In February 1868—I do not recall the date—hardened troops opened the way to Humaitá. On March 22, Curupayty and Paso Pucú were evacuated. From that time on, I formed part of the garrison at Humaitá.

We were completely cut off in Humaitá—by river and by land. The enemy bombarded us day and night from all sides. They made several attacks on our positions, which resulted in significant losses among their ranks. On July 16, 1868, they launched a major attack but were repulsed with huge losses. Whilst even a small defensive force remained, Humaitá proved extremely difficult to take.

In the end, our supplies ran out. Our daily rations consisted of one of three things: a cup of corn starch, a cup of manioc starch, or a strip of dried meat that we called *soó-juanchile*. On July 24 or 25, 1868, we abandoned Humaitá, moving by night to a place called Isla-poí in the Chaco. From there were began a further journey, crossing Lake Verá in canoes. Among the first we took across was Colonel Alén and other sick and injured men. Once we had landed them, we returned to Isla-poí to bring more people, always under cover of darkness. On Isla-poí we were attacked twice by forces that the enemy landed, but both times we drove them back. The place where they attacked was narrow and forced their troops to attack in close formation, which simply provided more fodder for our cannons. When we ran out of cannon balls, we packed the cannons with bayonets and fired them instead.

Our time on Isla-poí was extremely difficult. Many of us starved to death. We were forced to eat our leather whips and cartridge belts, as well as Colonel Martínez's lame horse.

When the enemy saw that we were making crossings via Lake Verá, they set up patrols of canoes and barges that would wait for us every night. We would fight our way through, disembark the wounded and dead and some healthy troops, and then fight our way back to Isla-poí. On each outward or return journey we would lose canoes until eventually we only had about eight or ten left. With these we tried to return to Isla-poí to bring across more people. On one of the canoes we placed ten soldiers, including myself, to act as a vanguard force for the flotilla, while the other canoes carried five or six. The enemy barges were waiting for us halfway across the lake. They let us come close and then unleashed a volley of fire. Of the ten soldiers on the first canoe, nine fell dead and the tenth (myself) was injured in the left arm. I fell into the bottom of the canoe, but then one of their barges ran over it, and I found myself in the water. I began to swim through the wreckage of canoes and barges, making good progress until I approached the shore, which was blocked by a dense swathe of waterlilies. With only one good arm, it was impossible for me to climb over them. I thought all was lost, but decided to try to swim under them, coming up for air between the tangled bunches of lilies. After three or four such dives, I reached the shore. I sat down, semiconscious at the foot of a large tree. From there I could hear the cries and screams of my unfortunate comrades who were like toys for the emboldened crews of the enemy barges. I had managed to escape thanks to the darkness of the night and the useful knowledge of how to swim.

After that, the route from Isla-poí was closed. Those who remained, more or less half of the garrison that had retreated from Humaitá, were surrendered by Colonel Martínez two or three days later.

Notes

1. *Caña* is Paraguayan rum. A *guampa* is an empty cow horn or gourd, used for drinking mate, a tea made from yerba mate.
2. This was a heavy fixed cannon, with great destructive capability, of which the Paraguayan artillery had very few.

The Lomas Valentinas Note

Francisco Solano López

This note was sent by President Francisco Solano López to the allied commanders on December 24, 1868, during the Lomas Valentinas campaign, which marked a turning point in the Triple Alliance War. Following the allied capture of the Paraguayan fortress at Humaitá, the remaining Paraguayan troops had withdrawn to fortified positions along the River Pikysyry, south of Asunción. But a renewed allied attack, which included the battles of Ytororó, Avaí, and Itá-Ybaté, led to the decimation of the Paraguayan army. In the note, written in these desperate times, López highlights two aspects of the war that would become part of the popular discourse in Paraguay in years to come, namely, the belief that the allies were determined to destroy the existence of Paraguay as an independent nation, and the extraordinary heroism of the Paraguayan soldiers against the enormous numerical superiority of the allied forces.

To Their Excellencies,

MARSHAL THE MARQUES DE CAXIAS,

MAJOR COLONEL D. ENRIQUE CASTRO,

BRIGADIER GENERAL D. JUAN GELLY Y OBES.

The Marshal President of the Republic of Paraguay ought perhaps to decline sending a written answer to Their Excellencies, the Generals-in-Chief of the Allied Army, in war against the nation over which he presides, on account of the unusual tone and language, incompatible as it is with military honor. . . .

These are precisely the sentiments which, more than two years ago, moved me to place myself above all of the official discourtesy with which the elect of my country has been treated during this war. At Yataity-Corá I then sought, in an interview with His Excellency the General-in-Chief of the Allied Army and President of the Argentine Republic, General Bartolomé

Portrait of Francisco Solano
López. From the collection
of Milda Rivarola.

Mitre, the reconciliation of four sovereign states of South America which
had already begun to destroy each other in a remarkable manner; but my
initiative met with no answer but the contempt and silence of the allied
governments, and new and bloody battles on the part of their armed representatives, as you call yourselves. I then more clearly saw that the tendency
of the war of the allies was against the existence of the Republic of Paraguay
and, though deploring the blood spilled in so many years of war, I could
say nothing, and, placing the fate of my Fatherland and its generous sons in
the hands of the God of Nations, I fought its enemies with loyalty and conscience, and I am disposed to continue fighting until that God and our arms
decide the definite fate of the cause.

Your Excellencies have thought fit to inform me of the knowledge you
possess of my actual resources, thinking that I have the same knowledge
of the numerical forces of the allies, and of their everyday increasing resources. I have not that knowledge, but I have more than four years' experience that numerical force and those resources have never influenced the
abnegation and bravery of the Paraguayan soldier, who fights with the reso-
lution of the honorable citizen and of the Christian man, and who opens a
wide grave in his country rather than see it ever humiliated. Your Excellen-

cies have thought fit to remind me that the blood spilled at Ytororó and at Avay should have determined me to avoid that which was spilled on the 21st instant: but Your Excellencies doubtless forgot that those very actions might have shown you beforehand, how true all is that I say about the abnegation of my compatriots, and that every drop of blood which falls to the ground is a new obligation for those who survive.

After such an example, my poor head will bear the burden of the ungentlemanly threat (if I may be allowed the expression) which Your Excellencies have considered it your duty to notify to me. Your Excellencies have not the right to impeach me before the Republic of Paraguay, my Fatherland, for I have defended it, I am defending it, and I will yet defend it.

My country imposed that duty on me and I take glory in fulfilling it to the last; as for the rest, I shall leave my deeds to history, and I owe an account of them only to my God.

If blood is still to flow, He will lay it to the account of those who are responsible. For my part, I am still disposed to negotiate for the termination of the war upon bases equally honorable for all the belligerents, but I am not disposed to listen to an intimation that I lay down my arms.

Inviting Your Excellencies, therefore, to treat of peace, I consider that I am, in my turn, fulfilling an imperious duty towards religion, humanity, and civilization, as well as what I owe to the unanimous cry that I have just heard from my generals, chiefs, officers, and troops, to whom I have communicated Your Excellencies' intimation—and also what I owe to my own name.

I ask Your Excellencies' pardon for not citing the date and hour of your notification, as they were not on the document which was received in my lines at a quarter past seven this morning.

God preserve Your Excellencies many years,

Francisco S. López,
Marshal President,
Republic of Paraguay

Memoirs of the Paraguayan War

Gaspar Centurión

Very few of those called up to defend Paraguay at the outset of the war survived until the end. One of those few was Gaspar Centurión, a sergeant major in the Medical Corps. Present in many of the most bloody battles, in which he was on the frontline tending to wounded comrades while the fighting raged around him, Centurión was witness to the desperation, the annihilation, and the heroism of the Paraguayan forces and followers.

I was born on January 6, 1843, in Trinidad, in the old family house of my ancestor Don Juan Valeriano Zeballos. I attended the local primary school, along with my ten brothers and sisters, almost all of whom died in the war. After primary school, I went to the capital where I studied at the College of Philosophy under Padre Maíz.

When war broke out, everybody was called up to defend the country, each of us obliged to undertake whatever role fate held for us. My classmates were sent into different services, some to the army, and others to the military hospitals. I was sent to the Medical Corps, and was put straight into active service.

During the long campaign, I was an assistant to Doctors Skinner and Stewart, when I was not on duty with the vanguard corps or on special commissions. While my permanent post was in the operating hospitals where there was no respite, I frequently operated on the battlefield where I had a lot to do. I was active in the battles of Tuyutí, November 3, 1867; Paso Espinillo, March 21, 1868; Ytororó, December 6, 1868; Abay, December 11, 1868; Lomas Valentinas, December 21–27, 1868; and Rubio-Ñu, August 16, 1869.

In these terrible battles, in which the heroism of Paraguayan soldiers shone, I found myself among the troops in the midst of the fighting, trying to offer medical help under a hail of bullets, amid the clash of lances and bayonets, often under the hooves of horses and always exposed to a multitude of dangers. It is one of the greatest sources of pride in my life that I helped so many brave men, saved so many lives, and relieved the suffering and agony of those who gave their lives for our homeland. I witnessed many things in those horrific days. Perhaps I was in a better position to see events than those who were actually wielding the sword in battle.

Withdrawal from Lomas Valentinas

Following the battle of Lomas Valentinas, which lasted for seven consecutive days, we found the road to Yaguarón blocked by the enemy and thus had to seek refuge in the great marshes between Villeta and Carapeguá. In this unforgettable place, López had ordered us to open a path and secure a rope across the main channel of a fast running river, to help facilitate the movement of troops. Along this improvised path, made rapidly for a forced withdrawal, the army of López was able to retreat.

The deep lake known as Ypecuá was crossed first by the healthy troops, then by the wounded, among whom I recall many with recently amputated limbs, then by women who carried one or two young children, and finally by young children, some abandoned, others simply following their parents. I calculated the length of this *via crucis* to be about two leagues. One had to actually see the line of people to be able to appreciate the true bravery, determination, and patriotism of the Paraguayan people. Nobody was forced to undertake this cruel retreat. The army had been scattered, yet the soldiers made every possible effort in the middle of the jungle to reach the other side of the deep swampland and rejoin their divisions.

And the civilians? Despite the hunger and unimaginable suffering in the rearguard, they carried on, resigned to their long Calvary, refusing to abandon the army. Out of sight of the Marshal, the High Command, the officers and the troops, and amidst the confusion and pain, they could easily have left the path, surrendered to the enemy, or simply gone home, tired of so much martyrdom. But such a decision seemed inconceivable to these people after all they had been through.

We reached a small hill to the north of the path at sunset, with the intention of continuing the following morning toward the road to Carapeguá. Throughout the evening and the night people continued to arrive, asking for news of friends and relatives, and the path that the Marshal had taken, with the idea of following him. Thus, the new army of Azcurra was formed. In the following unequal battles, it was this army that defended the national territory, palm tree by palm tree, all the way to Cerro Corá.

The Battle of Rubio Ñu

Surrounded and vastly outnumbered by enemy troops, we fought without respite until our battalions and regiments had been completely annihilated. By this time our army was a mere shadow of what it had been, made up as it was of old men, the wounded, and children aged between twelve and fourteen. Even so, we held back the constant enemy charges and fought with such bravery that it was as if our troops were battle-hardened veterans.

The survivors, barely 20 percent of those at the outset of the battle, were almost all wounded. Such was the deluge of projectiles fired by the thousands of enemy troops that surrounded us, and our complete lack of cover on that open field, that we thought it would be impossible for any of us to survive. Just before the call to retreat, I was hit by a bullet in the left leg. I managed to get to a small river, and there found hundreds of comrades along its banks, all trying to clean their wounds. River water was the only medicine available. I did the same and then hurried on.

At nightfall, near a small mountain, General Caballero, commander of the battle of Rubio Ñu, and the rest of the troops, stopped in order to gather together the stragglers. One can only imagine that scene of suffering. From all sides, soldiers and officers emerged out of the night, exhausted from the battle and the retreat, but relieved to have done their duty. Many of them even arrived with smiles on their faces, making jokes and cheerfully telling stories about the battle. What a long-suffering, selfless people. Their good humor, a balm against pain and suffering, never seemed to abandon them, even in the darkest moments.

I met a young soldier from Carapeguá called Rojas, who offered to act as my assistant, and we found a small house where we spent the night, half a league from the encampment. With only the light from the fire to work by, Rojas helped me cut open my leg with a knife and take out the bullet that was still there. I bandaged my leg as well as I could, and at daybreak we rejoined the rest of the army and continued onward—toward where, nobody knew or could guess.

In the North

Once I had recovered from the wound I had received at Rubio-Ñu, I was ordered to join a vanguard division in Santa Rosa de Carimbatay, under Colonel Rosendo Romero, His Excellency's aide-de-camp, with Commander Pérez second in command. On October 16, 1869, we reached Tandei-y, where we rested for two days before continuing our journey toward Villa Ygatimí, where the main encampment had been set up. Here, the Marshal ordered the officers to meet to receive their orders, about two hundred yards from the troops. Moments later, the Marshal, accompanied by his High Command, arrived, and addressing himself to those present, spoke at great length about, among other things, the need for a division to step forward and take on an important mission. And for this reason he was calling upon the Army Corps whose officers were present, since they had already shown their bravery and patriotism on many occasions. . . . His speech, delivered in a shaking voice and in such a desolate place, moved us deeply. He then explained what our mission would be.

We were to head toward Panadero, until we got to "Tacuarita" and "Tacuara Guazú," the large farms owned by the García-Corvalán family, and there collect and bring back all the available cattle for the troops. The Marshal warned us that in those parts there were many well-armed enemy troops and we should be prepared to make any necessary sacrifice should we come into contact with them. We should be sure to leave the battlefield victorious and collect as many enemy arms as possible for our own troops. Following the meeting, the bugle gave the signal to march at about 3 PM.

A few hours later we followed the path into the great forest of Itanará where we spent the night, continuing the whole of the following day until sunset. On the third day we passed a fort called Sanjita, reaching the trenches of Río Verde at nightfall. From there we proceeded to Tacuatí and then Tacuarita, from where Major Clemente Montiel and Captain Aquino were sent forward with eighty men to Tacuara Guazú. The next day, as we set off to rejoin Montiel, we heard gunfire and stopped. A little later a messenger arrived, requesting reinforcements, which the colonel denied, instead ordering a retreat. What had happened? Major Jacinto Bogado of the Thirteenth Cavalry Division had received orders from above to support us; but before he could reach us, he had run into enemy troops and his force had been completely wiped out. After four days of fighting, the remnants of the Thirteenth Cavalry under Major Bogado managed to reach us, in a truly lamentable state, near Aguaray. Just twenty soldiers remained.

After passing through Tacuatí, toward Lima-Tuyá, our division began to disintegrate due to the lack of orders and food. We did not know where to go or even which direction to take; the enemy was blocking all the roads and the stragglers that joined us all brought conflicting reports, which sowed panic among our already decimated division. A lot of the time we spent in the forest, where the starving soldiers searched for something to eat in the thick jungle.

In these miserable conditions, with no hope of getting back to the High Command, and in danger of capture by the enemy, eight of us decided to look for a way out of the dense forest. We followed a path, which, after about two leagues took us to the banks of the River Jejuí near Tupí-Pytá. Realising where we were, we began our long trek, resting during the day and marching through the night until dawn. In this way, each one of us finally made it to his final destination, our homes.

The Women of Piribebuy

Juan O'Leary

As many historians have argued, the Triple Alliance War was perhaps the only example of "total warfare" between nations in Latin America, in the sense that the entire Paraguayan population, rather than merely its army, was involved in the defense against the advancing allied forces. This was in great part due to the widespread belief that the Triple Alliance sought to destroy Paraguay rather than simply to remove the dictator Francisco Solano López. Such fanaticism was also fueled by the sheer brutality of the war, especially during the final campaigns, when few prisoners were taken. The battle of Acosta Ñu (1869), in which the allies defeated an army largely composed of Paraguayan children wearing beards, has become part of the Paraguayan national epic, as has the involvement of women in every aspect of the long defensive campaign.

The following extract is written by Juan O'Leary (1879–1969), who, as a member of the Generación del 900, played a key role in the revisionist interpretation of the nationalist period, and especially of the Triple Alliance War, which he sought to transform in terms of collective memory from a national catastrophe to a heroic national defense—the epic encounter of the Paraguayan nation. In the following extract, which recounts the desperate defense of Piribebuy in the last year of the war, the heroism of the Paraguayan defenders—and especially the women—is set against the cold brutality of the victorious assailants.

It was August 12, 1869. The cannons had been thundering since dawn and Piribebuy burned under the terrible enemy bombardment. The Prince of Orleans [Count d'Eu, son-in-law of Pedro II] was infuriated by the resistance put up by the small town and the losses that his troops had suffered. What could be done to take the Paraguayan trenches and storm the town? The resistance was inexplicable. Around the long defensive perimeter, we had just 1,600 men, twelve bronze cannons, and one howitzer. And the enemy was attacking from all sides.

The hours passed and still the assailants saw no sign of any weakening of the resistance in Piribebuy. The Imperial Prince fumed. This was his

This anonymous photograph of Paraguayan prisoners of war was probably taken by the Montevideo-based U.S. photo company W. Bate. Photographer unknown. From the book *La Guerra del 70: Una visión fotográfica* (Asunción: Museo del Barro, 1985), 56.

first military operation in Paraguay, and with the reputation of the Crown of Brazil at stake, failure was inconceivable. He could not afford to even doubt success. He was accompanied by two of the bravest generals of the Empire—Osorio and Mena Barreto. And his troops, who outnumbered the Paraguayans by ten to one, were hand-picked veterans, accustomed to holding their own against Paraguayan heroism.

However, against all expectations, his optimistic calculations had been upset by the stubbornness of the defenders. Piribebuy continued to hold out with a ferocity that shocked the assailants. What could be done? For his part, General Osorio proposed a final assault by hand-to-hand combat that would decide the day. His slogan was the same as ours: Victory or death. And, as with Humaitá, just one year before, he proposed launching one powerful strike against our trenches to end the momentous struggle for once and for all. Osorio was more exasperated than anyone. He was ill and the wound that he had received in Abay had still not healed. His foul temper got steadily worse under such frustrating circumstances.

The Prince of Orleans was nervous and unable to overcome his powerful instinct for survival. He was unconvinced by the audacious plan proposed by General Osorio. Above all, he could not forget what had happened to Caxias after the disaster of Osorio in Humaitá, when he had been accused of sending Osorio to certain defeat because he was jealous of the reputation of the intrepid gaucho from Rio Grande.

The Prince knew he could not afford to underestimate the Paraguayans, who after all had five years' experience of defensive warfare.

Under such circumstances, the Prince devised a tighter and less risky strategy. He ordered all the carts to be loaded with provisions and then sent them forward toward the destroyed central Plaza of Piribebuy. Under the cover of the carts several divisions of assailants would advance, opening up a path through the trenches. Then he would launch the final grand assault.

The allies advanced thus, avoiding our cannon fire. But when they emerged on to open ground to charge they were met by a deafening volley of fire that forced them to retreat. Three times they were thrown back and three times they charged again, urged on by their officers. In one of these assaults, General Mena Barreto was killed by a single shot from Corporal Gervasio León. Osorio stepped over his body and charged on toward our trenches.

Chaos reigned in the center of Piribebuy. We had run out of ammunition and had no more troops able to repel the attacks. Major Hilario Amarilla, our most famous artilleryman, fought on, loading his cannons with small coconuts, having already used all the rocks, remains of guns and even bits of bayonet that he could find. Our Commander in Chief, Pedro Pablo Caballero, had used all the resources available to sustain the resistance, but there were simply no longer any soldiers or ammunition left, and the enemy troops were fast approaching the last lines of our defensive trenches. The bombardment intensified.

In the town nowhere had escaped the bombardment and the battle seemed to be nearing its conclusion. Nothing else could be done and everyone seemed either to have been killed or lay defenseless, crushed by fatigue and with no more ammunition. . . . But not everyone. . . . A group of several hundred women gathered, who had witnessed the agony of their children, and they stood ready to consummate such sacrifice, to seal that heroic, romantic page in our history with their own blood.

With no guns, the women moved forward to the trenches to fight and to die before the countless guns of the enemy. By now, the cannons had fallen silent and the gunfire had ceased. The Brazilians advanced victoriously into our trenches, with the sun reflecting from their sharpened bayonets, believing that the battle was finally won.

But a long cry of rage and desperation from hundreds of voices met the first Imperial troops who entered our positions. And this roar that seemed to rise from the depths of the earth was followed by a volley of empty bottles and a cloud of sand that temporarily blinded the assailants. The women of Piribebuy had risen up as one.

Huddled in the depths of the trenches, hidden among the corpses, they had been invisible to the enemy. And now they arose to fall beside those they had loved in life, to accompany them in the journey into the unknown. Armed with empty bottles, with pieces of glass, their nails and their teeth, they fell upon the enemy. The bottles broke Brazilian skulls, the glass sliced open their cheeks, the teeth tore out chunks of flesh, and the nails scratched out their eyes.

The soldiers from the three nations, those war-weary troops of the Triple Alliance, were unable to escape the fury of those desperate women. Their bayonets and swords were no match for such an enemy. Blinded by the sand in their eyes, they struck out uselessly into thin air, while the heroines of Piribebuy bloodied their hands, wreaking vengeance on behalf of those who had fallen.

"A scene straight from Zaragoza!" exclaimed a Brazilian historian who could not help but admire the epic nature of the scene, which was worthy of being ranked alongside the most heroic struggles of history. The Prince coldly noted events in his campaign diary, as could only be expected from such a cruel monster.

How did it end, this struggle between men who fought like women and women who fought like men? The heroines of Piribebuy were wiped out, almost to the last one. Those who survived were taken before the Prince. Having witnessed the sacrifice of the Paraguayan defenders, they were now forced to watch as the wounded had their throats cut and the hospital, still full of patients, was burned to the ground.

The wife of Commander Caballero was forced to watch the execution of her husband. For the crime of having held out and having refused to surrender, his hands and feet were tied to the wheels of two cannons and then, with his body suspended in the air, his throat was cut.

Thus ended a struggle that not even the massacre of Zaragoza could match, and which was more akin to the barbaric times when the savage conquistadors did something similar to the unfortunate Tupac Amarú in Peru.

Of course, no reference to the massacre was ever made by the Prince of Orleans in his minutely detailed campaign diary.

The Death of López at Cerro Corá

Silvestre Aveiro

Colonel Silvestre Aveiro (1835–1918) was born in Limpio. From humble origins but of great intelligence he rose to be a confidant of President Carlos Antonio López. He was the last person to speak with the president before his death, and read his will to Marshal Francisco Solano López. He then became an advisor to the Marshal and fought alongside him in the Triple Alliance War until the final defeat at Cerro Corá. This extract is taken from his "Military Memoirs, 1864–70," and recounts the final moments of the war. Aveiro does not accept the standard version that López was killed by a lance thrust by a Brazilian corporal but maintains that he saw him captured alive.

We reached the encampment at Cerro Corá on February 14, after a long march during which it rained every day, either in the morning, the afternoon, or at night. As soon as we arrived and had rested, General Caballero's force set off for Colonia Dorado in search of cattle. But he did not find them, as a Brazilian column, sent to prevent López from advancing any further while the main army advanced on his encampment, came across Caballero and his small force and captured them.

López had placed a small vanguard force on the River Tacuaras, about a league or more west of the River Aquidabán. From Cerro Corá (a field surrounded by hills) Colonel Carmona, Lieutenant Villamayor, and Surgeon Solalinde escaped together with two doctors, but were captured by the Brazilian column. Solalinde refused to go with them by feigning illness, but the others changed their uniforms and acted as guides. Thus it was that at dawn on March 1, 1870, the Brazilians managed to take the small vanguard force without firing a single shot. However, a woman managed to escape back to the Paraguayan encampment and shortly after sunrise informed López of events.

López ordered a battery of four guns to be set up on the Aquidabán ford and organized the few remaining units that he had, in readiness for the coming battle. He also called a meeting to deliberate on how to deal with the crisis, to see whether we felt it would be better to seek refuge in the surrounding mountains or to await the Brazilians, ready to fight to the death. At that meeting were General Resquín, General Delgado, Colonel Centurión, Padre Maíz, Commander Palacios, Fathers Espinosa and Medina, Colonel Aquino, Colonel Abalos, and myself. We agreed that we should fight to the death so as to end the war for once and for all.

López ordered me to get together as many men as possible, prepare the oxen for Madame Lynch's carriage, and to await orders. At about 11 AM I remembered that there were troops still guarding his mother and sisters, and sent an officer to fetch them. As we retreated along the Aquidabán, a few yards after the main body of troops we passed López's mother and sisters. When his mother called out to him, "Help us, Pancho" (as she referred to him), the Marshal replied laconically, "Trust in your sex," and we carried on.

We proceeded eastward down to the river and followed the bank toward Chiriguelo. I was about thirty or forty yards behind the Marshal, and after me, further back, was Captain Cabrera with the bugle. He was followed by several others, who faded from sight as we entered the forest.

Suddenly, six enemy cavalrymen, including the corporal who led them and was armed with a lance, galloped toward our left flank. At a little inlet formed by the river, they were able to cut López off and called on him to surrender. Captain Arguello and Second Lieutenant Chamorro, López's former groom, galloped toward the Brazilians and attacked them, but they were forced back, badly injured, to a short distance from the enemy, many of whom were also injured.

However, just before this occurred, two Brazilians, including the corporal, had ridden up to López with the aim of grabbing his arms. But López drew his sword and tried to strike the corporal, who avoided the blow and thrust his lance into López's stomach while the other Brazilian struck him a blow to the right temple. It was just at this moment that Chamorro and Arguello had arrived.

After the skirmish, the Brazilians stayed back about ten yards in front of López. When I arrived at his side, López was furious, still mounted on his bay, and shouting, "Kill those monkeys!"

Touching his leg, I said in Guaraní, "Follow me, Sir, and save yourself." Asking whether I was indeed Aveiro, he turned his horse and followed me. I was exhausted and starving and although I had a sharp sword I no longer had the strength to cut through the undergrowth. I managed to make a path just by pushing forward with my body, following the tracks that the soldiers had made earlier whilst foraging for fruit. But just ten yards from the river, on an east-facing slope, I fell. The horse passed over me, fortunately without trampling me, but López also fell from his horse, head first down the slope. I got up, and López stretched out his hand for me to help him up.

He was so heavy that, try as I might, I did not have the strength to pull him up. At that moment the young Ibarra arrived, but even between us we were unable to get him to his feet. Then Cabrera joined us and the three of us managed to get him up and headed toward the river. As we approached the waterside, Cabrera said, "If you want I can bring more men, from over there," pointing to the south, from where we could hear more gunshots. Since I did not know how many men we had there, I gave him the benefit of the doubt and said in Guaraní that he should fetch help as quickly as he could. He left but never returned.

Ibarra and I carried López down to the river and crossed it, over slippery stones. On the far side we tried to lift him up onto the high bank, but when López saw that we could not, he said "Go and see if there isn't somewhere lower. . . ." We left him sitting on an uprooted palm that lay across part of the river.

When I was about eight yards away, Brazilian soldiers emerged from the forest onto the opposite bank of the river and opened fire. I climbed the bank and sat down in the undergrowth; then General Cámara appeared from where we had come, shouting the order to cease fire.

At that moment Surgeon Estigarribia emerged from the forest, his leg badly wounded, and tried to escape along the river. A Brazilian soldier ran after him, and right in front of me, speared him in the chest. He fell dead into the water.

The soldier turned toward me and since more Brazilians were emerging onto the riverbank all the time, I got up to try to reach López. But they had already taken him, and when they saw me get up they fired. I sat down and the shooting stopped.

I heard General Cámara and López exchange a few words, but I was unable to make out anything except for the word "country." Later I learned from an account published in Rio de Janeiro that when General Cámara had called on him to surrender, López had said, "Will you guarantee my demands?" When Cámara replied that he could only guarantee his life and nothing more, López had replied, "Then I die with my country!" He raised his sword but fell into the water, from where the Brazilians grabbed him and pulled him out, still alive. He was not speared by a corporal in the river as they say.

Seeing that they were taking López prisoner and were not interested in me, I escaped into the forest, and soon came across a group of about sixty women. I sent one of them to see if López was still alive and also to find out news of my family, but the woman never returned.

Hearing soldiers approaching, I realized that they must have remembered me and were now coming for me. I followed the tracks of others but I was unable to move up the slope with any speed. When I reached the edge of the forest I saw a Brazilian platoon with their guns at the ready. They came out of the forest, shouting, "He's escaped, that son of a . . . ." When they had gone, I carried on and by chance came across my family on the bank of another small river. Along with others who joined us, we spent the night near the same encampment in the foothills, then took the road to Concepción. After ten days we reached the Department of Concepción, and it was in Sanguina, one of our encampments, that we heard that the day before, two messengers had passed by with the news that López had died.

When I heard the news, and with my leg still injured, I decided to take the road to Concepción rather than to Corrientes, which had been our original plan. The following afternoon, General Cámara and his High Command overtook us. We were sitting by the roadside eating unripened oranges with Commander Palacios when General Cámara, whom we had known when he was still only a Colonel, approached us. I told Palacios not to get up, nor to stop eating his orange.

The General stopped and asked if I knew who he was. I told him that indeed I did and that he should also know who I was. He asked me if Palacios was an officer. I told him who he was, at which point Palacios stood up and said, "I am nothing, Sir." I shrugged my shoulders, as if to say that what he said was true. The General called over his Captain and said, "Take these men prisoner," and then rode away.

They told us to march, but I could only walk slowly, given the state of my leg. The Captain came and I told him that I could not go any faster. When he threatened to kill me, I said, "I am in your hands. You can kill me if you like, but I still cannot go any faster."

Impatiently, he ordered me to get onto a mule, and that is how I traversed the four leagues to Villa Concepción, where General Cámara had gone ahead. That was the first time I tasted manioc flour and salted beef.

A short time after we arrived, General Cámara summoned me to face serious charges. I answered them all with great dignity, since I felt resolute yet unsure of my fate. The first charge was to ask why, given my position, I had not taken the opportunity to assassinate López—whom he compared with Atila, Nero, Caligula, and others—since this would have been a great service to my country, liberating it from such a tyrant.

I answered that it was strange to hear such an accusation from his lips and that it ill befit him. Had I been in his position I might well have asked him the same question, because when all is said and done, López's government was as legitimate as that of the Brazilian Emperor Don Pedro II. Moreover, López had enjoyed the support of his entire people, who had sacrificed themselves for him in defense of a cause, the justice of which we were all wholly convinced.

Then he asked me if it was true that I had had the audacity to whip Señora Carrillo[1] and I said that it was true. When he asked me why, I replied that I had been carrying out an order. He then told me that the Señora had demanded that I be shot. I replied that it did not surprise me that she should have requested this of a foreigner, since she had also demanded it of López many times. In the end, I told him that he could do what he wanted with me; that I was in his hands, that I had dedicated my life to my homeland and it would make no difference whether I died now or later.

He dismissed me and called in Silvero. I did not see what happened to him or to Palacios. We spent the night guarded by eight sentries. I heard them say that they would bayonet these villains at the hint of a provocation.

Later they put me on a boat to Rio de Janeiro, and I returned to Paraguay five months later. I arrived back in Asunción in December 1870, having left in June 1865 to take part, as I eventually had, in the whole military campaign.

Note

1. The mother of Marshal López.

Sufferings of a French Lady in Paraguay

Dorotea Duprat de Lasserre

*In September 1869, President Francisco Solano López ordered the evacuation of
Asunción, as the allied troops advanced from the south, following the fall of the
Paraguayan fortress of Humaitá. The population of Asunción, consisting of mainly
women and children, were forced to follow López on the Vía Crucis, as the long
retreat came to be called, through the forests of northern Paraguay to the final defeat
at Cerro Corá. Many of these women, known as* destinadas, *were close relatives
of López's opponents. As such, they were prisoners and many died of disease and
starvation en route.*

*The following extract is taken from the account of one such "destinada." Doro-
tea Duprat de Lasserre was a French woman whose father, husband, and brother
had been executed following a series of show trials held throughout 1868 at the San
Fernando army headquarters, accused of involvement in a conspiracy to murder
López. A total of 368 alleged conspirators were executed as a result of the so-called
"tribunales de sangre" (blood trials). Among them were the younger brothers of
López, Angel Benigno López and Colonel Venancio López; his two brothers-in-
law—the finance minister, Saturnino Díaz de Bedoya and General Vicente Barrios;
the foreign minister, José Berges; Bishop Manuel Antonio Palacios; and General José
María Bruguez Ríos. This harrowing account describes Dorotea's arrest on January 1, 1869, and her suffering and privations on the forced march throughout most
of the year, which took her and her mother through Caacupé, Piribebuy, Yhú, San
Joaquín, Curuguaty, and Ygatimí. The following extract picks up the journey in
September 1869 as the exhausted, weak, and frightened Dorotea, after a brief respite
in Yhú, is forced on to Curuguaty and Espadín.*

We left Yhú at midnight and held out as long as we could through mud and
across *arroyos*.[1] All my provisions for the road consisted of fifteen pounds of
starch, one pound of black sugar, three pounds of grease, and a handful of
salt; three of us had to live on this for nobody knew how long. We arrived
at a spot where we lost the road; we were then about thirty and had to lay
down in the camp waiting for daylight. As soon as the day broke we got up

and saw the camp covered with fellow travellers who were also preparing to move; we soon discovered a small path, which we followed, hoping to meet somebody to give us *mate*; none of us had the wherewith to light a fire.

At last we fell in with a party better provided and we halted to breakfast; took *mate* and a cake which I hastily prepared. Afterwards having joined a party that knew the road, we reached long before sunset a house near the Ybycuí pass. All the women here were busy cooking, and I tried to obtain a small piece of meat, if it were only for my servant, who was not satisfied with cake alone, but nobody would sell me any.

From there we walked to the *arroyo*, passing through a marsh. I got my boots wet, and as everybody advised me to take them off, I did so. But as soon as I laid my bare feet on the ground I was seized with a frightful foot ache. We begged the sergeant to allow us to cross the *arroyo* in order to join some of our fellow-travellers; he refused to do, ordering us to sleep in some empty wagons that had been left there. Towards eleven at night several soldiers arrived, making a great noise and ordered us to cross the *arroyo* at once, because, if the officer found us there, we should be lanced. We stated to them the motive of our sleeping there, and this seemed to pacify them. They then told us that they were from Curuguaty, sent by López himself with strict orders to lance all the women that should lag behind from fatigue or that showed bad disposition.

Thus we crossed the *arroyo* Ybycuí at one in the morning. I had put on my boots again. From that hour we walked along narrow paths, through a thick wood in total darkness. I kept falling into some very ugly holes because I was going ahead to prevent my mother from stumbling; first I lost one boot and a little further on the other, so that I walked barefooted till we overtook our companions who were outside the wood. The day was not yet dawning, yet we were not allowed to rest; the others were made to rise in a hurry, under threat of being lanced, and we pushed on. At day-break we entered into another wood and did not stop till we had got out of it. It was then about two in the afternoon. None of us had even taken *mate*, and here we were made to halt to wait for the officer who had gone to Yhú to see if any women had remained behind. He shortly afterwards arrived. We had scarcely lighted fires when it began to rain hard. When the rain stopped, those who could changed their clothes. We did not get dry for two days, as we had to sleep in the rain. Mrs. Leite suffered greatly. I did not feel anything and seemed made of iron.

In short we travelled day and night till we reached Curuguaty on the 27th September at daybreak. Here they collected us under a tree, counted us, and made a list, after which they allowed us to rest that day. I spent it writing.

In the morning we heard that López had come and gone through the village the previous night, and that was why they made us sleep away from the centre. After being allowed to take *mate* and even make cakes we were taken leisurely as far as Ygatimí by a guide who was very attentive, allowing us to halt whenever we chose. On the second day, very late at night, we crossed the Jejuí. Here there was some hurry because it was stated that the enemy was coming by the river, but nothing happened.

It was raining, but we kept walking on till at last we reached our destination, wet through and through; here we passed in review, being ordered to build ourselves a house immediately. What was our affliction to see ourselves thus thrown with such barbarous orders, like animals in the middle of a wood without resources and without even a place where we could sit down. There I met a friend, Eugenia, wet to the skin, cooking for other people in order that she might give a mouthful to her little girls.

On the 23rd October we left the wood, and were kept that whole day in the scorching rays of the sun, as there were two thousand and fourteen people to be reviewed. About three in the afternoon the sergeant gave the order of marching, and we went along like sheep.

We occupied seven days to reach Espadín. The order must have been to make us march slowly in order that we might be debilitated on the road: finally we lay down to sleep the last night in a small wood before reaching the Ygatimí pass. It rained in torrents. I was suffering from toothache, and next morning we had not even a *mate* of yerba to take nor a morsel to eat. About noon, it was still pouring with rain, we were suffering greatly from hunger, and Mrs. Leite's servant was in a deplorable state of weakness, when suddenly a she donkey belonging to the *Señora* was delivered of a dead offspring. I told them that in France people eat donkey's meat, and proposed that we should try at once the abortion. They took courage and in a pelting rain cooked this meat. The sergeant called us together and gave us over to another sergeant, who did not seem to care much for his charge: he told us that we might go and seek wild fruit in the woods, but that we ought not for this to forsake our settlement; he marked out to each a piece of ground, and told us to make streets as in the capital since this was the spot where we were to spend the last moments of our lives, and added that anyone who should cross the Ygatimí would be considered a deserter.

Days passed thus, but the donkeys were all killed, and our condition became again desperate. A great number of people died of hunger; a spot had been selected for cemetery near the river, and in front of our house, so that every day we witnessed death from starvation, and burials that were truly heartrending.

We had an immense quantity of oranges, but we felt the want of donkey's meat: some families ate dogs, toads, and serpents. The boys walked about like living skeletons catching lizards, but the mortality continued very great among children and old women, especially on rainy days.

We kept forming every day new plans; but on the night of 21st December five families, ours included, joined cause and started on foot; we arrived at a place where the Indians were encamped, and laid down to wait till daybreak. About midnight it began to rain hard and we got wet through. When daylight came I went to prepare a *mate* for my mother, and I then parted with my last silver spoon in exchange for some honey. We started again after eating some roasted hide, and walked till we came across some women who had reached as far as the *cerro*[2] and seen there three spies driving before them a number of people.

For the second time we retraced our steps and walked till late in the afternoon, fearing to cross the *estero*. We laid down in the middle of the camp and woke next day wet through by the dew. We could not light a fire to make *mate*, and went back to the *rancho*[3] of some settlers who with difficulty allowed us to go near the fire; after taking *mate* I went with some girls into the wood to look for fruit.

In the evening news came that Josefa Rojas had come from the *cerro* to fetch us and that the Brazilians were waiting for us. We hesitated about going, fearing an ambush of López. We laid down very late, and we had scarcely gone to sleep when a voice awoke us saying, "Go to the pass, a number of ladies are waiting for you there." We got up quickly, took up our parcels and left. I was crying, and my mother asked me whether I thought it was López taking us away, and I replied, "No. It is our saviours." But I should know soon to what our hopes were reduced, and I could not help feeling strong misgivings, yet was thankful to have been saved from dying of starvation. Thus weeping I walked to where our deliverers received us. We crossed the *arroyo* and were welcomed on the other side by Commandant Moura's ordnance with kind words. Two spies were seized at the same time, who most probably had orders to make us march. This was on the night of 24th December.

We started with a clear moonlight, and walked two leagues; then we halted, took *mate*, and waited orders. At break of day we went and walked so fast as to be almost incredible. We reached the guard and then I learned from the Commanding Officer the fate of the prisoners. It was a severe blow to me, but I yet hoped. We walked all that day without stopping. The ground was like fire, and the pain to the feet was intolerable, but the anxiety to save ourselves was still stronger, and at last we reached headquarters and were presented to the Prince and staff, who received us with the most lively proofs of interest.

I had offers of a house from two Frenchmen, which I thankfully accepted, because I felt so lonely and abandoned in the world, that even to return to civilised life made me weep.

They made us to go to the Adjutant-General's Office to inscribe our names, then we went to the patio to wait for our ration of meat, salt, and *fariña*. Being seated there, some gentlemen came to converse with me, among them my distinguished host, Coronel Pinheiro Guimaraes, who took some notes. I dedicate to him this mournful record of my late misfortunes, which he has endeavoured to make me forget by his kind hospitality. The most delicate attention and the kindest care have been employed by him and his subordinates to make us forget our recent agony.

> *Signed*
> *Dorotea Lasserre*

P.S. On reaching Curuguaty I had the painful certainty that my three relatives had been executed in San Fernando—my brother on 9th August 1868, my father and husband on 22nd of the same month.

Notes

1. Small rivers
2. Hill
3. Small rural home

Declaration and Protest

Eliza Lynch

Eliza Alicia Lynch (1833–86) was the common-law wife of President Francisco So-
lano López, whose extraordinary and tragic life has inspired over a dozen novels.
Born in Ireland, she met López in Paris in 1853 during his official mission to Europe.
Unable to marry him because of her undissolved marriage to Jean Louis Armand de
Quatrefages, she nevertheless accompanied him back to Paraguay. Between 1855 and
1867 she gave birth to six sons. Her European elegance had a dramatic effect on tra-
ditional Asunción society. She remained faithful to López throughout the Triple Al-
liance War and buried both him and her eldest son, Colonel Juan Francisco López,
with her own hands after they had been killed at Cerro Corá. After the war, she
took refuge in Europe with her three surviving sons. She pursued a court action in
Edinburgh in a vain attempt to reclaim money from Dr. William Stewart, to whom
López had entrusted the family fortune. At the invitation of President Juan Bautista
Gill, she returned to Asunción on October 24, 1875, in order to reassert her claims
but was expelled by Gill within twenty-four hours following pressure from a group
of women from elite families who held her personally responsible for their suffer-
ing under López. Abandoning any hope of legal redress, she visited Constantinople,
Rome, and according to several accounts, Jerusalem. She divided her time between
London and Paris, where she eventually died. Although much maligned during the
liberal period, she is now regarded as a national heroine in Paraguay. Her ashes
were returned to Asunción in 1964 and buried in the national cemetery. The follow-
ing extract is taken from Exposición y protesta, *which she wrote in Buenos Aires*
in November 1875, following her expulsion from Paraguay. Here she defends her ac-
tions during the war and accuses her female detractors of lack of patriotism and of
simply wanting to get their hands on her family fortune.

For a long time I maintained a profound silence, though my name had for
six years been attacked by determined enemies, by individuals who sought
riches by writing pamphlets and books full of appalling filth, representing
me as the very essence of prostitution and scandal, as though I were one of
those human beasts who seek satisfaction in the extermination of society

Portrait of Eliza
Lynch. Photographer
unknown. From the
collection of Martín
Burt.

itself. I have been the target of the rage of those men who have taken power
in Paraguay to rule over the ruins of her wealth and of that greatness which
had been sacrificed to the defence of her independence and her dignity.

I have been accused of responsibility for the actions in domestic policy
of Marshal López and blamed for the war that three nations forced on Paraguay, as well as for the heroic sacrifice which immortalised this people, per-
ishing with their leader, in more than five years of warfare unexampled in
American history and which has been such a lesson to all nations, as great
as that of the Spartans at Thermopylae.

In their determination to smear my name all they achieved was to link it
to that very record that won the admiration of the civilised world and which
was repeated and exemplified for the French people when a million Germans laid Siege to Paris. I was far from being involved in the Government
of Marshal López or its politics, nor did I involve myself in anything during

the war beyond attending to the wounded and to the families of those who followed the army and trying to reduce the suffering I found; but I do not shrink from shouldering the responsibility that any would wish me to bear for the defence that the people of Paraguay offered of their rights and their territory.

I had departed Europe and returned to America after an absence of five years as I had finally managed to recover my papers and arm myself with the documents I needed to claim my rights. I came here resolved to go on to Asunción, because I wanted to answer the charges against me in a criminal case ordered there by the Government in 1870 and to confront my enemies in the very theatre of their power, even though the only support I could marshal would be my conscience and my actions.

My determination was only strengthened when *La Tribuna* of this city published so-called reports from correspondents in Asunción which were further embroidered here in Buenos Aires and which threatened me with death were I to venture to go to Paraguay.

Having spent three months in Buenos Aires trying to claim the price of my furniture, which today adorns the Palace of the National Government of Argentina, without managing to have the claim honoured, despite having presented the detailed accounts which evidence my claim, I did not wish to delay any longer and I set out for Asunción. There I came ashore and only hours later I was obliged to re-embark on the orders of President Gill.

All the lying telegrams that have been published about this journey, all the false accounts that have been circulated, all the deeds that were done and then misrepresented, all this obliges me to set out here a true account of what happened, a protest against the theft of my properties and a rebuttal of the calumnies endlessly repeated in books, newspapers and pamphlets. And if indeed these have created a black belief about me, they have neither silenced nor broken me, because my conscience raises me above them and fortifies me to confront my detractors.

On the morning of the 23rd we arrived at Asunción. On our arrival an officer of the English gunship which was moored in the port came aboard; I called for him and gave him a letter of introduction for his captain which I had in my possession, asking him that he should keep certain papers and documents for me but which I did not wish to expose when coming ashore. The officer went to talk to his captain and returned bearing his compliments. The officer went back, taking with him a box which contained my papers and which Enrique handed to him in front of everyone.

I remained awhile on board, awaiting the arrival of various women friends who had intended to visit me but who were not informed of my arrival; and after an hour and a half delay, I went ashore alone with my son and was received on the steps of the pier by many Paraguayan ladies, who almost drowned me with their affectionate embraces. The pier was literally overflowing with people, all of whom without exception saluted me warmly. I went on foot alone into this crowd (my son also walked surrounded by a large circle of well-wishers) as far as the Customs House, in order to have my trunks inspected. From there I continued on foot surrounded by people who embraced and kissed me and grasped my hands; all of them, men and women, wished to touch me and speak to me, and all of them had a friendly greeting for me. We arrived at the tramway, whose director had prepared and reserved a carriage specially for me; we boarded it and many ladies came in to express their happiness at seeing me return.

We moved slowly across the various streets that I had to pass through and all the people who were in their houses and who recognised me greeted me with affection. On arrival at the Station I was met by a large crowd which was growing by the moment. The lady street-sellers of the Plaza de San Francisco surrounded me with expressions of happiness and tenderness which moved me deeply. They all accompanied me and as we were passing in front of the Church of San Roque, the Major-domo and other personalities came out, congratulating me on my arrival. I went into the Church, because I could no longer control the emotions that were choking me, and I directed a fervent prayer of thanks to the Omnipotent.

From there I went to the house of Isadora Diaz, where I was going to stay, taking leave first of the multitude which had not left off pressing around me. All day there was a veritable procession of people, carrying messages from the most distinguished families who wished to visit me, and of poor people bringing little gifts showing that they had not forgotten me and that they had kind recollections of me.

At one o'clock there arrived the Delegate-General and the Secretary of the President, Don Antonio Baez. They were extremely incoherent and did not know how to express themselves. After many circumlocutions they finally said to me: "that the President wished me to know that it would be well that I should embark right away, that there was a decree to expel me, and that it was not desirable that I should remain in the country." At the same time they showed the Decree of Rivarola, dated 4 May 1870. I said that I recognised it and that if I had come to Paraguay it was because I had been invited—That I was greatly amazed at what was happening, and that if I were accused of any fault or crime, that I had come precisely so that I might be judged—That I was entirely at the disposal of the Government—That they should do with me as they wished, and they should arrest me whenever they wanted, even at that moment; that I was ready to follow them without the least resistance.

This I repeated several times.

They responded: "that they didn't wish to take me prisoner—that no one in their group wanted this—that this was a simple warning which the President was giving and that he wished me to depart."

I left the house at 11.20, having sent word previously to the General that I was about to embark and requesting that he should have the goodness to give the necessary orders to avoid delays in the port. We went on foot to the Station, passing in front of the Plazoleta de San Roque, which was filled with people, though nobody said a word—The Square and the neighbouring streets were lit up because of some important function that was being celebrated; many people could see me and some among them greeted me.

The following day was Sunday and many people came aboard to visit me, including poor women who brought me many gifts—I received an envelope which was sent to Isadora's house and which she in turn had delivered to me. It contained an old kitchen knife rolled up in a piece of paper on which the following words could be read

Margarita Barrios
The virgins lanced to death by
Elisa Lynch out of jealousy, Panchita Garmendia, Prudencia Barrios,
    Chepita Barrios, Rosario Barrios, Oliva Barrios, Pancha Barrios,
    Consolación Barrios—This dagger will pursue you as long as you
    live and after your death God will punish you.
Encarnación Valdovinos

A woman from Corrientes arrived to give me a report of the notification addressed to me by the Paraguayan Government of the embargo on my property, five years previously. For fully four hours, Gill stayed in the Captaincy of the port, observing the people who came and went from the gunship. When I was still on shore, the house in which I had been was surrounded by soldiers until after I left.

At three in the morning a band of musicians came to play me a *serenata*. They had not known that I had left, and they sent word that they wanted to recall for me better times that we all had enjoyed. On Sunday there was a banquet in the house of one of my friends at which enthusiastic toasts were drunk to my health and that of Enrique. We left early on Monday—on arrival in Corrientes [in Argentina] I went ashore, as I had no wish to cause problems any longer for the captain of the gunship, although he tried to persuade me to stay aboard for the remainder of the voyage. In Corrientes the Captain of the Port showered kindnesses upon me and accompanied me to the hotel where there was a festive party of Paraguayan men and women resident in that city. I left there at midnight and arrived again in Buenos Aires without further adventure.

This is an exact account of everything that occurred during the fifteen hours I spent in Asunción.

Those who sent telegrams to the Buenos Aires newspapers stating that I had been stoned in the streets of Asunción only gave further proof of how easy it is to depart from the truth and calumniate a whole people and a woman. Far from having been stoned, I was received with the most emotional displays by the women who live there by their toil and who have the virtuous strength to sacrifice themselves on the lances of those who would put the nation in danger, of those virtuous women and the mothers of that generation who taught their children to die for the fatherland.

Women friends from long ago, people who witnessed my behaviour during my time in Paraguay, whether in times of peace, whether in the cruelties of war, they all embraced me and came to welcome me; because those women remember very well that in the days of *the tyranny* everybody enjoyed happiness and freedom which they have not known under the rule of the famous liberators, who are bringing that beautiful country to its final ruin, as surely while "liberating it," burying it forever.

I left with two different impressions of Paraguay.

The first that was that six years of defamation against me had achieved nothing; that the Paraguayan people were the same people that I had known and with whom I had shared moments of happiness and of martyrdom; that there, deep inside these good people, were hearts that loved me and with their love they protected me from the prodigious calumny poured on me by those who speculate with the honour of others, by usurpers of my property and by traders who disguise themselves behind public office to loot the poor country even more and ruin and oppress it in the name of the Constitution and the laws they had promulgated.

My second impression was: that in that country there was a government that did not respect the organic or the civil laws, that it did not keep its word and that it placed itself at the side of those who attacked my rights, in order to cut the ground from under a person who had placed her trust in the written laws and in the promises made by the first magistrate [the president].

Those who laid this charge [of being a key supporter of the war effort of Francisco Solano López] against me were those who deserted the army, those who filled the cartridges of the allies to help them conquer their own fatherland, those who served as guides to give the Brazilians access to Paraguay, and to speed up the extermination of an entire people whose heroic grandeur has had to cover the dirty stains that the traitors to the Paraguayan flag have brought on its name. I have the intimate conviction of every son of England: when the fatherland is in danger, every citizen must run to die for his country without asking whether the cause is just or unjust, and even more so when it is a holy cause. I also have the deep conviction that that son who fires bullets at the breast of his fatherland must always and at all times be a traitor. If I have been accused of serving Paraguay, such an accusation might have come from anyone who was not himself Paraguayan, but it could never have been presented as a criminal charge against me by anyone who was born in Paraguay.

In their desperation to accuse me they have done nothing but make of me the target of the bullets of the degenerates of the fatherland, I who glorify a country which preferred death to surrender.

The time will come when the position I take today will be envied. But today the purer feelings are disturbed, the morale [of the country] is destabilised, and if a proof is needed of what I say, there is none more compelling than the petition of these ladies and the expulsion order of President Gill. The ladies' petition and the government's order only prove that there was a conspiracy among those who stole a great part of my property to prevent me from reclaiming it. An organised effort to hold the property of others, at whose head the President places himself, is what we see today in Paraguay.

The Psychology of López

William Stewart

The character of President Francisco Solano López (1826–70) continues to provoke considerable controversy to the present day. While many writers portray him as a crazed tyrant, others see him as the personification of patriotism. This firsthand testimony is written by one of the foreigners who knew him best: William Stewart (1830–1916). Stewart was a Scottish medical practitioner, appointed surgeon to the Paraguayan government in 1857, who set up the first medical school in Asunción and headed the national medical service. He quickly gained the confidence of López, who included him in his select circle of acquaintances. Stewart became the personal physician to López and his family. During the war Stewart worked under very difficult conditions, faced with a combination of extremely heavy field casualties; outbreaks of epidemics such as cholera, measles, and dysentery; the exhaustion of pharmaceutical stocks; and a dire shortage of trained doctors. After the battle of Riachuelo in June 1865 he was awarded the Grand Cross, the highest of the five grades of the Paraguayan Order of Merit. But soon afterward he lost favor with President López, who blamed him for a measles epidemic at Humaitá and a cholera outbreak in Asunción. Stewart continued to head the medical corps under insufferable conditions—by the end of 1867 deaths had reduced the number of doctors to just two, himself and Frederick Skinner. He accompanied the retreating army headquarters until captured by Brazilian troops on December 27, 1868, after the Pikysyry campaign. Stewart's scathing but dispassionate dissection of the psychology of López is published here for the first time.

The following is a detailed study of the psychology of López. There is no need to analyze his cruelty further, as many vivid descriptions exist, written by noteworthy people over the years, which save me the displeasure of having to repeat them. One may ask whether it befits a doctor to write the biography of a man such as Francisco Solano. However, while I maintain the detachment of a professional who approaches a highly interesting question, worthy of calm analysis, the fact remains that I spent a long period of time in his company and was able to study his character in great depth. In the opinion of many, there is a need for a more thorough explanation of the character and conduct of López, and I trust that the present attempt to produce this may be well received. In order to understand the laws of all animal creation, it is not sufficient to examine solely the character of the individual, but also the prior formation of that character. My method is to rely on both of these for the basis upon which to formulate a true and accurate analysis of López.

From the earliest expression of his intellectual faculties he showed an innate evil, which caused much sorrow to his mother, who often expressed in despair to the friends who witnessed his acts that she could do nothing to remedy nor correct such perverted instincts. The child enjoyed tormenting his pet animals, throwing them live into the hot oven in the kitchen.

His cousin, Felix Carrillo, who had been brought up with him, and was of the same age, recalled in 1857 that the favorite pastime of López consisted in constructing small barracks for soldiers, with an entrance made of sticks, into which he would make doves and other birds walk. If they did not walk in a straight line, he would seize them and take out one of their eyes with a needle. As he described this, it struck me that Felix Carrillo had been horrified at the thought of the cruelties that this depraved cousin, a child lacking in any good will toward his fellow human beings, might already be dreaming of, and which would multiply once he had accepted the reins of power from his father.

When his mother returned to Asunción at the end of the war in 1870, she asked me, "Why did you not save the life of my son Benigno?"

I replied, "If you, his mother, could not do it, how do you think that I could have done it?"

Then Doña Juana, although weak, declared that ever since his childhood, Francisco Solano had been extremely cruel; that he would throw live animals into the oven, and take out the eyes of chicks, enjoying the torture he inflicted upon them and laughing as they ran around in desperation. I included these observations, and other points, in my testimony for the Paraguayan Investigating Committee in Washington in 1870, and I stand by them today.

The unfavorable environment in which the character of López was formed, combined with his impulsiveness and his vanity, created a crucial defect in his personality. The mental deformation of López requires further explanation. We have already alluded to his almost complete lack of love or affection toward his fellow man, and it would be an easy task to cite numerous examples of this moral imbalance. As a young man he distanced himself from all contact or friendship with his peers, this due not only to his swift promotion through the military ranks, but also to his ingrained distrust of others. He was feared by all; the sole consolation for those around him was that Don Carlos Antonio retained power. However, when his father died, the thing which we had most feared came to pass: when Francisco Solano took power, he persecuted various members of Congress, and then likewise, little by little, many of our most decent and valued citizens, without any apparent justification. Madame Lynch, the only person in whom he had complete confidence, told her closest friends that the General suffered in his family. But the truth was that Francisco Solano mercilessly sought revenge on his brothers and sisters, as well as on their friends. The nature of the unlimited power which lay in his hands brought predictable results in regard to his mental stability. It is difficult to comprehend the internal mental processes of a man who wielded such power over the lives of the people around him, and who never heard a word of contradiction, or criticism of his follies.

The insensitive cruelty of the man is beyond doubt. I believe that all of the recent charges formulated against him by witnesses such as Masterman and Thompson are perfectly true. The hardness of his heart toward his family was not provoked, but the result of his selfishness. There was no such conspiracy as the one he invented in order to carry out his evil deeds. López was simply an example of the danger of intellect without moral character.

With regard to politics, López suffered a severe form of megalomania. His limitless power allowed him to lose himself in extravagant illusions. Such has occurred with other leaders of greater nations and under different circumstances; López unfortunately lost his way in trying to imitate them.

The dozens of incidents, recorded events and anecdotes regarding López are not sufficient to create a complete biography, however significant these may be. The arguments put forward by apologists of the tyrant, alleging that he was inspired by patriotic duty, given poor advice, or influenced by alcohol, are not as important as they would have us believe. Politicians and writers throughout the continent, who have accepted such theories, have done so in complete ignorance of the processes which made up his character. We should not delude ourselves with theoretical investigations and conjecture, whilst ignoring reality and human experience.

My opinion was formed while I was close to him, by the consistent impressions he created in my mind. I have never changed this opinion, based as it is on the well-founded observations I made, and have since analyzed. Without knowing the history of the man; without being able to constantly analyze his actions, it is impossible to understand completely his psychology.

Such a study provides the evidence which demonstrates that the behavior of López originated in an unstable mental state. When no boundaries are set, psychological actions are perverted, and natural impulses reveal themselves ever more vigorously. López became a victim of his own limitless self-aggrandizement. It prevented him from appreciating those pleasures of life which his position should have offered him. Once he had turned his back on society, the extent of his official coterie formed his only horizons, and absorbed all his attention. I understood my duty to cure this, but I confess my impotence. I never let pass an opportunity to try to awaken in him noble aspirations of political greatness, based on moral and material progress. But my efforts were rendered useless by the effects of neurosis, the central pillar of my diagnosis.

III

A Slow Recovery

Following the catastrophe of the Triple Alliance War, Paraguay sought to recover from the decimation of the adult male population, widespread destitution, economic collapse, foreign occupation, and demands for reparations. Defeat in the war also heralded the denationalization of the Paraguayan economy, and the selling off of the vast assets of the state. The independent road to development was erased and replaced by a growth process dictated by increasing foreign ownership of the nation's economic assets. Following the departure of the Brazilian occupying troops in 1876, a new *caudillo* élite of autocratic and charismatic political leaders, composed mostly of Paraguayans who had fought alongside the forces of the Triple Alliance and against López, grouped themselves into two opposing "clubs." In 1887 these formally declared themselves the Liberal Party and the Colorado Party (respectively the "blues" and the "reds"). The two parties reflected the international rivalry for political control over Paraguay, with Anglo-Argentinian capital generally supporting the Liberals, and Brazilian interests supporting the Colorados. Both parties were wedded to a laissez-faire economic doctrine, known as *liberalismo*, and these years saw a rapid growth in foreign control over the domestic economy, beginning with the massive sales of state-owned land in the 1880s, and associated investment in tannin production and cattle ranching. The Colorado Party ruled until 1904, when it was overthrown in a brief civil war by the Liberal Party. The years from 1904 to 1936 were characterized by political instability, with no fewer than twenty-two presidents in thirty-two years, as a result of internecine conflict between the various factions of the Liberal Party, which ruled until 1936.

Indeed, the whole period from 1870 to 1940 was marked by a tumultuous series of coups, countercoups, palace "revolutions," and two-day presidencies, as rival groups within each party fought over the rich pickings to be gained from association with the foreign economic interests that soon came to dominate the country. Altogether, thirty-eight presidents ruled during this seventy-year period, which was also marked by social unrest and conflict, fueled by poverty, inequality, and exploitation. Laws passed in the 1880s permitted the sale of vast amounts of state-owned land to foreign capitalists at extremely low prices, providing the basis for the highly unequal distribution of land, and foreign exploitation of the country's natural resources, which soon became characteristic features of Paraguayan agriculture. As recently as 1946 only twenty-five, almost exclusively foreign, companies still owned a third of the total land area of the country; two of these, the British-owned Industrial Paraguaya Company and the Argentinian Carlos Casado Company, together owned 13 percent of this land area. However, cheap land also contributed to waves of foreign immigrants wishing to escape their countries and found new colonies, often with a utopian (social, political, or religious) vision. The scale of immigration contributed to a changing demographic composition, especially in urban areas, influencing many areas of culture and politics, and bringing, for example, ideas of anarchism and socialism, which would flourish in the nascent trade union movement.

The period also witnessed the appearance of the Generación del 900, a group of young writers who brought about a cultural revival that laid the foundation for a subsequent re-evaluation of the achievements of the nationalist period. To a nation that found itself impoverished and downtrodden, the subsequent revision and celebration of the achievements of the nineteenth century restored a sense of national pride, and clearly had a resonance among the wider population. This resulted in a rapid rise of nationalist identity and opposition to the Liberal government, which was popularly viewed as associated with the victors of the Triple Alliance War. In the late 1920s, growing dissatisfaction with *liberalismo* led to the emergence of new ideological currents, as expressed by the Liga Nacional Independiente, the Nuevo Ideario Nacional, and a failed anarchist attempt to take control of the city of Encarnación. The nadir of the Liberal period was reached on October 23, 1931, when the army fired on students protesting the growing Bolivian threat to the Chaco.

Paraguayan Society in the Postwar Decade

Harris Gaylord Warren

The first decade after its defeat in the War of the Triple Alliance was traumatic for Paraguay. The country's already prostrate economy fell even further when attempts to resurrect it with dubious foreign loans and by European immigration failed. The political situation was in turmoil. Brazilian troops occupied the country for six years while relentless in-fighting fractured the political "clubs" of the elite that emerged after the war. Harris Gaylord Warren (1906–86) was one of the foremost academic historians of Paraguay and in this extract from his book Paraguay and the Triple Alliance *he describes the appalling social conditions that survivors of the war had to endure.*

War is a great social catalyst from which neither victor nor vanquished can escape. In conflicts that result in catastrophic loss of life, the very foundations of society are seriously weakened. But so long as a viable remnant of the old order remains, historical continuities are not completely destroyed and the opportunity exists for starting anew. These generalizations are especially applicable to Paraguay. Old families, some whose ancestors had come with founders of Asunción in 1537, were decimated and some disappeared entirely. Others, more fortunate, survived in the persons of those who had miraculously escaped death or who had been out of the country during the terrible conflict. They would become the rulers of Paraguay, not of a new Paraguay but of one in which profound changes were inevitable.

A new order of things was the vision of the young Liberals who, safe from the war, exhorted their fellow citizens with the cry of *Manos a la obra!* (Hands to the task!). There was much work to be done. New political institutions must be established, and they needed time to build a body of precedents, to gain respect and acceptance. Even while these new institutions were being created, as in the Constitution of 1870, old attitudes persisted. Tolerance of dissent, freedom of the press, and protection of political liberties enjoyed no more than feeble support during the post-López years. Very few men of any age with political experience survived the war, and among these few the moderates were almost non-existent. A new generation would have to be trained, hopefully imbued with ideas and convictions harmonious with the Paraguayan psyche.

A shattered economy must be restored. Immigrants must be sought to replace thousands of people destroyed by war. Paraguay had never been a haven for immigrants, and the disastrous result of the French colony of Nuevo Burdeos (now Villa Hayes) under the elder López made European governments hesitant about endorsing new ventures. The fiasco of the "Lincolnshire farmers" was the only venture of its kind during the postwar decade but in the 1880s agricultural colonies brought industrious immigrants who were to exert an exceptional influence on Paraguayan society.

The dictatorships of Francia and the Lópezes had held crime to a very low level, but after the war law enforcement disappeared in much of the country. Argentine troops maintained order in Villa Occidental and its immediate neighborhood, but Brazilians left a much poorer record in Asunción and its satellite villages. The postwar decade witnessed the worst outbreak of individual crime and revolts in more than four centuries of Paraguayan history.

Despite their poverty and uncertain tenure, postwar governments were ever mindful of the need to create an educational system. A few foreigners were attracted to the country, but most of the teachers were native Paraguayans, many of whom had been educated abroad. The best elementary and secondary schools developed in Asunción and Villa Rica, while village schools varied in quality from very poor to almost worthless. Paraguay desperately needed a free and responsible press, a need still unmet at the end of a decade. However, the many newspapers that appeared provided outlets for literary efforts, and copies that have been preserved are invaluable sources of information. They reveal clearly that a decade was altogether too short a time for the solution of the many social problems that all but overwhelmed Paraguay.

The Church, a powerful institution in colonial Paraguay, was reduced to impotence by Francia and failed to regain much of its power under the Lópezes. Dominated by foreigners during the occupation, the Church also met opposition from the Liberals. The native clergy and Congress struggled to regain control and finally recovered the right to nominate their own bishop.

Health, Morality, and Crime

Aside from the physical condition of the country and the destruction of its economy, the most obvious effects of the war involved health and personal relationships. The population as a whole was unable to withstand diseases that had previously been kept under control. Undernourished and even starving people offered little resistance to gastrointestinal, pulmonary, venereal, and other infections. To prevent a smallpox epidemic, the Brazilians offered free vaccination, but there was little they could do about other dread diseases. A group of Paraguayan prisoners of war, repatriated in 1870, started an epidemic of yellow fever that physicians diagnosed as "bilious icteroid." The death toll was heavy, several died on ships quarantined in the harbor, and fear of the disease drove many out of Asunción to seek safety in the country. To a survivor it seemed that "the hand of God is against poor Paraguay." In this emergency early in 1871, the Junta de Higiene (Health Commission) ceased to function when its members resigned. President Rivarola fled to the country; Vice-President Cayo Miltos died. The Buenos Aires *Standard* insisted that the disease was not yellow fever but a gastric epidemic and considered as trifling the daily death toll of twenty-five. Two years later, President Jovellanos made Humaitá a quarantine station to prevent yellow fever from being brought again to Asunción.

Sanitary conditions were terrible. The city government lacked resources to organize essential services. "The town of Asunción," wrote one correspondent, "is still in a horribly filthy state, and is likely to remain so, until the energetic commander-in-chief pays it another visit." People threw trash, garbage and filthy water into the streets, undeterred by stern threats of heavy fines. Brazilian troops were notorious offenders, as they allowed huge garbage dumps to accumulate by their quarters. All of the filth from the Argentine hospital was carried to the street by a sewer that emptied into the Rio Paraguay. In contrast, the Brazilian naval hospital was praised for its cleanliness.

Disposal of the dead presented an annoying problem. Refugees not only died on roads leading to Asunción but also fell in the streets, victims of hunger and disease. With packs of hungry dogs roaming at will, removal of corpses was of paramount importance, yet the dead often lay for hours where they fell. Government carts did make daily rounds to pick up the bodies, but this was slow business. The streets were "immense foci of infection."

Attempting to do something about health and sanitation, the Provisional Government appointed a Council of Medicine and Public Hygiene. If this council tried to do anything, it made little or no impact on the horrible conditions in Asunción. There were so few doctors in Asunción in 1871 that Brazil permitted three of its army doctors to serve on the council. Later governments continued to make gestures. President Gill in 1876 appointed another Commission of Public Hygiene with Dr. William Stewart as president. Such commissions made little progress, and years were to pass before sanitary conditions could be deemed acceptable.

Shocking social conditions could be expected after the war. There was no police force of any consequence for several years, and Allied troops were a rowdy lot. Travelers in the suburbs of Asunción and in rural areas encountered "gangs of deserters and hungry Paraguayans." Vagabonds and criminals roamed the streets, serious crimes occurred daily in Asunción, and rape was so common that no woman was safe without a strong male escort. Child-stealing occurred frequently as kidnappers attempted to obtain ransom from distraught parents; but the result generally was to turn the children into "the streets and roads to starve and die." Vandalism was common while there was anything left to smash or steal. Even street lamps were stolen. Indignantly an editor asked: "How long must we endure this condition, and how long will the perversion and vice of these creatures continue?"

Truly, the Provisional Government had an immense task as it strove to curtail banditry, prostitution, and gambling. *La Regeneración* never tired of urging greater efforts, of providing remedies in the form of work, resettlement of families, public relief, and better policing. Although these deplorable conditions improved with the passing of time, there were still so many women without gainful occupation in 1873 that the chief of police ordered them to be collected and sent to rural areas. Another order required every citizen to have an identification card, which would show up vagrants, and unemployed persons were to be put to work on public projects.

Moral laxity could be expected during the postwar period when Allied troops occupied the country. However, one should understand that nothing like a Puritan morality ever had prevailed in Paraguay. The numbers of "natural" children were always high, and little if any stigma attached to such origins. The extraordinary surplus of women was in itself sufficient explanation for looseness in family ties. Perhaps a French writer was correct: "But the women saved Paraguay, since they bore nameless children, and that liberty of morals that they instinctively practiced in place of marriage . . . assured the continuance of the race." When Benjamín Balanza, the French botanist, visited Asunción in 1877, he observed that there was one man for each twenty-eight women. The imbalance between males and females continued for many years, although by 1900 at least the numbers of each sex should have been about the same. A factor sometimes overlooked was the tendency in postwar years for males to seek employment in Argentina and Brazil. These emigrant workers, although they might return to Paraguay, generally were unmarried.

Paraguayans, like any other people, had their share of immoral men and women: but common law marriage, or pairing off in more or less permanent alliances, was never generally considered immoral. Priests from time to time inveighed against the practice, but these men of God frequently indulged in the same custom. The Paraguayan woman had an excellent reputation for her attachment to her man, "to whom she is rarely united by the sacred ties of marriage, and for her great sobriety of speech, her fastidious neatness, her industry and her intelligence."

Security of life and property was precarious in postwar Paraguay. No reliable police force existed in the country; indeed, a civilian policeman was a rare sight. The police force in Asunción, a paramilitary organization, confronted a task of mammoth proportions with meagre resources. No matter how often the press might deplore lawlessness, crimes of violence continued. Brazilian troops kept a degree of order by maintaining a guard under arms. Late in December, 1871, a riot developed in the port when police arrested a Portuguese sailor for attacking a Paraguayan woman. Such sexual attacks in full daylight and in plain view were so common that the arrest infuriated a gang of fifty sailors, among whom Italians and Portuguese (or Brazilians) were prominent. The mob marched on the office of Benigno Ferreira, captain of the port, and threatened to shoot him unless the sailors were released. The mob cut down the flagstaff, threw the flag into the street, and probably would have lynched Ferreira had not a Brazilian patrol charged the hoodlums. Loaded with irons, the ringleaders spent some time in jail. Unable to depend on police protection, citizens who could afford the expense carried firearms; others were never without a knife. The chief of police tried to stop the practice by levying fines and confiscating the weapons, an effort doomed to failure.

One would think that in Asunción, at least, a sound basis for order would have been established by the Brazilians if not the Paraguayans. But shortly after the last Brazilian troops had embarked for Mato Grosso in 1876, near anarchy prevailed in the capital. "Paraguay is in a state of complete social dissolution," the Brazilian chargé complained. "Not a day passes without serious crimes of every sort, which are committed with impunity because of complete lack of action by police." Courts were inept and corrupt, arrested criminals generally went free, and nearly all murderers were found innocent. "Thefts, disorders, and murders occur with alarming continuity," *Los Debates* asserted. While the press called for more severe measures to protect life and property, the Brazilian chargé wearied of reporting "the innumerable crimes that are daily perpetrated with impunity in this miserable country." That these conditions prevailed should have surprised no one. The court "system" existed merely in outline, and few judges had formal training in the law.

Society and Diversion

Profound changes in Paraguayan society occurred as a result of the war. A very large percentage of troops were *mestizos* of various mixtures, and it is unlikely that there were many "pure-blooded" Indians in the armies of López. By 1864, when the war began, Guaraní blood had been thinned by *mestizaje*, or miscegenation. Military occupation may have intensified the negroid strain somewhat, since there were many Brazilian Negro troops. This was not a new strain in the Paraguayan people, for there had been Negroes in Paraguay throughout the colonial period and there were still a few hundred slaves in the country when the war began. Slavery was not abolished until the Provisional Government issued the necessary decree in 1869, despite the law of 1842 which decreed "freedom of the womb" effective on January 1, 1843. A more ironical situation would be hard to find, in view of Paraguayan propaganda against the Brazilians because of slavery in the Empire. Although accustomed to racial mixture, Paraguayan women probably had few children as the result of liaisons with black Brazilian soldiers.

Upper-class Paraguayans boasted of their *limpieza de sangre* (purity of blood), and the presence of some racial prejudice is indicated by the charge that Carlos Antonio López had Guaycurú blood. Many who were "pure" European, whatever that might mean, had fled from Paraguay before the war. Many Paraguayan women of the upper class were not so fortunate. Dr. William Stewart's wife, Venancia Triay Yegros, was one among many who were forced to leave Asunción and suffered great privation in the interior. There was only a sprinkling of such fine women, but they played an important role in postwar Paraguayan society.

An almost new set of social relationships had to be established in postwar Paraguay. Many of the old and honored families had been wiped out by the war; others had lost their wealth and with it their prestige and position; a few had survived, some in exile and some by various miracles in Paraguay itself. Until 1876, Brazilian troops occupied Asunción, and, for a time, Argentine forces shared occupation tasks with Brazilians in villages near the capital. These men would find entertainment somewhere and what was left of the Paraguayan population could not avoid close relationships with the conquerors. That immorality was rife cannot be denied: but there is considerable evidence that Brazilian and Argentine soldiers were strongly attached to their half-Paraguayan offspring, and when they left the country many Paraguayan women went with them. Liaisons were not confined to the lower classes. Doña Rafaela, sister of Francisco Solano López, who had been widowed by her brother's command, married the Judge Advocate General, Dr. Milciades Augusto de Azevedo Pedra.

Inevitably there were clashes between Brazilian soldiers and Paraguayans, some of which were violent. Murders occurred with alarming frequency, both in Asunción and the interior towns, with the score of dead Brazilians and Paraguayans appearing to be about even. These incidents, unimportant individually, in the broad picture had a cumulative effect that increased Paraguayan animosity. Argentine troops, most of whom were held at Villa Occidental, not only avoided these conflicts but also provided protection for refugees from across the river.

An almost constant stream of complaints poured in from Brazilians in the interior. So many crimes occurred that a Brazilian living in Villa Rica complained: "The rights and guarantees that the Constitution of the Republic bestows upon all of its inhabitants are a chimera for the Brazilians." Criminals escaped punishment because officials ignored their crimes, pleading lack of resources to punish them. More than 300 Brazilians living in Villa Rica, Caazapá, and Yuty feared that they would lose their investments. The number of Brazilians seeking financial gain in the interior in 1872 is surprising, and Paraguayan resentment was to be expected. Elections were farcical, with government candidates always winning. Calling such officials barbarians, Azambuja described arbitrary confiscation of Brazilian property in Humaitá and Piribebuy, and complained that the freely roving Chaco Indians indiscriminately seized Paraguayans, Argentines, and Brazilians.

Despite the poverty, crime, disease, and resentment, that weighed so heavily on Paraguayan society, people did find a measure of entertainment. Asunción, much better off than interior towns, was far from being surfeited with opportunities for interesting diversion. Cockfights continued to be popular. Brazilian and Argentine officers occasionally staged amateur theatricals for their own amusement, and a few groups of players made the long trip from Buenos Aires and Montevideo: but Asunción was a drab place during the first years of occupation. The *Sociedad Paraguaya*, whose members have not been identified, staged a dance for foreigners late in September, 1869. Every woman, the reporter wrote gallantly, was queen of the ball. Dances celebrated the end of the war, the birthday of Pedro II, the founding of Asunción. Dances sometimes ended in brawls, as did one on Saturday, April 26, 1873, when a group of rowdy Paraguayans chased twenty Argentines through the streets to the Brazilian barracks, where the pursued found refuge.

The "Lincolnshire Farmers" in Paraguay

Annie Elizabeth Kennett

Several European emigration schemes were launched to Paraguay in the aftermath of the Triple Alliance War. None was as bizarre as the so-called Lincolnshire farmers scheme. The first postwar government tried to raise funds for reconstruction by launching a bond issue on the London market. But the Paraguayan consul in London, Máximo Terrero, and the brokers Robinson, Fleming and Co. diverted part of the proceeds from the sale of bonds to finance an emigration scheme to Paraguay in the hope that publicity about the scheme—by suggesting that Paraguay was an excellent place for British colonization—would keep up the price of the bonds. Stories were planted in the London press suggesting that the colonists were farmers from Lincolnshire, at the time one of the most prosperous agricultural regions of England. In fact they were mainly impoverished families from London and northern Germany. The scheme was a shocking indictment of how the urban poor were used as pawns by international financiers during the Victorian period. Three ships left England in October–November 1872 carrying a total of 888 emigrants to Paraguay, of whom 336 were children.

On arrival in Asunción, they were disowned by the Paraguayan government, as well as by Robinson, Fleming and Co. Eventually over 700 colonists were sent to the village of Itapé, and 140 others to the village of Itá. Mr. Seymour, the representative of Robinson, Fleming and Co., described them as "paupers, mostly from large cities, and totally incapable of living in the countryside—tailors, shoemakers, watchmakers, cane-makers and from all kinds of trades except farming." Housed in tents located in "a low place partially underwater when it rained," they suffered so much from fever that by the time the Italian consul visited them in June 1873 "the number of graves was equal to the number of those alive." In the end, the British colony in Buenos Aires collected £1,800 for a "rescue fund" and at the end of 1873, the survivors were brought down from Paraguay by ship.

The following is an edited abridgment of a previously unprinted document written by Annie Elizabeth Kennett, who was seven years old when she went to Itapé.

EMIGRATION
TO
PARAGUAY.
CAUTION TO EMIGRANTS.

In the month of October last the Emigration Commissioners, under instructions from the Secretary of State, put out a Notice cautioning British Emigrants against proceeding to Paraguay. As, notwithstanding that Notice, it is reported that arrangements have been made to establish a regular Emigration from this Country to Paraguay, the Emigration Commissioners have been desired again to point out to the ꞏꞏꞏꞏ losses ꞏꞏꞏ ꞏꞏꞏ ꞏꞏꞏ to that Country. It is right ꞏꞏ intending Emigrants should know that the Emigrants who ꞏꞏꞏ

So dire was the economic situation immediately after the Triple Alliance War that the British government posted billboards in London, such as this one dated February 13, 1873, warning potential emigrants about the rigors of life in Paraguay. But these warnings did not dissuade over eight hundred people, known as the Lincolnshire farmers, who were duped into emigration to Paraguay. Image by Government Emigration Board, London.

Arrival in Paraguay

Well at last we arrived at our destination, and now we have got to travel up country in bullock carts. We start from Asunction, and then we get nearly to w[h]ere our ground is, we stop there a good time. We each had to pitch our tents and sometimes in the middle of the night, there came a swarm of ants, and then we woke up in a fright with them all over us, especially in our hair, and they sting us something cruel. Then we jumped out of the bed, did not stop to dress, threw a blanket over our shoulders and ran over to a Roman Catholic chapel, and sat down around the porch until the men came to say they had gone. We never stopped for boots but we used to run across the grass with our bare feet, and there was one poor woman so ill, and she had a lot of little children, and when the ants came her husband had to bring her in our tent and put her in my mothers bed until they had gone from her own tent. She always used to crave for some of mothers cold tea, poor thing, she died soon after.

Arrival in the Jungle

At last we make another start for the piece of ground, each man was to have so much, we are in bullock carts again. We camp of a night and hear the growls of the wild beasts of the forest. The next morning we start again, we arrive very near our ground with[in] eyesight then we stopped near some trees, and then Mr. T. [Mr. T. or Mr. G. is Thomas Godward, stepfather to Annie] had to set to work and cut a path to the ground through so high weeds higher than our heads, and we carried all the things from the cart then pitched the tent, and we put them in, and by the path, there was the bed [and] some large wild beast. So Mr. T. had to watch that. The only neighbours we had was Mr. & Mrs. Bailey and family. One night Mr. T. kept watch and the next Mr. Bailey, on account of the wild beast and they kept such huge fires to keep them away, as we was only a few yards off a large forest. We used to see plenty of monkeys in the trees and snakes in the grass.

Storm

The next thing I shall write about was a terrific storm we had in the middle of the night. When we was in bed the wind tore a hole in the tent and Mr. T. held an umbrella to prevent the rain coming in. Presently there came such a gale of wind, down went the tent split in pieces. We all had a blanket around us and there was a natives hut some distance off and we had to walk there, we go along a path one by one and if it had not have been for the lightening we could not have possibly found our way. How it did pour rain and hail, we went with our feet bare, with just a blanket around us. We arrived at the hut at last. The native women are a kind-hearted lot. They took us in, gave us their beds until we got another tent. They was very kind to us, in those parts the women do the work while the men take it easy. They think nothing of climbing up a tree for oranges. Their costume is made of calico because it is very hot.

Pests and Disease

Another pest was jiggers, a tiny insect that got into our feet and some of the peoples had it. It is a little red insect and it get under the skin and lays eggs, and it is the size of a pea and it is round. My poor brother burned his foot so he got such a lot in he had to have his heel, at least a thick piece, cut quite off. Mother had all her toe nails come off three times, another complaint was the ague [fever]. I used to have it every two days and I used to sit over the fire and keep fanning it with my hat for it is a horrid feeling.

Food and Water

The food chiefly consisted of boiled rice and meat so many times a week and a kind of cake the natives used to sell us called chipas, made of maize like chaff to eat so very dry. I remember one day I was so wet the woman could [not] come around, so we had not anything to eat and we ate oranges, for they grow in abundance, large groves, they are so plentiful. Now the water is so scarce we are obliged to get it out of ponds or ditches anywhere we can and sometimes it is so dirty. We came across a spring and we got our water from there until we discovered there was such a lot of snakes we had to leave off. The flies and mosquitoes are something dreadful and the heat. The English people are thinking of coming nearer England to Rosario or Buenos Ayres.

Return to Asunción

But first we must again go in bullock carts. They are rather difficult to get. They send eight at first and a lot of families go, but there are some left. We are amongst the number. Mrs. French and family are gone for they had a kind of round hut, after they had gone we and another family went in until they could get some more bullock carts to bring us away. Mrs. Brownlow and family lived in a tent farther away from the galpon [shed], and they came up to the galpon so as us few could be more together, and left their things in the tent packed up ready for the bullock carts. During the night some bullock carts passing the men helping themselves to a lot of things.

Travelling by Cart

There are plenty of young parrots. Mr. T. often shoots some, and mother stews them up. At last they procure three carts but the women are to go and luggage and the men come afterwards, so we had to be pretty tightly packed. There was mother and Charlie and Lilly and myself, Mrs. Brownlow and two children, and two more children in one small cart. First in goes the luggage and then we sit on the top and a man to drive the bullock, he has a stick and a nail in the end so if he does not go fast enough he pokes him with the stick. The cart is covered over with tarpaulin.

Sold Wedding Ring to Buy Food

So we camped for the night just beyond them, and when we got there we had not had anything to eat, and not any money to buy any with, but we made a fire, and then some natives, pretty well to do, came and brought us some milk. They had a farm just where we was stopping, was just outside Asunción, and mother and me went in the town, such as it was, and tried to sell her wedding ring that my father gave her, to buy us some food, and she sold it for 10 pence.

Another Bad Experience

We still stop outside the town until we go in the train to be shipped. When we was in the train, it was just like being in cattle trucks, and a poor woman Mrs. Slater tried to jump out of the window, because her son Mathew was gone away with some natives. They had to hold [her] back or she would have got out. At last we have got to the shipping place and we go on board a ship and sail for Rosario, a weeks voyage. We shall be glad when it is over, for the ship is so full.

Safety at Last

At last we arrive, and go in a home until the husbands arrive, as they are to come by the next ship. Then the clergyman takes a house for several families to go in, and supplies us with food. My poor mother is taken ill that she has to go to the hospital, and Lilly and myself go too, for Mr. G. has not yet arrived. The nurses in the hospital are very kind to us, the clergyman comes and brings mother some Menephacy wine.

My Pilgrimage to Caacupé

Norman O. Brown

The Virgin of Caacupé is the most widely revered religious image in Paraguayan Catholicism. The shrine to the Virgin is located in the town of Caacupé, fifty-four kilometers east of Asunción. The annual pilgrimage on December 8 to worship at the sanctuary of the Virgin is the most important popular religious festival and is a public holiday. In recent years the festivities have been widely questioned for the introduction of excessive commercialism, gambling, and prostitution. This is a far cry from the situation in 1900, when the Englishman Norman Brown, a resident of the Paraguayan capital, made a pilgrimage on horseback from Asunción. Brown wrote an article for a contemporary magazine describing some scenes in Caacupé.

Like Lourdes in the Pyrenees, and Lujan in the Argentine Republic, Paraguay also has its place of religious pilgrimage in the beautiful little village of Caacupé. And, by the way, I may be permitted to mention here that these immense States of South America are for the most part far less well known than Central Africa. Bolivia, Ecuador, Paraguay, Brazil—these vast territories are indeed terra incognita to the average European.

But to my pilgrimage. The date of the festival is December 8th, which is, of course, the feast of the Immaculate Conception of the Blessed Virgin, and for weeks beforehand the "promeseros"—or those persons who for various reasons have made vows to pay tribute to the Virgin of Caacupé—start from all parts of the Paraguayan Republic on foot, on horseback, or in bullock-carts, to fulfill the good resolutions they have made.

As may be supposed, the roads and tracks at this time present animated scenes, and one would think that emigration, on a large scale, was being encouraged by the Republican Government. The Paraguayans are of a deeply religious temperament, and in time of sickness or trouble they make most solemn vows that, if all goes well with them and they are restored to health, they will undertake a pilgrimage to Caacupé from no matter what distance, and pay substantial tribute to the image of the Virgin as a kind of thank offering for being relieved of their troubles.

Even the very poorest of the poor—those who can afford no tribute in money in fulfillment of their vows—will actually carry for many miles a huge stone balanced upon their head. And outside the church at Caacupé, which I will show you presently, there are many piles of these extraordinary tokens, some of which weigh as much as 30 lb.

The more well-to-do pilgrims take with them a large quantity of paper money, mainly, however, in five-cent notes, each worth about a half-penny in English money. These imposing documents, whose intrinsic worth is out of proportion to their elaborate appearance, are intended for distribution among the beggars who naturally come in hordes to reap their annual harvest. Other pilgrims again—in this case of the pastoral class—offer sheep, goats, or cattle to the Virgin; and it is essential that these animals shall be of a pure white color, gorgeously decorated with flowers and ribbons. After the formal presentation these offerings become the property of the priests.

The village of Caacupé is situated over the Cordillera through which one has to pass on the way from Asunción, the capital, to this Paraguayan Mecca. And truly Caacupé is one of the prettiest villages in all Paraguay. Its population is about 3,500. There are, however, very few well-built houses, and it is only within the last four years that some of the wealthy families of Asunción have built dwellings of the better class there.

The great objective point in the village, naturally enough, is the church, which stands in a spacious plaza. This edifice is out of all proportion to the size of the village, being a large and fine structure capable of accommodating more than 1,500 people. A kind of corridor runs all round the sides, and this on the night of December 7th is brilliantly illuminated by countless candles, kept alight and replenished by hundreds of pilgrims, who sit round the church all night for this express purpose. Now and again these fervent pilgrims burst into a weird kind of chant, the effect of which from a distance is strange and almost unearthly.

There are some quaint and beautiful anecdotes told as to how the healing powers of the Virgin of Caacupé were first discovered, and also respecting the miraculous journeys she is said to have made. Some years ago, according to the tradition, for some reason or other, the figure was to be taken to Asunción, and was accordingly removed in a bullock-cart for that purpose by some devout priests. The first night they camped among the Cordillera Hills; but in the morning, just as they were about to resume their journey, they found to their dismay that the beautiful image had disappeared, and on their hurrying back to Caacupé it was found standing serenely in its old place in the village church. Many other attempts were made to remove the Virgin, but always with the same result; and it was ultimately decided that she must be allowed to remain where she was. The pilgrims are only too ready to tell the stranger these things in the beautiful Guaraní language— the native tongue of the Paraguayan Indian.

Last year, owing to poverty, there were, I should judge, not more than from 10,000 to 12,000 persons at the festival. In 1897, however, it was stated that some 22,000 at least took part in the great procession on the afternoon of December 8th. The figure of the Virgin, placed on an ornamental stand, is carried round the church and the plaza, followed by priests in gorgeous vestments bearing candles, etc., and accompanied by a full band, which plays appropriate music all the time. The crowd of worshippers—mostly women, owing to the notorious and peculiar condition of Paraguay—follow bare-headed, occasionally singing a musical chant, until at length the Virgin is borne into the church and placed on a stand near the high altar. Now for some of the most interesting details. The interior of the church is highly decorated, and during the festival the floor round the image is sometimes actually 2 in. or 3 in. deep in paper money, consisting of notes ranging in value from five cents, to 100 dollars. Amongst this extraordinary heap of paper money, and tributes from the "promeseros," may frequently be seen some gold coins, and, occasionally a ring, or bracelet, or other piece of jewelry. And nearly every year five or six English coins are found among the offerings.

One of the most curious features of the festival is the crowd of women who go to and from the Virgin's Well, carrying water in earthenware jugs on their heads, and offering a drink to everyone they meet. All persons favored by a water-holder have to drink from the same jug, and the pilgrims are deeply offended if their offer is refused. I chanced to come suddenly upon a friend of mine who accompanied me to the Caacupé festival for the first time last year, and noticed that he was looking thoughtful and melancholy. I asked him what the dickens was the matter with him, whereupon he shook his head and said, disgustedly, "Too much water!"

It is a remarkable fact that in a country where intoxicating liquor is so cheap, a great festival like that of Caacupé can be celebrated without the slightest disorder or drunkenness—and that, it must be remembered, in spite of the great heat, the temperature often being as high as 85 deg. or 90 deg. Fahrenheit in the shade.

What It Is Like to Work in
the Yerba Plantations

Rafael Barrett

Rafael Barrett (1874–1910) was an Anglo-Spanish anarchist, journalist, and social critic who spent four years toward the end of his short life in Paraguay, where he was instrumental in setting up the first national trade union body, Federación Obrera Regional Paraguaya. The following extract is the introduction to Lo que son los yerbales *(1908), his powerful denunciation of the living conditions of bonded laborers, known as* mensú *or* mineros *(miners), who were employed by the yerba mate companies in the Paraguayan forests. He became the scourge of the Liberal establishment and wrote a damning critique of effects of Paraguayan liberalism in* El dolor paraguayo *(published 1911). Expelled from Paraguay in 1908, and suffering from ill health, he returned to his native Spain, where he died.*

State-Approved Slavery

The world needs to know once and for all what has been happening in the yerba plantations. It is imperative that when someone wishes to cite an example of the essence of human greed, they should speak not only about the Congo, but also about Paraguay.

Paraguay is being depopulated; it is being castrated and exterminated in the seven or eight thousand leagues that have been handed over to the Industrial Paraguaya and Matte Larangeira companies, and to the tenants and owners of the *latifundios* of Alto Paraná. The exploitation of yerba mate is built on slavery, torment, and murder.

The information that I present in this series of articles, for publication in the civilized countries of the Americas and Europe, is based on personal testimonies, and has been checked and cross-referenced. I have selected not the most horrendous episodes but simply the most frequent; not those that are the exception but those that are the rule. And to any who may doubt or

The *mensú* carried enormous loads of yerba mate, as shown in this picture postcard. Photographer unknown. From the collection of Martin Romano.

deny these facts, I would simply say, "Come with me to the yerba plantations, and see the truth for yourselves."

I do not expect justice from the State. The State rushed to reestablish slavery in Paraguay after the war. After all, at that time it owned yerba plantations. Here are the key points of the decree signed on January 1, 1871:

"The President of the Republic, mindful of the fact that the beneficiaries of the yerba plantations and other sectors of national industry suffer constant losses caused by workers abandoning their place of work with unpaid debts. . . . hereby decrees:

"Art. 2. In all cases where a peon wishes to temporarily absent himself from his workplace, a written permission must be obtained and signed by the owner or manager of the said establishment."

"Art. 3. The peon who abandons his work without said permission will be arrested and returned to his place of work, if the owners so wish, and have charged to his account the necessary costs involved in ensuring his return."

Signed
Rivarola [President]
Juan B. Gil [Vice President]

The way in which slavery operates is as follows. A peon is never recruited without first having a sum of money advanced to him, which the poor wretch usually spends right away or leaves behind with his family. He signs a legal contract before a magistrate in which the amount of the advance is stated, and which stipulates that the owners will be reimbursed in the form of labor. Once herded off to the forest, the peon remains a prisoner for twelve to fifteen years, the maximum time that he will be able to endure the work and the privations that await him. He has sold himself into slavery. Nothing can save him. The advance has been cleverly calculated in relation to his rate of pay and the price of food and clothing in the plantations, such that even if he works himself to death he will always be in debt to the owners. If he attempts to flee, he is hunted down. If they are unable to bring him back alive, they kill him.

This is how it was done during the time of President Rivarola and this is how it is done today. It is well known that the state sold off its yerba plantations. The Paraguayan territory was carved up among the friends of the government and thereafter Industrial Paraguaya gradually bought up almost all of it. The state even gave one hundred and fifty leagues to one influential person as a gift. That period was infamous for the sale and renting of land and the buying-off of surveyors and judges alike. But we are concerned here not with the political behavior of this country, but rather with the issue of slavery in the yerba plantations.

The regulations of August 20, 1885 state that:

> "Art. 11. Every contract between the yerba processor and his peons, in order for it to be legally recognized, must be signed in the presence of the respective local authority, etc."

There is not a word there to say which contracts are legal and which are not. The judge still gives his authorization to slavery. Rivarola's decree was specifically abolished in 1901, after thirty years. But the decree that replaced it is yet another authorization for slavery in Paraguay, albeit more subtle, given that the state no longer owned yerba plantations. The peon is forbidden to abandon his workplace under pain of compensation to his employer. Yet the peon is always indebted to the owner; it is impossible for him to pay, and so he is arrested legally.

The state had, and still has, its inspectors, who usually get rich quickly. In theory, the inspectors visit the yerba plantations in order to:

> "1. Supervise the complete jurisdiction of his sector. 2. Inspect the processing of yerba. 3. Ensure that the industrialists do not destroy the

yerba plants. 4. Require that each leaseholder present him with the certificate of the house being leased, etc."

But he has no orders to verify whether slavery exists in the plantations, nor whether workers are victimized or shot.

This legislative analysis is itself rather naive as, despite the fact that slavery is not legally permitted as such, it is practiced anyway. In the forests the slave is as unprotected as if he were on the high seas. Don. R. C. said in 1877 that the writ of the Constitution ends where the Jejuí River begins. If we were to imagine that a peon could summon up just an ounce of independent spirit and the necessary strength from his aching body to cross the immense forests in search of a magistrate, he would still only find a judge who is in the pay of Industrial Paraguaya, Matte Larangeira, or the *latifundistas* of Alto Paraná. The local authorities are bought off every month with a "bonus payment," so the honorable accountant of Industrial Paraguaya informs me.

Hence the judge and the owner eat from the same plate. They are often simultaneously authorities of the state and leaseholders of yerba plantations. So it is that Mr. B. A., a relative of the current President of the Republic, is the political head of San Estanislao and at the same time local representative of Industrial Paraguaya. Mr. M., also a relative of the President, is a judge in the lands owned by the Casado company and also an employee of the same company. The Casado family exploits the *quebracho* forests through slavery. We still remember the assassination of five of its peons who tried to escape in a boat.

So we must expect nothing from a State that has reestablished slavery and profits from it, and which sells justice as if it were a commodity. I only wish that I were mistaken.

Now let us examine the details.

The Press Gang

They [the yerba companies] are now forced to look for young Paraguayans in Concepción and Villarrica. The departments where the yerba plantations are situated—Igatimí, San Estanislao—have become cemeteries: thirty years of exploitation has decimated Paraguayan virility between the Tebicuary and Paraná rivers. Tacurú-pucú has been depopulated eight times by the Industrial Paraguaya company. Almost all the peons who worked in Alto Paraná from 1890 to 1900 have died. Of the three hundred men taken from Villarrica in 1900 to the Tormenta plantations in Brazil, no more than twenty returned. Now it is happening in Misiones, Corrientes, and Entre Ríos, Argentina.

In Paraguay only children remain, and even they are often taken. Some 70 percent of those press-ganged to Alto Paraná are minors. From 1903 to the present (1908) over two thousand have been taken from Encarnación and Posadas, of whom seventeen hundred were Paraguayans. Only seven hundred remain, of whom hardly fifty are in good health. Naturally, no one objects to such a scandal. The awful truth is: we must defend our children from the clutches of the greedy speculators that are carving up the country.

Degeneration

Look closely into the forest: you will see a huge bundle walking. Look below the bundle and you will find an oppressed creature in whom all trace of humanity is gradually being erased. This is no longer a man, but a peon of the yerba plantations. There may still be some rebellion left in him, some tears. The "miners" have been seen to cry with the *bale* on their backs. Others, unable to bring themselves to commit suicide, dream of escape. Remember that many of them are barely adolescents.

Their salary is illusory. Even criminals can earn pay in some prisons. Not these men. They have to buy everything they eat and the rags they wear from the company. In another article I will describe the prices. They are so exorbitant that the peon has no possibility of extracting himself from his bondage of debt even if he dies working. Every year slavery and misery blend more irredeemably into a single curse. Some 90 percent of the peons of Alto Paraná are made to work for no other recompense than food. Their fate is identical to that of the slaves of earlier centuries.

And what food! Usually it is nothing more than *yopará*, a mixture of corn, beans, *charque* (old meat), and fat. *Yopará* in the morning and at night, the whole week, the whole month, the whole year. Food so awful and so indigestible that it is sufficient in itself to cause serious harm in the most robust organism. But in addition, and especially in Alto Paraná, where the horrors I describe reach an unimaginable degree, the food is half rotten. The *charque* prepared in southern Paraguay contains soil and maggots. The corn and beans are of the worst quality, and rot during transport over long distances. This is merchandise reserved especially for the poor souls of the yerba plantations, and smuggled from one country to another by the honorable bandits of the banking fraternity. That is how they are fed in the "mines": no civilized worker would deign to feed his pigs with such swill.

Living quarters on the yerba plantations are a hut shared by many workers, and covered with palm branches. To live there is to be at the mercy of the elements. They sleep on the floor, on dead plants, like animals. The rain soaks everything. The deathly mist of the forest penetrates them to the bone.

On top of hunger and fatigue there is illness. This horde of alcoholics and syphilitics shivers constantly with fever—the so-called *chucho* of the tropics. A third of the peons become consumptive under the mule's load they carry on their backs. And other delights? The *yarará*, a swift and deadly snake; the centipedes and scorpions that fall from the roof; the *cuí*, an invisible insect whose bite burns the skin; the *yate'i pytá*, a red tick that leaves festering sores; the *ura* of the *yerba* plantations, a large hairy fly whose eggs, when laid on clothes, fertilize in the sweat and create enormous boils under the skin that devour muscle; the terrible swarms of mosquitoes, from the *ñati'u cabayú* to the microscopic *mbigüí* that rise in clouds from the puddles and torment those wretched souls, denied even the soothing balm of sleep. Of course, a mosquito net is too expensive for a slave in the yerba plantations; only the slave-driving financier of capital uses one.

A most horrific degeneration oppresses the peons, their women, and their little ones. The yerba plantations extinguish a whole generation in fifteen years. By the age of forty a man has been turned into the miserable waste left by the greed of others. Only skin and bone remain. Decrepit, brutalized to the extreme of not remembering even his own family, he is referred to as an "old peon." His face has transformed from a pale mask, to the color of the soil, and finally to that of ash. He is the walking dead. He is a former employee of Industrial Paraguaya.

But an "old peon" is a rarity. The workers usually die in the mines before they get "old." One day the foreman finds his habitual victim lying on the ground. He tries to get him up by hitting him with a stick, but in vain. He abandons him. As his workmates set off for the shift, the dying man is left alone. He is in the forest. He is an employee of Industrial Paraguaya, returned by evil slavery to savage Nature. Nobody will hear you. For you there is no help. You will pass away without another's hand holding yours, without a witness. Alone, alone, alone! Even jailed criminals have medical attention; when they are sent to the gallows they are offered a glass of wine and a priest. Alas, you are not even a criminal; you are a mere worker. You will die in the solitude of the forest like wounded vermin.

Since the Triple Alliance War, thirty to forty thousand Paraguayans have *benefited*, or rather, been annihilated in this manner in the yerba plantations

of the three nations. With regard to those who are still suffering this yoke—
many of them minors, as I have explained—one fact will suffice to illus-
trate their state. They are much lower than Indians in intelligence, energy,
dignity—in fact, in any aspect that one may wish to consider. This is what
Industrial Paraguaya has done to the white man.

The Treatment of Tree Fellers and Timber Workers

Reinaldo López Fretes

During the first half of the twentieth century, nine ports were established along the western bank of the River Paraguay, dedicated exclusively to the production of tannin for export. Tannin produced from the quebracho tree soon became one of the most important industries in Paraguay. The trees were felled, then dragged by oxen to meter-gauge railway lines for transport to the factories, where the wood was sawn and shredded by machinery, and boiled in water to release the tannin. The red-brown juice was drawn off from the vats, and allowed to cool and congeal into a hard mass. The solidified tannin was then packaged and shipped downriver for export. The industry prospered during the First World War, when there was a boom in international demand for tannin extract, mainly for the curing of leather for army boots. From the 1930s onward, the industry began to fight a losing battle against declining world demand and local supply problems. This decline was punctuated only by the Second World War, when a second temporary boom in demand occurred, with British and United States armed forces arranging direct purchase from freeport facilities at Buenos Aires. Competition from mimosa extract in Kenya and the replacement of leather by synthetic footwear products hastened the eventual demise of the tannin extract industry in the 1970s.

These tannin ports were "company towns," operating as autarkic enclaves with indentured labor and had little impact on the surrounding hinterland of the Chaco. Workers were tied to the purchase of goods in company stores by a system of coupons, and perpetual indebtedness of workers was commonplace. Reinaldo López Fretes worked in the Chaco from 1938, first as an accountant for the U.S. tannin company International Products Corporation in Puerto Pinasco, and subsequently as justice of the peace in Puerto Sastre. His book, What I have Seen in Northern Paraguay, *published during a brief nine-month period of democratic freedom in 1946, provides a rare firsthand account of the semifeudal conditions and injustices suffered by the lumber and factory workers in the tannin companies.*

Fábrica de tanino Puerto Pinasco (Alto Paraguay)

Between 1889 and 1910, nine ports were established along the Chaco river bank of the River Paraguay, dedicated to the production of tannin extract for export from quebracho ("ax-breaker") trees. These tannin ports were "company towns," autarkic enclaves with a perpetually indebted labor force tied to the purchase of goods in company stores by a system of *vales* (tokens). The industry prospered during the First and Second World Wars, when there were booms in demand for tannin extract, mainly for the curing of leather for army boots. It declined, however, from the 1960s when the plastics revolution brought about the replacement of leather by synthetic footwear products and the chemical industry developed alternatives to natural tanning products. The U.S.-owned Puerto Pinasco was the major tanning port during the 1920s and 1930s. This view of the tannin factory from across the river shows its characteristic high chimneys. Back of postcard states: "Colección del explorador Ls. De Boccard." From the collection of Andrew Nickson.

Each of the companies uses gang masters, people sometimes even on the company payroll, who travel to towns such as Concepción, Belén, Horqueta, Loreto, and San Pedro with enough money to attract new workers—most of whom are inexperienced in lumber work—by offering them pay in advance. At the end of this preliminary contact, and after the customary "little speech" in which the gang master explains the virtues and great prospects of work under their future employer, and having obtained the number of personnel that the boss requires, he boards ship with them—along with their families, if they have them. Before they embark, the gang master will hand the men another certain sum of money: the day they get on board they have already assumed a considerable debt, this in addition to the cost of the boat trip for the whole family, transport of personal belongings, etc. Once

Indian workers dance at Puerto Pinasco. The caption reads: "Like a ballroom 'Paul Jones' is this traditional Indian dance—Workers in the American quebracho factory at Puerto Pinasco, on the Chaco side of the Paraguay River, stage a show for the manager and his photographer guest. Their reward was a feast provided by the company." Photograph by Fenno Jacobs, from the article by Christopher Gibson, "Through Paraguay and Southern Matto Grosso," *National Geographic Magazine* 84, no. 4 (October 1943), photography section "Color Cruising in Paraguay," 6.

on board, either the recruiter himself or some professional shark working with him will organize gambling, and take care that the new personnel are ensnared and indebted by handing them more and more money. At first they will ask him for five guaranies, then ten guaranies, and so on, until the gang master has complete control over them.

Once they reach their destination, they are set down in a house called *chata corá*. Puerto Pinasco now has a house close to the harbor for workers in transit. It is wretchedly inadequate, but at least offers some protection from the elements. But in Puerto Casado, Sastre, and Guaraní, the new recruits are simply left in the open around the harbor. Whether it is hot or cold, raining or not, they remain there for up to twenty days while the paperwork for their contracts is processed. During this time, they eat at the company canteen, amassing even more debt to the company.

One might imagine that the managers and administrators would be concerned that this personnel, who will soon be producing profit for the company, should be well looked after. On the contrary, the Paraguayans are their very lowest priority. When foreign staff members are contracted, however, they are well treated and there is even someone to carry their luggage from the ship. They receive many other attentions even though the Paraguayan workers deserve much more.

Once the paperwork is completed, the recruits are taken to the area of forest where they will work, already with a debt of 80–100 guaranies—a small fortune for a timber worker. When they arrive there, the administration gives them the necessary work implements and food rations for between eight and fifteen days, depending on the distance to their designated lot, as well as working clothes, a mosquito net, and other small items only available in the stores at Pinasco, since at Casado, Sastre, and Guaraní there are only beans, flour, salt, moldy biscuits, pieces of cloth, and the ever-present rum. From the sawmill office, they travel in a cart, ill-named a *lecho*, a word from which language I cannot imagine, because in the land of the author of Don Quixote, *lecho* means a bed suitable for sleeping or resting on, according to the Spanish Academy, whereas the *lecho* in Alto Paraguay is not like that at all, useless for resting, let alone for sleeping. It is yet another brilliant invention of the tannin companies . . . only they know its real origin, so we must leave them with the privilege.

How is it possible to imagine that any new worker should take up his post with a debt of over 100 guaranies to his employer already hanging over him?

When they enter the forest they find themselves faced with the enormous quebracho trees (as hard, almost, as steel), and are unable to fell even one in a whole morning (the usual case with novices), and even if they do succeed in cutting one down, the reward for the labor of felling, stripping, and leaving it ready for haulage is entirely insufficient, for the simple reason that the price that the company pays them is little more than an insult. Indeed, an insult: the price they are paid is 3.50, 5.80 and 6.00 guaranies per tonne respectively from virgin forest, exploited forest, and reexploited (stripped) forest where no tree of more than forty to forty-five kilos must be left in the lot.

It might be argued that the price paid for the timber is sufficient. It would certainly be so if the worker could regularly cut half a tonne or a tonne per day. But there is currently almost nobody in the whole of Alto Paraguay who is capable of cutting that quantity, and as a result the vast majority of lumberjacks are constantly in debt.

As well as finishing the logs from the quebracho or urundey tree, the lumberjack is required to provide the necessary conditions so that the logs can be hauled for delivery to the official receiver of timber. These conditions involve cutting wide tracks through the forest for the haulage cart or carts.

The lack of care toward these poor devils, this human dross, is continuous, and they think only of the hell of the quebracho forest, provider of their sustenance, in order to cheat their stomachs, which turn in their desperation to recover energy, and are offered only greenish yerba water, the sedative liquid of tereré.

On arrival at the place indicated for receipt of the timber, the lumberjack asks to see the official receiver, and almost always has to wait at least a week to effect delivery. In Puerto Guaraní, for example, a wait of ten days is the most normal thing in the world. The receiver eventually comes, and he measures the logs with a tape, a practice which is always to the cutter's disadvantage, as only three measurements are taken into account, namely the circumference of the two ends of the log, and its length. But if the width of the log is uneven, the receiver measures the narrowest, not the thickest, part. This can produce a difference of several kilos per log, which, when a number of logs are received, can add up several kilos, and so to several guaranies. There is much evidence of this practice, which I intend to include in a report begun in Puerto Guaraní.

After the logs have been handed over, the famous settlement of payment in the sawmills of Alto Paraguay is carried out. I say famous because when an axe man cannot read nor write, and even if he can, in the final settlement the company will dock him charges for such things as receipt of goods that the paymaster knows full well he has not received.

From the inspectorate, he then goes to the accounting office, where, as before, he must wait a couple of days—although in Puerto Pinasco they now sign off payments more promptly.

So what is the final amount remaining to the timber worker, who has waited, from the day that he asked to see the receiver to the day he is finally paid, a total of at least two weeks? In fact it can only be in the negative, because, while he has been waiting, he has been accruing more debts. With nothing left to him, he is obliged to enter once again the primeval forest which is the source of so many of his sorrows, and where he will leave the rest of his miserable, ragged life, a creature left behind in the terrible solitude of old-fashioned brutality.

I have omitted to mention the train ticket that the workers buy to reach their place of work. This is payable according to the distance traveled, from one cent to one guaraní, as if they were traveling in comfortable carriages rather than what are in reality dilapidated covered wagons.

The lumberjack, the carter, the water carrier, the drover, and all the other sawmill workers are the personification of abandonment and neglect.

No further explanation is necessary, and it remains only for me to say that all these companies should be nationalized—completely, and without exception. I will not hear that they would not be able to continue operating, because the people who really make them function are the Paraguayan workers and employees in the factories: if those people did not work, then the companies would indeed cease to function.

The Golden Age (Without a Nickel)

Helio Vera

The "golden age" was the construction of the Generación del 900, a preeminent group of writers who emerged in the early twentieth century and sought to construct a new historical memory. They challenged the dominant Liberal view of the nineteenth century as one of despotism and authoritarianism leading to the catastrophe of the Triple Alliance War and then to a new Liberal era based on constitutional rights and freedoms and laissez-faire government. Instead, they argued that the so-called nationalist period (1814–70) had been a golden age of state-led, autonomous development and national greatness. As part of this narrative, the Triple Alliance War was transformed from ignominious defeat to become the national epic—a heroic defense against the overwhelming forces of an international conspiracy to destroy the Paraguayan revolutionary model and thus the nation itself.

While the following extract is written in an accessible and humorous style, typical of the author, it also represents a strong critique of the Generación del 900 and the dangers of political construction of historical memory.

According to Mircea Eliade, the principal objective of all of the rites associated with the myth of the Eternal Return is the regeneration of time. In other words, the unconscious reconstruction of a Golden Age lost in our past. However, this reconstruction is incompatible with the existence of historical memory, with its abuse of prosaic detail, its vulgar chronologies, its tiresome reconstructions of events, its boring protagonists of flesh and blood, and individuals who, as well as uttering famous words and carrying out memorable acts, suffer from toothache, drink, love and hate, and suffer from mothers-in-law as well as parasites. They are simply human. And as such they are capable of making an enormous mess of things.

The Troubadours of Our History

For this reason, the past in Paraguay does not exist as history but as legend. This is why we do not have historians but troubadours, emotional singers of epic tales, tear-jerking, guitar-playing poets of the past. This is why we do not have human heroes, but have instead marble statues, without even the smallest stain of birdshit which, dropped by some iconoclastic pigeon, might blemish their pure white surface.

Some say that this attitude constitutes an act of deliberate falsification of the truth, a product of malign inspiration, a move by cardsharps, a dark conspiracy of imaginative rogues. It is no such thing. This way of presenting the past with its peculiar structures—"categories instead of events, archetypes instead of historical figures"[1]—corresponds to an archaic society that has still not emerged into modernity.

We should not be shocked by this, nor should anyone infer that we are criticizing our nation as a whole. For no one has shown definitively that the cosmovision of an archaic society is better or worse than that of a modern society. It is just different. I do not believe that anyone can prove that such a cosmovision should be rejected in favor of another presumably more "modern" one, sanctified by three centuries of rationalism; a period of time that shrinks into insignificance when compared to the weight of the millennia of human existence. There is nothing that gives us the authority to anoint and crown computers instead of our beloved stereotypes.

This way of seeing things is rooted in every activity of our time. This in turn naturally explains the tenacious rejection of every attempt to reconstruct the historical memory of Paraguay, understood, according to Eliade, as the "memory of events that do not derive from any archetype."[2] This is why the past in Paraguay does not exist as history, or a "succession of irreversible, unforeseen events of great autonomous value," but rather as a harmonious, rousing tune, composed to the beat of lutes and angelical flutes, while those who play them are as good as the Archangel Gabriel or as evil as Satan. No middle ground.

Why this need to embellish history? One very important reason is the need to evoke the shining Golden Age in the present. That is why Paraguayan history, understood as a tiresome timeline, interrupted by progress and regression, assailed by sporadic crises, but recognized as a definite ascending line, does not exist. What takes its place is a perpetual succession of black periods and white periods. The former are not relieved by even a drop of whiteness, the latter allow not even a speck of cosmic dust. Our history is the ideal of makeup artists; not a blemish. Its skin will always be black or white, with no concessions to mixture, especially to grey, since one never really knows whether it is a darkened white or a diluted, pale black.

The aim of all of this is to imitate and reproduce the archetypes of the Golden Age in an eternal struggle against the forces of darkness. Our acts will be given legitimacy only to the extent that they imitate the archetypes. In this way "we comply with the order of the great leaders of the past";

"we lay claim to the motherland"; "we continue the legacy of Cerro Corá," etcetera. If one does not establish a clear connection with archetypes, the legitimacy of one's argument is weakened.

Our Golden Age

Our Golden Age was in the nineteenth century. Most of the writers of the Generation of 900 agree about this. It is clear, however, that those who lived in the Golden Age were not aware of this and had no idea that they were walking on sacred ground. The map was drawn up later by Juan O'Leary, Moreno, Pane, and other eminent Paraguayan intellectuals, as well as by foreigners such as the wise Swiss naturalist Moisés Bertoni, who arrived in our Arcadia to revive himself with its pure air. From Europe came anarchists like Eliseo Reclus or dilettantes such as Thomas Carlyle whose eulogies helped to strengthen this discourse, whether taking as their main inspiration the devastation of the War of the Triple Alliance or the enigmatic personality of Dr. Francia.

The terrible experience of the war inevitably pushed human experience to the limits. Seemingly irrational and inexplicable sacrifice, as well as extraordinary deeds seemingly straight out of classical tragedy, prepared the ground for the emergence of the Generation of 900. The epic myth picks up this unrepeatable experience and provides clues that should not be ignored.

We recall for example "Cerro Corá" by Felix Fernández, one of the most beautiful songs of Paraguay's national heritage. Its words say it all: "After the Marshal, again the Marshal / Where could there be any greater than you? / . . . They sacrificed you; you never surrendered / You are the legend of Paraguay / . . . After death we will again hold our heads high in pride / When we hear the voice of the Marshal."

The Generation of 900 opened the way for the return of the Golden Age, their work infused with nostalgia, to the cry of "the greatness of the past, the misery of the present." Even the intellectual Left paid tribute to this discourse.

A certain curiosity may arise in the reader regarding whether the Generation of 900 was simply a response to the strong Liberal tide that swept over our land after the Triple Alliance War, or whether it arose from deeper, more personal feelings, rooted in our subconscious. With the irresponsibility of someone who has no proof or evidence, I will opt for the second. The archaic concept of the Eternal Return and the search for the Golden Age are more substantiated in our collective spirit than the abstract ideas that entered Paraguay in the backpacks of the soldiers of the Triple Alliance. It was no coincidence that the governments that came to power immediately after the defeat included a significant foreign influence—or at least individuals who had been influenced by foreign ideas.

As with the cycles of the moon, each period of shadow will be replaced by an age of shining light. Each paradigm of evil will be overthrown inevitably by a solar hero. The moon will regain its rounded brightness and time will have been regenerated. This is the myth of the Eternal Return.

Where Poetry Intervenes

The author Josefina Plá explains the efforts of the Generation of 900 in a different, but no less illustrative, way. For her, theirs was nothing more than a way of reconstructing or perhaps constructing a Paraguayan literary genre. Under the guise of writing history, the writers of this generation started to write fables. The results were perhaps poor from a scientific perspective, but excellent in terms of aesthetics. Whether their work had anything to do with historical fact, as positivists who were dominant at that time might have demanded, is another issue altogether.

The Generation of 900 was the first that had the opportunity to work with some kind of intellectual continuity. They got around poetry, novels, and theater by "considering them superfluous or simply ineffective in the task that interested them: the definition of a historical consciousness, the elucidation of a system of universal values that would give meaning to the future. It was clearly a matter of urgency to give this devastated, disoriented people faith, a set of values, a path. When they did it, however, these writers failed to appreciate the value of literature in promoting consciousness as a receptacle of collective historical memory which documented the spirit and climate of the times."[3]

The writers of this brilliant generation took it upon themselves to construct a new historical memory. Or put another way, following the ideas of Eliade, they constructed a perspective of the past that erased genuine memories and allowed us to see, without shadows or deformities, the perfect, glowing Golden Age. This position was not confined to a certain ideology. In turn, all the political parties in the country, from the Left to the Right, from Oscar Creydt to Juan E. O'Leary, began to adopt this perspective.

Notes

1. M. Eliade, *El mito del Eterno Retorno* (Barcelona: Planeta, 1986), 72.
2. Ibid., 250.
3. J. Plá, "Contenido humano y social de la narrativa," *Panorama* (Mexico City), no. 8 (March–April 1964): 86.

The Causes of Poverty in Paraguay

Teodosio González

The Misfortunes of Paraguay *is a biting critique of Paraguayan society during
the Liberal period. Its author, Teodosio González (1871–1932), was an administrator
renowned for his honesty and also the author of the country's penal code, which remained in force until 1998. In the book he expresses his contempt for what he sees as
a corrupt political class, whom he holds largely responsible for the country's backwardness, in particular the weak administration of justice, inadequate health and
education, and very poor public services. In this sense, his approach to the problems
of governance has a strikingly modern ring to it, and much of what he says is still
relevant today. However, in his chapter on the causes of poverty, reproduced below,
he is also very critical of the attitudes of Paraguayan men in general toward work,
the accumulation of wealth, and family, which he sees as important cultural factors
behind Paraguay's underdevelopment.*

Paraguay, at once the most heroic and the poorest country in the Americas, a country in continual contemplation of its past, lulled by the gentle
murmur of its epic history, looks very much like a restaging in the New
World of the role of Sparta in the Old. God save us from such glory. As a
modern writer has said, "Poor nations are like tramps; they live on crumbs
and past glories." Paraguay is arguably the archetype of this phenomenon.
All of Paraguay's problems—its lack of immigration, its administrative dis-
organization, its lack of public works, its anarchy, the exodus of peasants
to neighboring countries in search of a better life, etc.—can be attributed
almost exclusively to the chronic poverty that afflicts the nation, the causes
of which we will examine below.

Paraguay is probably the weakest country, economically, in Latin America relative to its civilization, history, size, and population, and its treasury
is certainly the poorest. There is no great wealth in Paraguay. Two hundred
thousand gold pesos are considered a fortune, and generally only foreigners
possess that much. Poverty reigns from one end of the country to the other.
More than half of the rural population lives in precarious, squat, one- or

two-room huts with no furniture and no conveniences of any kind, eating little and badly, and going half naked. And if the suffering this implies is not too keenly felt it is because, given the Paraguayan's natural frugality, the abundance of food that nature provides in return for absolutely no effort, and the generosity and hospitality of the people, hunger has not yet become widespread, and nakedness is no burden in a benign climate.

What is the cause of this generalized poverty? There are many, but in particular, two defects in the Paraguayan character (defects that are equally to be found among all mestizos or *criollos* of Spanish-Amerindian descent, as has been observed in Latin American countries from Mexico to Tierra del Fuego) are consistent with the lack of two indispensable qualities for the production of wealth: a love of work and the capacity to save. The vast majority of Paraguayans are profoundly lazy. Incorrigible laziness, taken at times to the extreme of a horror of work, is the norm throughout the country. Thousands of people prefer living seminaked, sleeping on the ground, and eating what they can reach with their hands to putting a tool to work. They often work only in order not to avoid starving to death, two or three days per week, and then rest until they have eaten everything they have earned.

An anecdote by way of example. A friend of mine, a dealer in animal pelts, arrived on one of his trips at a small hut near the River Tebicuary in a place where he knew there was a large number of *lobopé*. He found a strong young man and offered him $500 for every skin he brought him. Armed with an old rifle, the lad went off, and soon returned with a beautiful specimen he had hunted. He was paid his $500. My friend said to him "I'll be back in two weeks, and I want you to have twenty skins for me. I'll give you $10,000." My friend left, but on his return did not find the young man in his hut. Since receiving the $500 the lad had not lifted a finger, and spent all his time visiting neighbors. He still had some money left when my friend returned: the explanation for why there were no more *lobopé* skins.

Indolence, lack of initiative, and total inertia pervade the majority of the population, especially the peasantry. They look on with complete indifference as their huts fall to pieces and the weeds and accompanying snakes and vermin reach the doors of their homes. Very occasionally the deathly idleness lifts and brief enthusiasm for some task emerges. But these sparks are short-lived and soon fade and disappear without trace save for the bitter taste of yet another failure. Perseverance and tenacity, so necessary for productive work, are largely absent among Paraguayans. In vain one attempts to rouse them from their lethargy or to encourage them to follow the example of the colony of foreigners next door, to see how the gringos live, how

1904 Revolution street scene. In August 1904 the Liberal Party, reunited by Benigno Ferreira after years of division, organized an invasion upriver from Buenos Aires. With strong support from the Argentine navy, the rebels launched a war of attrition from their base at Villeta, south of Asunción, eventually forcing President Escurra of the Colorado Party to resign in December. The Revolution of 1904 was a political watershed, bringing the Liberals to power for the first time since the Triple Alliance War and ushering in the long period of their political domination, which lasted until 1940. Photographer unknown (E. Bloch and Co.). From the collection of Jorge Rubiani.

they want for nothing and progress with next to no effort. The Paraguayans understand and consider, but cannot be bothered to do the same.

Laziness is also apparent among the governors and politicians, who leave everything for tomorrow apart from collecting their wages and bonuses. In terms of foresight and economy, the Paraguayan is generally lacking. No one saves a cent; no one thinks about tomorrow. No one bears in mind that he might become ill or old or be injured or lose his job, and that he cannot expect the assistance of others or the Paraguayan state, the poorest of the poor.

In contrast, the vice of wastefulness, the love of amusements and of external appearances is commonplace. A peasant who works a tiny rented patch of land will spend his whole year's earnings on a wedding or a church function, even become indebted, rather than use the money to buy the land he works with the sweat of his brow and perhaps even put a little by. In miserable dwellings, with no furniture other than beds made from strips of leather without mattress or sheets, broken boxes, a wooden table, and four or five basic chairs, where the owner does not own an ox or a plow, I have seen saddles edged in silver and genuine Smith & Wesson revolvers with mother-of-pearl grips worth thousands of pesos. When the great influenza epidemic struck Asunción, doctors observed that the majority of poorer households lacked mattresses, sheets, furniture, and rudimentary utensils for the family, but never silk dresses and stockings, patent leather shoes, powders and perfumes, and luxury umbrellas and parasols:

> There exists a unique form of luxury and ostentation that leaps from poverty to conspicuous extravagance. It does not first achieve family welfare, safety, and comfort before going on to reach levels of super-fluous spending. Rather, it jumps, and we have gone suddenly from hardship to fascination with a luxury which, since we do not have the means to make it real, becomes a gaudy pretense, a false splendor that will nevertheless lead us to ruin. (*La Nación*)

For the sake of truth and justice, I should clarify that the Paraguayan woman, even if she might enjoy luxury like all women, is a hundred times more hard-working, diligent, economical, and persistent than the Para-guayan man. Intellectually and morally she is his superior. Her capacity for self-sacrifice, her loyalty, and her devotion to her spouse and children are exemplary, equal to those of the women of any other country. The vice of gambling, though, pervades the Republic with no exception for sex, age, so-cial condition, or fortune. The poor worker who shuns an honest day's work will spend his days and nights gambling, and if he has no money, watching others gamble.

In Paraguay there appears to be no way of putting an end to these evils. It is well known that work is a sacrifice, a form of suffering that everyone who is able avoids. One works in this world for fear of an evil—for fear of poverty, the worst of all evils. But the Paraguayan, like every Spanish-Amerindian mestizo, has never been afraid of poverty. He has been more afraid of work. In the time of Francia and Carlos Antonio López, he worked out of fear of punishment. In those days, as soon as the slacker came to his attention, a foreman would call the culprit and in the name of the Supreme Dictator warn him that he had to work for himself or for the nation. If he did not obey the order, he would get twenty strokes; if it happened again, fifty. And he was careful indeed not to risk the hundred strokes for a third offense. There were two options: work or be beaten to death. Nowadays, with constitutional articles guaranteeing free will, the frugal and resigned Paraguayan, who knows no fear of poverty, slacks at will and is the most zealous promoter of the modern principle that the clever man lives off the idiot, and the idiot lives by his work.

How many times, during trips around the country, have I tried to instill into the peasantry the love of money as a means to living life as pleasantly as possible? I have waxed lyrical on the pleasures of a good bed, good food, comfort, good clothes, the awareness of property, and the independence that money brings. . . . But my warm and enthusiastic exhortations go in one ear and out the other.

The Mennonites Arrive in the Chaco

Walter Quiring

The Mennonites are the largest and most successful of all non-Latin American im-
migrant groups to settle in Paraguay since it gained independence from Spain in
1811. Between 1928 and 1948, three waves of immigrants, comprising a total of 6,245
persons, established remote agricultural colonies in the central Chaco on 150,370
hectares of land that had been purchased from the Carlos Casado company by the
Corporación Paraguaya (referred to as C. P. in the excerpt below), a company owned
by a U.S. financier, Samuel McRoberts. The Paraguayan government was keen to
promote immigration to the Chaco because of the growing tension with Bolivia over
its ownership. The Mennonites are still the only people to have founded success-
ful large-scale agricultural and cattle-ranching communities in the Chaco, which
are based on cooperative principles. Today the Chaco Mennonites number over ten
thousand, and they own over one million hectares of land. They enjoy a high stan-
dard of living and their colonias *are the major supplier of dairy products to Asun-*
ción. This account tells of the extreme hardships suffered by the first group that
reached Paraguay in December 1926 and founded Colonia Menno in April 1928. Fol-
lowing the eventual success of the first, two more colonies were subsequently formed
in the central Chaco, at Fernheim in 1930–32 and at Neuland in 1947–48.

The total number of the immigrants who left Canada was 1,765, distributed among 279 families. Upon arriving in Asunción the immigrants were
warmly welcomed by the President of Paraguay, Dr. Eligio Ayala. The first
group reached its goal in Puerto Casado on the 30th of December 1926. Very
little had been done by the C. P. for their reception at Puerto Casado and
nothing at all for their further transport and colonization in the Chaco.
The new arrivals were temporarily located in five emergency barracks near
the river but most of them voluntarily relinquished these dwellings which
would naturally have to be surrendered with the arrival of later groups anyway. They began to live in tents which they had brought along, or later in
small huts which they built and for which the C. P. furnished lumber free
of charge. A sixth barrack which was somewhat larger than the others was

made to serve as a kitchen in one end and as a meeting place in the other end.

The new immigrants waited impatiently to press on into the Chaco but the C. P. made no moves to aid them. Months went by without anything being undertaken, either by the immigrants or the C. P. In the meantime the typhus epidemic which had broken out, the return of some disillusioned immigrants to Canada, and the attempt of a small, more active group to colonize in Eastern Paraguay, diverted the group in general from its most urgent task, namely, that of pressing forward into the Chaco.

The health of the group, which at the first had not been bad among the adults, gradually became less and less satisfactory. The time for the immigration was the least favorable imaginable, since the colonists came out of the severe Canadian winter directly into the high summer of the tropics. The change was so extreme that on the very first day after the arrival a child died, and on the third three children died. Frequent deaths of children occurred for months thereafter. In January and February alone 26 children were carried out to the cemetery. Soon adults began to take sick. The living in close quarters, the dirty and always lukewarm water, the unaccustomed and generally inadequate diet, the unsanitary toilet facilities which were located near to the barracks, the lack of the least opportunity for bathing and, finally, not the least, the flies and other insects, prepared the way for the catastrophe which was to cost almost 200 human lives. In April 1927 the first adults died, apparently from dysentery. However, all the symptoms pointed to abdominal typhus although Casado and his physician, Dr. W. Walter, did not want to admit it. In September after 83 people had already died, the C. P. secured a second physician, Dr. Karl Meilinger, from Encarnación on the Parana River. Dr. Meilinger was to give medical care to the colonists on their way into the Chaco. He at once determined that the disease was typhus and ordered the most stringent quarantine and isolation of those who were sick. He also took other measures to stop the epidemic, but little could be done. The disease laid low one victim after another. Soon mound after mound appeared in the cemetery. Everyone who could started out into the Chaco, if only to escape from the infected harbor. But death pursued those who fled. People went about as in a dream with certain death before their eyes.

The plague continued until February 1928 and then gradually died out. It had raged terribly among the immigrants. Parents were sorrowing for their children and children were sorrowing for their parents. By the end of 1928 a total of 185 persons had died. This number was distributed as follows: On the journey to Paraguay, 6; in the port of Casado, 121; on the way into the Chaco, 48; in the newly established villages, 12.

But let us go back to the beginning of 1927 again. With each passing day after the arrival at Puerto Casado, the immigrants became more and more restless and inquired more and more impatiently about the further movement into the Chaco which had been dragged out so unconscionably long. They demanded that Fred Engen should act but he hesitated. Many blamed Casado but he had nothing to do with the immigration. Nothing seemed to be of any avail. At last the immigrants wrote to Canada and requested the home group for speedy help. The home folks stirred up the C. P. and informed McRoberts. The latter, after trying in vain to handle the matter by cable, sent one of his best associates, the Vice-president of the C. P., Alfred Rogers, to Paraguay.

Rogers reached Puerto Casado at the end of May 1927 and immediately took up the leadership energetically. However, he failed to move the settlers to determine the boundaries of their land with even the most primitive means so he returned to Asunción to negotiate with the survey office. On the 16th of June, he returned to Puerto Casado, accompanied by McRoberts, who had meanwhile come himself to Paraguay, called the immigrants together and decided with them to send an expedition at once into the Chaco to make the final selection of the land. But it was July before the 12 representatives of the group got started and reached kilometer 216 (mile 135) on the trail which had already been traveled three times. They followed the example of their predecessors, made short trips to the left and right of the trail, dug wells, tried to find building lumber in the forest and finally chose a territory about 200 kilometers (125 miles) west of the port as the place for the settlement. Here they found larger pampas and observed that the land was not swampy as it was in the region near the river. On the 14th of August they returned to the port and secured the consent of the entire immigrant group to their choice.

It has already been mentioned that several families had pressed on into the Chaco to get away from the harbor and in order to be near to their future homes in the interior. Already on the 12th of February, 1927, six families with 31 persons had started out to settle down somewhere. This group had been used to work and could no longer stand the idleness at the port; they also hoped no doubt to be safer from sickness away from the port. After 12 long hard days on the journey, they reached kilometer 112 (mile 70), also called Pozo Azul, constructed emergency dwellings, began to clear the open pampas of the few scattered trees and bushes on them, and prepared to plough the first fields in the Chaco.

Finally at the end of August 1927, the survey of the land was begun. The immigrants took new courage and soon hoped to be able to settle on their own land and not waste any more time and money and above all physical strength, which is so important in the tropics. But the firm of Insfrán and Bibolini, which was to do the surveying, was moving at a snail's pace. By the end of December, that is, four months, they had only progressed 53 kilometers in one direction; consequently, the C. P. cancelled the original contract with the company for the surveying and agreed upon a price of $90 per kilometer. From that time on the work suddenly went forward with speed and dispatch. But it was the middle of April 1928 before the outer boundaries of the Mennonite area were surveyed and marked by trails cut through the forest.

In February, before the surveyors had completed their work, the locations of the villages were chosen and the inner boundaries surveyed so that by the first of March the tracts of land could be assigned to the individual families. Each village was to consist of 16 to 20 farms of 160 to 200 acres in each. Each family was permitted to join the village of its own choice provided the village would receive it.

Finally, in April 1928, 16 months after the arrival of the first immigrants in Puerto Casado, the great hour struck when the group as a whole were permitted to actually locate on their own land. The colony which was now founded received the name of Menno after Menno Simons, the early leader of the Mennonites in Holland. One village after the other was located in the forest and soon 14 were established. In the following four years (to 1932) four additional villages were established.

A long row of graves marks the road of these peaceful conquerors on their way into the wilderness of the wild Chaco. At the expense of tremendous sacrifice of lives, of strength and of health, these pioneers opened for themselves and for others the hitherto undeveloped and unexplored regions of the Chaco. After six years of the most severe labor, the pampas which have been settled and a small portion of the forest have been transformed into cultivated farms, and the settlers have learned to win their daily bread from the prevailingly light soil in quite different agricultural conditions than they were previously accustomed to. But their economic future is still uncertain and the market for their products is far away and probably inadequate. So far the colonists have had a modest income through the cultivation of cotton.

The Paraguayan Character

Juan Sinforiano Bogarín

Monseñor Bogarín (1863–1949) was a towering figure in Paraguay during the first half of the twentieth century. Born in rural poverty during the Triple Alliance War, he was orphaned very young when his father was killed during the defense of Humaitá and his mother died of cholera. Brought up by an aunt, he became bishop of Paraguay in 1894, and was the first archbishop of Asunción from 1930 to 1949. When he was appointed at the age of thirty-one, he was the youngest bishop in the Americas. He served for a total of fifty-four years as head of the Catholic Church in Paraguay, and was instrumental in reorganizing its structure, which had been decimated during the nationalist period. He undertook extensive "pastoral tours," traveling the length and breadth of the country three times on horseback. As a result he knew his country far better than almost any politician during his lifetime. Renowned for his eloquent oratory in Guaraní, he was also a political and religious conservative. He made strenuous efforts to counter anticlericalism and promote the "moral reconstruction" of the nation in response to the widespread practice of fathering illegitimate children. His analysis of the Paraguayan psyche appeared in his brief autobiography, Mis Apuntes *(My notes), published posthumously. Its harsh criticism of Paraguayan men should be viewed in the context of the gross gender imbalance in the decades following the Triple Alliance War.*

It is very difficult to really get to know the character of a person, and even more so that of a people, or a nation. One of the essential requirements in attempting such a task is to be completely dispassionate in assessing the particular ways of being of a people. In the absence of such an approach, any affirmation would constitute an irritating injustice rather than a reflection of reality, and be tantamount to peddling false concepts.

My conscience tells me that I can indeed write in *Mis Apuntes* the *modus essendi* of the Paraguayan: I have lived among my compatriots and have always had a marked inclination for, and indeed taken pleasure in, observing their behavior, both good and bad. I love my Paraguayan brothers and sisters, with their virtues and their defects, and their pleasant and ill humors,

Bolichera ambulante

Bolichera ambulante. Until the 1960s Paraguayan women were famed for their cigar smoking, as shown in this 1910 picture of one of the traveling *bolicheras*, men and women who operated as brokers in rural areas, buying cash crops from the peasantry in exchange for clothing, kitchen items, and alcohol. As powerful intermediaries, they still play an important role in "bringing in" the vote for traditional parties at election time. Photograph by José Fresen.

but my approach will cause me neither to exaggerate their merits nor underestimate their defects.

I repeat that it is difficult to know the character of the Paraguayan, and even more difficult to govern him if you lack this knowledge. Generally speaking, the Paraguayan's character is good, and even excellent, but one must get to know him. He is peaceful by nature, and of a happy disposition. He is impressionable and obedient, even humble, toward authority and his superiors, so long as they treat him with kindness and give fatherly advice and encouragement. He accepts everything from authority and his superiors with edifying submission and humility, so long as he is approached gently. He accepts a reprimand and receives punishment with resignation, so long as it is handed down after he has been convinced of its justification, and been made to understand that he was punished only because he contravened the law.

However, when a superior or authority behaves in a despotic manner, when he orders, commands or punishes in an angry tone or brandishes force, then—my word! Then, he will submit to the punishment because he has little alternative, but will feel no guilt, and will, as soon as he is able, incur again in the very same, or worse, misdemeanors, with the sole aim of annoying, or poking fun, as he would say, at the boss, superior, or figure of authority.

It is for this reason that inexpert or clumsy authorities, who seek to govern Paraguay with severity, achieve nothing more than the hatred of those they govern, thereby discrediting the government itself, and causing the citizen, against his natural inclination, to disrespect established authority. So with the Paraguayan one must proceed *fortiter et sauviter*, in other words, with strength of character and gentleness of manner.

God made the Paraguayan to be in the home, to work and to obey; he is neither restless nor argumentative nor callous; he is peaceful, and even rather timid, so long as his nerves are not agitated. But these positive qualities disappear completely, and he displays just the opposite if the latent pride—with which he is considerably endowed—is aroused. If he joins a political party, he loses his head: a complete change takes place in him; he becomes the "reverse side" of the coin. Once he is given an opinion to defend, that peaceful soul, obedient enemy of disorder and of brawling, metamorphoses into a restless, irate, stormy, argumentative individual. Having joined a political party, he will do everything to ensure that his party wins; he becomes fearless in the face of danger—even appears to seek it out. And at election time, propelled by his pride, he will not stand down in the face of his adversary but will prefer to wound or be wounded, to kill or be killed.

And all this, to what avail? Solely for the victory of the party or faction that he belongs to. He does not realize, does not care in the slightest, whether his party is working or will work for the good or the ruin of the country. The only thing he knows full well—but which he does not stop to think about—is that from all his efforts, from the dangers to which he exposes himself, he will derive neither material nor moral benefit. Oh, Paraguayans!

If he is given a position of authority, he will not be a success, since, if he is an embarrassment and even a liability as a member of a political party, then as a figure of authority he is a complete failure—and indeed prejudicial. From the moment he takes up a post, he undergoes a transformation; he begins to show a marked tendency, or facility, for unjust and arbitrary behavior and the abuse of power. It is as if the post triggers in him a huge flood of pride or vanity. Thus it is enough for the government to name him as an authority for him to be seized by disproportionate self-satisfaction and take to boasting, without thought for the obligations and responsibilities inherent in the job he is undertaking. He views the position he occupies not as a burden which requires him to maintain law and order, but as a privilege which grants him the right to impose his will and to indulge his every whim. He commits injustices against his subordinates and takes revenge against those for whom he previously held a grudge or some ill will. He takes advantage of any pretext to send them to prison, to commit them to manual labor, to humiliate them, or to send them to do military service, even when they are exempt.

This kind of behavior brings him not only antipathy but the hatred of his departmental staff, and provokes protest on all sides: his irritating acts of injustice are made public, and finally, unable to occupy any longer the post that has been granted to him nor secure the support of his superiors, he is forced to resign or is fired . . . such that he ends up in a vacuum, surrounded by enemies. This, in general terms, is a Paraguayan in authority; there are exceptions, but the more honorable they are, the rarer they are.

The Paraguayan is generous and hospitable, but he is also ungrateful. He will help those in need to the best of his ability. He considers generosity to be a noble act which elevates and gives esteem to those who show it. He will happily invite the traveler to share his frugal meal, and even—a not unusual occurrence—offer him his bed, and such comforts as he is able in order to ensure him a good rest. However, those who receive favors are, generally, ungrateful and indifferent to the acts of generosity they have received. With a curt "Thank you very much" they feel that they have more than repaid their benefactor. So while it is true that the Paraguayan will be generous without expecting anything, material or moral, in return, the fortunate person does not trouble to show any form of recognition to the one who has favored him. Hence, as this is the normal run of things, the benefactor should not be surprised by such conduct.

The Paraguayan is distrustful. He seems to have learned by heart the Spanish saying "Distrust and chicken soup never harmed anyone." This is why he is unlikely to be open with strangers or persons in authority; it is necessary that they warm to each other first; that is to say, he must see a reason for trust so that he feels sufficiently at ease to be honest. In reply to questions or requests that—for good or ill—are addressed to him, he almost always responds in an uncommitted way, or even completely denies what is being asked of him: he can lie as adeptly as he can peel an orange.

The way to overcome his reticence is to begin by discussing mundane topics that have nothing to do with what one really wants to know about from him. This preamble is much more effective when one engages him on things which are important to him, for example, his smallholding, how his work is going, the kind of crop that he plants, his family, whether his children are attending school, and so on. Once he is convinced that one is concerned for his welfare, and for that of his family, then he will be disposed to openness and honesty.

The Paraguayan is noble. When in the hands of the judiciary, through some offence or crime, he will confess, so long as the authorities proceed carefully with their questioning, and thus mitigate his perhaps graver errors; however, in the case of robbery, it is unlikely that he will tell the truth, and will do so only under exceptional circumstances. He will go round and round in circles—from which itself his guilt may be presumed—but a Paraguayan will never admit that he has robbed. This is because robbery is considered the most despicable act, more mean and contemptible than the most horrendous crimes. Another feature, which does demonstrate his nobility, is that he recognizes his illegitimate children and his debts. He will neither support the former nor settle the latter, but he will not deny either.

The Paraguayan neither knows nor wishes to know the advantages of saving. The absolute lack of aspiration to improve his material and social standing means that he lives always for today, worrying little about tomorrow. He is a good worker, not frightened by the burden and fatigue of the job, and, when required, he is resilient; he can cope with eight to ten hours of hard labor per day with ease, and repairs his weariness with laughs and jokes with his workmates. But does he submit himself to such sacrifices in order to save his wage for the future? Not at all. When the next national holiday comes around he will spend his whole week's wages on amusements, games, and parties, and what is more, glory in his lavishness and his carefree attitude to the fruits of his labor.

What I have said above refers both to single and married men; the latter are few, as men tend to abandon their farm and their family and go elsewhere in search of adventure. Once they leave, most of them are oblivious to the needs of their families. They earn money and spend it without consideration that their parents, wives, and children might be in great need. And if they do pay an occasional return visit, they arrive empty-handed as if they were penniless. Among married men who live with their family, there are many who are devoted to their agricultural or professional work. These men are more far-sighted; they think about the future, and place the sweat of their brow at the service of the family.

So this is, broadly, what I have learned from twenty-four years' constant observation of the Paraguayan *modus essendi*. Naturally, there are exceptions, but I believe that my appraisal is not far from the truth.

The Paraguayan People and Their Natural Tendencies

Natalicio González

Natalicio González (1897–1966) was one of the leading figures of the Generación del 900, a group of writers and intellectuals that included Juan O'Leary, Fulgencio Moreno, Manuel Domínguez, and Antolín Irala, who emerged in the early twentieth century. Besides being a politician (president 1948–49), poet, historian, and journalist, González was a political philosopher and a leading figure behind the "rebirth" of Paraguayan nationalism. A fervent member of the Colorado Party, González rejected the liberal antiauthoritarian discourse that was prevalent at the time and sought to forge a national identity that could make sense of the destruction and violence of the past, as well as the instability of the present, and offer Paraguayans a new sense of national pride.

His nationalism was based on a reinterpretation of the nationalist period (1814–70) under the dictatorships of Dr. José Gaspar de Francia, President Carlos Antonio López, and President Francisco Solano López, as a golden age characterized by peace, growth, and independence, as well as brilliant leadership, which only came to a brutal end with the Triple Alliance War, seen as an anti-Paraguayan conspiracy. However, his reinterpretation of history not only included the past but also the future, and Paraguay's destiny of greatness (under a Colorado government). He celebrated the Paraguayan "race" that was allegedly the result of the fusion between the indigenous Guaraní and the colonizing Spanish that produced the "warrior farmer," the selfless, noble Paraguayan, committed to the common good and to national values.

Although seen as a leading exponent of nationalism based on the ideas of "race, land, and history" and as a brilliant intellectual by his supporters, his works have been widely criticized in terms of style (the quality, complexity, and verbosity of his writing) and detail (the reinvention of the past taking priority over historical accuracy). However, his writings were fundamental to the emergence of a revisionist view of history that emerged as a dominant nationalist discourse after the Chaco War and that became the official discourse under the long period of Colorado Party

*rule (1947–2008). Above all, it was a discourse used and manipulated by President
Stroessner (1954–89) to highlight his own role as the continuation of the great leaders
of the past and his regime as the continuation of the golden age of the nationalist
period.*

In the following extract from El Paraguay Eterno *(written while Paraguay was
still under a Liberal government), González offers a summary of Paraguayan history since independence, highlighting its fall from greatness into decay following
the Triple Alliance War. He also includes a justification for authoritarianism and a
eulogy for the "true Paraguayan" (the mix of Spanish and Guaraní) before alluding
to Paraguay's destined return to greatness.*

The Paraguayan people arose from the synthesis of opposing forces operating at the very heart of the colony. Shared traditions, ideals, hopes, sufferings, ethnic unity, the development over centuries of the agrarian and
warrior-like features of the race, all meant that when independence was
declared, Paraguay was already one unique, organic entity with a set of
individual characteristics. While neighboring countries found themselves
consumed by a descent into anarchy, in the land of the Guaraní a strong
state arose. This state identified itself with the collective destiny, was conscious of its direction and its objectives, and acted as the motor of national
greatness.

Surrounded by external threats, and witnessing the political storms and
the seeds of dissolution that spread throughout the New World, Paraguay
withdrew into itself under the dictatorship of Francia and watched from
its position of splendid isolation as neighboring countries tore themselves
apart. The dictatorship of Francia did not tolerate the slightest attempt to
distract the people from the goals of the national interest. Francia not only
suppressed the aristocracy in order to lay the foundations of Paraguayan
democracy, skillfully exploiting the deep sense of inequality among Paraguayans, but he also declared himself head of the church, thus resolving the
religious problem through his absolute supremacy over the state. His policy
of isolation did not respond to an imitation of some missionary desire, as
some observers have superficially argued, but was born out of necessity. Perhaps nothing illustrates this better than the words of an inquisitive and analytical geographer: "A civilization can benefit enormously from an isolated,
narrow, and protected environment. There are cases in which extreme
isolation, distance from commercial routes, and inaccessibility represent a
positive advantage for peoples or societies, from which they may benefit."[1]

When Francia died, first Carlos Antonio López and then Francisco Solano López stepped forward. The two regimes overlap to such an extent

that in reality they can be considered a single entity. In a famous address, Francia alluded to the evolving character of the Paraguayan political system and its ability to continually transform itself in order to respond effectively to political realities.

"Time has shown," he wrote, "that our institutions contain some features which it is necessary to correct; time has also shown that before the Republic of Paraguay can organize itself, it is necessary that this provisional order and system should continue for many years, since this will allow institutions already in existence to slowly improve and be perfected, and others to be established as necessity dictates. In this way, the people will gradually become accustomed to the regular and moderate exercise of rights which as yet they do not know. If we do not proceed in this way, Paraguay cannot enjoy peace, and will suffer the great calamities that have tormented neighboring states.

"The government is convinced that this provisional regime is the only protection against such calamities: it is the only political lightning conductor that can render harmless the thunder and lightning of the storm clouds gathering throughout the world, and especially over the new continent.

"All of the newly independent Republics, with the exception of Paraguay, have been torn by a desire for liberty that they did not understand, and have hastily established fundamental laws and organized themselves within a constitutional framework. All of these theoretically perfect states are based on the most enlightened principles and the most elevated, just and liberal ideas. All grant their citizens broad and important political rights; all guarantee the fundamental rights of man: liberty, prosperity, security, and equality before the law; all are marked by the seal of permanence and immutability. Yet all have seen their authority undermined, and with the intent of avoiding despotism have only facilitated a descent into anarchy. None of these Republics has escaped often bloody and brutal despotism, or frequent revolutions and disorder. This is the incontestable proof that in order to conserve peace, public order, and freedom, something more than an easily discarded constitution is necessary."

In the cultural and economic realms, the regimes of the two Lópezes stand out for the audacity of their achievements. Primary education is made compulsory; schools and workshops spread across the Republic; the Literary Academy and the School of Medicine are founded; students are sent to Europe and material progress is developed in a variety of ways. State monopolies on the production of yerba mate and timber for construction are established by decree on the grounds, according to the decree that "they are natural resources which neither fall within the private domain, nor are fruit

Mercado, Asunción

This Asunción market scene, dating from around 1900, prominently displays the *mandioca* (cassava) that remained the major staple of the Paraguayan diet until the last quarter of the twentieth century, when rice, pasta, and bread challenged its pre-eminence. Photographer unknown. From the collection of Andrew Nickson.

of individual labor," and should thus benefit the collective interests of the people rather than one individual or any small group.

There is a perfect harmony to be found between the López regimes and the ideals of the Paraguayan people. The state manages to produce a magnificent synthesis of Paraguay's past. It combines the political legacy of the *conquistador* with the spiritual work of the catechists, developing national culture on solid and natural foundations. It defends the wealth of the country from foreign greed and makes the greatest efforts of all Spanish American states to use natural resources to produce industrial value. It redirects rivers and constructs railways and roads; it establishes an iron foundry where products ranging from military weapons to agricultural ploughs are wrought; it organizes the merchant navy, whose vessels fly the Paraguayan flag in European waters; it resolves the agrarian problem; and instead of opening the gates to the immigrant masses whose lust for wealth and greed for money supplant moral values and patriotic fervor, it imports teachers of the arts and renowned scholars who explore the subsoil, study the flora and fauna of the country, manage industry, and teach the people about European technology.

During an era in which international capitalism made its first concerted efforts to gain control of the wealth of the New World, a state that defended its economic and political independence and its cultural autonomy with such stubborn energy risked the formation of foreign alliances against it. This is indeed what happened. The Empire of Brazil, with a monarchy related to the dynasties of Europe, acted as the principal aggressive force behind a war of annihilation whose bloody epilogue took place on the stage of Cerro Corá.

The survival and development of the regime, destroyed in 1870 by foreign aggression, would have allowed Paraguay to progress as a state free from all servitude, beyond that which it naturally imposed for the good of the people. And this was what the allies wished to avoid at all cost. The role of the Treaty of the Triple Alliance as an instrument of international capitalism eager to colonize Paraguay can be seen in its own articles, which state in a preamble that the signatories, "persuaded that the peace, security and welfare of their respective nations would be impossible whilst the government of Paraguay remains in power," concluded a treaty of alliance whose articles stipulate the monstrous aim: "The allies are solemnly obliged not to lay down their arms . . . until they have overthrown the current government of Paraguay."

Triumphant, the allies set up a new state designed to serve not the ideals of the nation, but rather the foreign interests behind it. The peasantry was dispossessed of the lands of its ancestors; state lands became the property of bankers from London; foreign companies took control of the press and the natural wealth of the nation; debts from companies of dubious origin were charged to the state; and civil war, real or latent, ate at the nation like a cancer. Governments put their own consolidation of power above the territorial integrity of the Republic, and the army became involved in domestic politics and the struggle between political parties, instead of acting as an organized arm of Paraguayan international affairs. The warnings of history found no resonance among the ruling classes. Despite seeing Paraguay suffer a war every fifty years due to a form of geographical fatalism—in 1810 against Buenos Aires, in 1865 against the Triple Alliance and in 1932 against Bolivia—the state born from the 1870 Constitution did not learn from the lessons of the past.

But the people, excluded from the drawing up of the Constitution imposed on the country by the victors of the Triple Alliance War, kept alive their creative capacity and the ancient virtues of the race. Behind a weak state breathed a strong people. The error of Bolivia was to believe that the weakness of the State was synonymous with the weakness of our people. The victorious campaigns of the Chaco War were a bloody rejection of such an assumption based on a superficial understanding of Paraguay.

One cannot judge Paraguay without the risk of grave error, since its current political organization does not reflect its real strength, which is built on permanent rather than temporary foundations. Paraguayans are a unique people, who have created their own culture through the development of national values. The Paraguayan is not individualistic but gregarious, and the figure who encapsulates the ideal is not the loud-mouthed citizen of the political stage, but the warrior-farmer, the dynamic achiever, selfless and quiet, who transforms the indomitable forces of nature and the destiny of his land into cultural values. He loves the discipline of patriotism and is willing to sacrifice his own life for the sake of the collective community. He personifies the idea of the eternal Paraguay. And one day, he will advance with silent tenacity to project his character onto the forms of our civilization and the structure of the state. That day will bring to an end a tragic cycle of our history and the nation will have rediscovered the path of its destiny.

Note

1. As with another, longer quotation in the text, from a "famous address" by Dr. Francia, González gives no source for this quotation in the original. [Eds.]

Cultural Exile

Agustín Barrios

Agustín Barrios is a celebrated figure in modern classical guitar music and one of Paraguay's leading cultural figures. Born in 1885 in Misiones, in the south-east of Paraguay, far from the centers of early twentieth-century art and musical education, Barrios's life was in many ways one of cultural exile. He was largely self-taught, and pursued his itinerant career almost in isolation. He made some of the very first recordings of classical guitar music, and during the final years of his life the post of professor of guitar was created for him by the National Conservatory of El Salvador; he is buried in that country's capital, San Salvador. Yet during his lifetime he never achieved recognition outside Latin America, nor, notably, in Paraguay itself.

Barrios's political ideology was in line with the opposition Colorado Party in Paraguay in the early 1920s, and his alliances among the bohemian poets and playwrights of the Generación del 900 were well known. Through magazines such as Crónica, the group published scathing critiques of the Liberal government. These alliances were enough for the government to turn down Barrios's request in 1924 to found a guitar conservatory in Paraguay. He appears to have been black-listed: he left the country for the last time eight months later, having been unable to secure concerts at any of the city's major venues.

Since it was brought to the attention of the world in 1977 by John Williams, the music of Barrios has come to occupy a prominent place in the classical guitar repertoire. Barrios is widely accepted as the greatest composer-guitarist ever to have lived, and there is now a museum dedicated to his life and work in Asunción.

This text is one of the dozen or so known surviving letters written by Barrios. He writes to tell an old friend about his very promising professional circumstances. However, Barrios's own mention of another letter, shown to him by a mutual friend, triggers a flood of nostalgia. Behind the excitement is revealed the deep sadness he feels as destiny carries him ever further from the country of his birth. In 1929, waning success obliged him to leave the Rio de la Plata region, never to return.

Buenos Aires, July 23, 1928
Mr. Norberto Cardozo
San Juan Bautista (Misiones)

My dearest friend and neighbor,

   I have been back here in the capital for a short while now, after a
long tour of South America, with the intention of doing some concerts,
and to make a series of recordings for the Max Gluckman label, with
whom I have a four-year contract. Among other things that have happened during my brief stay in Buenos Aires, without doubt one of the
most pleasing has been to meet our dear old friend José, who, on finding that I had arrived, "looked me up" and very kindly invited me to
spend a few days relaxing at his house—which I most certainly needed,
with this restless life of mine, constantly on the move. So here I am,
my dear Norberto, enjoying days of serenity and of true happiness in
the generous and charming company of José and his delightful family.
He showed me a letter in which you wrote the kindest words about
me. I only wish you could imagine the pleasure I felt when I read them;
they are the mark of the nobility that beats in your heart. Believe me
that for it you have my sincerest gratitude. It is many years, Norberto,
since I left San Juan Bautista—that modest, picturesque little town
that was the scene of our beautiful and memorable childhood. Who
would have thought then, as we sat together on the school bench, that
destiny would have your friend leave to travel the world! How wonderful it would be to go back to those places, to see things whose beloved
memory time cannot erase! But I do not know if that pleasure will be
afforded me: I shall soon have to move yet further away from Paraguay,
as I now have contractual obligations that will take me to Europe. In
any case, please be so kind as to pass on my very warmest greetings
to each and every one of the old friends and companions who still live
in San Juan, and tell them that the joyful memory of those friendships
remains with me, deep in my heart, in spite of the inexorable passing of
the years and of the vicissitudes of this artist's life. Norberto, I wish you
and yours the very best that this world can give. You are a gifted musician, and it is my fervent hope that divine art will bring you spiritual
delight and material prosperity always.

   My best wishes to you and all your family, and a fond embrace from
your old friend

A. Barrios

Profession of Faith

Agustín Barrios

In 1930 Barrios adopted the stage persona of Nitsuga Mangoré: Nitsuga is simply Agustín spelled backward; Mangoré is the name of a Guaraní chief of the precolonial period who, according to legend, died for love and honor. Barrios began performing dressed in "Indian" regalia, including feathers, headband, and bare chest, billing himself variously as Cacique Mangoré, the Prodigious Guaraní Guitarist, the Paganini of the Guitar from the Jungles of Paraguay, and the Aboriginal Soul That Sings on the Guitar, among others.

This may have been a business decision: Barrios may have felt that he would attract a larger audience by conforming in caricature to stereotypes—including those within Latin America—of Paraguay. On the other hand, an analysis of his identity and of his work may have led him to a reinvention of himself as an artist consciously identified with indigenous heritage. Certainly, Barrios is one of the first Latin American cultural figures to engage the international audience within a frame both overtly Amerindian and at the same time artistically modern and highly sophisticated.

"Profession of Faith" (ca. 1930) is a poetic reflection that Barrios wrote at the beginning of this period in his career. He turns to Guaraní mythology to explain his calling to the guitar, declaring himself a willing servant of the gods and a part of the living essence of Latin America itself.

Tupá, the Supreme Being and protector of my race
Came upon me one day in the midst of the flowering forest
And he said to me: "Take this mysterious box and discover its secrets"
And enclosing in it all the songbirds of the jungle
And the patient soul of the vegetation
He left it in my hands.

I took it, obeying Tupá's command
And, holding it close to my heart
Embraced it as I lay for many moons by a spring.

This photograph of Agustín Barrios was taken around 1933, probably in Venezuela or Central America, and shows Barrios dressed in one of a variety of "Chief Nitsuga Mangoré" Indian costumes in order to conform with the cultural stereotype of Paraguayans as primeval jungle-dwellers that was prominent among Latin American concert-goers at the time. The suitably exotic-sounding name, Nitsuga, is simply Agustín spelt backward. Photographer unknown. From the collection of El Museo del Cabildo, Asunción.

And one night, Yasy,[1] reflected in the crystal water, and
Sensing the sadness in my Indian soul,
Gave me six silver moonbeams
With which to unlock its distant secrets.
And the miracle occurred:
Out from the depths of the mysterious box
Flowed the marvelous symphony
Of all the virgin voices of the forests of America.

Note

1. In the indigenous Guaraní tradition, Yasy is the spirit of the moon. [Eds.]

A New National Ideology

Oscar Creydt, Obdulio Barthe, Anibal Codas, and others

An inflammatory proclamation, "Nuevo Ideario Nacional" was published in Asunción in August 1929 by a group of young intellectuals who called for a popular insurrection in order to carry out a social revolution in Paraguay. The document advocated a total rejection of the existing political parties and the parliamentary system, which it said had only served the interests of a small elite. It also condemned the authoritarian regimes of the nationalist period and rejected Marxism, envisaging instead a highly decentralized society based on a mix of trade unions and popular councils organized on anarchosyndicalist lines. It argued that a social revolution in Paraguay would also involve an ethnic conflict between the Guaraní-speaking rural masses and a largely Europeanized elite.

Its ideas were propagated by a weekly newspaper, La Palabra, *of which fifteen issues were published in Asunción between October 1930 and January 1931. Its rapid spread among students and trade union militants reflected both the ideological vacuum created by the demise of* liberalismo *and the crisis of international capitalism at the time. A hurried uprising in February 1931, which included an attack on Encarnación, was aborted when a general strike spearheaded by construction workers in Asunción collapsed following the arrest and deportation of its leaders. Although the "Nuevo Ideario Nacional" represented a major intellectual current of opinion at the end of the Liberal period, its utopianism was gradually abandoned in favor of Marxism during the 1930s, and two of the original signatories of the proclamation (Obdulio Barthe and Oscar Creydt) later became leaders of the Paraguayan Communist Party. This final section of the proclamation offers a synthesis of the eclectic and sometimes contradictory mixture of ideas that it embodied.*

Our Call—Workers and Youth from All Parties, Unite!

We have nearly reached a dividing line that marks the end of one road and the start of a new one. With a heroic, collective, and simultaneous effort we will see the chains that oppressed our people for over four centuries fall into pieces. We have suffered with unimaginable stoicism a whole historical period of servitude, humiliation, and suffering. When we tried to free our-selves from the sword of the Iberian conqueror and from the Jesuit crucifix, we fell under the scourge of the dictator's whip; today the heavy yoke of capitalism has added to the already unsustainable burden of our age-old op-pression. For four centuries we have been waiting for our liberation. Long, too long has been the Calvary of our race. Now is the time for he who was executed to come down from the cross in order to speak of justice among men.

A long tradition of insurrections, which dates back to the first arrival of the Spaniards in the land of the Carios tribe, a branch of the powerful Guar-aní people, and continued throughout the turbulent colonial period, culmi-nating in the glorious Comuneros rebellion, and finally giving way to the May Revolution, has had the virtue of educating the Paraguayan people in the school of heroic defiance. Brutally repressed and temporarily suffocated under the merciless rule of three generations of tyrants, who drowned in blood the slightest breath of freedom, the spirit of our race was quick to re-vive as soon as the chains were broken by the events of 1870 that put an end to the dictatorship. From that day to the present, the Paraguayan people, victim of its naive illusion of redemption, was forced to offer its lifeblood a hundred times in a storm of deceitful promises with which the different po-litical parties tried over and over again to conceal their petty ambitions for power. Fortunately, this cruel sixty-year-long sacrifice was not completely without purpose. It served as a lesson for our workers and peasants; a hard lesson written in letters of blood. Each new uprising that occurred was a signal that germinated new hopes for a collective liberation and was also motive for a new and painful lesson in disappointment. However, today the people have lost faith in the promises from the party leaderships and com-mittees, and instead have faith in themselves. Military uprisings and pitched battles have followed one another with great frequency, some carried out by the Liberal Party, some by the Colorado Party, and some by persons or fac-tions within both traditional parties. And now, after half a century of sterile convulsions, the people sense with clear intuition that a new revolution is coming, the final revolutions: the social revolution.

This one will not be, like its predecessors, a party-based movement, re-sponding to the plan of one or other faction or political cabal. Rather, it will be a general insurrection with a popular character and a nationwide cover-age, against those parties and political groupings that have governed the country so badly and against the oligarchy that has usurped the sovereignty of the people. Our experience of democracy has taught us that, despite all manner of abstract theorizing, the political parties—instead of working as supports for democracy—are nothing but schools for personal ambition. The real aim of every party grouping consists of limiting and violating the freedom to vote, which is the theoretical foundation of any majoritarian democratic system. By regimenting the citizens' vote and subjecting it to the will imposed by a ruling clique, the regime of the parties has led to the maximum expression of centralized government and destroyed the fundamental principle of liberalism: the sovereignty of the people, stripped away in favor of the governing elite, made up of men born and educated in the spiritual atmosphere of the wealthy class. For this reason we have come to understand that the political party, a necessary complement to a parliamentary and majoritarian democracy, in practice does not mean anything other than the formula and basis for the political organization and domination by the bourgeoisie. Our struggle for the abolition of the traditional parties, responsible for all the nation's ills, cannot, therefore, start off from the foundation of another party that is similar in its organization to that of the existing ones. This would be tantamount to a contradiction in its very principles. *Our movement does not pursue as its objective the triumph of a new party, even if it were reformist, over the conservative parties, but rather the supplanting or suppression of the latter by professional unions and communal councils that constitute the true representation of the popular will.* That is why both revolutionary action and the work of reconstruction must be carried out by the people themselves, organized in this system of councils, unions, and federations.

We have lived for more than half a century under the control of the political parties. The voice and vote of the masses have never had a means to express themselves because the disciplinary party regimes obliged them to put their complete trust in the local committees and central leaders, who continue to the present day to be their only means of expression. That is why all of our governments, presidents, parliament, and tribunals have to date been governments of factions, cliques, or coteries. An objective analysis of the stormy and chaotic political panorama today convinces us that the regime of political parties, after such enormous failure, cannot nor should not be continued. National unity will never become a reality while the principles of political and economic organization that inform the legality of the old social order remain in force. The government of a people can only legitimately call itself "national" when it is the people themselves who govern. And this will be achieved only when the nation rises *en masse* against the oligarchy and the parties, against politicians and exploiters, demanding the restitution of its political sovereignty and the reintegration of its economic assets.

FINE CATTLE
...IN PARAGUAY

GOOD FOOD
...IN BRITAIN

Because the grasslands of Paraguay can nourish millions of cattle, a massive meat-packing factory has been built up by Liebig's Extract of Meat Company, whose products add both nourishment and richer flavours to the world's cooking. Liebig's, a subsidiary of the Brooke Bond Liebig Group, looks forward to handling an increasing supply of fine Paraguayian cattle, so helping to maintain and improve the economy of the lovely country immortalised by its President, Don Alfredo Stroessner, in one simple but memorable phrase, "The People and the land are Paraguay"

"The People and the land are Paraguay"

Liebig's in Paraguay
PARTNERS IN A NATION'S PROGRESS

Liebig's in Paraguay. Liebig's Extract of Meat Company was a major company in Paraguay from 1898 to 1980. In 1922 it began to export corned beef from its meat-packing plant at Zeballos-Cue near Asunción and it soon became one of the major exporters in the country. By the 1950s it had become Paraguay's largest cattle-ranching company with 525,000 hectares of land. But as the world demand for corned beef slowed down Liebig's gradually sold off its landholdings in Paraguay to associates of the Stroessner regime. From the collection of Andrew Nickson.

There is no doubt that the poor majority of inhabitants of the country will make up the true driving force of the Revolution, due to both economic circumstances and ethnic or racial considerations. We believe that this vast multitudinous insurrection will coincide with a formidable resurrection of the native or *criollo* spirit, that the violent and sudden uprising, welling up from below from the lower orders of society, like a volcanic eruption, will lead to the rebirth of the legendary ancestral spirit of our race, which has long been suffocated under the unbearable weight of oppression. Prostrated, suffocated, anesthetized from the first days of its existence, this mysterious collective spirit has never ceased having a decisive influence on the destiny of the nation. The persistence of Paraguay in the international arena as an independent state is due precisely to those initial demonstrations of the indigenous spirituality, as expressed in its native language, its local customs, and folk art, which all together comprise a firm and resistant desire of a free people that does not want to be destroyed. And this *criollo* or native idiosyncrasy will also be that which in a short time will lead to the complete emancipation of the Paraguayan people, as well as the definitive destruction of the old feudal and colonial organization that prevails today, supported by foreign and mestizo elements, as a legacy of the conquest. Just as in European history, the French Revolution signified the insurrection of the Gallic-Latin spirit that had survived against Germanic feudalism, so our revolution will have the flavor of an uprising by the typically Guaraní or American element that has been conserved in latent form in the broad mass of the people, against the predominance of the European or Aryan spirit, represented by the bourgeoisie and the governing caste.

It is in such circumstances that the Paraguayan people, given life by all new, healthy, and virginal forces that make up its essentially indigenous character, must begin its historic rise, displacing the dominant class, whose moral breakdown is nothing but a sign of the universal decadence of the European spirit in the twentieth century. This epic revolutionary gesture alone with be the product of a close and trustworthy collaboration between the working class and the young generation of our intellectual elite. From this fruitful combination of all the pure and uncontaminated elements of our nationality, a new Paraguay will be born, free from the ignoble stigma of slavery, purified in the flames of the revolutionary blaze, and rejuvenated by a new ideal of life, that turn our people into the vanguard of a multitude of workers and students who are struggling throughout the lands of Latin America for social regeneration and international fraternity.

Signed: Oscar Creydt, Obdulio Barthe, Anibal Codas [and others]

IV

From the Chaco War to the Civil War

Following skirmishes between Paraguayan and Bolivian troops over control of the disputed Chaco region, Bolivian troops steadily advanced toward Asunción during 1929 and 1930. Because of the Liberal government's policy of appeasement, when war finally broke out in July 1932, Bolivian troops were just 130 miles from Asunción. While conventional explanations for the cause of the war emphasize the Bolivian desire to obtain a secure trade route to the Atlantic, an alternative explanation that remains widely believed in Paraguay cites conflict over ownership of the petroleum resources of the Chaco, exacerbated by competing foreign companies. Paraguayan knowledge of the Chaco terrain and the guerrilla warfare tactics used by its troops nullified Bolivian advantages in personnel and firepower, and after three years of heavy fighting incurring the deaths of some thirty to forty thousand Paraguayans and fifty-five thousand Bolivians, the Paraguayan army was able to repel the Bolivian forces from almost the whole of the Chaco region, and push them back to the foothills of the Andes. Paraguay agreed to an armistice in June 1935, ostensibly because their lines were over-extended, but just at a time when it seemed that the Bolivians were about to surrender, leading to widespread anger at the decision in Paraguay.

Popular resentment at the ineptitude of the Liberal government with regard to preparations and conduct of both the war and the peace treaty led to a military coup in February 1936 (from which the Febrerista Party takes its name). The popular war hero Rafael Franco was made president, at the head of a diverse nationalist coalition. Although the Febrerista government began by announcing plans for a serious land reform, it soon alienated supporters from left and right by jailing labor leaders and expelling pro-fascist sympathizers. With the Febreristas' political base rapidly eroding, Liberal supporters within the armed forces carried out a successful coup in August 1937.

The return to power of the Liberals proved to be short-lived. Following the sudden death of General José Félix Estigarribia, the head of Paraguayan forces during the war, only months after he had assumed the presidency, General Higinio Morínigo assumed power. Taking advantage of the new constitution of 1940 that the Liberals had just introduced, and which was weighted heavily in favor of the executive, Morínigo proceeded to ban all political parties, at the same time severely repressing the trade union movement. The Allied victory in the Second World War provoked a military movement against the fascist supporters of Morínigo. A brief period of political freedom in 1946, in which Morínigo was forced to accept a Colorado-Febrerista coalition government under his nominal control, saw intense activity as the previously banned parties vied with each other to fill the political vacuum. Endangered by the rising tide of popular mobilization and the growth of left-wing parties, Morínigo excluded the Febrerista Party from government and openly sided with the Colorados. This led to an uprising against the government in Concepción, in the north of the country, by an alliance of Liberals, Febreristas, and Communists and a brief but bloody civil war that lasted just six months. In the "red terror" that followed the Colorado victory, armed Colorado militias or *pynandí*, wrought vengeance on their defeated opponents throughout the country, producing the first of many waves of mass emigration to Argentina and setting the scene for the political dominance of the Colorado Party over the subsequent six decades.

Capturing Volunteers

Carlos Federico Reyes

Carlos Federico Reyes (1909–2002) was an outstanding musician, as well as a talented (and award-winning) poet, writer, and painter. Self-taught in both music and writing (he only reached second grade at school), he traveled the Americas, from Argentina to Canada, before temporarily settling in the United States, where he founded a guitar school. His two-volume memoirs cover the first thirty years of his life.

When the Chaco War broke out in 1932, the Paraguayan army was mobilized and recruitment offices opened throughout the country. According to popular myth, the wave of nationalism that swept the country meant that forced recruitment was unnecessary. However, as can be seen from the following excerpt from Reyes's memoirs, conscription was not popular and many tried to avoid it.

In 1932 the Chaco War with Bolivia broke out. When I heard the news I went straight to enlist in the Military School Band, under the directorship of the legendary Remberto Giménez, with his nephew Herminio Giménez as assistant director.

Once I was in the band, I spoke to the director, Remberto Giménez, and asked him whether he would take on as an apprentice a young boy that I had met in Ñemby, the brother of a good friend. His parents had asked me several times if I would put in a good word for him, since they thought that if he enlisted as an apprentice musician, he would run less of a risk on the front line than if he was a soldier.

With the permission of the director, I went to Ñemby to bring back the young boy, who was called Félix Rolón. I had not visited his family for a few months, but there had been talk of war in the Chaco for over a year. When I arrived at my friends' house, I had a very pleasant surprise: they were celebrating the wedding of my friend María Rolón to a boy from the neighborhood. The priest was just about to begin the ceremony when I entered the large patio, which was decorated for the occasion and full of guests.

I walked toward where they had set the altar, as I had still not realized what they were celebrating. Suddenly my friend María, the daughter of the owners of the house, dressed all in white, caught sight of me and with a shout of "Carlos!," left the guests she was with, came over and hugged me. It was only then that I realized that it was María who was getting married. She introduced me to her fiancé and, of course, they insisted that I stay for the party after the ceremony.

I went over to say hello to the hosts and explain the reason for my visit. They were very grateful that I had remembered their boy. When the ceremony ended, we all went over to the tables, which had been prepared with great care, as was the custom in those days. There was a huge spread of delicious food and drink. Everybody was so happy, enjoying the party, even though war had just been declared.

Then, at about 2 AM, the party was suddenly interrupted by the appearance of the famous "Jagua Pero," the nickname of the head of the Recruitment Service, surrounded by a large group of soldiers. Jagua Pero was about thirty years old, short, fat, dark, very smartly dressed, almost overdressed. He always smelt of cologne, which was an extravagance in those days, especially for people of his class. That, combined with the arrogant and overbearing tone he adopted for official duties, made him particularly unpopular. Since his job was to recruit men for the front, he demanded that everyone of fighting age should present their documents; those who did not have them would be taken immediately to the barracks for conscription.

Everyone at the wedding who was of recruitment age and who did not have their documents with them (the majority) fled in all directions or just hid wherever they could, in an attempt to avoid being conscripted. Jagua Pero's soldiers began to gather together the guests without papers, who they flushed out from the most extraordinary hiding places. Since I was already a member of the military band, I would not have had a problem. However, since I was dressed as a civilian I did not identify myself, but decided instead to try to help my young friend Félix avoid being sent to the front.

One of the guests had hidden inside the huge, empty—but still dirty—cooking pot in which the main dish for the party had been cooked. Somehow he had managed to turn it over and curl himself up in a ball inside, leaving a little stick propping it open so that he could still breathe. Someone must have helped him hide. One of the soldiers went over to the pot and after examining it said loudly: "You can come out now, my friend. The wedding's over."

Jagua Pero recruited twenty-five soldiers that night, all of them elegantly dressed. With them, and others he had previously captured, we all set off back to Asunción.

I was among the group of new recruits along with Félix. After about an hour of walking, we arrived at a police station in Tres Bocas. Here they ordered us to go into a small makeshift cell with no windows, where about sixty men were crammed in together, standing room only. I am short, so it was not long before I felt desperate for air and began to panic. We stayed in there for two hours until, to our relief, they opened the doors and let us out into the fresh air. We were marched to the Recruitment Office near San Roque church in Asunción. Suffice to say that the recruits from the wedding were in a terrible state, as they were all wearing their best suits and most had new shoes on.

In the office I waited my turn with Félix, who had not left my side. When the officer interviewed us, I showed him my documents and they allowed me to leave and take my friend, under my responsibility, to go and sign up for the military band.

The Battle of Boquerón

Alfredo Seiferheld

The battle of Boquerón was one of the first major battles of the Chaco War. After the Bolivians captured the Boquerón fort in July 1932, the Paraguayans launched a huge counteroffensive in September involving 13,000 troops. The small Bolivian force of about 600 under Lieutenant Colonel Manuel Marzana held out for twenty-three days, suffering constant artillery bombardment, repeated frontal attacks, and a lack of food and water. The Paraguayan troops found themselves ordered to make almost suicidal attacks on Bolivian lines, and also suffered from a shortage of supplies and water. The battle left 5,000 Paraguayans and 150 Bolivians dead.

On September 29, the Bolivians finally surrendered after a three-week siege. On entering the fort, one Paraguayan official wrote: "The triumphant entry of our troops into the historic fort of Boquerón was dampened by the horrific tragedy suffered by the defenders; 20 officers and 446 soldiers (including the wounded) were at the extreme of human suffering. All around lay dead bodies and human remains. In a dark shed, covered in rags, dirt, blood, excrement, and worms, lay more than a hundred wounded, with no medical attention, no bandages, and no water." While the terrible human suffering involved in the battle would turn out to be characteristic of the next three years of the war, both governments hailed it as a heroic victory. In Bolivia, Boquerón went down as one of the most heroic defenses in the nation's military history, while in Paraguay it was seen as a vital first victory, giving the country and the military the belief that the Bolivians could be defeated.

The following extracts are taken from La guerra del Chaco *(The Chaco War), by Alfredo Seiferheld (1950–88), one of the most prolific and respected historians that Paraguay has produced. Seiferheld painstakingly weaves together diary entries from an array of combatants to give an authentic taste of the first major battle of the Chaco War, always with an eye for the human, rather than merely military, experience. The extracts cover five days—from September 18 through 22, 1932.*

Paraguayan troops moving guns during the Chaco War. Photographer unknown. From the collection of Andrew Nickson.

Sunday, September 18, 1932

WHY DOESN'T THE FORT FALL?

The Paraguayan Ministry of War confirmed in the morning that progress had been made by the army in its advance on Boquerón: "We continue to fight successfully in the fields of Boquerón. We are tightening the encirclement of the enemy positions with attacks carried out by newly arrived troops. Yesterday we held off renewed attempts by the enemy to relieve and reinforce their besieged comrades, inflicting heavy losses on the Bolivians. The spirit of our troops remains high."

The Paraguayan artillery continued to bombard the machine gun nests at Punta Brava. Jose Daza, a Bolivian lieutenant, stationed at Boquerón, wrote in his diary: "The enemy bombardment began at 8 AM. A shell fell on the position of Sublieutenant Aguirre, injuring him and several soldiers. The damned Paraguayan artillery makes our life impossible and the wounded keep arriving."

Alberto Taborga, a Bolivian lieutenant also stationed at Boquerón, wrote in his diary; "This war, whose end is not in sight, will lead us to ruin. It will destroy our economy. An impoverished people like ours should never trust their destiny to the whims of a *caudillo*. Unfortunately we are simply guinea pigs in a new experiment."

In his diary, Lieutenant Colonel Manuel Marzana, the Bolivian commander at Boquerón noted: "16:10 hours. A new attack is launched on the Cuenca sector with heavy artillery support. It lasts one and a half hours. The assailants are making superhuman efforts to reach our trenches, but we managed to repel them, leaving many dead and wounded in the field. On our side, five dead and two wounded."

The exasperation of the Paraguayan High Command is reflected in the diary of Lieutenant Heriberto Florentín, who, having been to report to Major Carlos Fernández, found the latter nervous and in a bad mood: "Without even giving us the chance to read out our reports, he asked a series of questions that left us completely confused. 'How come this fort doesn't fall? Where are the Bolivians getting their reinforcements from?'"

Monday, September 19, 1932

THE DRAMA OF THIRST

The horrors of thirst could be seen everywhere. The madness for water led our own soldiers to attack water trucks in fights for liquid that couldn't be broken up. "The battle lines were abandoned by soldiers overcome by thirst," wrote Major Carlos Fernández, adding: "In ten days of fighting, the long-suffering soldiers have taken on the appearance of skeletons. Dehydration and tension have taken their toll at an alarming rate. The battle lines were held only thanks to the invaluable service of the heroic but ignored water carriers, who braved the front lines, crawling on their bellies to collect the soldiers' water bottles."

By September 19, the lack of water had reached breaking point. Most of the Paraguayan troops besieging Boquerón had left their posts, retreating along the road to Villa Militar in search of water under a merciless, burning sun. The Paraguayan lieutenant Hernán Velilla, who a few weeks later would die heroically on the battlefield, wrote on that desperate day: "The heat began to rise at dawn . . . my tongue is dry and bloated; our rations of bread and meat made us even thirstier. There is a general exhaustion. More than just my own situation, what grieves me is that of the soldiers in my company who are suffering sunstroke and stretched out desperately on the ground. The vile war; the hell, the desert, the agonizing thirst, the infernal heat that envelops you, the stench of rotting bodies left for days on end . . . this kind of war is a terrible crime."

At 13:40 hours, the commander of the Fourth Infantry "Curupaity" Regiment, Major José Ortíz, wrote the following report; "The troops are suffering from thirst. They are leaving their positions in search of water. We should strictly monitor the distribution of water, because according to the soldiers who went back to look for water, it is all being distributed deep behind our lines, rather than reaching the front lines which ought to be our priority. The soldiers who are fighting need it much more."

Thirst ravaged the defenders of Boquerón who so admirably held off the Paraguayan advance. Bolivian Lieutenant Colonel Manuel Marzana noted in his campaign diary: "Two of our planes came straight over and after launching three bombs at the enemy positions, returned to base. We desperately signaled with boards: 'We have no water!'"

Antonio Arzabe Reque, a private in the Bolivian Sixth Infantry Regiment summarized in his diary entry for that day the horrors of war. "Like every other day, Boquerón wakes up to a fierce exchange of fire. Our soldiers are no longer able to stand. Their ears are buzzing and in many cases bleeding. Their shoulders have become bloody wounds, from supporting the rifles and machine guns. They go to the first aid point to get cotton for their ears and they make pillows for their wounded shoulders. Blood flows from their noses and their decrepit bodies suffer the agony of dysentery."

Tuesday, September 20, 1932

TIME IS RUNNING OUT AT BOQUERÓN

In the stronghold of Boquerón, time was running out. The wounded lay piled together in a large shed, while the troops, suffering from hunger and thirst, seemed like a regiment of ghosts. "One well has been destroyed by a shell. The only other well was subject to constant fire from the enemy. It was only possible to get there by crawling, under the cover of night. The reservoir of putrid water was even more dangerous; on its banks lay several dead bodies," wrote Querejazu Calvo.

The Bolivian lieutenant Alberto Taborga noted in his war diary: "Our planes fly overhead, dropping bundles, which I imagine contain food and munitions. But the pilots, under intense heavy and small arms fire from the Paraguayan troops surrounding the fort, drop their load far away from our positions, in enemy-held territory; we can see the Paraguayans merrily distributing the contents of our supplies."

Thursday, September 22, 1932

OUR FORCES REPEL NEW ATTACKS

The hour of victory at Boquerón was approaching. With a vast numerical superiority, thousands of Paraguayan troops converged on the besieged fort, whose position had become desperate. The Bolivian efforts to relieve the fort by land had been repelled, and all roads had been cut by Paraguayan troops.

The official diary of the Sixth Infantry Regiment confirmed this: "Day 22: we heard that the Second Infantry had made significant progress and captured the well near the fort. At 16.00 hours the Santiviago Battalion advanced without resistance, as did the Pagliera Company."

Bolivian military sources revealed the difficult situation at Boquerón. The telegram from the Fourth Infantry Division stationed at Arce, replied to a high-level request for information: "Boquerón is under intense bombardment on a daily basis. Morale among the troops is low and they have rations for only another two days; ammunition is low and they are unable to get the necessary provisions to all their troops. They can only hold out for two more days. Much will depend on the offensive plans of Paraguay after Boquerón because they have a clear superiority in terms of firepower and numbers. . . . Signed: Peña y Lillo."

The Bolivian High Command warned of the significance of any retreat from the fort. There would be no valid justification for defeat. It is not surprising that the commander of the Army Corps, General Carlos Quintanilla, wrote the following at midnight to Colonel Francisco Peña from his base at Muñoz: "The High Command orders that Boquerón should not be abandoned. Supplies should be delivered by plane, including the three-engine plane that should arrive tomorrow. Time permitting, two planes should be able to fly, taking 200 kilos of salted beef to drop over Boquerón. Upon their return they will land at Arce to pick up more supplies that you should have ready on the airstrip, well packed and ready for dropping."

In his campaign diary the Bolivian lieutenant Alberto Taborga reflected the harsh conditions in the besieged fort: "The remaining well has been closed off by the Paraguayans; they have two pieces of heavy artillery trained on it. In the puddles of water nearby, I can see the bodies of two soldiers, who beside themselves with thirst, had managed to reach there, desperate for a few drops of water."

Memoirs of a Man from Concepción

Carlos María Sienra Bonzi, as told to

Roberto Sienra Zavala

Carlos María Sienra Bonzi (1906–2006) was born in Concepción. He joined the Six-teenth "Mariscal López" Infantry Division at the outbreak of the Chaco War, rising to be a decorated officer (lieutenant), and seeing action throughout the conflict. A so-cialist and revolutionary, he joined the Febrerista Revolution in 1936, and remained a member of the Partido Revolucionario Febrerista, surviving the disastrous 1947 civil war and the Stroessner dictatorship.

Carlos Sienra's memories of the Chaco War are particularly interesting since they are written by a man with a keen eye for detail and the ability to convey the reality of war in a few, carefully chosen words. Rather than an account of heroic actions or military tactics, his memoirs constantly return to the human side of war, remind-ing us of the daily experience of the troops who fought under terrible conditions. The extracts chosen below reflect not only the brutality of the war and the horror of thirst, bombardment, and torture, but also the heroism, the humanity, and—in the case of "Puerto Casado"—the social awareness of the soldiers themselves.

Thirst

When a man gets sunstroke he loses all control over reality. Some just look for a little shade and don't care about anything, just waiting for the relief of death. The tongue comes out of the mouth, breathing becomes more dif-ficult, and men begin to make strange animal-like noises. I saw many Boliv-ians shoot themselves in the head rather than meet such a terrible death. In the war I saw so much death, and so many terrible, unbelievable injuries. One soldier in my Company had his lower jaw blown off by a mortar explo-sion; even though his tongue hung down like a tie, he still survived. But nothing compares to the request "Please, Lieutenant, piss in my mouth." That beat everything. In the end, to see a comrade, a friend, dead or badly wounded, with his lungs collapsed by a bomb, you think, "Well, that could have been me"; but to hear that request, to piss in the mouth of a comrade, left an impression that I will never forget.

Puerto Casado

When our leave of absence ran out, a lot of us, officers and soldiers, were sent on a boat to Puerto Casado. Puerto Casado had a special significance for many of the troops. A lot of them had worked for the company before the war, as factory hands or other workers, and had been treated like animals; many had been whipped and beaten by the so-called *capangas* (overseers) who were like a group of some kind of demigods who ruled over the lives of the humble workers. The troops that were going to defend the Chaco were also of course defending the vast landholdings of the company. The troops were transported in the company trains, but incredibly, instead of putting the transport at the service of the army, the company charged the government every last cent, down to the fare of the last soldier who was going to his death in defense of the company land. In Asunción, when hundreds of trucks were decommissioned for the war, the owners were offered war bonds. Puerto Casado was the exception, since the government offered it not only bonds but also millions of pesos in cash.

Carlos Casado bought his lands for "100 pesos a league," a ridiculously small amount—and then sold a large part of them to the Mennonites for a much higher price. Even so, at the end of the war he still owned more than three million hectares. We once saw the arrogant and bad-tempered Dr. Carlos Casado as we walked down towards the railway station. I remember he was wearing brown trousers and jacket, shiny black boots, and a white hat, and standing with his hands on his hips, casually watching the troops go by. Some of his "capangas" were with him, all of them carrying revolvers. Their smart clothes were a big contrast to our faded uniforms; many soldiers went barefoot, simply because they did not have enough money to buy boots. It crossed the minds of more than one of us just how much we'd like to kill them all.

The Terrible Years of War

I do not want to talk about this, or rather I do not want to remember it. War scars a man forever, and it is not easy to get over the images left by so much death, with the knowledge that you were part of that mad war machine. All of us went to the Chaco as youngsters. Instead of killing each other in that ridiculous war, we should have been writing love poems, working peacefully with an eye to our futures. We thought war would be an adventure, but we were confronted with a brutal reality. I had always been a pacifist and was brought up to believe in chivalry, education, love, and respect for others. It would have been much more constructive for everyone to have had friendly trade relations with Bolivia rather than killing each other like we did in those three terrible years of war.

Brutality

I think that both sides committed acts of brutality against prisoners, but probably more so in the case of the Bolivians. Once a group of our men came across the bodies of six Paraguayans who had been captured and then killed, but not before being horrifically tortured. They had cut off the soles of the feet of one of them, stripped him naked, and then just left him. He had no other wounds, but he couldn't walk, so he had tried to reach our lines on his knees. The others had been castrated and shot in the back of the head. I heard that in revenge the commander of a Paraguayan regiment gave orders that for a week we should take no prisoners. This is probably not written down in any official records, but I can assure you that it happened. Coming from the tranquility of the countryside, seeing such brutal things completely changed me as a person.

The Battle of Strongest

At first, there was some sporadic gunfire; then it began to increase, rapidly becoming a long thunderous roar. It was as if all the guns were firing at once, just in that area. I do not know how to describe it . . . the mortar shells were falling constantly. It was complete chaos, and I cannot think of any words to convey the scene.

At Strongest, both sides had artillery, but our side stopped using it almost straightaway because, to be honest, we did not know where the enemy was, and we remembered how at Boquerón our artillery had wiped out hundreds of our own men. Toward the end of the battle there was an artillery duel that I can remember as something strange and macabre. . . . In the inferno of Strongest everything was constantly changing. One minute we were advancing and the next retreating; advance, hold positions, retreat. Advance, hold positions, retreat.

Between May 25 and May 26 the Bolivian attack slowed until finally it stopped. Thanks to Joel[1] and his boys, the Paraguayan forces managed to avoid the enemy pincer movement. The Bolivians took just over 2,000 pris-

The harsh conditions of the Chaco War are exemplified by this picture of a barefoot Paraguayan soldier with torn trousers; the mule is carrying his water. Photographer unknown. From the collection of Andrew Nickson.

oners. We felt quite downcast, especially those of us in the Mariscal López Division, the unit that had held back the main Bolivian thrust. We found out from soldiers who had managed to escape at the last moment that just 175 men from the First Battalion of the Mariscal López Division had managed to hold off 5,000 Bolivians in triple encirclement, for five whole days. Imprisoned in that circle of steel and fire, with no water, with their worm-infested wounds, and despite being completely outgunned by a vastly superior enemy, Joel and the other officers and soldiers held out, perfectly aware of the disaster that would befall them if they were taken; every minute that they held out gave another minute more for the rest of the Paraguayan forces to escape the deadly trap.

We soon heard some of the details. Joel's unit had been surrounded, but their tiny force of just 11 officers and 164 men had held their position against all the odds. They had been surrounded by a whole Bolivian division, about 5,000 men. Machine-gunned by planes and under fire from every kind of weapon imaginable and from every direction, they managed to hold out lying flat against the ground, until finally they were overcome.

Yrendagué

With our water supplies calculated down to the last spoonful, the Eighth Infantry Division set off on a long fifty-kilometer march under an unforgiving sun and with no chance of retreat due to the lack of water. During the endless march the water soon ran short and I remember the soldiers lying stretched out on the baking sand. The water finally ran out and we halted the advance.

We took Yrendagué, annihilating the Second Bolivian Army under the famous David Toro. We took thousands of prisoners. Thousands more fled, only to die of thirst on the famous "Road of Despair." They say that between 5,000 and 7,000 Bolivians died, just from thirst. Many committed suicide, shooting themselves in the throat. Others were found dead, huddled together under the pitiful shade of thin trees.

Note

1. Joel Estigarribia (1911–37) was a lieutenant in the Mariscal López Division of the Paraguayan army.

A Visit to Villa Hayes Military Hospital Number 16

Reginald Thompson

The Chaco War was fought on most inhospitable terrain. On both sides, more combatants died from thirst than from enemy fire. The treatment of the wounded was limited by the extreme shortage of medical personnel and supplies, as well as by the very stretched supply lines as Paraguayan troops pushed the Bolivians back to the foothills of the Andes. This rare firsthand account of conditions at a military hospital close to Asunción was given by Reginald Thompson, an English freelance journalist who traveled to Paraguay and Bolivia in 1934–35 to cover the Chaco War for the Morning Post *newspaper of London.*

We followed the major and chief surgeon into the hospital. The building, as usual, was built round a large central courtyard. This courtyard was large enough to be called a barrack square. It was deserted.

The major gave the lead to the surgeon. The stench of ether came in heavy puffs from open windows; foetid, nauseating in the heat. It could not disperse. It simply hung there. The plaster walls seemed ready to crumble in the heat. Sweat stood on the major's fleshy face and beaded his upper lip. His grey eyes flicked at me.

"Hot, eh?" He sniffed—"Ether—ha—"—and in that "ha—" I could almost feel limbs being chopped off.

The surgeon opened a door that had paper gummed over its glass panels and ushered me into a small room. There was more paper gummed over the outer window. The air could be seen; a yellow *hum*. The ether became almost overpowering so that it was an effort to keep one's senses. There was a rough plain wooden table; a sink; forceps, scalpels and saws—the dull plated tools of amputation and internal delvings. There was no blood to be seen but blood seemed to be in the room. There was a mutilation of bodies in the very atmosphere.

The surgeon's voice was explaining, apologetic.

"It is the best we can do here: operations, amputations, arms, legs," his voice gathered pride, even defiance—"day after day; every day. We do our best."

Bodies went on that table. It was still warm from the bodies. They went on to it with smashed limbs and came off without limbs. Often they came off dead and went under the hot soil. Day after day, all through the Chaco, in this ghostly, foetid, yellow light, in field tents and wooden shelters in the wet heat-soaked shade of trees, the scalpels were cutting, the probes probing, the saws sawing. I felt as though I were in a well of pain.

"Scarcely any gangrene," said the major in his loud voice. "Very little gangrene, eh, doctor?"

"Very little."

We passed on. Long rooms, dim and full of sickness, legs in ponderous cradles, brown faces with a curious greyness of suffering, dark heads on hard white pillows; beardless faces. Always the stench of surgery, iodine, ether, raw wounds.

There were no words to say in this place. We passed on in silence. There were no thoughts in my head; simply a kind of hopeless feeling; impotent, sullen fury; a struggling against powerlessness.

Some of the rooms were brighter. Young men in simple white smock-like garments sat up in or on their beds, their naked feet swinging. They would soon be ready to fight again.

I said to the major: "May I ask their ages?"

"Surely!" His grey eyes ranged the long room and its rows of cots.

"*Miguel—cuantos años tiene? José? Juan?*"

"*Diez y seis*—sixteen," "Seventeen," "Seventeen."

We asked a dozen at random. The oldest was twenty; the veteran of these veterans, all with wounds; all with devil knows what internal disorders, results of bad water, fever, poisoning. The rising generation of Paraguay, living as their grandfathers had lived and died, but now—victorious!

A squad of Bolivians marched with slurring steps in the heat of the yard and formed a double row in the shade against a wall. We passed slowly along the lines; their eyes stared dully from heavy fat-cheeked faces, dusky brown, almost chocolate.

"*Cholos*, mostly," said the major. "Poor devils."

But some were different. One had red hair and nearly white skin.

"You," said the major. "Where do you come from, *Rubio?*"

"Santa Cruz."

"We get a lot from Santa Cruz now," said the major. "They're a different breed from the Alti-Plano Indios." His laugh grated. "Irish father, that *Rubio.*

Those Irish. You'll find their work here, there, all over." The prisoners were marched away.

"A good little hospital," said the major. "Efficient as may be. Surgeon works hard."

A young officer was dragging an alligator towards the shade: "Shot him with revolver," he announced.

The major put his large, hairy hand on the evil-looking muzzle of the reptile. The teeth were murderous.

"Are they dangerous?" I asked, thinking of Señora Cohen.

The major made a champing movement with his jaws; "Dangerous! Try one and see!"

A number of young officers were presented. All were dark faced, intense, young men, scrupulously polite. We walked round a few buildings, a straggling group. An officer came from the prisoners' barracks with a long brush, made of grass fibre by the prisoners. It resembled a giant's shaving brush and the handle was large enough to hold a dozen signatures.

"*Recuerdo del hospital militar, número diez y seis,*" said the major when the handle had all our autographs.

Three of the young officers and Mercédes de Fiendra climbed into our launch to escort us across the river to inspect the meat works and the six hundred prisoners at *Piquete-cué*.

Among a small group of white-overalled, sober-faced *médicos* and a few urchins, the bulky, boisterous figure of the major stood out like a rock.

"*Adios! Adios!*"

Major Fiendra's full-throated, chuckling laugh came to us over the water.

Scenes of Thirst

Hugo Rodríguez Alcalá

Thirst and disease took more lives in the Chaco War than bullets and shells. The heat and lack of water sources in the region meant that keeping the armies supplied with enough water was a constant logistical problem. The Bolivian defeat at the battle of Yrendague and the retreat from the fort at Picuiba in November 1934 was symbolic of the horrific conditions under which both sides were forced to fight. Obliged to march fifty-seven kilometers under a burning sun with no supplies, the Bolivian Cavalry Corps suffered huge casualties due to thirst. In the words of the historian Bruce Farcau: "The heat that day was intense and the men stumbled blindly to the north. All units soon became thoroughly disorganized. Men threw away their rifles and packs, and most had been shoeless and dressed in rags for weeks. Panic infected the men and some began to wander off into the bush, crazed by thirst, or to commit suicide, or to simply die of thirst. Others threw themselves under the wheels of passing trucks to end their agony quickly."[1]

Hugo Rodríguez Alcalá (1917–2007) was one of the renowned Generación del 40, a group of outstanding Paraguayan poets and literary critics. In his work on the Chaco War, the themes of loneliness, as well as the horror and the futility of the conflict, stand out, as in this poem written in 1938.

A whole army corps
Defeated at Picuiba,
Perished on the roads from thirst

The roads, littered with bodies
And burned-out trucks
Speak of that *via crucis*

The greatest strategist
In the immense, horrific solitude
Was a ghost: thirst

Awaken memories, I wish to talk of thirst

Desperate soldiers
Furiously attacked the trucks

To drink the water bubbling
From the burning radiators.

Like baited tigers
Five unarmed men advanced
Devouring the distance
On a truck, as the driver tried to save himself.

The struggle was terrible
Between the men and the machine

One fell under the wheels
Trying to hold it back

Another jumped onto a running board
And the driver gunned him down

Another clung desperately to
Mudguards with battered hands

And all for the boiling dirty water
That the machine carried in its belly!

Another man, maddened,
Struck the driver with a spade;

But over the soft, bloodied sand
The truck went on and on

Death came to
The survivors of battle

In the end thirst claimed victory
On the road
The truck lay enveloped by flames

The boiling water had evaporated
From the scorching radiator

Across the tracks of the truck lay
Five thirsty corpses

Note

1. Bruce W. Farcau, *The Chaco War: Bolivia and Paraguay, 1932–35* (Westport, Conn.: Praeger, 1996), 216.

A Handful of Earth

Hérib Campos Cervera

Although he wrote only one published volume, Ceniza redimida *(Liberated ashes),
Hérib Campos Cervera (1905–53) is considered among Paraguay's great poets, and
one who influenced and inspired a generation of other writers and poets, including
Augusto Roa Bastos and Elvio Romero. As a politically engaged poet, in his writing
he touched on themes of war, politics, and social issues, whilst as an exile, his poetry is often nostalgic, reflecting the pain of distance and separation. "A Handful of
Earth," one of his best-known poems, is written from exile, and expresses his love,
passion, and longing for his country.*

I

A handful of earth from your profound latitudes,
From your place of eternal solitude,
From your brow of clay,
Pregnant with seminal weeping.
A handful of earth
With its simple salt caress
And the desolate sweetness of roots;

A handful of earth that carries on its lips
The smile and the blood of your dead.

A handful of earth
to draw to the warmth of its embrace
all the cold of the time of dying,

And a patch of shade in your slow wood
to watch over my sleepy eyelids.

I have yearned for your nights of orange blossom;
yearned for your warm and wooded meridian;
yearned for the mineral food that lies

The Chaco War produced a resurgence of popular nationalism, exemplified by the circulation of a poetry magazine *Okára Poty Kue-mi*, which circulated widely among the troops, and by musical bands, such as the one shown here, which played for the troops. Photographer unknown. From the collection of Andrew Nickson.

along the hard shores of your buried body
and yearned for the wood of your breast.
This is what I have yearned for,
Land of my happiness and my sorrow.
This is what I have yearned for.

II

And now again I am naked.
Naked and desolate
on a clifftop of memories;
lost in dark misted paths.
Naked and desolate;
far away from the firm symbol of your blood. Far away.
No longer can I see the distant jasmine of your stars,
feel the nightly siege of your forests.
Nothing. Neither your days of guitars and knives,
nor the timeless clarity of your sky.
Alone, like a rock or like a cry
I call to you, and when I seek
to return to the stature of your name,

I know that the Rock is rock, and that the Water of the river
flees from your startled waist, and that the birds
use of the lofty refuge of the humiliated tree
as a precipice for their song and their wings.

III

But, as I walk thus under different clouds,
through the artificial profiles of other lands,
suddenly, I find you again.

Amidst the insuperable loneliness
or along blind roads of music and wheat fields,
I discover you stretched out by my side,
with your martyred crown
And your crystal memory of *guaranias* and orange trees.
You are within me; you walk in my steps,
you speak in my throat; you rise in my lime,
and you die, when I die, each night.

You are within me with all your banners;
with your laborer's honest hands,
and your small, irremediable moon.

Inevitably—
with the punctual constancy of the constellations—
There come to me, ever present and primordial,
your torrential hair of rain,
your nostalgia for the sea
and the vast grief of your thirsty plains.
You dwell in me and I in you:
submerged in your wounds,
I keep my vigil at your brow, that, in dying, dawns.

I am at peace with you;
neither crows nor hatred
can tear me from your side:
I know that I carry your Beginning, and your End
on the mountain peaks of my shoulders.

And that is what I have of you.
A handful of earth:
this is what I have yearned for.

Proclamation of the Febrerista Revolution

F. W. Smith and Camilo Recalde

On February 17, 1936, an insurrection by discontented veterans of the Chaco War toppled the Liberal government of President Eusebio Ayala, thereby initiating the short-lived Febrerista government led by the war hero President Rafael Franco. The misnamed Febrerista "revolution" reflected widespread discontent with the Liberal Party despite the fact that it had led the country to victory in the Chaco War and was part of a growing rejection of liberalism throughout much of Latin America in the 1930s. The insurrection also marked the first break in the two-party system that had dominated Paraguay since 1887. The political ideology espoused by the febreristas was an uneasy mixture of socialism and corporativism—its very name, taken from the month of the insurrection, reflects this lack of political definition and ideology. The new government attracted support from the right and left of the political spectrum, and the proclamation itself, furious in its condemnation of liberalism, was written by a fascist sympathizer, Gomes Freire Esteves, who became minister of the interior in the short-lived government.

Proclamation of the Liberating Army

Paraguayans!

Illustrious nation of Antequera, of Rodríguez de Francia and of the Lópezes! Your soldiers in arms have assumed the honor of protecting the national colors, our sacred soil and the immortality of the Fatherland.

We announce to you that we have heard the mandate of the solemn deeds in our nation's history

 . . . as in the armed plebiscite of Antequera's militia, which established the creed for the spiritual formation of the Republic;

 . . . as in the summons of the army on May 14, 1811, which gave us our sovereignty;

 . . . as in the support of those same troops for José Gaspar Rodríguez de Francia, affirming the collective oath to continue as an inviolable and independent nation in the Río de la Plata throughout the centuries to come;

. . . as in the juntas of the Asunción militia in 1842, which engendered by their swords the best governed nation on earth under their united idealism and its faithful interpreter don Carlos Antonio López;

. . . as in the Plebiscite of the Armies in 1865, at the beginning of the great national epic, to triumph or die at the side of Marshal don Francisco Solano López—preserving on this earth the principle of nonintervention as the only norm of international law for America and ensuring all free, civilized nations the right to live together in peace;

. . . so is the pledge of your armies, which have just finished three years of battle, defending our inviolable Chaco from one end to the other, sweeping before them remnants of hordes fallen on our open plains—having invaded us with the intention of snatching the inheritance that has been ours since Ñuflo de Chávez and his soldiers arrived at Parapati from our glorious Villa de Asunción.

Now we come, in our turn, to speak for all the men and women who love this land, to voice the indignant protest of the entire Republic against a regime of frock-coated bandits and cold-blooded assassins who, after many decades of violent domination, have ended by becoming the infectious force for even greater crimes, both within and outside the country—crimes which may never be righted, and which now threaten to destroy the nation's moral and material welfare.

That group of declassed politicians' long hegemony, which has brought this nation to the brink of disaster, can only be explained by the fact that the Fatherland scarcely existed: only special interests, always conspiring against the general welfare.

The whole nation knows about the shameless dictatorship and politics-as-a-business that the Paraguayan government has practiced since it fell into the hands of that group of treasonous politicians of that party which the military arm of the people has now cast from power.

We need not repeat this charge for the present, except to offer some concrete examples. President Eusebio Ayala built a tissue of criminality that offered to public opinion the limitless audacity of his all-powerful mafia. In 1913, in connivance with the leading politicians and their agents, he signed the Treaty of April 5, establishing with the seal of the Republic the lie that Bolivia was confining herself to those possessions she had held in 1907—knowing all the while that this was false. Later, he proclaimed the country's disarmament as the desideratum of so-called Paraguayan pacifism, while in the meantime Bolivia pursued her systematic advance toward the River Paraguay.

He did not have to wait long for his reward for this defeatist doctrine. The negotiator of that faithless treaty soon appeared vested with the job of high representative of the same foreign interests who were supporting the Bolivian invasion. He became the steward of foreign companies and a fifteenth-century slave trader at their service, strangling the Paraguayan workers and buying up the highest political offices.

The corruption of that negotiator, who was bribed by foreign gold, gradually caught on in all the leading circles of the regime. Defeatism and surrender became not just the seraphic-pacifistic theories of he who signed the Ayala-Mujia Treaty, but the very program of that party to which he was the Word Incarnate.

And then came the expatiation of that horrible crime of conspiring against the external security of his own land. The savage war broke loose over our people, who were manacled by the satrapy of Puerto Pinasco and its occult machinations. Through the irony of fate, he was the president and commander in chief of the nation's armies, whose men went off to leave their bones in the blood-stained fields of the Chaco, already the home of enemy machine guns. And then not a day passed when the compromised agent of foreign bosses did not try to diminish by every means in his power the miraculous victories of a Paraguay revived.

We will omit the innumerable examples of his deceit. But there was one unmistakable gesture, the proof of treason carried to its maximum: the offering of an armistice to Bolivia after the victory of Campo Vía, in order to prevent the capture of the remainder of the invading army. All that he did afterward, including the ridiculous Protocol of Buenos Aires, is nothing but the crowning of the continuous crime of hurting his country, which begins with the Treaty of April 5, 1913, and ends with the final diplomatic machinations of the said president, who will pass into history with the notoriety of a trafficker in the blood and patrimony of his countrymen.

If such is the worth of that mafia chief in international affairs, what should be said of his impudence in domestic matters—he who fought in 1922, with his famous veto, the law to convoke presidential elections, so as to remain in office. And the entire Republic has been a witness to his recent attempts to have himself reelected. Here is a specimen of born traitor to his country—he who managed to corrupt with gold the Paraguayan general who helped him achieve the armistice of Campo Vía, in order to convert the army's high command into his palace guards. And he dared buy off this general so that he could imprison and proscribe from the soil of the Fatherland *our only authentic leader: Colonel Don Rafael Franco,* living symbol and mirror of the highest virtues that live within the ranks of our Liberating Army!

As a result, President Ayala cast himself into the arms of his political cronies, the political assassins of the "23rd of October," the criminals responsible for the massacre of students. He planned the destruction of the Liberating Army in order to replace it with a prison guard. We will not mention the people's anguish and desperation, which the vampires dwelling in the presidential circle sharpen day by day in order to enslave them. Hunger strikes every home. Thirty thousand Paraguayans died in the Chaco, thousands of millions of pesos have been spent, yet in the postwar period they casually debate the most urgent problems and ramifications of this international catastrophe brought upon the country by the regime.

And they speculate in hunger with impunity, while the people curse the criminals who burn the sugar fields in order to raise the price of sugar and speculate with the rising price of food. There is no chance to protest through the press, for it is in the exclusive service of the government. All constitutional guarantees are ended. Outside of the governing clique all Paraguayans are pariahs, without the right to publicize their ideas, or to assemble, or to enjoy the rights of citizenship.

But all this might have been sufferable had it not been for new plans by the people's unfaithful president and his accomplices to pare down the Republic's territorial sovereignty and to irredeemably frustrate all the victories of our armies in the Chaco War. We shall not lend ourselves to this. One more day of inaction on our part would have been a desertion of our urgent duty to assert the sovereignty of the Paraguayan people and provide the vital necessities for their organization and security. And on these grounds we declare to the world, in the name of the people, that we take for our guiding principle the finest justification that contemporary Europe affords: "No State can be sovereign over itself and compromise its future for the benefit of another State."

We decree, therefore, that the President of the Republic, Doctor Eusebio Ayala, and all the personnel of his administration in the three branches of government, cease in the performance of their official functions.

Paraguayans!
Your soldiers in arms swear to comply with their mission. The Nation will be restored to the level of its past history in the Río de la Plata, to the free dominion over its soil, and to the grandeur of its future.

Asunción, February 17, 1936
Lt. Col. don F. W. Smith
Lt. Col. don Camilo Recalde

How Beautiful Is Your Voice:

Accounts of the History of

the Enlhet of Ya'alve-Saanga

Compiled and edited by Ernesto Unruh

and Hannes Kalisch

During the 1920s, the world of the indigenous communities of the Chaco was suddenly and irrevocably exploded by three consecutive events: the arrival of the first Mennonite settlers, the arrival of Paraguayan and Bolivian soldiers in preparation for war, and a disastrous smallpox epidemic.[1] Their history since has been one of continual invasion and dispossession. The following four firsthand accounts, by Metyeeyam', Savhongvay', Seema Maalya, and Kenteem of the Enlhet community, give an invaluable and unique viewpoint on these violent events. The texts are taken from a compilation of personal accounts, by Enlhet elders, of the history of the Enlhet indigenous people. Both authors and compilers (Ernesto Unruh, an Enlhet native, and Hannes Kalisch, a German-born linguist) live in the central Paraguayan Chaco; their team, Nengvaanemkeskama Nempayvaam Enlhet, has carried out extensive work in the collection, publication, and radio broadcast of linguistic and cultural patrimony in order to strengthen and protect indigenous self-determination.

Who Showed Him Our Land?

In the early twentieth century the center of the Paraguayan Chaco was inhabited almost exclusively by its indigenous peoples. In order to populate the northern areas bordering Bolivia where oil deposits were thought to lie, the Paraguayan government encouraged Mennonites to settle in the Chaco. In 1919 the Mennonite community of Manitoba, Canada, approached a New York real estate agent, who employed Frank Engen to find suitable land for them in the Chaco where they would have the freedom to practice their way of life.

Engen, called "Meste [Mister] Engke" by the Enlhet, arrived with a small party in the central Chaco in 1920. *This was the first contact that the Enlhet had had with foreigners in their land. Their openness is characteristic of the Enlhet concept of peace; they had no interest in private ownership of the land for themselves. Only later did the Enlhet realize that the friendship offered by the settlers was a fraud, and that the intention of the new arrivals was to take their land from them. The Canadian Mennonites founded Colonia Menno in 1927, and more Mennonite settlement followed in the next five years. The following decades have seen a litany of dispossession and marginalization of the indigenous people.*

It is important to the Mennonites' historical view that Engen's report stated that the Enlhet were not, as the Mennonites understood it, "making the most of the land." That is, they were not farming it. Thus the Mennonites merely sought to put to good use what the Enlhet had chosen to disregard, and to bring Christianity to them. This argument is still prevalent in discussions with the Mennonites on egalitarian land distribution between the indigenous and immigrant communities in the Chaco.

Metyeeyam' was about ninety years old in 2011. His accounts of Enlhet history run to many hundreds of pages. Here, he offers a rare and precious insight into the start of the tragedy of the Enlhet's contact with the white man.

Right at the beginning an *Elle* [2] came, an Englishman. I wasn't there; I didn't see him. But my father told me a lot about him. My father, who was his guide, was Apveske', an important person, a leader. The Paraguayans called him Kapata Poko. The Englishman, the *Elle*, was the first white man to see this land. Fred Engen was his name—"Meste Engke." It's because of him that the Mennonites and the Paraguayans came. They say Meste Engke came from the north; the telephone probably brought him news of our land. He must have flown over us in an airplane and then told them in Asunción that he'd seen us, the Enlhet who lived there.

"There's a lot of open grassland there. That's a good place. There are people there. There are no houses, no roads, nothing," he probably said. "But I don't know whether they might be dangerous," he thought. "I'll go and see," Meste Engke decided. And so he came into our land.

First he went to Maklha-Nempeena, Puerto Casado. From there he came this way. It was probably the river people, the Toba, that brought him from Maklha-Nempeena, but it could have been the Koonaapoklhe', the Guaná, too. And he brought Paraguayans with him. That was in the time before the train. The railway wasn't there yet, and he came on a big oxcart looking for the *amyep*, the grasslands he must have seen from above. But he couldn't find them.

"Where are the grasslands?" he asked as he traveled further and further. In the east, where he started his journey, only *taayet* grows. It's a completely different landscape from here. It was all *yengman*—marshes—where he was looking. Meste Engke finally reached Haalhama-Teves, beyond Kilómetro 145, but he still couldn't find the *amyep* however hard he looked. Then he reached Kemha-Pamlhek, still looking for the open fields he'd seen from the air, but he still didn't find it. So he kept heading west, toward us, and reached Yelhnaklha-Pa'at. There he met an Enlhet—Meseng, the Paraguayans called him. In Enlhet his name was Seeyeta'ay'; he was a wise man, a man with powers; he lived there. But Meste Engke didn't find any fields in Yelhnaklha-Pa'at either, just *yangkomelh*, lakes.

Meste Engke carried on toward us, and arrived at Pongkat-Napoolheng, Hoffnungsfeld, and there he came across a small field. After that he came to the edge of the place where the grassland was; in Kenma-Gaaga he finally found real open land. But he kept on going and came to Kenmaa-Paapen', where Lichtenau, the Mennonite colony, is today, and found a big settlement.

"Who is the leader here?" he asked.

"He is," they said, and pointed to my father.

"Right. Tell me where the fields are. Where is the open grassland I saw, where the Enlhet live, people without clothes, like you?" asked Meste Engke.

"They are here," my father said to him.

"Good. Take me to them."

There were some Paraguayans with Meste Engke. They say there were four. The Enlhet stood around Meste Engke.

"What do you want in exchange for letting us onto your land?" asked the *Nolte*—that means the one from the north—"Do you want money? A car?" That was what he must have offered them, but nobody understood what he was saying because in those days the Enlhet only spoke their own language.

"Do you want us to pay you in money? Or do you want things?" he'd have asked. But the Enlhet didn't know that because nobody understood foreign languages. If the Enlhet had understood, they'd have a lot of possessions today, but no. . . . He just carried on; Meste Engke spent some time traveling around the land, and wherever he met the Enlhet they killed goats and sheep, and he and his companions ate meat. In exchange Meste Engke gave them *yerba*, but no one had ever seen *yerba*, and he gave out flour as well, but the people threw it away when he wasn't looking. Even though with time the Enlhet got used to the *yerba*, and then to the flour, at first they threw them both away. My father told me that many times. Meste Engke made my father his guide, and my father always told us how he received a long skirt as a gift. "He is my guide," said Meste Engke.

When he left here, Meste Engke took some earth with him. He filled a can with soil and took it north with him.

"What's he doing? Why is he taking the earth?" people asked.

Meste Engke answered, "I'm taking this with me. Some people are going to come, called Lengko—Mennonites," he explained.

He took the earth with him, and when the Lengko in the north saw it they wanted to come right away.

"See how good the Enlhet land is," said Meste Engke to the Lengko. "And the Enlhet are not dangerous."

After he spoke to the Enlhet, Meste Engke left, but before he went he marked the place where the Mission was going to be. We call it Nevkev'a, Loma Belena. He walked over and put a mark on a big *maaset*, a quebracho tree. The quebracho is still there.

"This is where the Enlhet will live. This will be the Mission," said Meste Engke, the *Nolte*. "The Mennonites will live all over this land. They will multiply and live everywhere. They will own everything. But the Enlhet will live all crammed together here. They will come here from all around." And he marked the *maaset*.

"You will all live here. Your people will come from all over—Toba, Sana-paná, Nivaclé." That's what he said, at Nevkev'a, where the Mission would be later for a while. Then Meste Engke went back to his country. I didn't meet him. My father told me about him. Then the Mennonites settled all around here and the Paraguayans were given money for the land, but the Enlhet didn't get any.

Who showed Meste Engke our land? He came when there weren't any Paraguayans here yet. The Paraguayans only came after Meste Engke—the people who kill; the soldiers. They followed the Mennonites.

When We Were Eaten by Dogs

The smallpox epidemic that struck the Chaco immediately after the Chaco War was almost fatal to the Enlhet-Enenlhet nation. It left an entire generation of orphans to face the changes of the twentieth century. They knew of no medicine against it, and were terrified by the cruel death that it brought. People are said to have been driven to madness by having witnessed it. Here, Seema Maalya describes how, having spent years running from war, the Enlhet now ran from the plague and communities were forced into behavior that shocked even themselves.

Both Paraguayan and Bolivian military outposts provided vaccines against the sickness, but the Enlhet were divided between those who chose to accept the medicine, thus bowing to the white man's power, and those who preferred to die with their dignity untarnished.

The Enlhet were almost wiped out. They died of the sickness. People would start feeling sick when the sun was still low in the sky, and by the time it set they'd already be dead. That's what my mother told us. I wasn't there—I'm still young now—but my mother always talked about it, about when the jaguar ate our people's corpses. He'd wait until we died and then he'd eat us. The dogs ate the dead bodies too. You'd be relieved if you got little blisters on your skin because that meant you'd get better, but if the sickness came like fire, as if you had burns all over your skin, then it was bad. I heard people would writhe around on the ground as if they were breaking into pieces. Soon you'd turn white, and then big pieces of skin would start to come off your arms and your knees and your hands.

People left the sick alone straight away. Yes . . . when they were still alive, they left them. The ones that were still well ran away even while the sick person was still calling after them. They'd leave a little water with them and go; and if the sick person still had the strength he'd drink some of the water. They'd leave the water in a clay jug propped up next to him. That's what I was told. And so he'd die alone. It was because of the sickness that people behaved like that. The Enlhet were very afraid of the sickness. But it was no good running; the sickness followed us. People were very frightened of catching it.

And the children. . . . This was before the sickness started killing people, when people were running, when the Paraguayans came—soldiers, men who shot other men. People were very frightened, but even if you told the children to keep quiet some of them didn't listen.

"Kill those children!" someone said. "The Valay will know where we are!" So the adults sometimes killed the children. Then the people ran away again, far away, far away to the middle of the forest. Today we couldn't run away. If it had been then like it is now we'd have all died, because now there's no forest. But at that time the forest was strong and we could hide there.

Why I Left My Home

At the beginning of the twentieth century the Enlhet population of the Chaco was nomadic, practicing periodic migration around a central area that was their "home" land. During the late 1920s this traditional pattern began to change for two reasons. First, there was the imperative to escape, as they found themselves in increasing fear of being killed in the escalating clashes between the Paraguayan and Bolivian armies in the run-up to the Chaco War. Second, there was the spread of the Mennonite colonies. Although they were initially drawn to approach the newly arrived settlers with whom they now shared space, the Enlhet's autonomy became increasingly constrained by the presence of the colonies and their power of self-determination slowly reduced.

With the founding, in their homeland, of Colonia Neuland in 1947, the family of Savhongvay' found itself, like many others, caught up in this frightening, shrinking world.

When we lived in Kemha-Maaneng, around where Lichtenau, in Neuland, is today, there were no Paraguayans yet. And then one day these Valay—Paraguayans—appeared, doing reconnaissance of the land. I've told you about them; there were two Paraguayans and an Enlhet. And that was the beginning of when the Valay came. Before that there weren't any; no Mennonites either.

So we left our home—Kemha-Maaneng—because of the Paraguayans; the Valay ruined the Enlhet's home. It makes you sad, this place—this isn't Paraguayan land. This land belongs to the Enlhet. There's no question. The Valay's home was over there in the east. This land here, they took it—but it all belongs to the Enlhet.

So we left Kemha-Maaneng, although the Paraguayans didn't come that far, only the two that I mentioned. But we kept hearing about them.

"The Valay want to shoot each other," people said.

"Where can we go? They're going to fight their war here," they said. "Where can we go?"

"We could go to the Mennonites."

And everyone went to the Mennonites. The soldiers only arrived in Kemha-Maaneng, in our home, later. It was on one of their soldier roads.

We ran from the war. We went to *Lhaptaana*—Friedensfeld—and to *Kemhaytaava-Amyep*—Schönwiese. I was still a child; I was only about ten years old. The Enlhet were afraid of the Valay. The Valay were at war with the Yaamvalay, the Bolivians. They didn't care about the Enlhet; they just killed them. The Paraguayans didn't help us. Only the Mennonites helped us, once they came.

I didn't go back to my home after the war finished. I made my home with the Mennonites. I lived in Toopak-Amyep—Gnadenheim. At first we settled in Lhaptaana. We went to Matna-Maaleng, to Schönbrunn as well. That was where we met the soldiers that killed my grandfather. I was left on my own, because my parents died too, during the epidemic. That's why I didn't go home to Kemha-Maaneng. I had no one left there to go to.

The Enlhet thought they'd be safe with the Mennonites during the war, but it was bad there too. Even when we were with the Mennonites a Paraguayan would kill an Enlhet when he saw one. That's why the Enlhet ran again, back to the forest to hide. Not one Enlhet stayed with the Mennonites. Only me. I slept at a Mennonite's farm, and worked for him. The reason I stayed on my own was because the soldiers had caught me after they'd killed my grandfather, but I escaped and went to this Mennonite. He disguised me—he put a big straw hat on me so the Paraguayans wouldn't recognize me; so they'd think I was a Mennonite that worked there.

That's how it happened. It was terrible. Terrible. That's why I say that compared to that, things are good now. Of course, I often worry the Enlhet might be hunted again.

We Have to Give Up Our Way of Life

By the mid-twentieth century, cultural and religious imposition, loss of geographical space, population depletion through sickness, and the savagery of the Chaco War had combined to cripple the Enlhet's livelihood and symbolic universe. They had been forced into an untenable situation. They finally took the decision to renounce their previous life in order to survive. Here, Kenteem describes the consequences of the loss of the Enlhet universe and of the store of wisdom that the people once held.

We used to have a lot of goats in Lhaapangkalvok, in Filadelfia. We don't now; that's all gone. We used up all the sheep and goats, and we don't have animals now. But it's not just a recent thing—the Mennonites started getting angry years ago about our sheep. They always said they didn't like our animals stealing their crops.

Around that time the festival of Yaanmaan finished as well. We held the last one on the far side of Filadelfia. We killed the last goats and sheep, so we had no more; that was the end of them. And that's when the Enlhet elders met and talked together.

"We have to give up our way of life," said one of them.

And after a while the Enlhet converted to the Mennonites' religion.

Our way of life really disappeared. It's all different now. But the Mennonites still ask us, "When's it going to rain?"

It's obvious they don't understand our situation. What's wrong with the Mennonites? They don't get it. They'll think I'm attacking them when I say this, but they just don't understand. They don't realize our way of life has disappeared. In the old days, with the elders, when a Mennonite asked, "When is it going to rain?" they'd answer, "Tomorrow afternoon," and it really did rain.

The old people had powers; wisdom. That's all gone now. Nowadays the Mission rules everywhere, nowadays everyone's a Christian, nowadays none of that's left. And the Mennonites don't understand that. What's wrong with the Mennonites? They don't understand any of it. That's why when a Mennonite asks me about the rain I say, "We've lost that knowledge now."

In the old days the Enlhet knew when rain was coming, and it always turned out the way they said, but now the Enlhet will say, "You need to watch the television to find that out."

When a Mennonite asks me, "When's it going to rain?" I say, "No one can tell." The Mennonite will say, "It'll rain in the morning."

But it doesn't always. So I say to the Mennonite, "The television lies. It was different before with the Enlhet. They knew exactly when it was going to rain."

The television tells lies. But the Enlhet's way of life—that has gone.

Notes

1. Although there is no clear evidence of the exact nature of the epidemic, smallpox seems the most likely, although some sources suggest that it may have been typhus.
2. Although Engen was in fact Norwegian, the speaker, Metyeeyam', believed Engen was English and so used *Elle*, the Enlhet term for the English, derived from the Spanish *inglés* (Englishman).

The Revolution of 1947

Carlos María Sienra Bonzi, as told

to Roberto Sienra Zavala

The 1947 civil war was the most serious and prolonged domestic conflict in the post-independence history of Paraguay. Lasting from March to mid-August, an estimated fifty thousand people were killed as a largely peasant militia of the Colorado Party defeated a major part of the armed forces. The conflict began as a purely military insurrection by disaffected officers in Concepción, who feared the growing partisanship of the armed forces under the autocratic presidency of Higinio Morínigo, who was increasingly sympathetic to the Colorado Party. As this testimony suggests, the influence of Febrerista officers who were ex-combatants of the Chaco War and activists of the Paraguayan Communist Party, enabled Morínigo to access U.S. support by labeling the insurrection a "communist conspiracy." Although the attitude of the Liberal Party hierarchy toward the insurrection was ambivalent, Morínigo began to accuse the Liberals, Febreristas, and communists of involvement in an unholy "triple alliance" against his government. The ferocity of the vengeance wrought by the victorious Colorado militias, especially against the Liberals, provoked the first of many subsequent waves of emigration to Argentina. The civil war left a legacy of deep political divisions in Paraguayan society and ushered in the subsequent six decades of Colorado hegemony within the political system.

To understand the Revolution of 1947, we have to be clear about the particular circumstances that we lived in at that time. Most of the population resented President Morínigo's decision to allow the Colorado Party into government (thus breaking previous agreements with the military) and his inability to resolve the country's problems. We must not forget that he had a lot of support from the United States; President Roosevelt had encouraged him to declare war on Hitler's Germany, although we never sent a single soldier to the front, and the eventual declaration of war on the Axis powers brought an avalanche of dollars.

One morning, Concepción woke to the news that Captain Bartolomé Araujo had led an uprising in the city. Today, years after the event, I personally think that Araujo rushed into it; the uprising should never have taken place in Concepción, but in Asunción, where it would all have been over in a few days or even hours. Our city is so far from the capital that the uprising would have needed fantastic logistics to have had any chance of success. Crucially, the government in Asunción had more than enough resources to defend itself, and in that situation, the element of surprise was vital for the insurgents; when the revolutionary forces set off in boats from Concepción under cover of dark, Morínigo's forces were left stranded near Horqueta and on the outskirts of Concepción. The revolutionaries entered Asunción swiftly, sweeping through the government's defenses and reaching as far as the Olimpia football stadium. But because of disagreements between the commanders, the revolutionaries divided their already meager forces. This was the worst strategy they could have adopted, as they were up against an enemy that was vastly superior in both numbers and resources.

The Revolutionary Capital

Another mistake that the revolutionaries made was to allow the Communist Party into their ranks. The United States, in its international struggle against communism, was never going to allow the Communist Party to take hold in the heart of South America. My friend Arnaldo Riella was sent by the Revolutionary Government to the Brazilian border to buy medicines, but the second time he went, he was not allowed to buy anything; the Brazilians had been ordered by the Yanks not to have anything to do with the Paraguayan revolutionaries.

To soften up the revolutionaries, the government forces began to send planes to drop bombs and indiscriminately machine-gun the population. Where the statue of the Indian stands today, one of the rebel regiments— the Second May Regiment I think—was stationed, and it was attacked a number of times by these planes. They tended to fly very high; I don't know why, because the revolutionaries did not have antiaircraft guns. One of the most important victims of these bombing raids was the mother of my friend Blasito Echague. Dropping bombs on military targets is one thing, but to do it against innocent civilians can never be justified.

The fighting was fierce around Cororó, in the Department of San Pedro, where Colonel Alfredo Ramos launched a surprise attack and overcame vastly superior government forces. There were also fierce clashes below La

Caída to the south of Concepción. But over this period, the revolutionaries lost the element of surprise and it was Morínigo's forces that went on the offensive while the revolutionaries tried to hold their positions. In the whole war, the revolutionary forces never had more than about two thousand men, while the government had around twelve thousand. Even though the Chaco army joined the revolutionaries and many young volunteers came from neighboring countries to join the effort to overthrow the dictatorship, the insurgents never got to grips with problems of logistics, arms, and rations, and some troops began to desert through hunger. We all hoped so much that this would be the last revolution in our country, and that it would put an end to anarchy and injustice. With all my years of experience, I can say that the 1947 Revolution was the hardest in our country's history.

With the final defeat of the revolutionaries, the Colorado Party came to power, marking the beginning of a dark period for anybody that had not supported them; even dissident Colorado leaders were imprisoned and then exiled. I still do not understand today why the Colorados supported Morínigo: they could easily have won free and fair elections and come into power by the front door rather than through the back door. I think they would have won an election because we had all had enough of the Liberals.

The Collapse

The revolutionary troops that headed south to take Asunción were hardly babes in arms—most were seasoned veterans of the Chaco War. Unfortunately there just were not enough of them. The plan was simple and feasible, but a lot of precious time was lost in "liberating" each port as the army went down the river. When the troops disembarked on the outskirts of Asunción the commanders made another mistake, opting to take all the neighboring towns around capital city one by one and then divide their small force for the final assault.

Eventually the revolutionary forces lost any kind of cohesion, and the coordination that is so vital for any offensive or defensive strategy was missing, which led to confusion among the commanders. Having at one point virtually held the capital in the palm of their hands, the revolutionary troops were finally forced into retreat by vastly superior numbers.

A large number of the revolutionary forces retreated south with their commanders and several politicians, while another group fled to Argentina across the Chaco and then the River Pilcomayo. Many did not make it, and were taken prisoner or shot. The remainder of the army retreated toward Villeta under the command of Juan Martincich, the mythical hero of the Chaco War. Some of them managed to cross to the Argentinian side in small boats and on rafts, while the rest fought hard, inflicting a lot of casualties on the government forces. When they were finally surrounded and could not hold out any longer, they threw down their weapons and waited with their hands up as an unmistakable sign that they had surrendered.

But when the advancing government forces began simply to cut the throats of the first revolutionaries they reached, the others reacted and resumed the fight. Some dived into the water as a last resort, to try to swim to the Argentinian side, and a lot of them drowned in the attempt. Several nurses were repeatedly raped and then murdered. Martincich refused to cross in the last boat and no one knows how he really died. Only his murderers know, but the cowards never revealed anything. Most likely he dived into the water too. Morínigo's forces, drunk on rum, went out in boats and shot any men that were in the water and unable to defend themselves. Martincich's body was never found. As the poet Hérib Campos Cervera said, "It needed that much water to put out so much fire."

And so ended the Revolution of 1947. Before the government forces entered Concepción, I fled with a large group of families. Despite the hardship, we managed to cross the Chaco, and then the River Pilcomayo into Argentina. I went on to Formosa where I was later reunited with my family. Concepción was left defenseless, open to looting and vandalism. People fled as best they could. Most headed to Brazil across the River Apa in the Cachueira Pass. Whole families emigrated and left behind everything they had.

As a result of the defeat, the names of all the units that had joined the revolution were removed from the archive of the armed forces; erased from the record. That is what led Lorenzo Medina to say: "A dictator can erase the names of those glorious regiments from the national archives by decree; but he can never erase their actions in the Chaco War (Military Prison, 1948)."

That was the end of an adventure that should never have started in Concepción and which instead of liberating us from Morínigo punished us with another even more terrible dictatorship. Paraguay today is not the Paraguay we dreamt of during the war in the Chaco, during the February Revolution, nor during the 1947 Revolution. Paraguay today is a discredited country, where to be honest is to be a fool, and where, as the tango "Cambalache" puts it, "Everyone's a lord; everyone's a thief."

A Half Hour in My Childhood

Eva Bichsel

At the midpoint of the twentieth century Paraguay remained a backwater in Latin America and was hardly known outside the subcontinent. Human development indicators were among the lowest in the region and even Asunción, the capital city, did not have a water supply system. The highway network was almost nonexistent, hardly any roads were asphalted, and internal transport still depended heavily on a railway from Asunción to Encarnación. Eva Bichsel (née Ramírez) grew up in the small town of Ybytymí, which, despite being on the railway line and only one hundred kilometers from the capital, still had neither electricity nor telephone. She evokes the slow-moving and unchanging nature of life in rural Paraguay at the time she lived there, as a seven-year-old child, and the strong sense of isolation felt by its inhabitants.

Thursdays, two o'clock in the afternoon, became a magical time for us. My two sisters and I waited happily for it each week during the summer of 1950. Going to our town's railway station turned out to be the single most important event for us children, because it allowed us to feel transported for a few minutes to another world inhabited by other people, different from those we saw daily on the dusty streets of the town. An hour before the train's scheduled arrival, we used to run towards the station along the "Zanjita Trail," a dusty, treeless, bumpy one-mile stretch, deeply engraved by ox-drawn cart wheels, the hooves of cattle and horses and the most diverse size of human foot-steps. This trail resembled a relief map and it made running difficult but, in our excitement, we never reduced speed until we reached the station. We usually perched ourselves high on top of a heap of cut oak stacked by the side of the railway tracks and strained our eyes towards the sandy, red plain. Suddenly, a long chain of dark dots would appear in the distance advancing rapidly and, as they came nearer, these dots turned out to be the long awaited train!

My sisters and I counted as fast as we possibly could the number of compartments until the train came to a full stop. The stifling heat of the summer allowed no closed windows and, from our position, we could look right into

The Paraguayan Central Railway, one of the first in South America, was inaugurated in 1861 and gradually extended to Encarnación (441 km) by 1909. It became the major means of internal communications until displaced by an emerging highway system in the 1950s and had ceased to operate by the late 1980s. Photograph by Ben Cavanna. Used by permission of the photographer.

the compartments, which were always very crowded. We observed strange, tired faces, young mothers nursing their babies, young men stretching their cramped legs, white-haired old men and women holding large fans made out of bamboo leaves. From time to time they glanced towards the platform where a large crowd of townspeople stood staring at the passengers. We were never sure whether these townspeople were there expecting some visiting relatives to get off the train or whether they were there out of curiosity just as my sisters and I were.

We had an irresistible desire to go into the cars and ask these passengers just what made them travel, where were they coming from, where were they going, what kind of villages, towns or great cities have they left behind or were they going to visit, how long had they been sitting in that train and so on. Through our minds raced the most fantastic stories in which each passenger could fit. We were told that the starting point of the Thursday train was Buenos Aires and then rolled some 1100 kms through half of the northern part of Argentina and the greatest part of Southern Paraguay before it reached its destination, Asunción, some 95 kms from our town, Ybytymí. We imagined ourselves among its lucky passengers and pretended we were travelling to faraway places.

We observed that some of the women of our town, dressed in long, flower-patterned skirts and immaculately clean white aprons, came to the station carrying large straw baskets full of freshly baked corn bread to sell. They carried these baskets gracefully on their heads using a skilfully rolled towel as cushion to balance their nourishing cargo. Others carried buckets full of water from the local well or freshly squeezed fruit juices to sell. Walking very erect from one end of the platform to the other they shouted "homemade bread, 5 cents a loaf!" or "water, water, orange juice, pomegranate!" Some of the hungry and thirsty passengers stretched their hands out of the windows and, in no time, emptied the baskets of bread and buckets of water. The town's women then stood in small groups counting their hard earned cash stuffed in a cloth bag, tightly tied around their waist. They chatted happily among themselves, perhaps planning what to sell next week and how much they expected to earn, now and then wiping the pearls of perspiration off their faces.

Once the rush of activities ended, the mail sack and other cargoes were loaded or unloaded, the travellers returned to their seats and made themselves comfortable for the rest of their journey. The doors closed with a deafening clink, the train whistled loudly, and then rolled slowly out of the station. As it gained speed, it looked like a great centipede rushing through the dusty plain. All eyes followed the departing train and white handkerchiefs were waved until it disappeared on the horizon. Later, my sisters and I realized that none of the townspeople had travelling relatives or friends. Waving handkerchiefs was just a gesture, which made the people feel a bit closer to outside civilization since the Thursday train and its passengers were the only link to the world beyond our small town. We had no electricity, no telephone, no radio or television. We felt very isolated and forgotten by the wider world, except on Thursdays.

When we heard no more whistling or rattling of the train and the crowd dispersed, my sisters and I used to look at one another silently, with big question marks in our eyes. The arrival and departure of the International Train gave us an opportunity to observe and enrich our imagination, yet, it almost always left us in a pensive mood. Each one of us knew then that there were other ways of life, other kinds of people and languages and places far away and we dreamed of seeing them one day.

At about 2:30 in the afternoon the thrill was over. We pulled ourselves together and from our unique position on top of the pile of logs, we jumped down to earth and followed the crowd of townspeople, horse riders, ox-pulled carts and barking dogs towards home. After a long mile along the "Zanjita Trail" under the scorching sun, we arrived home thoroughly tired but happily waiting for next Thursday afternoon.

V

Dictatorship and Resistance

In May 1954, the commander in chief of the armed forces, General Alfredo Stroessner, overthrew the government of Federico Chaves in a military coup. Stroessner went on to rule Paraguay from August 15, 1954, to February 3, 1989. Also known as El Rubio, Mburuvichá, and El Segundo Reconstructor, he became the longest-serving head of state in Latin American history, putting a temporary end to Paraguay's notorious political instability and leaving an indelible mark on the country's psyche. The Stroessner regime relied on five major mechanisms in order to maintain itself in power for so long—a democratic facade, an effective system of repression, institutionalized corruption, the use of nationalist ideology, and the support of the United States government.

The longevity of the regime depended crucially on the tripartite alliance that Stroessner forged, as president of the Republic, with the armed forces and the Colorado Party. As a veteran of the Chaco War and as a supporter of the government of President Morínigo during the 1947 civil war, his own nationalist and political credentials were well suited to the role that he chose to play during the subsequent three decades. Under his regime, the edifice of a corporativist state, the foundations of which had been laid by Morínigo in the 1940s, was subsequently completed. The Colorado Party and the armed forces henceforth developed a symbiotic relationship, which was overseen by Stroessner in his capacity as head of state, commander in chief, and honorary president of the Colorado Party.

Stroessner used purges and repression of perceived and real opposition to gain control of the Colorado Party through the 1950s, converting it into an authoritarian political machine that would guarantee mass allegiance to him, and strengthen his control of the country through its comprehensive national network of party branches. Membership of the Colorado Party was made obligatory for all public employees, including teachers and officers in the armed forces, and the party increasingly presented itself as the true party of the nation.

Despite his singularly uncharismatic nature, a strong personality cult developed around the figure of Stroessner, which sought to identify him with the nationalist heroes of the nineteenth century, and manifested itself in various forms: the lending of his name to towns and public buildings, the display of his photograph in all public offices, the annual pilgrimage to the presidential home by thousands of acolytes on his birthday, and the extensive use of propaganda in the media, which praised him to excess. However, Stroessner did not conform to the stereotypical image of the Latin American *caudillo*. Indeed, the Stroessner cult emphasized not only his dull persona, but also, more significantly, the importance of the alliance between the Colorado Party and armed forces to the maintenance of *Paz y Progreso*, which became the ubiquitous propaganda slogan of the regime.

Economic growth from 1954 until 1973 hardly matched the increase in population. The highly unequal land tenure system remained untouched, and a rapid increase in smuggling combined with a lack of state-sponsored reform aborted all attempts at domestic industrialization. Repression combined with a lack of access to land generated a continuous emigration of the rural poor to neighboring Argentina. However, the construction of the massive Itaipú hydroelectric project on the border between Paraguay and Brazil led to rapid economic growth in the 1970s. Growing migration of Brazilian colonists into eastern Paraguay led to a boom in agricultural export production, but also to land conflicts due to the displacement of small farmers and indigenous people.

In the context of the Cold War, Stroessner portrayed himself as a bastion against communism (thus assuring material and diplomatic support from the United States for most of his rule). Opposition was repressed, exiled, or tolerated, this last in order to give a democratic facade to the regime. Following the Cuban Revolution, a number of armed guerrilla groups attempted to establish a presence in the country, but with little popular support, they were wiped out by counterinsurgency units in a series of brutal campaigns. A nonviolent peasant movement (the Ligas Agrarias) emerged in the 1960s supported by progressive elements of the Catholic Church, demanding access to land. However, following rapid growth, it was brutally repressed in 1976 when Stroessner accused it of links with an embryonic guerrilla movement, known as the Organización Primero de Marzo (OPM).

Economic slowdown in the 1980s added to the growing opposition toward the regime, alienating the previously compliant private sector. By the late 1980s the church and the United States were openly criticizing the dictatorship, while domestic opposition was also beginning to take advantage of an apparent period of liberalization. This led to splits within the regime between loyal *stronistas* who favored continuity, and traditionalist Colorados who were willing to open up the political system in order to retain power. In February 1989, Stroessner was overthrown in a putsch led by his foremost military aide, General Andrés Rodríguez, with the support of the traditionalist wing of the Colorado Party. He left the next day for permanent exile in Brazil, where he died in 2006.

Toward a Weberian Characterization
of the Stroessner Regime

Marcial Riquelme

Several attempts have been made to characterize the Stroessner regime, ranging from "traditional caudillo," and "traditional-authoritarian" to "transitional from a caudillo-type régime to a modern bureaucratic-authoritarian régime." But the most appealing characterization to date is that offered by the Paraguayan sociologist Marcial Riquelme (1937–2007), who argues here that the nature of the regime was similar to what Max Weber called "sultanism," a variant of patrimonialism, in which power is centralized and based on the discretion of the ruler. The violent overthrow of the regime in 1989 is consistent with Riquelme's characterization of "neosultanism," given its lack of institutional mechanisms for the peaceful transfer of power.

Stroessner's regime was closer to what Max Weber (1978: 232) called sultanism: "Where domination is primarily traditional, even though it is exercised by virtue of the ruler's personal autonomy, it will be called *patrimonial authority*; where it indeed operates primarily on the basis of discretion, it will be called *sultanism*." Like patrimonialism, sultanism is a personalistic and centralized government in which functionaries are recruited on the basis of personal loyalty to the ruler. And in both types of regime the incentive to that loyalty lies not in the ruler's personal charisma, but in his ability to dispense and suspend material rewards and privileges. But whereas the exercise of power in patrimonialism is circumscribed by traditions and custom, in sultanism it operates under no such constraint, but proceeds on the basis of the leader's absolute discretion.

Since this characterization is formulated as an "ideal type," it does not necessarily imply the existence of any referent. Nonetheless, it is worthwhile to point out that the majority of defining traits of sultanism put forth by Weber in *Economy and Society* and re-elaborated by Linz (1975) can be found in Stroessner's regime, sometimes purely, sometimes in association with other forms of domination.

Relying on Linz's model, we will cite several salient operative traits of the Stroessner regime that correspond to features characteristic of sultanist regimes.

— Power was exercised in a discretionary form, in other words, without legal constraints and without subjection to a system of values or a specific ideology. To be sure, appeals were repeatedly made to legalistic arguments in order to conceal the true discretionality of power. Formal institutionalization was merely a façade since independent institutions did not in fact exist. The Judicial and Legislative powers were, under the constitution, mere appendages of the Executive branch. And the head of State, through unilateral decisions, constantly, and with absolute impunity, subverted such rules which nominally did regulate the functioning of the state's institutions.

— Implementation of decisions of the head of State rested on the strength of non-institutional, partisanized armed forces, and on a party of patronage which administered the system of prebends and privileges.

— Public administration relied on a small core of elites and civilian technocrats and a relatively specialized bureaucracy; in terms, however, of recruitment, payment, promotion and layoffs, its members more closely resembled personal servants of the head of State than public functionaries within a legal rational administration. As is well known, the latter are appointed, and redeem themselves on the basis of universalist criteria (such as competitions based on merit and aptitude, the rational description of duties, etc.), which do not exist in authoritarian regimes of the sultanist sort.

— Loyalty of civil and military servants to the head of State was purely personalistic, based as it was on fear of his displeasure and on striving to acquire the material rewards which he dispensed to his unconditionally loyal followers.

— The country represented the head of State's largest property. This appropriation was made possible by the personalistic and discretionary exercise of power on the part of the head of State and his closest collaborators. The patrimonialist administration of the State's real assets translated into a conflation of the political sphere and the economy, and into the absence of well defined boundaries between *public* and *private* property. The result of this was that the head of State and his immediate cohorts freely disposed of public funds, services and properties, and placed their relatives and cronies in various key administrative positions often within anti-economic state monopolies. In other words, the head of State and his civilian and military following effectively treated public property as if it were their own. The distinction between public and private wealth was further blurred by the practice of exploiting the state's licensing power to extract bribes and commissions from even wholly privately owned enterprises.

The economy, as a consequence of this conception of authority, was continually manipulated, not, however, for purposes of central planning, but plainly and simply for the acquisition of personal benefits. This explains in turn the lack of a coherent, global economic policy, which is one of the traits that distinguish sultanist regimes from those of a totalitarian orientation (Linz 1975).

Finally, as Linz points out, this class of regimes is generally suited to arise in small countries with essentially agricultural economies, with a high percentage of rural residents and with few key urban centers, which usually operate in conjunction with several commercial and industrial establishments. Such factors facilitate the sultanist ruler's total control of society.

If Stroessner's regime was neither totalitarian nor bureaucratic-authoritarian, neither was it simply a traditional dictatorship headed by a military *caudillo*. His domination was based on a calculated system of rewards and punishments that left nothing to improvisation or chance. The legal ordinance which shored up the regime could be tinkered with as much as necessary in order to adjust it to the discretionary aims of the head of State. The entire process was further guaranteed by an efficiently repressive state apparatus based on modem technology. The uncovering of the contents of the police archives in 1992 (known in Paraguay as the *Archivo del Terror*), provides systematic evidence that Stroessner was informed of even the smallest events that took place in the country. Paraguay was in fact fully integrated into the international project known as Operation Condor (Buffe 1993). On the basis of the documents in Asunción, it is hard to imagine that, if and when the corresponding archives compiled by its Southern Cone neighbors should ever come to light, Paraguay's participation will prove to have been any less systematic and methodical than that of the bureaucratic-authoritarian regimes with which it so eagerly and efficiently collaborated.

In short, from the traits we have just described, the most appropriate term, using Weberian typology, for this regime would be "neo-sultanism." The prefix "neo" serves to emphasize that this was not a regime headed by a "traditional *caudillo*" running on the legacy of the Spanish authoritarian political culture but rather a well-articulated regime based on a partisanized army, a party of patronage which fed the loyal bureaucracy, and a modern repressive apparatus systematically used to crush dissent.

Consolidation, Expansion, and Decomposition of a Neo-Sultanistic Regime

In characterizing the regime as neo-sultanistic, we do not treat it as a static construct. On the contrary, our characterization makes it possible to periodize and reinterpret the different phases undergone by this regime.

In the period of *consolidation* (1954–1967), political aspects came to the fore; purges were carried out within the ruling Colorado Party and the armed forces, and a "loyal opposition" was institutionalized. During this period the regime laid down the legal framework for what Delich (1985) called "republican despotism."

During the *expansion* period (1968–1981), the patrimonial components of the regime were extended (Riquelme 1989). With the construction of the binational Itaipú hydroelectric plant, an unprecedented flow of foreign capital was infused into the economy. Simultaneously, the regime embarked on a program of modernization of agriculture through the expansion of the agricultural frontier and measures calculated to foster the emergence of large agribusiness. This is the period in which public resources were distributed in a prebendary fashion to subsidize the loyalty of a large clientele of party members via the private enrichment of the regime's cronies in the civil service and the military.

Eventually (1982–1989), the regime began to show signs of *decomposition*. With the sudden drop in foreign investments, rising unemployment rates and the shrinkage of the Argentine labor market—a "safety valve" for tens of thousands of Paraguayan workers who emigrated every year to that country—patronage could no longer be extended to all of those who had benefitted from it in the past.

In the absence of resources, a regime based on patrimonial practices becomes increasingly difficult to sustain. As some authors have suggested, this form of domination seems to work well in small agricultural countries, with a relatively limited population and small-scale economy (MacDonald 1981; Snyder 1992). However, the country under which Stroessner's regime emerged in 1954 had by 1989 changed tremendously. Its population had almost tripled, more than 50 percent of the population were now living in urban areas (as compared to only one-third in the 1950s) and the economy had undergone a process of modernization.

Ironically, the strategies used by the regime to expand its patrimonial practices also contained within themselves elements conducing to its own demise. The regime's limited capacity of distribution issued in economic crisis contributed to a re-activation of civil society and, ultimately, to a violent schism within the ruling party. And, indeed, even the bourgeoisie godfathered by the regime through state largess became increasingly distressed by the failure to institutionalize clear rules of the game.

The neo-sultanistic nature of this regime made it virtually impossible to reform itself through negotiations with the opposition. In contemporary Latin American history, neo-sultanistic regimes, lacking the institutional mechanisms for peaceful political transitions, have been removed from power by violence (Snyder 1992).

It is important to bear the above periodization in mind, since the value of employing ideal-type constructs is lost if one insists on projecting them as "stable essences" into empirical reality. To be useful, an ideal-typical concept must be historicized within a context of socioeconomic and political processes.

Works Cited

Delich, Francisco. 1985. "Estructura agraria y hegemonía en el despotismo pepublicano." In *Hegemonía y alternativas políticas en América Latina*, ed. Julio Labastida, 470–86. Mexico City: Siglo xxi Editores / unam, Instituto de Investigaciones Sociales.

Linz, Juan J. 1975. "Totalitarian and Authoritarian Regimes." In *Macropolitical Theory*, vol. 3, ed. Fred Greenstein and Nelson Polsby, 175–411. Reading, Mass.: Addison-Wesley Publishing.

McDonald, Ronald H. 1981. "The Emerging New Politics in Paraguay." *Inter-American Economic Affairs* 35, no. 1: 25–44.

Riquelme, Marcial A., and Carlos Martini. 1989. *Hacia la transición a la democracia en el Paraguay: Entrevistas, análisis y documentos*. Asunción: Fundación Friedrich Naumann / Editorial Histórica.

Snyder, Richard. 1992. "Explaining Transitions from Neopatrimonial Dictatorships." *Comparative Politics* 24, no. 4: 379–99.

Weber, Max. 1978. *Economy and Society*. Vol. 1. Berkeley: University of California Press.

The Revolutionary Spirit
of the Colorado Party

Luís María Argaña

The dictatorship of General Stroessner used the Colorado Party (National Republican Association—ANR) as an instrument of social control and mass mobilization in support of the regime. Stroessner developed the party into a highly efficient, vertically organized political vehicle that permeated and dominated all aspects of Paraguayan life. By the mid-1960s Stroessner had successfully created a unified party which, with its control of the media, its system of patronage, and immense grassroots support, represented one of Latin America's most powerful political machines.

The dictatorship, like the Colorado Party, lacked any firm, guiding political ideology, beyond a virulent anticommunism. To fill the ideological vacuum, both the party and the regime developed and manipulated a fierce sense of nationalism based on the revisionist writings of some of the Generación del 900, a group of intellectuals and writers that emerged at the beginning of the twentieth century. The glorification of the past sought to enhance the standing of the party, the military, and the heroes of the nineteenth century, above all the presidents of the nationalist period, José Gaspar Rodríguez de Francia (1814–40), Carlos Antonio López (1840–62), and Francisco Solano López (1862–70). General Stroessner went out of his way to associate himself with these heroes, encouraging nationalist references to himself, such as the Second Rebuilder of the Nation, the Great Benefactor, and the One Leader.

The following extract is typical of much writing from the Colorado Party, with its verbose and overblown rhetoric, its references to a glorious past, and its "doublespeak" when describing the dictatorship in terms of freedom, democracy, peace, and revolution. It was written in 1983 by one of the "ideologues" of the dictatorship, Dr. Luís María Argaña, a leading conservative figure within the party. Argaña became a member of the Junta de Gobierno in the 1960s, was leader of the Chamber of Deputies in the 1970s and served as president of the Supreme Court in the 1980s. As a leader of the traditionalist faction of the party that supported the overthrow of Stroessner in 1989, Argaña subsequently reinvented himself as a democrat. He headed one of the most powerful factions of the Colorado Party throughout the

1990s, narrowly losing the presidential party nomination in both 1992 and 1997, and serving as vice president of the country from 1998 to 1999. In March 1999, he was assassinated in one of the very few acts of political violence of the transition, an event that sparked the heroic marzo paraguayo.

The Colorado Party is revolutionary in the most authentic and noble sense of the word. Indeed, if in the historical sense revolutionary Coloradoism symbolizes a revisionist stance against an ideology that destroys our fundamental national values, and lays claim to our national heroes as superhuman figures due to their bravery and sacrifice, in the social sense, revolutionary Coloradoism also implies reclaiming human worth. It is the recognition of the value of the Paraguayan; it is the concern of the state for the reestablishment of balance in labor relations; it is the painstaking search for truth and harmony between the powerful and ambivalent forces of development: capital and labor, labor and capital.

For this reason, the National Republican Association, even though its formal existence spans nearly one hundred years, is a revolutionary party that grasps the potential of each era. It is revolutionary not only in the metaphysical expression of an ideology or of a political program, but also in terms of the pragmatic realism of its everyday actions. It is revolutionary in the permanent interplay of the three great periods of humanity: past, present, and future.

In the past, it defended our sovereignty, allied itself with our national heroes, and fought, through justified historical revisionism, to plant in the hearts and consciences of our people the truth regarding the lies told about José Gaspar de Francia and Francisco Solano López. Through the efforts of the Colorado Party, patriotism and *lopismo* become central facets of nationalism through the ages. Furthermore, in the short period in which it ruled, the party began the great process of the transformation of our institutions and our way of life. Political parties were organized, the National University and the Faculty of Law were founded, and the nation was guided along a democratic path. Indeed, if the traitors to the nation had not embarked on the "Sajonia" on that sorrowful day in 1904,[1] our process of development, today rekindled by the Colorado Party, would have been more successful still.

Today, its revolutionary, reformist, and innovative attitude is constantly evident; it is written in books and evident in events. It struggles against illness, misery, poverty, and backwardness and, above all, it is present in something that is written with deep gratitude, with the heartfelt emotion of mothers, with the absence of the anxieties and uncertainties which impede initiative, work and production on all levels. This reality, written every day in a spirituality which produces material wealth, is called PEACE. Peace among brothers, peace among Paraguayans.

Thus, in the past and in the present, the Colorado Party has redeemed the nation. We are preparing the future foundations of permanent greatness. We are living in a great era of progress, of true and deep transformations that penetrate the deepest social fabric. However, it will be for future generations to reap the bountiful rewards of the sacrifice and effort of the government of General Stroessner.

One cannot think of industry when there is no energy to move machines. One cannot talk of colonization when there are no roads connecting towns in the countryside. It is utopian to talk of exports or trade balance when we have to pay for holds on foreign ships that traverse our national rivers. We will never make progress that way. Coloradoism, in practice and not just in lyrical revolutionary action, broke down these obstacles. It built the hydroelectric dam that produces energy at Acaray. It acquired ships for our merchant fleet and undertook wide ranging public works, such as the Trans-Chaco highway and the road to Ciudad Stroessner. Today it is undertaking hydroelectric projects at Itaipú and Yacyretá that will transform our country in unimaginable ways.

This is part of the revolutionary legacy for the future of the nation.

The Colorado Party is a revolutionary party, but with its own characteristics. It is deeply rooted in what is ours, what is Paraguay. It is not a heretical, iconoclastic, or international revolutionary party. It is revolutionary not in terms of destroying the past, but of understanding it. It is revolutionary without following imported doctrinaire lines, because Paraguay has never imported liberators; it has produced them.

Thus, with this epic history and this skill in confronting problems, we are carrying out a revolution, accompanied on our journey by José Gaspar de Francia, Carlos Antonio López, Francisco Solano López, and Bernardino Caballero, the revolutionaries of their age. They foresaw the obstacles and devised ways of overcoming them. We have updated their thoughts and their dreams for our age, for our times.

Poets say that clouds take the forms of the country that they are crossing, and mould themselves over the valleys, plains, and mountains, retaining the impression they make and carrying it into the skies. That is the image of certain men, whose collective genius is modeled on the age, and embodies in itself the individuality of a nation. Thus, in its moments of need the nation produced men such as Francia, the Lópezes and today the figure of General Stroessner. Coloradoism gave the ideal, the principle, and the dream; General Stroessner took it, gave it form and made it reality, consubstantiating himself with the Colorado Party.

To better understand and evaluate the Colorado Revolution we need to recall its past. The Colorado Party arose from the midst of the rubble; self-interest, sectarianism, intolerance, and exclusiveness made peaceful and harmonious cohabitation impossible in our nation. Coups d'état, treason, military revolts, and rebellions were the only thoughts of the opposition. But in the long run, morality won the day. Victory is always for the good. Reason was restored and harmony triumphed. The eternal enemies of freedom and justice were forced—whether definitively or not we do not know—to renounce their fratricidal pacts and alliances and enter through the only door to national harmony and greatness: THE DOOR OF DEMOCRACY.

That great master that is called Nature, in whose laws we seek and find the mysterious alchemies of human events, shows us that just as dead, dry branches fall from the trees, so too will fall forever those patterns of civil or uncivil behavior that lack democratic or patriotic usefulness. Thus, the Liberal Party has fallen, along with its retinue of injustice, administrative dishonesty, pillaging oligarchies, and intellectuals by decree; and in this way too has crumbled and fallen away the neofascist Febrerista movement. And in this way too will disappear from the stage of national political life all those vain, foreign-inspired ideologies that lack the warmth and heartbeat of the people and the nation.

But the Colorado Party will live for eternity, because it is a revolutionary party whose strong arms are filled with life-giving sap: because it knows that the truth lies in its own constant transformation; because it is the fire in the veins of the earth of the nation; because it gives heat, essence, fertility, and life to our nation.

Note

1. This refers to the extraordinary events of August 1904. On August 4 a small group of Liberals overran a merchant ship, the *Sajonia*, in Buenos Aires harbour. They then armed and manned the ship, traveled upriver, overran the defensive stronghold of Humaitá, and took a government ship, the *Villa Rica*, that had been sent to block their path. On August 16 they reached Asunción, where they forced the Colorado government to resign under threat of bombardment. The successful coup d'état marked the end of the Colorado era (1878–1904) and the beginning of a period of Liberal control that lasted until 1936.

The Tragedy of Fram

Jorge Rubiani

In 1955, just six months after the inauguration of President Stroessner, a colony of Ukrainians, Poles, and Byelorussians who had fled to Paraguay from the terrors of Stalin's purges and Nazi occupation, was brutally repressed for supposed communist influence. Keen to demonstrate its anticommunist credentials in order to access U.S. foreign aid at the height of the Cold War, the new regime sought to find subversives and communists even where they did not exist. The Eastern European immigrants of the peaceful and thriving colony of Fram, in the southeast of the country, were an easy target. They spoke Russian, and they received mail and some newspapers from home—the Soviet Union.

The events described here were almost completely unknown in Paraguay until they first appeared in 2004 in a book entitled Tierra, trabajo y religion (El Lector, Asunción) *written by Roberto Zub. They were then published by Jorge Rubiani over three days in April 2006 in the* ABC Color *newspaper. The articles provoked an immediate reaction, with descendants writing in from around the country, offering further details and photos.*

Fram is just one example of the catalog of human rights abuses committed by the Stroessner regime in the name of anticommunism. However, it is also symbolic of the legacy of fear that remained years after the events described. Indeed, when the articles were published, many expressed outrage at the silence that had descended over the events and why such a tragedy had almost become forgotten. As Rubiani states, "This massive reaction just goes to show that Paraguay still has areas that are sealed by silence, fear, or resentment. Or perhaps they remain in the darkness because, to quote the words of the Argentine historian Ramón J Cáracano, they do not have 'the poet who signs the epic.'"

General Alfredo Stroessner had been in the presidency for only six months when the "strong man" of Paraguay began to show his teeth. An innocent community of Ukrainians in the colony of Fram would become the very first victims of a barbaric repression.

The memory of a distant homeland often binds immigrants to nostalgia for the past. The poor collectively seek to rediscover something that they have left behind—a common language, food, music, or some traditional celebration that might mitigate their sadness. This is what we Paraguayans do when we find ourselves far from home, and it is what colonists who come to Paraguay do too. It is what the Ukrainians did in the remote colony of Fram—never imagining the dire consequences.

Since settling in the area in the mid-1920s, they had struggled against everything from the impenetrable forest, wild animals, and the absence of communications to the lack of such basic items for their survival as bread and salt. They would have had ample reason to celebrate from time to time. But with the onset of the Cold War and the emergence of a bunker mentality in the "Western, Christian bloc," the dictators of South America interpreted the metaphor as best suited them, and madly waved the banner of "anticommunism." At that time Ukraine was still part of the Soviet Union, and to the simple mindset of Alfredo Stroessner—a military man of extraordinary brutishness and ignorance—the Ukrainians toiling in the inhospitable and isolated colony of Fram "were all communists."

Vladimir Kuczer: "General Store, Post Office, and Bank"

In a world almost entirely alien to them, the immigrants nevertheless worked hard. By the 1950s some of them, like Vladimir Kuczer, had achieved a reasonable standard of living. Kuczer owned a successful "general store" in Carmen del Paraná. Together with his wife Olga and little daughters Viera, Lidia, and Amanda, he was doing well: his fellow colonists in Fram brought him animal fat, eggs, cheese, cotton, corn, and whatever else they managed to produce, and Kuczer sent it by train for sale in Asunción. In exchange, the colonists took farm implements, utensils, and cloth from Kuczer's store. It was logical that he should be the person tasked with receiving correspondence. As his widow Olga, now living in Posadas, explains, "The letters came from Europe to the store because the post office was closed"— that is, on Sunday, the only day of rest for the immigrants, and so the only time they could "come down" to Carmen.

"We had a lot of clients, and all of them used Kuczer's store as their mailing address," recalls Olga. And close to tears, she ends, "And for passing on letters and newspapers, they tarred my husband as a communist." The elderly woman, now eighty-three, shows us precious photographs: "He left Ukraine as a child. He could hardly read and write. He didn't know anything about communism."

The Terror Begins

"Carmen was much prettier then," says Mrs. Kuczer of Carmen del Paraná. "It went downhill after they built the highway, and it finally died when the train stopped coming through." In Fram, the situation was the inverse. When it ceased to depend on Carmen, the situation improved greatly. But few of those who suffered "the repression of '55" stayed to experience the difference.

Previously, the colonists had occasionally organized town celebrations, in part perhaps to help ease the pain of nostalgia. But during one of these celebrations in early March 1955, the Soviet and the Paraguayan national anthems were sung. The colonists' outlook turned suddenly dark: word had already reached the authorities that among the correspondence that the Ukrainians regularly received, were newspapers written—shockingly—in Russian. All the colonists had done was to sing the national anthem of what was at the time, after all, their country of origin, and had done so in the presence of invited officials, including the town police chief, Scappini.

But as would happen repeatedly in the following decades, the repressive *stronista* apparatus felt an obligation to magnify any incident out of all proportion in order to justify terror. The newspaper *Patria*, in its edition of March 26, 1955, carried the headline "Itapúa: Shock Uprising of Communist Colonists." The accusation was official. Now all that was needed was for the "institutions of the Republic" to apply the sentence. This would, without a shadow of a doubt, be brutal.

After the arrests that followed the "celebration of dissent," the women took to the streets "to cry and shout," creating a public disturbance; *Patria's* comment on the colonists' reaction was as follows: "In the wake of the detention of the Russian agents, other colonists organized violent demonstrations in the town, inciting many of their number to attack the municipal building and demand at gunpoint the release of the prisoners."

The number of "insurgents" arrested—the official organ of the Colorado Party goes on to inform the reader—reached four hundred, practically the whole male population of Fram and part of Carmen. Through the subsequent "interrogation"—intimidation, torture, and beatings—police were able to identify the "ringleaders" and to reduce the original figure to one hundred according to the March 26, 1955, edition of *Patria*. These detainees were transported to Encarnación, and finally, fifteen of the most "dangerous" leaders of the "movement" were taken to Asunción—Vladimir Kuczer among them.

For the widowed Olga, the worst part of all is the torture that Vladimir suffered in Asunción. "They beat him and beat him. They put ice on him." The widow explains that long blocks of ice were strapped over the whole of Kuczer's body; as he neared the point of freezing to death, electric shocks were applied.

"Spit it out! Spit it out!!" they shouted at him. "But what could he possibly tell them if he didn't know anything? They just ruined his health—he never recovered. He was only forty-one when he died."

The poor man was beaten to death. Indeed, Stroessner and his horde were initiating with these colonists what they would later "perfect" with political opponents, and with any innocent who had the misfortune to fall into their hands.

The majority of the colonists who had come from the Soviet Union were in fact anticommunist. Although many had suffered the excesses of the tsarist regime, the Bolshevik revolution did not bring the redemption they had hoped for, and when, as discontents, they decided to emigrate, whole villages headed into China, traveling on foot through the Siberian steppes. Once in China, and finding themselves faced with the emergence of Mao Tse Tung's new system, they were forced to resume their march. This time they went to the Philippines, and from there by sea to an Italian port, to pick up a ship bound for São Paulo. From here they flew directly to the colony at Fram. The twin-engine aircraft that formed this original "shuttle service" landed in the middle of the forest; a part of the landing strip remains to this day. In just one day there might have been up to three flights, the last of them arriving late in the night. As it approached the improvised airport, the aircraft was guided by local amateur radio enthusiasts, the landing strip marked at either end by the headlights of a parked truck. A genuine odyssey. They suffered all this and other hardships in order to escape from communism: they had hardly come to Paraguay to replicate the Bolshevik experience.

Back Home

Kuczer left prison a very sick man. But as he did not feel moved to escape while he could—seeing that he had no reason to do so—he resolved to stay in Paraguay. He was dead within two years. Like almost all the other colonists, he left prison with broken ribs and dislocated arms and legs, his morale broken. Many suffered illnesses that were the direct consequence of the mistreatment they suffered in the dungeons in Asunción, and died soon after returning to their homes. "They didn't die of old age," says Olga, "they died young, like my husband, because of what they did to them in jail."

The Exodus

After the nightmare, however, others did decide to leave. "The exodus had an effect similar to that of a great storm," writes Zub. "It was noisy, sudden, and massive." The government added its part, by expelling some of the recently released colonists from the country. By this time all the settlers knew that the authorities would never leave them in peace: "Intimidated and harassed, they abandoned their belongings and fled the country in panic, never to return."

In their flight, and with what little they were able to take with them from the colony, they resorted to any means available to help them. A large number of them made use of the fragile boats that crossed the Paraná River. But fate was once again against them in their race to reach the Argentine side—they were attacked by the people who they thought would help them, or even drowned during the crossing.

History Repeats Itself

Paraguay has seen practically no organized foreign colonization. What little there was during the twentieth century was continually frustrated by "revolutions" or by armed militias protected, in most cases, by local parties or politicians. Settlers recall fearfully the "confiscations" of the 1922 civil war (many of which are documented in the registers of local justices of the peace), and the aggressions and violations of the Civil War of 1947, among many tragic incidents of Paraguay's "democratic skirmishes." All of these had the "virtue" of discouraging immigration to our country, even through projects organized privately, without government help, and under which the colonists who dared to come still faced all manner of hardship that brought back to them the trials and tribulations they had suffered in their own countries—precisely the suffering they had sought to leave behind. For most of them Paraguay was a dead end. Given the impossibility of reemigrating, the settlers sought refuge in silence. Curiously, a similar strategy was adopted by Stroessner, who would eventually impose the same silence on the rest of the Paraguayan people.

Be Careful, Dictator

Elvio Romero

Elvio Romero (1926–2004) is recognized as one of Paraguay's greatest poets. He was a member of the Generación del 40, along with Augusto Roa Bastos, Josefina Plá, and Hérib Campos Cervera. He joined the Communist Party and went into exile after the Civil War of 1947, forced to abandon what he termed "our profound land." Like many of Paraguay's greatest artists, he lived and wrote in exile throughout his life. His writing makes frequent reference to the flowers, trees, and birds of Paraguay but it is also socially and politically committed, addressing issues of poverty, repression, and inequality. In this sense, his poems at once reflect the pain of suffering and protest in exile as well as the constant hope for change.

This poem was written in 1960 at a time when exile opposition movements based in Argentina tried unsuccessfully to overthrow the Stroessner regime. It reflects the optimism of the time and the conviction that the days of the dictatorship were numbered. Indeed there was little to indicate that the rule of Stroessner would break the cycle of chronic political instability that had led to no fewer than thirty-four presidents between 1900 and 1954. In his first six years of government, Stroessner faced significant opposition from within the Colorado Party, as well as from unions and political opposition, and the first of a series of guerrilla incursions. Understandably, few predicted the longevity that would come to characterize his rule. However, Stroessner was highly adept in the field of political conspiracy and was aware of the dangers of the "concealed daggers lying in ambush" referred to in the poem.

This is a different fight, Dictator,
A different force.

Today, as the prisons shake
And flags ripple in a different wind
And the red horror of your torturers' slaughterhouse recedes,
Little remains of your arrogance.
Little is left to you;
Nothing more than that poor black pistol in your belt,
Cold in the premonition of what approaches.

Dictator:
No bayonet can stake out your sad shadow.

It is no use now.
It will be of no use that for a few coins
You sell our heritage, our bread, our homeland, what the people
hold—because it belongs to them—that prison dogs, bolts,
    and pickaxes guard you.
No use, the barbed wire fencing.
No use, the misery of military epaulettes.

Other horsemen, Dictator,
Are putting on their spurs.

Brave men and burning barricades,
Here the future is born
A future that still tastes of suffering,
Of dark foliage and bitter sadness,
Bravery, indignation.
And the pace of certain change quickens with every step!

Be careful, Dictator. A high sun
Rises burning at its edge,
A razor-sharp scythe,
A steel blade in the splendor of thundering captains,
An issue of charred valleys,
A question of blazing fires.

Be careful, Dictator. Your very shadow
Conceals daggers lying in ambush.
The dark slaughterhouse retreats.

The stars move in a different orbit, Dictator.

The Worm inside the Lotus Blossom

Graham Greene

The second half of the 1960s was the zenith of the Stroessner regime. The guerrilla incursions had been defeated, military discontent had been bought off by the parceling out of lucrative contraband activity, and political prisoners languished in jail outside the spotlight of the world community. The English novelist Graham Greene was one of the few foreign writers to visit Paraguay during this period, and the country would later feature in his Travels with My Aunt *(Harmondsworth, England: Penguin, 1972). In this article Greene describes the quiescent political and social scene, which superficially appeared so attractive to foreigners, but which thinly concealed simmering social tensions and a climate of fear under the dictatorship.*

The empty house was beautiful. Colonial in style, it had a great tiled terrace, and they assured me (but we had no keys) that there was a "marble bathroom." The garden stretched out below us for some 80 yards—shadowy with orange trees—some in fruit and some in blossom, lemon trees, grapefruit, palms; there were roses and jasmine and a great flare of pink lapacho flowers. After a good lunch with my two writer friends at the village inn, and several glasses of *caña*, I had reached the hour for day-dreams.

"How much would this house cost?" I asked them. The smell of orange fought the smell of jasmine as it had done every day since I had landed from the river boat in the capital. It was to the smell of orange blossom I woke every morning in my hotel, which had once been the house of Martha Lynch, the mistress of the monstrous López, and below my window a bush of jasmine grew blue and white flowers simultaneously.

One of my companions gave me the price in *guaranís*.

"About £3,000," I calculated. "Or nearly that. But what a staff one would need."

"Oh no, it could be run with one maid, a cook and a gardener."

"And that would cost a small fortune?"

Again he gave me the price in *guaranís*. "A week?"

"No, a month of course."

"Forty dollars a month!"

Somebody rode by on a horse, silent on the dirt road: our car was the only one we had seen in the village, and the stillness of the universal siesta lay among the garden trees. A few days earlier on the main road to the south, more than half of it unpaved, I had made my statistics between two towns, Carmen and San Ignacio, 105 kilometres apart. We had seen 26 cars, 24 horsemen, and 16 carts pulled by horse or oxen. The cars had only just won.

The elderly, cheerful, alcoholic writer, who told me that he began to drink at 9.30 in the morning, said he would like to end his days here in this house—it was his pipe-dream . . . but the difficulties of a writer in this country were immense.

"And yet there is no income tax?"

"No income tax, no."

"And no censorship?"

"Certain limits," he said, "are understood. One mustn't attack the President—or the United States, of course. But for a writer it is very difficult to save. We are a small country, there is much illiteracy."

"You write in Spanish. There's all the Spanish world."

"It's hard to find a publisher outside."

In this river-bounded inland country one thinks of the world always as outside. Richard Burton called Paraguay "the inland China," Cunninghame-Graham "a lost Arcadia." Now, of course, there are jet planes to the United States and Argentina, to supplement the railway built to the south by Englishmen in the 1860s with some of the old rolling stock still in use, and the river steamers which take four days and nights from Buenos Aires mounting against the current—the most suitable way to arrive, for on the wide Paraná river, between the low unchanging banks, one is gradually prepared.

It might seem daunting otherwise if one dropped down too quickly by jet from the noise and rush of Buenos Aires or New York into this land of deep tranquillity and the smell of flowers, where wind-blown oranges lie ungathered along the country roads. (They are three-a-penny in the market.) "A land where all things always seemed the same."

What price is the lotus-eater prepared to pay for his tranquillity? Here he will pay not in dollars for a luxury suite with double windows against the traffic (there is no traffic), only with the half-closed eye and the prudent pen: to live here one would be charged in the quite small currency of the conscience.

One price, of course, is life under a military dictator, but in Paraguay there have always been dictators, civilian, military, ecclesiastical, the cruel and the kind. In the 17th century there was the benevolent Communist rule of the Jesuit missions who protected the Indians from the Spaniards, so that the native language, Guaraní, endures to this day and it is imprudent as well as useless to speak Spanish in the countryside.

The magnificent red baroque churches, the size of cathedrals, lie in ruins on both sides of the great Paraná river with their slitted watchtowers erected against Spanish slavers raiding from San Paulo and the wide colonnaded plazas where the Indian labourers lived in front of the church doors. Spain drove the Jesuits out, but more than the ruins attest their kindly influence now [. . .]

The second dictatorship came after Independence when Doctor Francia cut Paraguay off from the world—the cruellest dictatorship of all, the dictatorship of El Supremo, an intellectual, a mathematician and astronomer, and an admirer of Voltaire and Rousseau, a crueller man even than Marshal Solano López, who in his senseless war with Argentina, Brazil and Uruguay, reduced the male population to less than 30,000.

Paraguayan historians are busy now rehabilitating López's name, perhaps because praise of a past dictator is a safe way of diminishing the stature of a present one. The bust of López stands in front of the government building which he built like a *bon marché* Louvre, the military academy carries his name in large letters across its façade and his body lies in the Heroes' Pantheon [. . .]

Constitutional rule was never very successful; after the disastrous war of Marshal López there were 32 presidents in Paraguay in 62 years; and in 1948, after six months' civil war, the Red Colorados (the Conservatives) became the only party. In the civil war it was the peasants and not the divided army, who had at least the excitement of action, that suffered most, and it was with relief they found themselves under a dictatorship again.

General Stroessner, who in August celebrated the beginning of his third period of power, has the air of a fleshy, good-humoured and astute owner of a beer cellar who knows his customers well and can manage them. In his third term he is able to relax. There are ugly stories of his early days, of opponents thrown from aeroplanes into the forest and bodies washed up with bound hands on the Argentine bank of the Paraná—the dead are always lucky. Perhaps 150 political prisoners have been lying in the cells of police stations up and down the country for ten years or more, forgotten by all but their families and an occasional priest.

The ruling party is the Colorado and the Colorado is General Stroessner. The army and the political party, as in a Communist state, are closely integrated, and on the party's annual celebration I could have believed I was in a Communist state, for red was everywhere. The peasantry wore red scarves, the bourgeoisie more shyly bore a red handkerchief in the breast-pocket or sometimes a handkerchief carried in the hand like a passport. There was no blue (the sign of the Liberal party) to be seen anywhere.

Peasants poured noisily into town on horseback and in buses with their red favours—it was like a note of warning to the Liberals who had been allowed this year to fight an election and win a proportion of seats. If the strong man was not there, these crowds of *caña*-drinking peasants seemed to indicate, whose life would be safe?

If you can afford that old colonial house, with a cook, a housemaid and a gardener for 40 dollars a month, it's just as well to carry a red handkerchief when you walk in the street that day and forget the troublemakers in prison and the malnutrition you might find among the scrap-heap huts perched on the red cliffs of Asunción in the shadow of the white Shell bastions like the hovels which clung against the walls of a medieval castle [. . .]

"This is nothing," my host said, raising his head for a moment from his third steak, "I eat eight kilos a day." The better to forget—forget charity, forget curiosity, forget ambition.

A quarter of the population is said to live abroad, some of course for political reasons, like their finest writer, Roa Bastos, but most from frustration at home. I spoke to a dozen young students [. . .] They were curious about the outside world; they asked questions about Fidel Castro ("We only hear one side in the newspapers") and the Pope's Encyclical—their real ambition was simply to get "outside."

For inside, apart from a job as a Colorado man, only one career is really open to talent—smuggling—which, after the growing of *yerba mate* and the raising of cattle, is Paraguay's chief industry. On the Paraguayan side of the border it is quite a legal occupation. Whisky and American cigarettes are flown down from Panama "in transit" and transferred at the international airport under the eyes of the police and customs to private planes. A token transit tax having been paid, the planes, many of them Dakotas, then set off to the Argentine, landing on this or that estancia near Buenos Aires.

Sometimes they crash and scatter cigarettes over the countryside, sometimes, when the local police are dissatisfied with their rake-off, they are seized and the pilot ends in prison—there is enough excitement to attract a man of enterprise, and there are high, quick profits. A proportion of the smuggled goods always remains behind (the customs are not particular), and you can buy whisky openly in Asunción cheaper than in any other capital, while small boys sell the smuggled cigarettes on the steps of the Ministry of Defence itself—as the President wisely says, the commerce keeps them out of worse mischief.

Across all the frontiers there is trouble: serious trouble in Bolivia, student riots in Brazil, uneasiness in Argentina, general strikes and kidnappings in Uruguay. Paraguay is almost as cut off from the world outside as in the days of Doctor Francia. Not even the flying saucers which are reported daily in the newspapers and on the Saturday radio of Buenos Aires penetrate across the Paraná, and the tourists—they spend 48 hours in Asunción, visit the Iguazú Falls and move on. A few Jewish agents arrive looking for war criminals in the German colonies around Encarnación, but they get no help from anyone. No one here wants to stir up trouble.

There are no political demonstrations—except for the Colorado party—no students' protest. "It would be impossible here," a student told me sadly. The Communist Party is illegal: no one waves the little Red Book. I spoke to some members of the new Christian-Democrat movement (they have not yet been accepted as a political party): well-meaning men and women of the left, scholars and university teachers, they are not the stuff of revolutionaries. One of them even admitted to me that the military dictatorship allied with the Colorado party was the best government they could expect at the present cultural level.

To exchange Red for Blue periodically, as in the old days, would make no difference at all.

Only the Church (and the Jesuits in particular) seems sometimes to threaten the surface of the still pool. A priest said to me: "The new movement in the Church makes the President uneasy. He got on well with the old monsignors, but now he doesn't understand what is happening." Stories of Camilo Torres, the priest shot with the guerrillas in Colombia, seep over the frontier—he is the Catholic equivalent of Che Guevara.

The Jesuits in Asunción have instituted what is called an Open Mass, with Guaraní music played by harp and guitar, when sermons are preached by lay members of the congregation. On one occasion a student in his sermon criticised the President for spending money on a visit to the United States while children in his own country were dying of malnutrition. The police that time arrested the wrong student, who spent two days in prison. Priests' telephones are sometimes tapped: sometimes they are followed by agents . . .

[. . .]

I think again and again of the house in the sweet-scented garden in the land where oranges lie ungathered and no one pays income tax. Only 150 men in the police station cells to forget and the children dying of malnutrition—no evil comparable at all to the wholesale massacres in Biafra and Vietnam. Perhaps if one were sufficiently fond of beef . . .

A Short History of the
Northern Ache People

Kim Hill

The Ache are a tribe of forest Indians in eastern Paraguay. They eschewed seden-
tary agriculture in favor of a seminomadic existence engaged in hunting, fishing,
and honey-collecting and had resisted contact with outsiders for centuries. But be-
tween 1965 and 1975, they were "pacified" during the rapid deforestation of the Alto
Paraná. This prompted widespread international condemnation of the Stroessner
regime for tolerating the "genocide" of the Ache. The U.S. anthropologist Kim Hill
is the leading authority on the Ache. Here he traces their tragic history at the hands
of outsiders who have invaded their world, abused their rights, and decimated their
population, and highlights the seemingly insurmountable legal challenges that the
Ache continue to face in their struggle to obtain title to just a fraction of their origi-
nal land.

The Ache are an ethnolinguistic group whose language and culture is
related to the Guaraní of eastern Paraguay. Although "Ache" is the self-
denomination of these people, Guaraní speakers have called them "Guayakí." The Ache are linguistically, culturally, and biologically distinct from
the Guaraní. Early descriptions emphasized their white skin, light eye and
hair color, beards, Asiatic features, and practice of cannibalism (a typical
Tupi-Guaraní trait) as identifying characteristics. Their subsistence practices and technology were considered extremely simple and nomadism
made them secretive and evasive. Recent genetic studies have demonstrated
their genetic dissimilarity from the Guaraní and most other lowland South
American Indians.

From the earliest Jesuit accounts of the Ache in the 1600s until their permanent peaceful outside contact in the twentieth century the Northern
Ache were nomadic hunter-gatherers living in small bands and depending
entirely on wild forest resources for subsistence. In the twentieth century
four different ethnolinguistic populations of Ache were contacted and paci-

fied. They are the Northern Ache, the Yvytyruzú Ache, the Ypety Ache, and the Ñacunday Ache. Each of these populations was an endogamous dialectal group, consisting of multiple residential bands and no peaceful interaction between them. The largest Ache group, the Northern Ache, resided in the region between the San Joaquin Hills (Coronel Oviedo) and the Paraná River, and centered between modern-day Curuguaty and Salto del Guairá.

The Contact Period

After the expulsion of the Jesuits from Paraguay in 1768 there is no further information about the Ache until the end of the nineteenth century and early twentieth century, when several writers related the knowledge of local Paraguayan populations concerning the Ache (but none observed them directly). In 1959, after decades of persecution, the Ypety Ache were contacted in modern-day Caazapá and pacified by Manuel de Jesus Pereira. Pereira then used Ypety Ache guides to track down, contact, and pacify the Yvytyruzú Ache in the Guairá department in 1963. Both groups together numbered only about one hundred individuals when contacted.

Between 1963 and 1968 more than half of the Ache who had been recently pacified perished from disease while under Pereira's supervision. Despite the Ache deaths, and numerous reports of abuse, Pereira was given an honorary title of *coronel* in the Paraguayan army (Indian affairs were then under the supervision of the defense ministry) and provided with a monthly salary and funds for Ache food, clothing, and medicine. Reports indicate that almost none of the money was used to help the Ache. Instead Pereira embezzled the assistance, and rented out Ache men as field hands and women as prostitutes.

Meanwhile, colonial settlement was beginning to take place in the Curuguaty and Alto Paraná regions and the Northern Ache began to feel the pinch. Until the 1960s Curuguaty had been isolated and could be reached only by horse trail from San Estanislao. But in the mid-1960s, an ambitious road project began (funded by the U.S. government and international agencies) that connected Coronel Oviedo and San Estanislao to the river town of Salto de Guairá, passing through the village of Curuguaty. This road, completed in 1968, passed directly through the heart of Northern Ache territory and sealed their fate.

From the early twentieth century to pacification in the 1970s, the Northern Ache were constantly persecuted by Paraguayan colonists, loggers, and ranchers. Ache bands were systematically raided with the intention of killing the men, and capturing women and children. Ache children were sold openly in the region as late as the 1970s (something we personally observed). Systematic interviews show that eighty-five Northern Ache were killed in these raids and seventy-four women and children were kidnapped and sold or used as forced labor throughout the region. Only a handful of these individuals were ever returned to the Ache tribe after reservations were established. Most of the captured and purchased Ache were openly displayed by their owners who described them with the Paraguayan term *criado*, which means "the one that I raised." The last large raid took place at Silva Cué in August 1971 near the ranch settlement of "Naranjito." Four Northern Ache were killed and six children were taken captive and sold to third parties. Only one of the captured children was ever returned to the Ache.

Because of increasing hostile encounters with Northern Ache during the construction of the Salto de Guairá road, Manuel Pereira requested the creation of a new Ache reservation (Colonia Nacional Guayakí) in 1968, with himself named as "director." He moved with the Ypety and Yvytyruzú Ache to a site called "Cerro Morotí" in modern Caaguazú in order to track down and pacify the Northern Ache. In October, 1970, several Ache from the Cerro Morotí reservation were attacked while hunting. They routed their attackers using newly acquired shotguns, and captured a Northern Ache woman who was taken back to Cerro Morotí. At that time, when all Northern Ache bands still roamed free in the forest, there were approximately 560 individuals in the population. Within a month the captured Northern Ache woman led Pereira's tame Ache to her residential band, and the forest group was "persuaded" to move to the Cerro Morotí reservation in order to receive protection from "Papa Pereira." Twenty-four of the twenty-six adults in that band walked to Cerro Morotí from the headwaters region of the Acaray River, while two adults set out to spread the news to other Northern Ache bands. Within a year ten of the newly contacted adults had died from respiratory disease.

Between 1971 and 1978 at least ten different contact and extraction events of forest-dwelling Northern Ache took place. In this way the entire Northern Ache population was taken from the forested regions of Alto Paraná, Canindeyú, and Caaguazú, and moved to government- or missionary-sponsored reservations in the 1970s. A high percentage of those taken to the Cerro Morotí government-sponsored reservation (officially named the "Colonia Nacional Guayakí") died from respiratory epidemics within two years after first peaceful contact. In addition several large bands fled from contact and suffered almost total mortality in the forest. This included nearly all the followers of Betapa Vachugi and Krombe Pougi, two of the most powerful Ache leaders in the late twentieth century. The final free-living Ache band, which had fled from contact in 1972, 1973, and 1974, finally surrendered to fellow Ache in April 1978 at Carpa Cué inside the Mbaracayú Forest Reserve (MFR).

Detailed demographic data on the Northern Ache population (based on extensive interviews with survivors) shows that 38 percent of the population died from contact-related respiratory disease during this time period.[1] This included sixty-eight individuals who ran away from contact and died in the forest; ninety-three individuals who died at Cerro Morotí (Colonia Nacional Guayakí) under the supervision of Coronel Pereira and New Tribes Missionaries; twenty individuals who died at Colonia Manduví under supervision of "Divine Word" Catholic Missionaries; seventeen individuals who died in Laguna Pacová waiting for a truck to Cerro Morotí; and one individual who died at Colonia Mboi Jaguá, supervised by the German Protestant Mission, after the 1978 contact. In addition, forty-nine individuals were kidnapped by Paraguayans during the contact process and taken forcibly to be used as unpaid laborers or to be exploited sexually.

Because of the Paraguayan history of massacres and enslavement of Northern Ache during the precontact period and the fact that nearly 50 percent of the population died from epidemics or were kidnapped during the contact period, several prominent Paraguayan and foreign anthropologists accused the Paraguayan government of "genocide" in 1972. Mark Münzel, Padre Bartomeu Melià, Miguel Chase Sardi, and Luigi Miraglia all spoke out publicly accusing the Paraguayan government of "genocide." The Catholic Church echoed their dismay. The matter was brought up in the Paraguayan parliament and rapidly led to an international outcry. In the mid 1970s, the charge of "genocide" against the Ache was investigated by the Organization of American States' Inter-American Commission Human Rights, several international human rights groups, the U.S. State Department, and the U.S. Congress. While later careful investigations by reputable anthropologists and human rights groups revealed no evidence of "systematic and intentional" extermination of the Ache, most knowledgeable individuals agreed that "de facto" genocide was taking place and the Paraguayan government had taken no significant steps to protect the Ache from abuse and preventable infectious epidemics that killed hundreds. The Paraguayan government responded in the newspaper *ABC Color* (May 9, 1974) by stating that "genocide" was not the appropriate label for the Ache situation because there was no "intention" of extermination. Because of the events described above many international human rights groups and scholarly researchers still consider the Paraguayan treatment of the Ache during the late twentieth century to constitute a modern example of "genocide."

However, detailed interviews with Ache informants showed that many of the facts presented in support of the genocide charge were erroneous.

Recent History

The postcontact history of the Northern Ache began in September 1972 with the chaos at Cerro Morotí following the arrest of Pereira for systematic abuse and the disappearance of funds meant for Ache assistance and the newly appointed administration of New Tribes Missionaries. Small groups left the reservation almost every day and dispersed along the new road from Santa Rosa Cué to the Carapá River. Many joined Pereira for a short time at Ybyrycuá and then left again. Some reentered the forest and many were persuaded or coerced to stay on as laborers in small Paraguayan settlements and isolated rural houses. The situation changed dramatically in 1974–75 when a Catholic priest, Father Nicolas de Cunha, began to systematically collect these refugees into another settlement, the Mission San Agustín, later located at "Chupa Pou" in August 1978. For the next twenty years the Chupa Pou mission grew into the largest Ache settlement in Paraguay, while at the Colonia Nacional in Cerro Morotí, the population decreased in size, lost most of its original land holdings, and, increasingly intermixed and intermarried with the neighboring Paraguayans.

THE KUETUVY ACHE

In 1991 the legal decree creating the Mbaracayú Forest Reserve (MFR) recognized it as traditional territory of the Northern Ache and gave them permanent hunting and collecting rights inside the reserve. The Kuetuvy Ache are descendants of bands that were extracted from Finca 470 area in 1972–74. They announced their intention to move back to their traditional homeland (Finca 470) and began the process of soliciting expropriation of the property. They resided just south of Finca 470 with the Guaraní Indian community of Takua Poty and waited for permission to occupy it. On December 11, 2000, they received official recognition as a community by the Paraguayan Indigenous Institute (INDI) and on June 25, 2001, they received status as a legally recognized entity.

Initially, the Fundación Moisés Bertoni (FMB) intended to purchase Finca 470 from its Taiwanese owner with funds raised in the United States, Taiwan, and other foreign countries and then transfer the title of the property to the Kuetuvy Ache as an "Indigenous Forest Reserve." In June 2000, the FMB made a verbal agreement with Kuetuvy leaders that included the development of a sustainable management plan and a promise not to cut more than 5 percent of the forest for residential areas and agriculture. The FMB carried out an evaluation of the property and on January 15, 2001, the Taiwanese property owner accepted its offer to purchase the property.

But, in the months following the initial agreement between the FMB and the Kuetuvy Ache, the Ministry of Public Works and the Environmental Secretariat (SEAM) began negotiating independently with the property owner to purchase Finca 470 as part of a conservation land quota required by the Interamerican Development Bank (IDB) in order to meet conditions for a IDB loan for the Highway 10 project in Canindeyú. The Taiwanese owner notified the FMB that he was no longer interested in selling the property to any NGO because the Paraguayan government had offered a price twice the actual land value. When the Kuetuvy leaders discovered that the government intended to purchase the property as part of a conservation easement plan, they immediately presented a formal "request" for expropriation to INDI and SEAM. Because the IDB contract specified that Finca 470 must remain as a forest reserve, the Ache began meeting with IDB officials to persuade them to support their claim, and to agree that the settlement would constitute an "indigenous reserve" thereby meeting the loan criteria. IDB officials commissioned a sustainable management plan, written in 2001, which later became the basis of a long-term project funded by Conservation International.

But in January 2001 clandestine loggers working for Brazilian sawmills invaded Finca 470, aided by "landless peasants" and several families of Guaraní Indians who promised to protect them if they cleared roads and allowed for subsequent settlement on the property. The loggers were evicted in December 2001 and the landless peasants were removed in July 2002 after armed Ache warriors patrolled the southern boundary of the territory.

Between July 2001 and late 2003 Ache leaders attended dozens of meetings with representatives of IDB, government agencies, and NGOs interested in supporting their claim to Finca 470, all of whom assured the Ache that the land would be titled to them once expropriated by the government. The strong support was based on the fact that the Ache were the ancestral inhabitants of Finca 470 and that they had developed a management plan that stipulated that it was to remain as a forest reserve. In early January 2002 the Kuetuvy Ache received permission from SEAM to occupy Finca 470 and they permanently settled the property on January 8, 2002.

In June 2002, the Ache began systematic conservation work on Finca 470 funded by Conservation International. During June–July 2002 there was a second attempted invasion of the property by so-called landless peasants. Ache leaders called the national press and government officials and organized a show of armed resistance which was attended by representatives of all six Ache reservations. Over two hundred warriors armed with bow and arrow stood along the border of the property near the campsite of the would-be peasant invaders. The event clearly demonstrated their resolve to protect the forests of their traditional homeland.

FINCA 470 AS THE KUETUVY INDIGENOUS RESERVE

On July 24, 2003, the political leaders of Kuetuvy gathered their community and all adult members signed a document requesting that INDI obtain the legal title to Finca 470 from SEAM and transfer it to the Ache community. They proposed to conserve a large area of forest where activities would include sustainable hunting, collection of edible fruits and insects, collection of medicinal plants, enrichment of the forest with commercially valuable native tree species such as yerba mate, and "minimal-impact" forestry based on long-cycle rotation and low-impact harvest and transport. The forestry-based products would be primarily destined for internal consumption in the form of houses, school buildings, and clinics.

SEAM supported the proposal and signed an Agreement of Inter-institutional Cooperation for five years with INDI and the Ache leaders on September 2, 2004. The first clause stated that "the purpose of this agreement is to cede temporary use rights of the SEAM property called Finca 470, in the District of Ygatimí, Department of Canindeyú, to INDI with the ultimate intention that the Ache Indigenous Community of Kuetuvy can continue their customary subsistence activities, in agreement with principles of nature conservation. This taking into account that Finca 470, object of this agreement, is a forestry reserve of biological and botanical resources, considered part of the 'lungs' of the Atlantic Interior Forest, and located inside the buffer zone of the MFR. In this way we hope to establish mechanisms to guarantee the joint process of transferring land rights of Finca 470 to the native peoples located in that place, and in observance with the National Constitution and laws 352/94, 904/94, and 234/93."

In March 2005 the Ache presented a formal management plan for Finca 470 to SEAM, which it accepted in a reply dated May 3, 2005, and also agreed to begin the process of transfer of title from SEAM to the Kuetuvy Ache. Soon afterwards, on August 19, SEAM formally requested the Office of the President of the Republic to carry out the administrative processes necessary in order that the State Notary, INDI, and the Ache work together to guarantee success in the process of transferring the title of Finca 470 to the Ache Community of Kuetuvy.

Despite this 2005 request, no significant steps have been taken since then to further the land titling process. Instead, the Ache have fought endless battles against illegal loggers, speculators, and so-called landless peasants. In December 2005 the chief of the Kuetuvy community was arrested and imprisoned in Curuguaty along with members of the forestry patrol team who had tried to stop illegal loggers from extracting valuable hardwood trees from the property. During the following years SEAM officials confiscated approximately $70,000 worth of illegally cut timber that was removed and sold, but those funds were not used for protection of the property. Instead, all boundary defense and conservation of the forested property has been carried out directly by the Ache with outside funding from Conservation International.

Conclusion

The Ache have suffered unspeakable abuses by rural Paraguayan colonists, ranchers, and big landowners from the conquest period to the twentieth century. In recent times they have been massacred, enslaved, and gathered on to reservations where no adequate medical treatment was provided. This process was specifically carried out to pacify them and remove them from their ancestral homeland so that absentee investors (mainly Brazilian) could move in and develop the lands that once belonged only to them. At the beginning of the twentieth century the Northern Ache were the only inhabitants of nearly 20,000 square kilometers, yet by its end they were confined on two reservations totaling little more than 50 square kilometers of titled land. The fact that the Paraguayan government has never recognized the large-scale theft of Ache lands and forced displacement of Ache people is reprehensible. That the Paraguayan government has never rectified this situation or offered any compensation for these crimes is morally pathetic. But these actions have been consistently funded through loans by international aid agencies that are also to blame.

The Kuetuvy Ache were forcibly removed from the Mbaracayú region in the 1970s but managed to return to their ancestral homeland in 2000. Since that time they have begged, urged, and demanded that the government provide them with a piece of their ancestral homeland, but all to no avail. On Feb 10, 2004, religious and political leaders from Kuetuvy met with then president Nicanor Duarte Frutos, who assured them that they would receive title to Finca 470. They also met repeatedly with IDB officials who assured them that they would monitor Paraguayan government compliance with the conditions for the Highway 10 loan. Still nothing happened. Instead the Ache have heard one excuse after another concerning why the land cannot be titled until some other administrative or political hurdle has been cleared. They have been asked repeatedly to be patient in waiting for their human rights to be respected, in waiting for the Paraguayan government to comply with international law and to rectify the pilfering of their lands and the near extermination of their people. Meanwhile each month new incursions to the property are detected and always with the same intention—namely, clandestine deforestation and extraction of valuable hardwood trees.

Epilogue

In March 2010 SEAM canceled all prior agreements with the Ache and announced that it would divide Finca 470 between the resident Ache and nonresident Ava Guaraní communities that had previously claimed a portion of the land. Despite the fact that the Ache provided extensive documentation that this area was Ache ancestral territory and had not been inhabited by the Ava, SEAM refused to budge. In March 2011 the Ache organized a large protest in front of SEAM headquarters in Asunción. Subsequently the Paraguayan Congress voted overwhelmingly to transfer the title of Finca 470 to the Ache alone, and without cost. But in May 2011 President Lugo vetoed this law, citing the advice of his minister of environment. The veto was then overridden in August 2011 by a new vote of Congress. It remains to be seen whether the Paraguayan government will respect this law and comply with the titling process.

Note

1. These data are published in Kim Hill and Ana Magdalena Hurtado, *Ache Life History: The Ecology and Demography of Foraging People* (New York: Aldine de Gruyter, 1996).

The Testimony of Saturnina Almada

María Saturnina Almada (1924–) is a textile worker who was incarcerated by the Stroessner dictatorship in 1968 and held for more than thirteen years. The following extract is the harrowing account of her imprisonment, based on her own testimony. Imprisoned for her role as a unionist and for supporting political prisoners, María endured years of physical and psychological torture and deprivation before finally going into exile in Germany. As she states in her testimony, "In Paraguay, there is no need for any explanation to arrest someone, fire them, or throw them out of the country. The state only has to accuse them of being a subversive or communist to justify repression."

On Sunday, January 28, 1968, twenty plainclothes policemen arrived at her home. She was alone in the house. They said they were looking for her husband, Alfonso Silva Quintana, but she later learned that they had already arrested him. They ransacked the house and then arrested her. Thus began her long journey through the jails and concentration camps of the dictatorship.

She was initially taken to the Department of Investigations. There the interrogations began, along with the punches and kicks. They wanted to know what political organization she belonged to, who the leader was, and who she was working with in Paraguay. Above all, they wanted names. When she refused to reply in spite of the beatings, they tortured her. At that time, torture was carried out in offices located on Presidente Franco Street, as there were very few passers-by after about 7 PM.

Pastor Coronel, the head of the Department of Investigations, interviewed her personally. He advised her to tell him everything she knew, promising that nothing would happen to her if she did. He presented her with a document stating that her husband was a leader of the Communist Party and that there were plans to assassinate all of the heads of the government and their children. He demanded she sign it. He told her that if she signed she would be released and provided with work and protection by the police, as the communists would want to kill her. Tina repeatedly stated that she did not belong to any political party and that she was not afraid to die, but that she would not sign the document because the allegations were totally false. Pastor Coronel replied that if she did not sign the document, she would leave prison on crutches, to which Tina replied: "If I have to walk on crutches because I told the truth then I'll walk on crutches."

Coronel ordered her to be taken away, and she was brought before the head of the Secret Police, a man called Sánchez, renowned for his violence. He told her, "Stupid old woman—what d'you want to defend a guilty man for? You'd be better off cooperating with us." Tina replied that she would not cooperate with enemies of the people. She was taken away and tortured. This time she was allowed to see her husband, who had been badly beaten. They tortured each in the presence of the other. At one stage, between bouts of agony, she said that she had nothing to say because she knew nothing. That made her feel stronger. When they took her to the Police Clinic, covered in blood, there was not a single inch of her body that had not been beaten. They made her stand facing a wall for eight days, with her feet swollen from the torture. If she fell asleep they hit her ears with both hands (a torture they referred to as "the telephone"), a process that has left her hearing damaged to this day.

She spent twenty-two days in Investigations under physical and psychological torture. The worst thing for her was seeing the other prisoners dragging themselves across the floor, feet and hands tied, their whole bodies covered in cuts and bruises. Over and over she told herself that she was human, that she could endure it. She did not know whether the torturers were acting out of conviction or whether they were drugged, and she has often wondered since how it is possible that a person you have never harmed can beat you and treat you with such hatred.

Then she was taken to Police Station No. 1 in Asunción, where she remained for a year and seven months with no formal charges against her or judicial process begun. She was put with two other women who had already spent two and three years respectively in the same cell. In the adjoining cell lay a woman, Gilberta Verdún de Talavera, who had been there eight years charged with guerrilla activity, and was clearly mentally unstable. They had cut her husband's throat in front of her during the repression against the 14th May and the fulna guerrilla movements in 1960. She was in such a terrible state that the other three women kept up a hunger strike for thirty-three days in April and May, demanding that she be freed, which, finally, she was.

The police commissioner, Fretes Farías, treated them brutally. Every day he found new ways of persecuting them to keep them in a state of permanent psychological torture. The cell was narrow and damp, situated next to a gully. There were no beds, so they had to sleep on the floor on a folded

blanket. There was no toilet or water, and they could only relieve themselves when they were taken to the latrine in the gully, sometimes in the
middle of the night in complete darkness. Commissioner Fretes Farías ordered their cell to be turned over every two days. The guards humiliated
the women, rifling through their personal belongings, even waving their
underwear around like flags. They made them take down all the nails from
the walls where they hung bags with all their belongings in them; there was
no furniture. Sometimes, they did not take the women to the latrine for
several days. The women were forced to relieve themselves in empty dried
milk tins or in bottles that they threw out of the window into the gully. The
sergeant would amuse himself by rattling the bars of the cell, and when he
took them to the latrine, he would hold his pistol against their heads.

Visits from family members would last for less than a minute; when they
had scarcely been able to greet each other, an officer would arrive to say
that the visit was over. Tina had an aunt who traveled a long way to visit
her, but each time she came, Commissioner Fretes Farías turned her away.
Sometimes the guards refused to pass on to the prisoners food that visitors
brought; they made them take it back home with them. Other times they
would break everything on the pretext of looking for hidden weapons. The
commissioner even used to go into the cells and just empty out the jars of
coffee and sugar onto the floor.

Then they were moved to a cell in the police station in Fernando de
la Mora, eight kilometers from Asunción. When they climbed out of the
truck, they saw three men who they knew to be political prisoners being
brought out of a small cell. They looked as if they were emerging from a
cave. The women were put in the cell, which measured twelve square meters. It had an earth floor, and the humidity was unbearable. They had a toilet in the cell but there were no beds. The previous prisoners had made beds
out of old newspapers to avoid having to sleep on the ground. The women
were delighted to find the newspapers: in the nineteen months that they
had been in Station No. 1 they had not seen a piece of paper, nor a pencil;
both were strictly forbidden. If their families brought them sugar or yerba
mate wrapped in paper they had to pour it out onto a plate or into a jar and
the paper was confiscated. The isolation there had been absolute. Even the
officers were forbidden from turning up the volume on their radios to make
sure the prisoners wouldn't hear anything.

They had to live there, sleeping on the floor, in the humidity, with the
toads that would wander in and the cockroaches that would find their way
into their clothes and make them jump up screaming in the night. With
no water in the cell, they couldn't wash, and they were only occasionally

allowed outside to wash in the water from a well contaminated with oil that dripped from the pump, and infested with cockroaches. The heat in summer was unbearable and they slept with wet cloths over their faces in an attempt to relieve the suffocating heat.

In 1972, Stroessner allowed the International Red Cross to visit prisons where political prisoners were held. Through their mediation, the prisoners obtained the right to a bed, a small window in each cell, a fifteen-minute family visit and an hour outside each day.

On September 6, 1976, they were taken to the concentration camp at Emboscada, a former prison for minors, with thick, high walls, about forty kilometers from Asunción. More than five hundred prisoners, including ten babies and twenty-five children under fourteen, were crowded into twenty-four cells. There was even a seventy-eight-year-old grandmother there, with all her daughters-in-law and grandchildren, the entire families of her four sons, the López brothers from Misiones, who had been "disappeared."

In February 1978 Tina was released, under a torrent of threats and without ID papers. Her husband was freed in March along with many other peasants in groups of twenty or thirty. They tried to begin a new life after ten years of imprisonment without charge or judicial process. Her husband found work as a tailor. An aunt gave her a sewing machine and she began to work in their new home. However, on May 8, 1979, agents from the Department of Investigations called once again. Just like the first time, they took her and her husband to Investigations, where the interrogation began. When they asked her why she had allowed ex-prisoners into her house, she replied that they were like brothers to her, that they had been imprisoned together for so many years, and they knew each better than anyone else. When they asked why she visited three of the last prisoners still held at Station No. 3 in Asunción, she said that they had been held prisoner for nearly sixteen years and had no one else to visit them; she felt she had to do something for them, and took them medicine, and anything else they needed. The visits were always in the presence of police officers and with their full authority, and she had nothing to hide. Yet this was deemed a crime. "They accused me of offering 'logistical support' to the prisoners. I didn't know what that meant—we weren't at war and I'd never kept a gun or anything like that."

She was interrogated for almost a month at Investigations. "One day they sent me to the Central Police Station and I found out there that they were sending me to the Buen Pastor [a prison for women convicted of common crimes] and my husband was going to Tacumbú [the national penitentiary for common criminals]. They pressed charges against us both for the first time." During the trial, which lasted for two and a half years, she was accused of belonging to the Communist Party, of engaging in subversive activity, of aiding political prisoners, and of having traveled to the Soviet Union. In 1981 she and her husband were each sentenced to four years and ten months in prison. Her own sentence was reduced to three years on appeal, but her husband's was upheld—it was considered irrelevant that he had already spent ten years in prison without trial. The attorney general, Clotilde Jiménez, judged that he had not yet "recovered" sufficiently to reintegrate into society and rejected any further appeals.

On May 20, 1982, dirty and with her head thumping, having not eaten or washed for four days, Tina was taken across the border to the Federal Police Station in Foz de Iguazú, Brazil, and handed over to a young police officer. He was ordered to take her to São Paulo, where she had relatives. And she was told never to even think of returning to Paraguay.

An Interview with Corsino Coronel

*The Ligas Agrarias Cristianas (*LAC*)—Christian Peasant Leagues—was a coopera-*
tive movement among small farmers that arose in the 1960s, first appearing in the
Department of Misiones, the location of the former Jesuit missions. It represented
the first signs of independent political action by the Paraguayan campesinos. *Its*
inspiration came from two sources within the church. The first of these was the
urban-based Christian Democrat trade union body, Central Cristiana de Traba-
*jadores (*CCT*), which had been active in the formation of peasant cooperatives and*
which, in January 1968, organized the first congress of the Federación Cristiana
*Campesina (*FCC*). A second, more radical wing also emerged under the influence of*
progressive Jesuit and Franciscan missionaries. Loosely grouped in the Federación
*Nacional de Ligas Agrarias Cristianas (*FENELAC*), this organization emphasized*
the autonomy of grassroots communities, known as comunidades de base, *and*
the role of popular education in the process of social change.

By 1970 the LAC *had a national membership of ten thousand families, divided*
roughly equally between the FCC *and* FENELAC, *and organized in a regional network*
of ligas (leagues). The rapid growth of the LAC *began to sap traditional support for*
the ruling Colorado Party, upon which the rural stability of the Stroessner regime
depended. This political threat provided the backdrop to a sharp deterioration in
relations between the government and the Catholic hierarchy in 1969 and mounting
repression against the LAC *thereafter. Torture and imprisonment of peasant leaders,*
destruction of base communities, deportation of progressive clergy, and a media
campaign denouncing communist infiltration of the church ensued. In response, the
two wings of the LAC *came together in August 1971 in a new unitary organization,*
*the Coordinación Nacional de Bases Campesinas Cristianas (*KOGA*), but this was*
unable to halt the mounting repression. The repression reached a peak in April and
May 1976 when the government accused the LAC *of involvement in an embryonic*
*guerrilla movement, the Organización Primero de Marzo (*OPM*). Almost all the* LAC*s*
became inoperative as over 2,500 peasants were arrested in a series of raids through-
out the country, and twenty leaders were killed. Corsino Coronel, a leader of the
movement in Misiones, provides the following personal testimony of the suffering
endured by its activists.

Peasant League booklet. The pioneering use of educational materials in Guaraní by the peasant *ligas agrarias* movement was severely repressed during the Stroessner regime. These pages are taken from a publication commemorating the struggle of the Costa Puku base community in the Department of Misiones, the birthplace of the movement. Page 24 highlights the various elements of the work of the organization in improving the health, education, credit, and communal labor among its members. In contrast, page 25 recalls the efforts of the local authorities to identify and arrest its leaders. Image by C. E. B. Costa Puku, San Ignacio Misiones, from the book *Tekojoja Rekávo*, by C. E. B. Costa Puku, San Ignacio Misiones, 1990. Used by permission of the Centro de Documentación y Archivo "Casa de las Víctimas," San Ignacio Misiones.

"I'm happy, *compañero* Meaurio, that you have come to my farm here in Acaray Costa, in the depths of the Department of Alto Paraná. This place is part of the history of my life and of my family.

"I started working with the Peasant Leagues in 1962, soon after I got married. At that time I was in Potrero Alto, a hamlet of Santa Rosa. We started the League with our neighbors. We set up a Peasant School and a consumer cooperative, and we marketed our produce together.

"At that time I was a local activist and I took my first leadership course in 1963, in Itacurubí de la Cordillera. It was then that I really began to understand the problems that the peasantry faced and I became committed to the struggle. I saw it not just as a political obligation but also a duty as a Christian, as a way to improve our standard of living.

"In 1972 we had the idea of creating a Base Christian Community. We started with twelve families. We moved from where we were to form a small community in Potrero Alto. We lived there for a time trying to put into practice a new model of society, but we couldn't maintain it for long because we were all poor and we realized that the prevailing social situation wouldn't allow it. Nor did we have the financial resources that were needed for such an experiment. After that we formed the FERELAC, the regional federation of Peasant Leagues in Misiones, and I became a regional leader."

"How many base communities sent representatives to the Itacurubí meeting?"

"People came from FENELAC and from the Federación Cristiana Campesina (FCC). FCC covered the costs of the course and invited us all. All together there were representatives from thirteen communities at that meeting."

"Do you remember the names of compañeros who were with you there?"

"Yes, for example, Juan Félix Martínez, also someone called Alcaraz, Ladislao Solís, Rodolfo Romero. The course coordinator was a priest from Carapeguá (Father Acha Duarte, who has since died). Anselmo Romero, another activist from Misiones, was also there."

"How did the leadership operate in Misiones?"

"We started the Ligas in Santa Rosa. Then we spread them to San Patricio, Santa María, San Ignacio, San Juan Bautista, and even as far as San Ramón. We already had five base communities when we set up the regional federation, FENELAC. In order to do that, we held a big meeting and democratically elected our leadership. I was elected to the executive committee. In 1972 Monsignor Bogarín, bishop of Misiones, donated his farm to FENELAC so that we could use it as our headquarters. The federation entrusted the farm to me, to live there with all my family. At that time I had a house in Potrero Alto. After we moved to the farm, I was arrested several times. Even before that, they had arrested me once during a demonstration that we had organized. I was kept in isolation for seventeen days before they released me. And then the torture began. After moving to San Juan Bautista in 1973, I was rearrested because of my leadership role in the federation. I was taken to the Office of the Government Delegate in Misiones, where they tortured me with electricity, using a bare wire. It was Police Inspector Barrios who tortured me. The *compañeros* associated with the federation organized a demonstration demanding my release and thanks to them I was freed.

"During 1974 and 1975 we worked unhindered in the regional federation, making quite a lot of progress. We arranged joint marketing of produce, as well as holding group training courses. My wife worked on setting up a regional women's organization. We also arranged for mutual support between these different branches within the federation.

Peasant League demonstration. This rare photograph shows a public demonstration by the Christian-based *ligas agrarias* movement in 1970 in protest at the kidnapping of a priest by the Stroessner regime. Photograph by Andrew Nickson.

"Then in 1976 a wave of repression was launched to crush the Peasant Leagues. I was in San Juan Bautista at the time. Police officers came from Asunción to arrest me, accompanied by agents from the Office of the Government Delegate. A police inspector called Julio César Guillén was then the head of the Police Department of Investigations. He said to one of his officers, 'Take the opportunity of all this commotion and get rid of that communist, who has already caused me such a headache.' And when I was arrested, it was that officer who shot at me several times. Two bullets hit me. I was lucky because he shot quickly and didn't manage to kill me.

"Then they tied my hands and feet and took me the same night to the Department of Investigations in Asunción. At around 1:00 AM they took me before its chief, Pastor Coronel. Two of them started to torture me with whips. Even Pastor Coronel hit me and ordered his men to do the same, because it seems that he didn't want to be the only one doing it. They beat me from 1:00 AM until seven in the morning. Then they ordered me to strip (it was winter) and started to kick me. They knocked me to the ground and then they put me in a cell in the Department of Vigilance and Crimes. There I found several *compañeros* trembling in the cold, naked and covered in cuts and bruises. Melquiades Alonso was one of them. Every night they took us somewhere else to torture us and then brought us back to the cell at dawn.

"We were there for twenty days. Then they tied us up and transported us back to Misiones. They called together all the activists and exhibited us like trophies. Abraham-Cué was the name of the new prison, where we were kept in handcuffs. There were no seats at all and we were hardly fed—and the punishments never ceased.

"One night they called together eight of the prisoners—the chosen ones were the four López brothers, Rogelio Pinto, a *compañero* called Rodas, Sergio Espinoza, and myself. They said to us, 'You are all going to be freed.' Then out of the group they called back Espinoza and myself. 'You still have a matter outstanding with me,' said Sapriza, the torturer, and he took us back to be beaten again. And while we were being tortured, the other six disappeared. To this day, no one knows what happened to them. There are rumors that they were killed and buried close by. That's how two out of those eight 'chosen ones' survived.

"Then we were taken back to Asunción. In the Department of Investigations they shaved our heads and kept us in the so-called round cell. I lived in that cell for five months with seventy-three other prisoners. Quite a few of them died from the torture and others died of hunger. For five months I lived with my hands tied behind my back. I had to sleep like that, I had to dress like that and I had to eat like that. I even got used to it. They shaved our heads with a razor as an additional part of the torture.

"In September they moved us to a concentration camp at Emboscada. There we were no longer kept indoors, but lived in the open, and were able to walk around. I was there for twenty-one months. I was released from Emboscada after a hunger strike lasting sixteen days. That was the price of my freedom.

"When I had first been arrested, the whole of my family had fled from the police. My wife had nine young children with her. They came here, where we are now, to the forest of the Alto Paraná. They settled on a piece of land with no other protection than the trees. And later my wife built a little house with her own hands. That first home that she built for her nine children is still here. She survived for the two years that I was in prison.

"After my release, I found them here. So we started again from scratch. We had nothing—the little that we had saved had been stolen from us by Montanaro, Stroessner, and Pastor Coronel. They were thieves. Because of them, my children's education was sacrificed—we had no income so they had to drop out of school. One day we may be able to get compensation but it's difficult. My children are all grown up. Perhaps they could have studied but it's too late now. And I'm still convinced that the organization of *campesinos* is the only alternative, so even now I am still fighting for that."

"Can you tell us something about your wife?"

"My wife is called Pablina Acosta. The children that are still with us are Eliazar, Moisés, Cristóbal, Salvador, and Jorge Javier. They're the youngest, that's why they are still with us. And the rest are married. Each one has their own place."

Apocalypse

Alfredo Boccia

The Organización Primero de Marzo (OPM) was an incipient guerrilla movement that was formed in the early 1970s by radical students seeking to overthrow the Stroessner regime. The movement underwent a rapid growth in the mid-1970s and links were forged with some members of the independent peasant movement, the Ligas Agrarias Cristianas (LAC), which emerged during the 1960s as a reaction to the unequal land tenure system. However, such growth also allowed the regime to infiltrate the movement, leading to the arrest of the leadership in April 1976, which in turn provided a pretext for a wave of repression that destroyed the OPM and was extended to many other opposition groups. Some twenty OPM members died in police custody and over 2,500 small farmers were arrested throughout the country. In the following extract, based on interviews with the survivors, Alfredo Boccia describes the regime's chance discovery of nearly the entire leadership of the OPM. In what at times borders on the tragicomic, the absence of any serious security measures within the movement is striking.

> April is like an ax. It has left deep scars in our history.
> —OPM document, "The People Will Triumph in Their Righteous Struggle"

In April 1976, Stroessner's police would obtain the first pieces of information regarding the existence of a clandestine organization. The chance arrest of Carlos Brañas and the women who were with him in Encarnación would unleash a dizzying chain of events which in turn would reveal the extraordinary level of control the regime had over the whole country.

Afternoon. Saturday, April 3, 1976. Department of Investigations of the Metropolitan Police, Asunción

The prisoner who had just arrived from Encarnación was received by the officers on duty, Francisco Ramírez and Isabelino Pino, who applied the customary treatment of the establishment: he was beaten, robbed of all personal possessions, and left *incomunicado* in a cell before being subjected to a first round of interrogation.

"At first I lied," recalls Brañas. "I told them I had to meet a person at the corner of Eligio Ayala and Estados Unidos."

Brañas then invented a second meeting opposite the Corposana water tower on Eusebio Ayala Avenue. At that the police ran out of patience, and set about subjecting him to the infamous bathtub, as well as beatings. That night the police would find out that a few weeks before Brañas had been in a house in Lambaré that belonged to the organization. Meanwhile, several members of the OPM were in Sajonia celebrating the marriage of Victor Hugo Ramos and Olga Spirindoff, completely unaware of what was happening.

Dawn. Sunday, April 4. Valle Apuá, Lambaré

There had been a meeting in the house of Martín Rolón the night before, which Juan Carlos Da Costa and other leaders of the OPM had attended. At dawn, Martín went out in the Citroen, with Da Costa driving. He returned at 10 PM. In the house, apart from Martín, were his wife, Estela Jacquet, their three children, and her brother, Melchor.

The raid happened while they were asleep. The police arrived in force but Martín and Melchor returned fire. There was an intense gunfight, during which part of the house caught fire. Martín was killed in the exchange of fire, but Melchor managed to flee into the darkness firing his .38 revolver, and hid in undergrowth until late the next day. Police Captain Gustavo Giménez suffered minor wounds. The police found the first OPM documents in two powdered milk tins. Estela Jacquet was arrested and taken to the Department of Investigations, where she was brutally tortured. Martín's body was never handed over to his family, who maintain until this day that Martín was seen alive later in the Department of Investigations. Nor did the "Archive of Terror" shed any light on his death.

Morning. Sunday, April 4. Department of Investigations, Asunción

The whole of the police hierarchy was summoned to examine the information that had been gathered from the interrogations of Brañas and Estela Jacquet. Pastor Coronel and Alberto Cantero were surprised by the existence of this small subversive group, and imagined that it was already in a state of alert following the incidents in Encarnación and Lambaré. They were wrong on two counts: the group was not small, and it had not set up any system for internal security.

In fact, incredible as it may seem, nobody within the OPM yet knew anything. From Brañas the police discovered that two comrades from Corrientes were to arrive at midday on board the *Carlos Antonio López*. From Estela Jacquet they discovered the address of the house of Constantino Coronel in San Lorenzo. The two documents recovered in the raided house in Lambaré revealed the name of Aníbal Franco. Franco was not part of the OPM, but an internal report mentioned his name and assessed his political stance. That same morning, Aníbal and his wife Blanca Olivetti were taken to the Dept. of Investigations, along with Aníbal's father, a sixty-year-old engineer. All of them were tortured and imprisoned for months simply because their names appeared in one of the documents captured by the police. Also that morning, the women arrested with Brañas in Encarnación were brought to Asunción: his wife Ana, Teresa Aguilera de Casco, and Mary Alvitos de Zavala.

Just before midday, in the intense heat, the *Carlos Antonio López* docked in the port of Asunción. From the ship's bridge, Carlos Casco and Ricardo Schmalko were watching the docking manoeuvres as they approached port. A moment later the ship's captain announced that all passengers should wait in their cabins, which would be inspected by the police. That was when the two were arrested. "Seven guys in plain clothes came in," recalls Casco. "Didn't say a word, just beat the shit out of us. They took us to Police Headquarters. An hour later we were in Investigations."

The police confiscated everything that the men had brought with them in wooden boxes: personal belongings, books, documents, a typewriter, and a mimeograph. These latter two had been "liberated" by Teresa Aguilera and Ricardo Schmalko from the University of Corrientes.

The name of Carlos Fontclara came up almost by chance. "Among the things that Carlos Brañas brought from Corrientes was a suit of mine that I'd forgotten to pack—it had my name sewn on the inside pocket," remembered Fontclara almost two decades later when asked about his link to Brañas. For his own part, Brañas maintains that he did not realize that Fontclara was part of the OPM. "I didn't think he was part of the organization. I didn't know that a few months earlier Mario Schaerer had contacted 'Pombero' and that he was in. The police found his parents' address in my diary."

Afternoon. Sunday, April 4. Barrio Los Laureles, Asunción

Carlos Fontclara lived in a house that belonged to his parents-in-law and was planning to move out that afternoon. For that reason, he had gone earlier than usual to have Sunday lunch at his parents' house, almost opposite the Government Palace. "I even heard the ship's siren at midday, but I had no idea Casco and Schmalko were due to arrive at that time. I stayed until 1:30 PM and then left to get ready for the move. The police arrived five minutes later. They were in plain clothes and got into the house by saying they were friends of mine. My family didn't suspect anything; they even drew them a map of how to get to the house in Los Laureles."

A squad under Camilo Almada ("Sapriza") raided the house and arrested everybody inside. In a moment of police carelessness, Fontclara escaped and tried to reach the nearby Panamanian Embassy. The police chased him and opened fire. The bullet that grazed his leg, and a wooden fence shot to pieces a split second after he had jumped it, persuaded him that he had no escape. He surrendered and was beaten and kicked into a Department of Investigations truck. His wife, Teresa López Bosio, was also taken.

By late afternoon, the police could show very good results: several arrests and one dead subversive (Martín Rolón). But the interrogation and torture to which they would subject Fontclara that night would give Pastor Coronel another piece of information that might prove important: the prisoner knew of one of the organization's safe houses in Barrio Herrera.

Evening. Sunday, April 4. Barrio Herrera, Asunción

The house of Mario Schaerer Prono and Guillermina Kannonikoff was 2618 Sucre Street, just off Emeterio Mirando Street, one block from the University Hospital and close to San Cristóbal school. A meeting had been held there that evening, attended by the four leaders of the Eighth Column and Juan Carlos Da Costa. During the meeting, Da Costa had reprimanded them for the lack of discipline in the Column, and announced that he would be taking over as commander. Da Costa was particularly worried that a comrade who was supposed to have arrived from Argentina had not appeared at the *rendezvous*, or at the fallback point one hour later.

Next to Mario Schaerer's house was the New World cinema, which was showing two detective movies that night. Miguel Angel López Perito, who was among those who had stayed behind after the meeting, still remembers the details: "Juan Carlos and I used to climb up to the water tank in the back and from there we could watch the films in the cinema next door for free. That night we were watching a French detective film starring Jean Louis Trintignant. When it finished at about 10:30 PM I left with Diego Abente because I was staying the night at his house. Juan Carlos was staying at Mario's." In fact, Da Costa had secretly been staying at Mario's house for a few days, since he thought that the "headquarters" in Las Perlas Street offered less security. Guillermina Kannonikoff remembers clearly that after Abente, Abente's wife, and López Perito left, she stayed up to watch the last movie. "It was called *The Incredible Flight*. I'll never forget that name because that night Mario and I would make a flight of our own."

Dawn. Monday, April 5. Barrio San José, San Lorenzo

The police decided to wait until dawn before raiding the house of Constantino Coronel. There they found Constantino, his wife Pablina (forty-four), his sixteen-year-old son Hilarión, and their months-old baby. Constantino barely had time to reach for his .45 pistol before he fell, wounded by several shots. They were all taken away in a Department of Investigations 4x4. For a long time the Organization (or what was left of it) gave up Constantino for dead, but he was to survive almost miraculously.

Dawn. Monday, April 5. Barrio Herrera, Asunción

Under a thundery sky lit by distant flashes of lightning, the police squad, under Captain Alberto Cantero, arrived at Mario Schaerer's house. It was 2 AM. Da Costa was sleeping in the front room, and Mario and Guillermina in their bedroom. The only survivor of the police assault on the house in Sucre Street, Guillermina Kannonikoff, recalls the events. "Some time in the early morning I heard footsteps in the front garden. I woke Mario and he told me that it must be cows. That wasn't impossible, since the house had high walls but no front gate. But then, seconds later, we heard police officers shouting and then shots. Mario jumped up and ran to the room where Juan Carlos was while I got some clothes on, and then I instinctively ran into the passage to turn off the electricity. I still don't know how I did it, because the front door was full of bullet holes from the police advancing from in front of the house. We were in darkness. Juan Carlos had a .45 pistol and he gave Mario a pistol with a long magazine with eighteen bullets. Mario didn't manage to fire a single shot that night. And then Juan Carlos opened the kitchen door out into the back and tried to shoot his way out."

Da Costa only managed a few steps before he was hit by several shots to his upper body. He managed to get back to the house before collapsing dead at Guillermina's feet. The leader of the Paraguayan revolution fell, faithful to the beliefs to which he had dedicated his life.

The police were distracted for a few seconds when they realized that during the skirmish Captain Alberto Cantero had been hit in the stomach. That brief moment was enough for Mario and Guillermina to make a break for the back gate. Somehow eluding a frantic police search, Mario and Guillermina got as far as San Cristóbal school, four blocks from their house, where they were both teachers. They sought refuge in the Nuns' House, where they were taken in by the French Sisters Madgalena and Gabi. After cleaning Mario's wounds, and unsure of what to do, the nuns went to speak to Father Raimundo Roy, who appeared a few minutes later. The police, still surrounding Mario's house, had no idea where the fugitives were.

Early Morning. Monday, April 5. Barrio Las Mercedes, Asunción

At 875 Teniente Nuñez Street, the sound of the telephone ringing in the early morning woke Diego Abente, his wife, Stella Rojas, and Miguel López Perito, who had stayed there overnight. The phone call informed them that "Number 11 had fallen." According to the internal code of the organization, Number 11 was Mario's house. The three nervously debated what to do. Finally they decided to go over to Mario's house to check what had happened. They could not have made a worse decision.

Diego drove the Citroen van to Barrio Herrera. Next to him was Stella, with Miguel Angel in the back. Also in the back of the van they had stored part of the OPM archives and a number of books. "The previous Tuesday or Wednesday, Juan Carlos had told us to take most of the archives from my garage in Las Mercedes over to Mario Schaerer's house, which he thought would be more secure," recalls Diego Abente. "Mario borrowed a Volkswagen van and we took the papers in that."

As they neared the house they saw cars and lights, and almost immediately they were ordered to stop by a police car. "We tried to escape" says López Perito. "Stella passed me a pistol and I got ready to shoot. Then I saw that about five police cars were chasing us, full of police with machine guns." In a moment of lucidity, López Perito decided that firing would mean certain death for all of them. Diego stopped the van, which was immediately surrounded by the police. Stella Rojas was also heavily pregnant. It was almost 4 AM. The police were still looking for the fugitives from the raid. Frustrated at not being able to avenge their injured captain, they were suddenly presented with a gift from the gods: three new prisoners and what looked like a large quantity of important documents.

Morning. Monday, April 5. Barrio Herrera, Asunción

Father Roy returned shortly afterward and announced that it would be best for all concerned if Mario and Guillermina gave themselves up to the police.

He stated that he had taken measures to ensure that their physical safety would be guaranteed. Despite Guillermina's pleading, he said that the decision had been made and that the police would be arriving in a few minutes to take them. What made Father Roy hand them over to the police without protection? Inadequate understanding of the reality of what would happen to them once they reached the Department of Investigations? The naivety to believe that the promises made not to harm them would be respected? Fear of endangering his congregation? Whatever it was, that morning he made a terrible mistake and one which he would regret for the rest of his life. Mario Schaerer made his feelings clear to him as he was led away: "Father, you are a coward."

The police left a guard at Schaerer's house. The neighbours cautiously repressed their curiosity to ask what all the shooting had been about. There was a rumor that some neighbours had been taken to Investigations. People whispered in the safety of their own homes—everyone had had years of experience in keeping a safe distance from Stroessner's police. Or almost everyone. Mario Arzamendia was a man in his sixties, a veteran of the Chaco War, a devout supporter of activities in the parish of San Cristóbal who sold the weekly church newspaper *Sendero* to support the work of the church. When his curiosity got the better of him, he took the risk of walking past the front of the house. He was arrested and sent to the Department of Investigations. Arzamendia had absolutely nothing to do with the OPM, but he would later pay for his curiosity with his life.

Morning. Monday, April 5. Department of Investigations, Asunción

Mario and Guillermina were pushed into one of the winding corridors of the Department of Investigations. Some time later, Mario was taken to one of the rooms upstairs to be interrogated. Guillermina would hear him screaming from the torture. When they brought him back, she tried to hug him, but a kick from Captain Pino sent her crashing back against the wall. Guillermina remembers having seen Fontclara tied up, as well as her own mother-in-law, who had been arrested that morning when she had gone to ask what had happened to them.

María Esther Cerdan de Rodríguez lives today in Coronel Bogado. That Monday morning she was being held as a political prisoner in the Department of Investigations, and saw Mario Schaerer arrive. "I'd been held along with my husband Humberto Rodríguez since March 15; we were accused of belonging to a small organization of Paraguayan exiles in Argentina called PORA. I was in the corridor and I saw a young man dressed only in a dark hospital shirt come in. He was hopping on one foot—the other one was obviously injured. They made him sit on the floor. Because he looked badly hurt and the wound was bleeding I passed him a little pillow that I had for him to rest his injured leg on. He was completely lucid and didn't have any other injuries. Soon after that, an officer came and started asking him questions—at the same time he stuck his sword into the wound on the man's foot. He did this a few times and then came back in the afternoon and did it again. The young man, who I later found out was Mario Schaerer, didn't say a word. He stayed silent the whole time in spite of the officer twisting his sword into the wound. That night they came for him. They took him upstairs and tortured him. We knew because even though they put the music on at full volume, we could still hear him screaming."

In general in Latin America, the capture of a few members of an armed guerrilla movement would not normally mean the destruction of the whole organization. The compartmentalization of information would prevent the security forces from making too much progress, and win time for the organization to set up mechanisms of defence. However, no armed movement on the continent had experienced the disastrous and highly unusual situation in which the OPM was beginning to find itself. The first to fall were its main leaders, who held most of the information about the organization. Of these three, one had been killed (Juan Carlos Da Costa), another arrested (Constantino Coronel), and the third (Nidia González) was the subject of an intense police search. And as if this calamitous situation was not enough, the police also had possession of documents detailing the structure of the columns, the names of their members, and even cards with some of their personal details.

As the morning went on the list grew longer, with the arrest of more relatives of those previously detained. The documents captured were also extensive: those found in Valle Apuá, plus the ones from the Citroen and the ones found in the house of Mario Schaerer constituted the bulk of OPM records. When Brañas had been arrested in Encarnación, the police had had no idea of the existence of the organization. Less than forty-eight hours later, they knew almost everything about it.

Just as in a "join-the-dots" or a "fill in the blanks" exercise at school, the high command at the Department of Investigations and at Military Intelligence spent the next few days completing the jigsaw, putting together the information from the OPM archives with the information gathered through interrogation. The interrogations could be directed toward specific issues, lies could be quickly revealed and pseudonyms linked to real names, and any discrepancies between declarations could be clarified by putting the prisoners face to face. In short, it was hard work, but a lot more straightforward than anyone could have imagined.

Was the OPM a clandestine organization or a gang of kids playing at being guerrillas? Several members of the OPM rounded up over the following few days still ask this question today. During that catastrophic Monday, hardly anybody was alerted. In fact, everything carried on as normal: meetings were held irregularly, with a few absences as usual—nothing which might cause alarm. "Nobody was worried, and security was defective," is a phrase that we heard repeatedly during our interviews. What happened was serious: the arrest of the whole of the Corrientes group, shoot-outs in Lambaré, San Lorenzo, Los Laureles, and Barrio Herrera, and the killing of important leaders. Although many escaped thanks to the compartmentalization of information, which did work in some cases, it is incredible to find that the majority of members had no idea of what was happening that Monday morning.

The police made ready to launch the most extensive campaign to capture alleged guerrillas ever carried out in the country. The OPM debacle was a godsend to a regime that would now have something with which to refresh the tired rhetoric of the "threat of communism," and a perfect excuse to arrest, interrogate, and torture thousands of people linked to social movements, peasant organizations, unions, or opposition political movements. But this campaign would not bring any obvious change to most people's daily routine. Indeed, for many years, the only people who knew of it were the neighbours and relatives of those who were taken away. In Asunción, ordinary people were oblivious.

My Farewell Speech

Carmen de Lara Castro

Carmen Casco de Lara Castro (1921–93) was the leading human rights activist during the Stroessner regime. From 1965 to 1977 she served as a congressional deputy of the Radical Liberal Party. On June 17, 1967, she founded the Commission for the Defence of Human Rights in Paraguay, one of the first independent human rights organizations in Latin America. In the early years she worked almost single-handedly in defence of political prisoners, suffering repeated arrest and physical abuse from government authorities. During the 1980s she organized human rights conferences that drew inter-national attention to the violation of human rights. The regime responded by vilifying her in the media and subjecting her to constant harassment. This extract is from her farewell speech to Congress on December 15, 1977, following the decision of her "Authentic" faction of the Radical Liberal Party to abstain from the February 1978 presidential elections in protest at the Constitutional Amendment of 1977, which per-mitted the unlimited reelection of Stroessner.

Mr. President, Honorable Congressmen: My address today is a farewell speech and an examination of conscience. I was sent to this chamber by the vote of people for the Radical Liberal Party, with the commitment to defend the rights of citizens, make just laws, denounce abuses and injustices and see that the National Constitution is faithfully observed. I believe I have carried out this honourable mandate with dignity during my ten years of parliamentary activity. Parliament is the highest tribune to which a citizen freely elected by the people can aspire. The people only deliberate and rule through their representatives. These people are not mere spectators; they also know very well how to tell the difference: they understand that all that glitters is not gold.

That is why they are asking and demanding to know why it is that dur-ing the last ten years only two bills presented by the opposition have been passed; they are not satisfied with simplistic explanations. They want the truth, but we cannot give it to them because all the ways to do it are closed to us. We are threatened with imprisonment, persecution, marginalisation and obstacles to the exercise of the right to assembly and other common rights.

In these circumstances I have to ask myself whether or not I should continue to occupy a seat in Parliament while those who elected me are being victimized and there is nothing I can do to help them. Am I serving the people or am I forgetting them? My colleagues here can see that I am speaking with absolute sincerity just as I always do, but the smiles of disbelief or the strong rebuttals which are part and parcel of the job do not surprise me. I do not care about the first and I am not frightened by the second.

Political parties should take a special interest in strengthening the authority of Parliament and its members, respecting them and encouraging others to respect them. Parliament should be a school of civic training for young people. Laws cannot and should not be applied to part of the people only, nor are rights the exclusive patrimony of one group. All people are born free and equal and are also mortal. Only their deeds live after them, and time will judge each person. Due to ignorance or indifference few people attend the public sessions of Parliament; nor does the press give the sessions the coverage that they deserve, but rather gives greater attention to sound bites than to the treatment of important issues, and many people think our work does not justify the salary we receive.

At the beginning I said I would speak with my usual sincerity and thus I refer to a sensitive question for us Radical Liberals. True democracy cannot be disguised. True democracy is the continuous living-out of a civic conscience; it is a struggle, yes, but also a confrontation of opinions, with respect for ideas. But the government is calling its masquerade "democracy," a masquerade that conceals a frightful cannibalism (across all of society, including students, sports, universities and politics) in which only selfish ambition is recognized and virtues and merit are ignored. This explains why there is so much scepticism about the idea of elections. All of us are aware, even if we do not say so, of the enormous level of electoral abstention. Supporters of the ruling party know they will win anyway and opposition voters know they will lose. Because of this, the "Authentic" Radical Liberals are opposed to presenting a candidate and participating in the presidential election on 12 February next.

I want to make it very clear that we are not against a straightforward electoral contest, but we do oppose a fraudulent one. We have personally witnessed the latter many times. The preparations for the next election already indicate what the result will be. It is not possible for leaders who say that they defend the people to be involved in such a degrading episode or endorse such a mockery of the people by participating or accepting a fraudulent result.

The ruling Colorado Party has much to do with the scepticism surrounding elections. If its supposed majority really exists, why is it necessary for it to resort to such scandalous use of fraud and implementation of a state of siege? A whole generation has been deprived of its freedom by the periodic renewal of the state of siege every three months since 1954. Although it is officially applied to only three regions, in reality it covers the whole country. I am not exaggerating when I say that in order to hold any meeting of opposition parties or groups we have to depend on the whims of local police commissioners who are charged with the enforcement of the state of siege.

We have repeatedly tried to do what the constitution imperatively calls for: legislate regulations for the state of siege. We have presented legislative proposals to do this in every session—always with the same negative result. I ask: why, if there is peace, must we endure a permanent state of siege? And if, as the Colorado Party proclaims, the absolute majority is on the side of the government, who then is to be feared? Each time the state of siege is renewed the press barely mentions it. Instead it focuses on news about baby showers and gossip about sportsmen.

Another aspect which should be made clear, Mr. President, is that we in the opposition have been completely marginalised from important national enterprises, in which we should be included with no other condition than that of our competence. In the case of the Itaipú hydroelectric project, the opposition was correct in all its analysis, objections and arguments. Time now proves that we were right. Unfortunately there is a form of apartheid here, as damaging as a racial one, and that, Mr. President, should not be allowed.

I cannot omit from this judgement of my parliamentary life what has been my ongoing struggle: freedom for my Paraguayan brothers and sisters. It has not been an easy struggle; many times fear pursued me relentlessly. My fellow deputies, you will not have forgotten that I paid a high price for this commitment; because of it two of my sons were brutally tortured.

I cannot leave this chamber without appealing for a broad general amnesty. The clamour for an amnesty comes from all quarters. We hear this cry of the people and know we have a great debt to pay. We have remained silent before the death of *campesinos* and the imprisonment of colleagues, Radical Liberal deputy Ranulfo Gill, for one.

Let us show charity to Paraguayan mothers, to women, wives and partners; to children jailed with their mothers; to the more than two hundred political prisoners. Let us not forget those who died in torture cells: Mario Arzamendia and Juan José Farias, for example, who died without knowing of what they were accused. Let us not forget Arturo Bernal, a humble *campesino* tortured to death, nor the destroyed body of the teenager Joel Filartiga. Let us not forget Mario Schaerer Prono, one among many others massacred over the years. There are missing persons such as Carlos Mancuello, Agustin Goiburú, Amilcar Oviedo, the Ramírez Villalba brothers and many more about whom the authorities will give no information whatever, not even whether they are alive or not.

Let us also remember unfortunate women such as Maria Elina Rodas who has been in prison for many years, accompanied by her little grandson, Derlis Villagra; and innocent people such as Captain Napoleón Ortigoza, on the brink of insanity, and the poor innocent *campesino* Ignacio Chamorro in prison for nineteen years. Horror! a thousand times Horror!

Colleagues and friends (I think I have made some): I speak to you as a parliamentarian and also as a mother who has suffered pain. We have a beautiful country, with verdant forests and crystal-clear rivers and streams. It is a paradise, but we need to add to its material progress a concern for the human problem. Let us turn it into a country without political prisoners, where justice will reign so fairly that it will shelter everyone, without the cancer of torture carried out by men who get drunk on another person's pain as if they had taken drugs. With Christian love we should put an end to hate if we don't want it to have power over Paraguayans. May God grant that violence finds no inspiration in Paraguay. We must combat treasonous assaults in our country with justice and not with violence.

This is my last speech in Parliament but not my last denunciation. I will go on with my humanitarian work as I did before becoming a deputy, because my struggle for human rights was not motivated by ambition on the eve of elections. I did it and will continue it because of a Christian spirit and a human solidarity with innocent victims. I am satisfied by having done my duty and to receive as payment the kiss of mothers and the freedom of my brothers and sisters—including some who had previously attacked me—whom I have defended without partisan distinction.

I have faith and hope in the youth of our land. I have the inner conviction that the time is not far off when the young people of the Colorado Party will leave behind destructive fanaticism. I hope that soon they will open their arms to their brothers and sisters to live united and in a better way than we who have not given them the happiness of that union. Today more than ever young people deserve the gift of peace.

The Death of Somoza

Claribel Alegría and Darwin Flakoll

In July 1979 Anastasio Somoza Debayle, president of Nicaragua, was overthrown by a revolutionary movement led by the FSLN *(Frente Sandinista de Liberación Nacional). This put an end to the infamous Somoza dynasty that had ruled Nicaragua since 1936, supported by successive administrations of the United States government. Somoza sought sanctuary in Paraguay, believing that he would find protection from the anticommunist regime of his friend Alfredo Stroessner, and that in Asunción he would escape the international limelight. On September 16, 1980, he was assassinated by a small guerrilla cell of the Argentinian People's Revolutionary Army (*ERP*), which sought revenge on behalf of the Nicaraguan people for the brutal repression ordered by Somoza in the 1970s, which had left tens of thousands of civilians dead. The assassination rocked the Stroessner regime, and was used to justify another wave of repression against the growing domestic opposition.* The Death of Somoza, *written by the Nicaraguan poet and novelist, Claribel Alegría, is based on interviews with the members of the guerrilla cell and especially with its leader, Ramón (Enrique Gorriarán Merlo). It reveals the lack of basic security surrounding Somoza, the success of the guerrillas despite a series of quite astonishing mishaps, and the ineptitude of the Paraguayan police.*

Osvaldo tells the story as follows: "I was at the news stand, chatting with a man who always brought me *empanadas*. It was around 10 A.M., and I was sitting down when I saw Somoza's car coming. I stood up to get a good look. I recognized the license plate, but when I looked inside I couldn't make out anything. Or to be more accurate, I saw a man in the back seat reading a newspaper and another man sitting beside him. Another thing that confused me was that Somoza always sat in the front seat beside the driver. When he was only 10 or 15 meters away he lowered the paper and I identified him.

I headed for the toilets, stepped inside and transmitted the signal: "White, white, white."

I hadn't noticed that there was a man inside painting. I repeated the signal, and he looked at me as if I were crazy. He was painting over a poster with white paint, and he must have thought I was commenting on his work. I was wearing my windbreaker with my hand in the pocket pressing the Transmit button. I repeated the message a third time and then went into the bathroom and came out expecting to hear the sound of shooting, but I didn't hear a thing. I looked at my watch.

It was 10:05 in the morning of Wednesday, September 17, 1980. Julio Cesar Gallardo, Somoza's longtime chauffeur and bodyguard, was at the wheel of the Mercedes. In the rear, sitting next to the ex-dictator, was Joseph Bainitin, his North American economic adviser.

If God exists, he must be a *guerrillero*, Armando told us, because of all the tests we made, this one came through the clearest of all. I opened the door of the pickup, got in, turned the motor over and pulled out to the sidewalk. There was the white Mercedes pulled up at the stop light about 60 meters away. I reversed, pulled back nearly into the garage and waited for him to come to us.

I went into the garden and saw the car 60 meters away, Ramón told us. Armando was at the wheel of the pickup ready to cut the traffic. With practice, we had cut our time of getting into position to 13 seconds after we heard the signal. I had a reference point: when the front of the car drew level with a certain tree I would give Santiago a signal, so he wouldn't come out earlier and let someone see him with the bazooka. Armando was awaiting my signal to head into the street and block traffic.

I saw Ramón, Armando continued, waiting to give Santiago the signal to get into the firing position, and the truth is I didn't look at him after that. He was supposed to signal me when to pull out, but I was watching Somoza's car, and as a professional, I knew exactly when I had to make my move and how many cars I had to cut off. When I saw that the limousine had started up with five or six cars ahead of it, I let most of them go past and then I pulled out in the pickup and aimed straight for a Volkswagen Combi that was in front of the Somoza car. The driver slammed on the brakes and swerved into the middle of the street. As I set the brake and climbed out, I heard the first shots: "Bam, bam, bam."

In accordance with the preestablished plan, Santiago had to take the first shot with the bazooka in case the limousine was bullet-proofed. Ramón, from the front garden, watched the limousine pass in front of the marker tree and gave Santiago the signal to take up his attack position. Armando chose his moment and blocked the Volkswagen van that was just ahead of Somoza's car. The dictator's car braked. Ramón heard a noise behind him and turned to see Santiago on one knee, struggling with the bazooka. Thinking that Santiago had slipped and fallen, he swivelled, raised the M-16 to his shoulder and started squeezing off shots.

What had really happened was that the first bazooka charge was a dud. When a bazooka misfires, one is supposed to wait 30 seconds before removing the defective projectile and replacing it with another. Santiago didn't wait even two seconds. He knelt, pulled the projectile out of the mouth of the tube and replaced it with the spare. He got to his feet again and took aim but didn't fire. The Somoza limousine, its driver already dead, drifted aimlessly toward the operational house and ran into the curb exactly in front of Ramón, who kept firing methodically into the back seat. The limousine was not bullet-proofed, and each of the shots penetrated the car through the shattered back window. Ramón was so close to the Mercedes that a bazooka round at that moment would have killed him.

I started firing single rounds, Ramón continues his account, first at the driver who had already braked. The car kept drifting and came to a stop just in front of the door. I shifted aim to the other two. Somoza never knew what hit him, because he was staring straight ahead.

It wasn't until then that Somoza's bodyguards went into action. I hadn't so much as seen them. When I wanted to start firing at them, I discovered the M-16 was empty. Santiago had withdrawn into the entrance and was ready to fire. I ran over to where he was and said:

"Give it to him now."

He fired from inside the house. The explosion was tremendous. We could see that the car was totally destroyed. The bodyguards were hiding behind the wall of the next door house. They had stopped firing.

The pickup's motor stalled, Armando continued, and I climbed back in. The van I had cut off was backing and filling. The driver was desperate. I started the motor, and when I got out again, Bam!—a deafening explosion. The Volkswagen spun its wheels, found an opening and took off like a scalded cat. The explosion left me shaking.

With the Volkswagen out of the way, I could see the Somoza car blown apart, metal scraps and shattered glass all over the street. I was blocking the avenue in front of the house. Our getaway route was via a sidestreet off to the left about 10 meters beyond the operational house. The cars coming the other way were backing up and turning around. I had to cut off the getaway street before any of them could block it, so I got back in the pickup and pulled ahead 10 meters to cut off the street. When I got out again, I heard shots and I saw the bodyguards behind the wall of the next-door house, and one of them was firing at Santiago and Ramón. Flaco was behind the front door, firing the submachine gun that made no noise because it was fitted with a silencer. I brought the FAL up and shot at one of them. I don't think I hit him, but he dropped to the ground. I shouted at Santiago: "Come on, I'll cover you."

One of the guards raised his head to see what was going on, and I fired again. Pieces of the wall flew in all directions. Ramón came running and climbed into the cab. I let go four or five more rounds so they'd keep their heads down. I remember I said to Ramón: "We blew him away."

"Yeah," he replied, "he won't bother anybody any more."

Flaco came running toward us, and I shifted into first and took off. The pickup was already moving when he jumped into the back. I turned into the getaway street, accelerated and 30 meters down the street, pah, pah, pah, the motor died on me.

"This piece of shit has had it," I told Ramón. "Let's get ourselves another car."

Just then, a little Mitsubishi came down the street toward us. Ramón said: "Okay, let's take this one."

We got on both sides, and the driver slammed on the brakes and raised his hands. I opened the door and said: "Get out, or I'll blow your head off."

"Sure, sure," he said, and he went scurrying off.

This took about two seconds. The three of us climbed in, and we took off. We could barely squeeze into the car.

My Vote Is for the People

Alcibiades González Delvalle

Alcibiades González Delvalle (1936–) is a leading contemporary journalist and playwright. He joined ABC Color, the most widely read newspaper in Paraguay, when it was founded in 1967, and went on to become a member of the editorial staff. During the 1970s and 1980s he was widely respected for his acute observations on political affairs, and for his ability to defy the limitations of state censorship to produce scathing attacks on the Stroessner regime. His articles provoked the ire of the dictatorship, not only leading to brief periods of detention in 1979, 1980, and 1983, but also contributing to the closure of the newspaper from March 1984 until the fall of the regime in February 1989.

"My Vote Is for the People," written in 1983, represented a clear challenge to the legitimacy of the democratic facade behind which the dictatorship operated. The article, written in a highly formalized, quasi-religious style, offers a harsh criticism of the regime, and a strong and hopeful rallying cry for a new democratic order. In the imminent elections that the article mentions Stroessner went on to win 90.1 percent of the vote.

In the forthcoming elections it is predicted that the presidential candidate of the Colorado Party, General Alfredo Stroessner, will win approximately 90 percent of the vote. In the last elections, the percentage was 87.6. Given that over the past five years the party has enjoyed a flood of new members, which is not the same thing as authentic new Colorados, it is highly likely that the percentage will be even higher this time, despite a general discontent resulting from soaring petrol prices and other events that have quietly infuriated the general public.

Although they do not figure among the official candidates, I will be voting for the People. I will vote for them to be the subject, rather than the object, of future events, and in particular, of a political, social, economic and cultural transformation.

I will be voting for our primary school teachers. I will vote that their daily sacrifice, so poorly rewarded, might one day be recognized, not just in official speeches. And I will vote for them to be the ones who will lead our future citizens along the path of truth, love, and tolerance.

I will be voting for the teachers in secondary schools and higher education. I will vote for them to be able to instill in the minds and spirits of our youth a new, authentic understanding of peace, liberty, and democracy. I will vote for them to transform the strength of our young people into a creative force for moral and spiritual good.

I will be voting for our young people. I will vote for them to occupy a new place of honor in the rebuilding of the nation, and be confident in their own ability to forge a new path. I will vote for them to be able to cast off the obligation to follow torturous paths to false ends, on which they lose their sense of moral values and become accomplices to dishonesty.

I will be voting for the small farmers. I will vote for them to gain control over their own land, and to be free from the covetous gaze of those powerful enough to have the means to acquire it. I will vote for the end to the burning of their homes and settlements, and the unlawful arrests and persecution they suffer. I will vote for a fair price for their produce and that they may no longer be the eternal recipients of unfulfilled promises.

I will be voting for the workers. I will vote for them to have a decent standard of living; that their dignity may be respected; that they may be truly protected by labor laws and cease to be persecuted for their desire to form unions as the best way to protect their rights.

I will be voting for all working people, since they are the force that will move this country forward. I will vote for them to be able to carry out their jobs within the protective framework of justice, and be free from the burden of civil servants who live off the hard work of others.

I will be voting for those in exile. I will vote for this large and worthy group of compatriots to be able to return to their homeland and place their minds and bodies at its service. I will vote for the right of every Paraguayan to live and die in his country. I will vote for the disappearance of exile from the list of state punishments.

I will be voting that the priests, at the same time as offering up their prayers, roll up their shirtsleeves and involve themselves in social issues, so that they may understand our problems and find solutions. I will vote that among their commitments, that of worshipping the powerful will disappear and the clergy may have no powers beyond the social doctrine of the church.

And so I will be voting for the People. I will vote that one day they may triumph in elections, in which the issues will be their liberty, their dignity, and their moral health.

February 6, 1983.

Paraguay's Terror Archive

Andrew Nickson

The 1992 discovery of a major archive consisting of police records from the time of the Stroessner regime provided a unique insight into the day-to-day workings of the security system, as well as into the objectives and strategies of those who headed it. It also shed new light on the scale and nature of the repressive apparatus, raising serious doubts about the conventional view that it was cumbersome and poorly organized. On the contrary, as this report suggests, they show that the government kept an extremely accurate updated list of all political prisoners, even to the extent of providing code marking for those who subsequently died under torture. Following classification and microfilming, the archive is now housed in the Museum of Justice, located in the High Court building of Asunción. Access to the files has enabled relatives of disappeared prisoners and former political detainees who had been tortured to substantiate formal charges against leading members of the Stroessner regime.

The contents of the archive came to light following a tip-off from a police informant. On 22 December 1992, the Dirección de Producción of the Policía de la Capital in the residential suburb of Solares de Lambaré, near Asunción, was raided by a judicial team headed by Judge José Agustín Fernández and Luís María Benítez Riera, accompanied by Congressional Deputy Francisco José de Vargas. They were acting under the habeas data provisions, inscribed in Article 135 of the 1992 Constitution, under which citizens may have access to information on them held by the state. A habeas data writ to this effect had earlier been issued in favour of former political prisoner Martín Almada, an educationalist detained from November 1974 until his expulsion from the country in mid-1977. To the surprise of the judges, nearly two tonnes of documentation relating to the activities of the Department of Investigations (Departamento de Investigaciones de la Policia de la Capital—D.I.P.C.), and the nerve centre of state repression during the Stroessner regime, were discovered in a locked room. Acting swiftly and accompanied by the press and TV, the judges ordered the immediate confiscation of the documentation and its transfer by a fleet of vehicles to the Palacio de Justicia (High Court) building in Asunción.

This discovery led to two subsequent raids in the following weeks by judges acting on the basis of further habeas data writs. On 4 January 1993 the legal office (Departamento Judicial) of the police headquarters was raided. A wealth of documentation was confiscated on the repression of the peasant league movement, Ligas Agrarias Cristianas, and the case of Cpt. Napoleón Ortigoza, the longest-serving political prisoner during the Stroessner regime. This was followed on 8 January 1993, by a third raid on the Departamento Técnico para la Represión de Comunismo of the Ministry of the Interior, commonly known as La Técnica, which was established in the early 1960s with U.S. Government support in the wake of the Cuban revolution specifically for the repression of communism. In this case, however, relatively little documentation was confiscated, apart from a collection of some 700 books considered subversive which had been stolen from private residences during police raids. The raid confirmed that La Técnica had continued to operate long after the February 1989 putsch which overthrew President Stroessner. Following the 22 December 1993 raid referred to above, its senior officers, Antonio Campos Alum and Felipe Nery Zaldívar, disappeared, having apparently disposed of sensitive documentation.

The consolidated archive, commonly referred to in the media as *el archivo del terror*, is currently located in two cramped rooms on the 8th floor of the Palacio de Justicia. A small part of the archive, as yet unclassified, contains internal documentation of the security forces during the period from 1941 until the beginning of the Stroessner regime in 1954. Referred to as the *archivo muerto*, it is located separately in the basement of the Palacio de Justicia.

The archive may be divided into two broad sections. The first comprises material confiscated by the security forces, such as personal correspondence, political literature (leaflets, pamphlets, etc.), internal party documents, newspaper cuttings, and analyses of the economic and political situation. The second comprises material produced by the security forces themselves, such as reports by informants, internal reports on political and trade union matters, reports obtained through telephone-tapping, statements extracted from detainees, evidence submitted as part of legal charges, and lists of detainees.

The bulk of the contents of the archive derives from the first raid carried out on 22 December. Its core is the 500 bound folios (volumes) of internal documents of the D.I.P.C., which are arranged and internally classified by subject matter. In addition to a further 100 folios which have been bound and classified following their confiscation, they comprise approximately 300,000 individual pages. Among the documentation are:

   i) detention and release data on all political prisoners from 1952–89 (in 5 volumes)

   ii) *libros de novedades* of the Oficina de Vigilancia y Delitos of the D.I.P.C., where most torture activities were carried out, detailing the daily entry and exit of detainees from June 1976 to December 1990 (in 56 volumes)

   iii) internal correspondence between the head of the Departamento de Política y Afines (D.P.A.) responsible for political surveillance and the head of the D.I.P.C. during 1981–89 (in 21 volumes)

   iv) a total of 7,193 personal files, listed by alphabetical order, on political detainees, including photographs, fingerprints, information on the circumstances of their arrest, political, trade union and cultural activities, etc.

   v) large quantities of personal documentation and publications considered subversive which were confiscated during police raids

   vi) some 3,000 photographs of political dissidents, many taken during public events with the use of telephoto lenses

   vii) some 500 audio recordings of radio programmes or public meetings considered subversive

   viii) transcriptions of conversations obtained by telephone tapping

   ix) transcriptions of some 400 statements extracted under torture

   x) over 500 passports and identity documents of foreigners of different nationalities

The following random selection gives a flavour of the wide-ranging contents of the folios:

Vol. 4 Telephone tapping (Sept.–Nov. 1984)

Vol. 36 Surveillance of persons entering and leaving the country

Vol. 40 Surveillance of the independent teachers' union, OTEP

Vol. 47 Inaugural meeting of Operation Condor

Vol. 111 Surveillance of hotels

Vol. 179. Correspondence from Pastor Coronel, head of the D.I.P.C., to Stroessner

Vol. 203 Membership list of Christian Democrat Party which had been stolen from party headquarters in the 1970s

Vol. 216 Grupo de Acción Anticomunista (GAA)

EL PRESIDENTE DE LA REPUBLICA DEL PARAGUAY
AL COMISARIO ANTONIO CAMPOS ALUM CON LA
DISTINCION DE SIEMPRE POR SU DENODADA LUCHA
CONTRA EL COMUNISMO ATEO ENEMIGO DE LA PATRIA.
ASUNCION DEL PARAGUAY 11 DE SEPTIEMBRE DE 1970

Alfredo Stroessner gave this signed photograph in 1970 to Dr. Antonio
Campos Alum, the infamous head of the Technical Department for
the Repression of Communism of the Interior Ministry, where he was
responsible for the systematic torture of political dissidents during the
Stronato. The dedication highlights his "unswerving struggle against
atheistic communism, the enemy of the fatherland." Trained originally
in the United States by the Federal Bureau of Investigations, he played
a crucial role as a link between the Paraguayan secret services and the
Central Intelligence Agency in the fight against communism. Amazingly,
Alúm continued in office after the overthrow of Stroessner in 1989 but
disappeared immediately after the 1992 discovery of the "terror archive."
Photographer unknown. From the collection of Andrew Nickson.

Specifically, the archive contains detailed evidence substantiating allegations of human rights violations by the security forces, as follows:

   i) torture was a common practice against political prisoners

   ii) opponents of the Stroessner regime were kidnapped from exile, with the cooperation of the security forces of neighbouring countries

   iii) detainees who disappeared while under detention, were in fact murdered and were filed as such by use of a special classification, *empaquetados* (packaged)

   iv) the activities of leading opponents of the regime, both inside and outside the country, were closely monitored

   v) President Stroessner received regular written reports on surveillance activities by the security forces

   vi) an extensive network of informants (*pyragues*) was employed by the D.P.A. Some were well-known people, including a Catholic Bishop

   vii) Paraguay was an active member of the Operation Condor, a collaboration network set up by the military regimes which ruled Argentina, Brazil, Uruguay, Chile and Paraguay in the 1970s and 1980s

   viii) the police continued to monitor the activities of opposition leaders well after the February 1989 putsch which overthrew Stroessner, as shown by the *cuadernos de novedades* of the D.I.P.C.

On 26 March 1993 an agreement was signed between the Paraguayan Government and U.S.A.I.D. for initial classification by Micro-Isis and microfilming at a total cost of us$68,000, of which U.S.A.I.D. contributed us$40,000 for a six-month period ending in September 1993. Although the U.S. Ambassador, Jon Glassman, had earlier denied U.S. involvement in the state repression evidenced in the archive, at the signing ceremony he publicly recognised that members of the U.S. security services had collaborated in the establishment of La Técnica.

"A Hundred and Eight" and a Burned Body: The Story Not Told by the Truth and Justice Commission

Anselmo Ramos

Until very recently, human rights violations suffered by gay men during the Stroess-ner dictatorship remained outside the public domain. In a strongly machista soci-ety, the number 108 is still commonly used as a term of abuse in Paraguay toward homosexuals. Due to the repression and autorepression unleashed as a result of the cover-up of the murder of Bernardo Aranda in 1959, few of those who now use the term know of its origins. Such was the degree of self-censorship that even today hardly any of those named on the infamous "list of 108" have spoken of the suffering they experienced. The appearance of the film Cuchillo de Palo *(dir. Renate Costa, 2010) has helped to correct this, although, as the title of this article suggests, even the Truth and Justice Commission was allegedly unwilling to publish the findings of its own investigation into the Aranda case.*

It was 1959, around two in the morning of September 1. A violent explosion woke Lidia Alvarez at her home at Estados Unidos and 9a Proyectada. The blast had come from one of the pension rooms she rented out. Smoke and a smell of burning were coming from the room of the young radio presenter Bernardo Aranda. Loud rock 'n' roll music was the only witness to what had happened in that tiny room. Aranda, aged twenty-six, a highly regarded professional in the world of radio, had been murdered.

Blessed with an ideal voice for the airwaves, Bernardo Aranda had ar-rived in Asunción from the countryside. He worked at ZP9 Radio Comune-ros, and had his own early morning program. He was in charge of opening up the radio station in the early hours.

That tragic night, according to *El País*, a newspaper of the time, he ar-rived at 1:05 AM, parked his motorbike, and went to fetch a record by Bill Haley and the Comets, *La Revista del Rock*. He closed the door and windows of his little room, put the vinyl on the turntable, and turned the sound up full. It was the last thing he did. He was murdered, and his body was doused in petrol from his own motorcycle and set on fire.

Aranda had the unkind nickname *New Yorker* (the brand of a well-known sewing machine that worked from back and front). He worked professionally at the radio station, owned by Juan Bernabé.

Only one person was ever arrested for the crime, but was released after the search for incriminating evidence proved fruitless. The crime was widely talked about and carefully investigated. One of the strongest police hypotheses was that it was a crime of passion.

"Witnesses at the time said Bernardo complained constantly about a man who gave him all kinds of help with work and finances but at the same time harassed and stalked him," said the broadcaster's girlfriend, the person who might have suffered most from his "unusual relationship." Often when Aranda visited her house, a man would pull up outside in a car and sound the horn from the road. Aranda would go out, get into the car, and they would leave together. That man was arrested by police after the fateful night. As he began his statement to them, he "threatened to divulge the names of important persons in authority from different sectors of society, including the armed forces, in a short but important list of homosexuals."

A detective by the name of Fuster, who had been assigned by the dictatorship to investigate Aranda's death, resigned only weeks later. According to his own statement he felt powerless to proceed with any meaningful investigation "because the government knew everything."

The explanation that circulated among the public, although never actually voiced, was that this crime of passion involved the death of a man at the hands of another man who had close links to people at the highest levels of the church and government—all of them homosexuals. In any civilized society there would have been an investigation and the guilty would have been brought to justice. Instead, in 1959, the murder of Bernardo Aranda and the burning of his corpse led to the first great repression of the Stroessner era, this time against homosexuals.

The crime quickly gained notoriety in Asunción, a city of no more than 200,000 inhabitants at that time.

The Repression of the 108

Since the rumor cast suspicion principally on a close associate of the Stroessner leadership, the crime had to be covered up somehow. And as it was a crime of passion between two men, police strategy was, simplistically, to arrest all known homosexuals—or those said to be homosexuals—in the best style of the Salem witch hunts. Hairdressers, dancers, and ordinary citizens were arrested. One hundred and eight in total, all of them men. They were then tortured horribly.

Of the many humiliations that the group of 108 suffered, a poignant example is the parade that the police forced them to take part in outside Las Teresas school for girls. The aim was to show the pupils at the prestigious faith school, and anyone else who happened to be interested, exactly who these 108 men were. Among them were relatives, fiancés, and friends of the girls. Police raids targeted homosexuals at first, but later other names were added to the list simply because they had links in one way or another to the gay community of the time, even though they were not necessarily homosexuals themselves. For the 108, the parade lasted an eternity, but the mockery and denigration were only just beginning. After Las Teresas came Palma Street.

On Saturday mornings, Palma Street in downtown Asunción had a party atmosphere about it. A meeting place with a wealth of things to do and see, it was packed with people. That Saturday was like any other. But it was not to be like the others. The 108 were there. The men "considered sick." Their heads shaved—with all the Nazi connotations that that held—the police paraded them down Palma Street, to "show" the 108 to the people. The walk ended in front of Police Headquarters. There the 108 were exhibited, completely naked, lying face down and with stones on their backs. The first great lesson was about to be taught. Far away Bill Haley and the Comets were singing. Far away indeed was a crime that by now few people cared about.

The newspapers attacked homosexuality ferociously. It was an illness that had to be eradicated from the country. These 108 were the first outbreak and they had to be eliminated. There was a run of vicious press coverage as the papers exhorted citizens to put an end to this illness. It was presented as a foreign scourge, a disease that had come from outside.

The result was of considerable help to a dictatorship characterized in part by psychological repression. It was a way of spreading self-censorship: self repression works more effectively than repression itself. Mass psychosis took hold, and in the papers people like Botti wrote openly mocking and joking about the tragedy of the 108. The number 108 itself began to be used as a term of ridicule—the cartoonist actually boasted that he had created the catchphrase "108 and a burned body."

All that remains of the Aranda case in the press of the time is the terror instilled in the population during the following months, a time when there were even calls for a special police squad to be set up to persecute and re-move the threat of the hedonists.

Despite press reports that the person responsible for the murder had been identified, the authorities never released his name "for reasons of national security."

The Final Report of the Truth and Justice Commission

Andrés D. Ramírez

The Truth and Justice Commission (TJC) was established in 2003 with a remit to investigate violations of human rights under the dictatorship of General Alfredo Stroessner and to be completed by August 2008. The following extract is a summary of its findings published in the 2008 Annual Human Rights Report by CODEHUPY, a network of twenty-five nongovernmental organizations that work in the field of human rights in Paraguay.

The report was important for a number of reasons: it recorded the details of human rights violations from testimonies given by the victims; it categorized the nature of the violations as crimes against humanity, thereby opening the door to prosecution; and for the first time in the transition to democracy, there was a con-certed effort to confront the past by recording the atrocities committed under the dictatorship. As the article demonstrates, Stroessner did not rely on the mass disap-pearance or execution of opponents, as occurred during the Dirty War in Argen-tina, in order to strengthen his regime. Indeed, the total figure of 337 disappeared and 59 executed over a period of 35 years is very low compared with those from other Southern Cone dictatorships. Far more common and effective in Paraguay under Stroessner's strategy of "preventive repression" was the widespread use of arrest, detention, and torture by the police in order to create a culture of fear and mistrust among the population in general.

The Minister of Internal Affairs advises the Paraguayan people to cooperate fully with the law enforcement agencies to ensure that our National Security, which has come at so high a price, is not undermined by factions formed and indoctrinated by foreign terrorist organizations. Let it be known that anyone found to be complicit in any type of clandestine activity will be dealt with se-verely. At the same time, the National Government will leave no stone unturned in the fight to protect the well-being of its people and the democratic institutions that govern the Republic.

—*Diario Patria*, the official newspaper of the National Republican Association
(Colorado Party), Asunción, April 1976

We must never tire in our efforts to overcome the legacy of Stroessner, even now that he is dead. My father's life is the story of the determination of thousands of Paraguayans: suffering that increases our strength, and obliges us all to carry on, come what may, so that our dreams can be realized in a better nation where all are equal, where there is no discrimination and where no citizen is demeaned or humiliated.

—Testimony given in July 2007 to the TJC by Carlos Villagra,
    son of Cpt. Américo Villagra, missing

I am sorry. In the name of the Nation, I am sorry for the solitude to which these victims were subjected. For every ounce of pain that scarred the flesh, body, mind, and spirit of those who fought for our new homeland while the country lay in slumber, blindly cohabitating with an ignominious dictatorship. Will the law honor its purpose, and apply the balm of historical redress to heal the open wounds suffered by these victims in the name of heroic dignity?

—Fernando Lugo, president of the Republic, August 2008

State-Sponsored Terrorism

The strategic command of the repressive state machinery was held by the army general Alfredo Stroessner, who was simultaneously commander in chief of the National Armed Forces, president of the Republic, and honorary president of the Colorado Party. The other authorities, both civilian and military, in the chain of command were part of a structure designed for the planning, coordination, and implementation of human rights violations. In this regard the TJC found that one of the main features setting the repressive Paraguayan regime apart from others in the region was the total absence of clandestine military or police structures different from or parallel to the official public structures of the state. The various political, military, and law enforcement bodies that carried out serious human rights violations did so in full public view. Nor were there any clandestine centers for imprisonment and torture; instead these were publicly known facilities belonging to the police, the military, and to government and civilian authorities.

The dictatorship brutally repressed members of banned or clandestine organizations—both political and armed—members of communist organizations, popular opposition leaders, and professional military personnel opposed to the regime. The repressive state machinery oversaw the massacre of indigenous people and allowed the trafficking of indigenous boys and girls. Acts of sexual violence, predominantly against women, adolescents, and young girls, constituted a serious violation of human rights that was encouraged by the structures of the system, to the point where senior officers of the regime used young girls as sex slaves.

In the opinion of the TJC, the human rights violations perpetrated during acts of state-sponsored terrorism qualify as crimes against humanity: the crimes committed are indefensible and are not political in nature, meaning that those responsible have no recourse to judicial privileges, amnesty, or immunity in relation to them, and are not exempt from accountability under the penal system, should they claim to have acted under the Law of Due Obedience. It also means that the principles of universal and international law may be applied, with the result that another state or an international tribunal or court may pursue, capture, investigate, prosecute, and punish those responsible.

Victims of Repression

The TJC investigation enabled the total number of victims who suffered directly from human rights violations to be estimated at 20,090. Taking into account the different kinds of violations perpetrated, victims subjected to direct human rights violations can be grouped as follows: 19,862 arrested either arbitrarily or illegally; 18,772 tortured; 59 executed extrajudicially; 337 disappeared; and 3,470 forcibly exiled. It should be borne in mind that individuals may have suffered more than one form of violation, and it should also be noted that these broad headings encompass many different forms of human rights violation, such as violations of the rights of women of all ages, and rape.

From calculations based on the number of victims in relation to the total population of Paraguay, which was on average 2,500,000 (1,300,000 in 1950 and 4,100,000 in 1992), and in relation to the adult population which was on average 1,250,000, the following can be established: 0.79 per cent of the total population, that is, one in every 126 individuals or one in every 63 adults, was illegally or arbitrarily arrested. One in every 133 people, or one in every 67 adults, that is, 0.75 per cent of the total population, was tortured. One in every 6,345 people was "disappeared" or executed extrajudicially. One in every 721 people, that is, 1.4 per thousand of the population, was exiled. In total, 0.80 per cent of the population, that is, one in every 124 people, was subjected to the violation of one or more of his or her fundamental human rights.

The dominant motive for the perpetration of human rights violations was the victim's affiliation with a specific social sector, for example with the Agrarian Leagues or the student movement, with opposition political parties, or with armed groups. Members of political parties accounted for 52.59 percent of recorded violations, 37.47 percent of violations were perpetrated against members of social movements, and 9.94 percent against members of armed groups. The primary victims of illegal detention and torture were members of political parties and social movements, especially peasant men and women, while the majority of forced disappearances and extrajudicial executions involved members of armed groups.

Arbitrary Arrests and Illegal Detention

According to the information contained in the conclusions of the Commission, 19,862 people were arrested, accounting for 98.8 percent of the victims of human rights violations. More than one in ten of those arrested (10.7 percent) were deprived of their freedom on more than one occasion. Under the dictatorship, a yearly average of 626 illegal arrests were made, affecting 567 people per year, equivalent to almost two arrests per day over a thirty-four-year period. In this way, the dictatorship violated the right to personal freedom of one in every 126 people or one in every 63 adults. This violation also affected the relatives of those arrested, as well as their friends, unions, political parties, religious and ethnic groups, and neighborhoods.

Illegal detentions were not carried out in secret, but rather in official, public locations well known to Paraguayan society. Over the course of several decades, thousands of people were subjected to generalized and systematic arbitrary arrest and the unlawful extension of their period of imprisonment; the TJC maintains that, since it was a part of institutional state policy, this practice of human rights violation constitutes a crime against humanity.

Torture and Other Forms of Cruel, Inhumane, or Degrading Treatment

The TJC was presented with 2,691 testimonies containing reports of torture, accounting for 93 percent of the total number of testimonies received. It is estimated that at least 18,772 people were tortured during the dictatorship, which equates to 0.75 percent of the population, or one in every 133 people. Few of those arrested escaped torture. Of the victims recorded by the TJC, 86 percent (17,277 people) were subjected to at least one form of physical torture and 83 percent (16,675 people) were subjected to at least one form of psychological torture. Of those who testified, 93 percent (18,772 people) were tortured, accounting for 94.5 percent of those people illegally deprived of freedom.

Forms of physical torture recorded during the TJC's investigations included: beatings with and without instruments; hanging; being forced to assume extreme positions; subjection to asphyxia by immersion in water, known as the "pileta" or bathtub; asphyxia using plastic bags; passing an electric current through the body by means of electrodes or an electric cattle prod; burns or cuts; rape; other forms of sexual abuse (harassment and molestation); and forced labor. Other forms of torture were also employed (untypical forms, such as the use of insects, or those unspecified by the source).

A separate form of torture was classified as psychological, although in many cases this caused both physical and psychological suffering: extreme (individual) isolation; withholding of food; withholding of medical attention; unsanitary conditions; overcrowding; sleep deprivation; solitary confinement; forced witnessing of torture; mock executions; death threats; death threats against relatives; threat of rape; threat of rape against relatives; defamation of relatives, and humiliation—insults, degrading treatment and restricted use of sanitary facilities, among others.

Forced Disappearances and Extrajudicial Executions

The TJC was able to identify 423 people, by their first names and surnames, who were deprived of their right to life. Of the total number of victims, 337 disappeared, 59 were executed extrajudicially, and violations perpetrated against 28 were uncategorized. In its report, the TJC considered that the process of clarification should continue in Paraguay with a view to uncovering the whole truth regarding the circumstances, names, and number of people who disappeared or were executed. Forced disappearances were carried out by the repressive state machinery because, among other things, it sought to eliminate the physical and social identity of the victim, to eliminate any association with specific groups or sectors, to remove any physical trace of the victim's body and of violations perpetrated, such as marks or evidence of torture, and to keep secret the final whereabouts of a person executed extrajudicially or arbitrarily.

The TJC maintains that, because of the generalized and systematic nature of the violation of the right to life perpetrated over several decades as part of state institutional policy, including its coordination with other regional dictatorships, these human rights violations constitute a crime against humanity.

Alfredo Stroessner:
Revisiting the General

Isabel Hilton

After he was overthrown in a bloody putsch on February 2–3, 1989, Alfredo Stroess-ner went into exile in Brazil. Thereafter he rarely gave interviews but made an ex-ception for a British journalist, Isabel Hilton. That interview, "The General," was first published in Granta *magazine in April 1990. These excerpts were published in* Open Democracy *on August 17, 2006, the day after Stroessner died in Brasília. In the interview, Stroessner continued to deny all of the accusations against him, portraying his time in office as a period of peace and progress, just as the official propaganda did when he was in power.*

I can see now where this story ended, although for a long time I was play-ing with other endings, reluctant to let go. It ended with that moment of cinema, crossing General Stroessner's spongy lawn and looking back to see him, framed in the doorway, waving. I waved, went through the gate and into the General's car, and the world rushed in around me, hotels, luggage and airports—everyday people, everyday lives. . . .

But where had the story begun? It had been there for years, but I always found something else, wars, elections; Latin America was never short of events clamouring for attention. Except in Paraguay. Paraguay was a situ-ation, rather than an event. It was wrapped in a layer of clichés, and, when events poked through, they seemed only to reinforce the clichés. Josef Mengele was in Paraguay; fascist army officers from Argentina fled to Para-guay when their coup plots failed; Indians in the Paraguayan jungle were hunted by fundamentalist American missionaries with rifles. Stroessner had been there for ever and always would be.

Then, suddenly, in February 1989, he wasn't. I wasn't there either. I was in Jamaica, watching a more orderly change of government. I called my newspaper from Kingston, cursing my bad luck—a journalist in the wrong place. It was too late. Stroessner had been hustled out of the country and had gone to ground in Brazil, where he sat in his beach-house, under siege from a press corps in bathing-suits. No interviews, no comment, no recriminations. Nothing.

He had never been a great one for interviews, but now he had a further excuse. He was in asylum and that imposed silence. After an interlude of disorderly scenes at the beach-house—photographers on step-ladders peeping over the wall, helicopters chartered by TV companies chattering overhead—he was moved. Some said to São Paulo; others said Brasília. At any rate, he had vanished behind another set of walls, another set of guards. He was rumoured to be ill and had a brief spell in hospital, then silence.

Six months later, I decided I would try to find him, to talk to him, and I had mixed feelings about the prospect. I knew nobody had and I didn't really see why I should be different, though I also knew that the unpredictability of Latin America could precipitate you as easily into a president's office as into a jail. I had set out on similar quests before and knew that they followed no timetable and that you just had to go where they led you until you either gave up or found yourself pushing an open door. I also knew that the last door always opened on to another, that it was hard to stop going through them and that there was never going to be enough time; I would end up, I feared, with one of those hollow-hearted stories which reconstructs the drama without the main character.

But even with that risk, it was a tempting drama. I knew that Stroessner's Paraguay had featured a kind of rampant official gangsterism, racketeers masquerading as high officials, contraband pretending to be business. There was a constitution, a state structure; there were laws, elections: but none of them was real. What was real was power, cronyism, corruption, the righteous men in jail and the criminals in government. . . . I wanted to follow a thread to the Presidential Palace.

I set off for Asunción at the beginning of September 1989 with a suitcase of research I had only just begun to read and a list of names and numbers. Apart from one detailed academic political study and some slim volumes published by human rights organizations, there was remarkably little about Stroessner's Paraguay. . . . It was like the silent planet, on a different radio frequency from the outside world. It fought savage wars with its neighbours, in which thousands died; created passionate myths and legends, but who cared? It changed presidents so often that when Alfredo Stroessner staged his coup, in May 1954, then sanctified his newly acquired throne with rigged elections, he must have seemed like just the latest man through the revolving door.

When he fell, thirty-five years later, he held a number of records. He was the longest-serving dictator in the western hemisphere and the second longest in the world: only Kim Il Sung outlasted him. The world had lived through thirty-five years of history, but three-quarters of the population of Paraguay had known no other leader, and there was not an institution or political party in the country that had not been shaped by his presence.

[*Isabel Hilton traveled from Asunción to Brasília. There, a contact told her that the general would see her. Following a chat with Stroessner's son, Gustavo, a car was sent to bring her to his home.*]

I turned round from the garden at the moment the General made his entrance. It was as though the photographs had come alive. That heavy face, the pouchy blue eyes, the full underlip beneath the moustache and the slightly receding chin that folded into a flabby neck. His blue-silk suit was carefully buttoned over a paunch.

"Welcome," he said, "a great pleasure to receive you." . . .

Stroessner cleared his throat and began to make a speech. "In Paraguay," he said, "there was democracy. A fully democratic system, with absolute independence of the judges and the parliament. Then there was great progress. Great progress. Development." . . .

"We can't make any statements here. We can't talk about the internal politics of Paraguay." My heart sank. "A lot of people have asked for interviews, but we have said no. This is a special case. But we are in political asylum. We have to be careful." I wondered why they had made an exception. . . .

[*Stroessner listed countries he had visited, other leaders he had met, infrastructure improvements under his rule—and asked what people were saying about him in Asunción.*]

But the attempted revolutions in Paraguay? The guerrillas? . . .

"A few," said the old man. "But they were very small in number. They were of no importance." I thought of those peasant massacres, armed assaults on people seeking land-reform, tortured oppositionists, all condemned as communists. . . . Of the language of the Cold War, preserved in the rare air of Asunción. And he didn't believe it? Never had? "There was no reason for a revolution in Paraguay," Stroessner added, by way of explanation. I tried a few other ways of asking the question and gave up. Stroessner simply refused to worry about communism.

I tried another line of questions, on the problems of authority. Did he feel, always, that he was being told the truth by those who served him? "Yes, always," he said. Another dead end, I thought. "Though," he added, after a pause, "one can always be wrong, given what happened." I looked up at him. He was smiling at the floor. I hadn't expected irony.

He seemed to be thinking about it, talking from inside at last. "I was always confident that I knew. I never expected this . . . this"—he searched for the word—"this *cuartelazo*." For reasons that are not hard to find, there is, in Spanish, more than one word for a *coup d'etat*. The most derogatory is *"cuartelazo,"* a barracks revolt, a rabble got out of hand. . . . How did he feel about it, I asked him. . . . "Look, what can you do in these circumstances . . . 'A lo hecho, pecho'*—take it on the chin. It happened. Taking into account all the other things that happened in the past, what happened to me is not extraordinary." He returned to his consolatory recital. "Paraguay had a long period of progress, tranquillity and peace. It took giant steps."

[Isabel Hilton returned later to continue the interview, Stroessner in the same up-right chair, "with the same disciplined stillness."]

The General had dusted off the president, put on a suit and performed for history as well as his rambling old age would allow. . . .

. . . I had come for my second interview wanting to get some sense of how the General felt about the *coup*—what led to it? why he thought it had happened? did he think that things could have turned out differently?—but I was not to have much success.

There were so many things Stroessner clung to: that the army had not been unhappy; that he had never insisted that officers join the Colorado party; . . . that those who ousted Stroessner were members of a small clique who did it for no other reason than that of squalid personal ambition. Under Stroessner, life in Paraguay had always been marked by peace, order and an absence of serious social conflict. The problems with the Church were a matter of a few individual priests. The problems with the United States were some minor difficulties (with one ambassador). The problems with the "exiled" opposition were exaggerated. . . . The problems with the press were only because some members of it had been advocating violence. Para-guay, under Stroessner, was a fully democratic society. . . .

I was starting to see that, at the heart of it all, there were just too many things that could not be reconciled: a clear white space between the Para-guay of Stroessner's vision and the Paraguay I had got to know. There were also two Stroessners: one, the beloved father of the people, progressive and popular; the second, the man who, for thirty-five years, ran a state of terror

This postage stamp portrays the Itaipú hydroelectric plant as
one of the main achievements of the Stroessner regime. It was
issued in 1988 when Stroessner was reelected for the seventh
time, with 88.6 percent of the votes cast. Although the over-
print assumes that he would stay in power for a further five
years until 1993, he was deposed less than a year later. Image
by Correo Paraguayo (Paraguayan Postal Service). Used by
permission of Correo Paraguayo.

in the name of national security and the fight against communism. Now, in
exile, he chose to forget the second Stroessner: or, at least in my company,
he had chosen to forget him, and there seemed to be little that I could do
about it. . . .

[The next day, Isabel Hilton was to see Stroessner for the third and final time.]

I had little to lose, I thought, in confronting him with some realities. That's
what I decided I would do: I would make Stroessner confront Stroessner.

I would talk to him about torture. I began by citing Amnesty International. A simple statement: that Amnesty International had consistently reported that in Paraguay there was torture. "Rupture?," said Stroessner. "No,
there was no rupture. We always answered the questions." There was never
a rupture or there was never torture? I asked, deflated by this attack of deafness. "No," he said, "never a rupture. We answered all the questions quite
normally." But what about the allegations themselves? I said. The physical
mistreatment in the prisons? "No. Absolutely not," he said. "I don't remem-

ber any such allegations. Or any such information coming to me through such organisations."

"So the behaviour of the Paraguayan police was—"

"—Correct," he interrupted.

"Correct?" I said.

"Correct," he repeated.

What about the state of siege? I asked, determined to poke my finger through the ideal democracy of Paraguay. "Did not the state of siege act as an impediment to justice?"

I had made him irritated.

"Look," he said. "The state of siege was necessary. There was subversion in Latin America. It was more of a preventive measure. It wasn't used much." He said he would have preferred to have lifted it. It was not what he wanted.

But I had crossed the line.

"These are things that have already been judged. Things in the past," he said. "I have to think of my status as a resident in this country. But I do insist that in Paraguay there was order [*orden*]; the judiciary had the power of complete independence; justice was fully exercised."

I asked him if he regretted the way things had turned out.

"Oh, yes," he said. "I went in by the front door and had always wanted to leave by the front door. But circumstances didn't allow it. But I don't want to make any accusations. Everything that happened, happened, and, if I had known—well, we are all wise after the event . . ."

"Well," he said abruptly, "I think we have talked quite a lot. I was at the head of the government—by popular choice—and Paraguay progressed. That's all I can say, Isabel Hilton. . . ."

. . . His greatest gift had been his power to corrupt. His great good fortune that so many were willing to be corrupted. He had distorted meaning so far that finally there was none. How long would he last, I wondered, in this little domestic prison, adding up the mileage of asphalted roads?

. . . "I saw Stroessner," I said to one friend, a man who knows as much about Latin American dictators as anybody.

"Did he say much?" he asked.

"No," I replied.

"I'm not surprised," he said. "They never do."

VI

A Transition in Search of Democracy

In overthrowing Stroessner, General Andrés Rodríguez sought to reestablish the unity between the military and the Colorado Party that had been weakened in the final years of the regime, but he also initiated a process of democratic transition in order to end Paraguay's diplomatic isolation. Exiles were allowed to return, banned newspapers and radio stations were reopened, and all political parties were legalized. Rodríguez won a clear victory as the official Colorado presidential candidate in the snap elections held just three months after the coup, and in June 1992 a new democratic constitution was promulgated. Democratization also opened the door for stronger economic ties with neighboring countries, in particular with the creation in 1991 of Mercosur, the regional common market comprising Argentina, Brazil, Paraguay, and Uruguay.

Despite the new constitution and the introduction of free elections, the legacy of the past weighed heavily against efforts for improved governance. The Colorado Party managed to hold onto power throughout the 1990s despite bitter internal factionalism, a series of banking crises, economic mismanagement, and resulting economic stagnation between 1996 and 2002. The dismal democratization process saw three bouts of military instability (in April 1996, March 1999, and May 2000), the assassination of a vice president, Luís Argaña (in 1999), and the indictment of two former presidents, Juan Carlos Wasmosy (1993–98) and Raúl González Macchi (1998–99), on corruption charges. Powerful elite groups that had emerged during the dictatorship jostled to retain their power in the new democratic environment, often buying political influence. Corruption escalated as ill-gotten fortunes were rapidly amassed through the narcotics trade, counterfeiting, and the flagrant misuse of foreign aid inflows, while Asunción became a regional center for money laundering and contraband. With no efforts by successive Colorado administrations to introduce social reforms, indices of poverty, inequality, and rural landholding worsened throughout the decade, while indicators of access to primary health care and basic education remained among the lowest in the Americas.

The mid-2000s saw sustained economic growth that pulled Paraguay out of recession, based on the rapid expansion of soybean and meat production for export in response to soaring world prices. The area under soybean cultivation grew rapidly and by 2010 Paraguay ranked as the fourth largest exporter of soybeans and the eighth largest exporter of meat in the world. However, the benefits of this were captured by a small elite of soybean farmers, cattle ranchers, corrupt politicians, and urban professionals, while the vast majority of rural households were bypassed by the boom, and the environment suffered from overuse of chemicals on GM crops. Growth was accompanied by growing poverty: by 2007, 35.6 percent of the population was living in poverty, of which 19.4 percent were living in absolute poverty.

Growing resentment at the failure of the transition to deliver improvements in living standards was evidenced in the annual public opinion surveys by *Latinobarómetro*. Paraguayans consistently scored lowest of all countries in the region on almost all ratings of attitudes toward democracy, including support, government performance, and improvement to welfare, and Paraguay was the only country in the region where support for authoritarianism rivaled that for democracy. Such disillusionment found expression in a number of ways. Migration to Europe exploded, as young, poor rural Paraguayans sought work abroad: by 2008 there were an estimated 100,000 Paraguayans living (mainly illegally) in Spain. Security became the greatest concern for citizens in surveys, as violent crime soared. Support for the authoritarian populist leader Lino Oviedo continued, and in the mid-2000s, a small armed revolutionary movement, the Ejército del Pueblo Paraguayo (EPP), appeared in the Departments of San Pedro and Concepción, renowned for their high levels of poverty and landlessness, demanding radical land reform.

It was in this environment of disillusionment that a former bishop, Fernando Lugo, emerged at the forefront of the protests against President Duarte Frutos (2003–2008) and, soon after, as the leading presidential candidate. An electoral pact with the Liberal Party (PLRA) produced the Patriotic Alliance for Change (Alianza Patriótica para el Cambio—APC), giving Lugo the vital backing of the powerful Liberals, while his promises of long overdue social reforms in favor of the poor, his image as an honest and committed bishop, and his commitment to tackle corruption caught the popular imagination. His victory in the 2008 elections, which put an end to sixty-one years of Colorado Party rule, led to high—perhaps unrealistically high—expectations of, as he put it, a "new dawn" for Paraguay.

However, Lugo's commitment to progressive social and economic change, including land and tax reform, faced a range of almost insurmountable obstacles. Despite some significant progress in social welfare, including the establishment of free medical attention in public hospitals and a monthly conditional cash transfer program which benefitted over 100,000 of the poorest families, Lugo's popularity decreased considerably as his presidency proceeded. This was partly caused by a series of paternity scandals and by his indecisive leadership but primarily by the power of vested economic and political interests, assisted by a powerful media campaign, to block his key reform initiatives. This virulent opposition culminated in the express impeachment of Lugo on 22 June, 2012, only 14 months before he was due to leave office—a decision that received widespread international condemnation—and his replacement by his vice-president, Federico Franco, of the PLRA. Lugo's election in 2008 had shown a popular desire for change after over half a century of authoritarianism and Colorado Party rule. But his removal from office revealed the continuing fragility of the democratization process initiated in 1989.

We Have Left Our Barracks

Andrés Rodríguez

The first, short statement during the putsch that removed Alfredo Stroessner from office was made by its leader, General Andrés Rodríguez, on a local radio station, Primero de Marzo, at thirty minutes past midnight on February 3, 1989. Because of the euphoria generated by the end of the dictatorship, less attention was paid to what Rodríguez actually gave as the reasons for his decision. It is revealing that his often-quoted objective of initiating a process of transition to democracy came after two other priorities: the distancing of the armed forces from the Stroessner dictatorship (after thirty-five years of close support) and the reunification of the ruling Colorado Party, which had suffered from growing internal divisions in the final years of the "stronato." As subsequent events would amply demonstrate, the order of priorities was not random. A revitalized Colorado Party would set out the scope, nature, and limits of the democratization process, which it would then dominate from its position of power for a further nineteen years.

Dear compatriots and esteemed comrades of the armed forces. We have left our barracks in order to defend the dignity and honor of the armed forces; for the complete and total unification of the Colorado Party in the government; for the initiation of the democratization of Paraguay; for the respect of human rights; and in defense of our catholic, apostolic, and Roman Christian religion. This is what I am offering to you through the sacrifice of the Paraguayan soldier for our dear, brave, and noble Paraguayan people. I hope that our comrades in the armed forces will accompany me in these circumstances in the knowledge that we are defending a noble and just cause that will benefit our heroic and noble Paraguayan people. Thank you.

Reestablishing the Status Quo

Andrew Nickson

The overthrow of Alfredo Stroessner in 1989 gave rise to intense euphoria inside Paraguay that democracy had arrived and that with it, the country's many economic and social problems would soon be overcome. The following extract is taken from an article written in the heat of the moment that advised extreme caution. It pointed out that the prime objective of the putsch was to reaffirm the alliance between the Colorado Party and the armed forces, which had been the mainstay of the Stroessner regime. Although viewed at the time by many Paraguayans as unduly pessimistic, its prediction of a slow and complicated transition to democracy proved broadly correct.

At 9.45 P.M. on Thursday 2 February 1989 tanks rumbled out of the 1st Army Corps headquarters at Loma Pyta, four miles north of the Paraguayan capital of Asunción and headed for the city. The rebel troops, loyal to their commanding officer, General Andrés Rodríguez, soon occupied the city centre. Artillery fire and bombardment from cannons mounted on navy vessels in the River Paraguay quickly overcame resistance from the Presidential Palace and the main police headquarters. Meanwhile, troop commanders in military regions throughout the country pledged their support to the rebels. The elite 700-strong Presidential Escort Regiment was the sole military unit to resist the uprising. Its headquarters were overcome only after several hours of intense bombardment. At 8.00 the next morning General Rodríguez was able to announce the complete surrender of government forces and by 5.00 P.M. he had already sworn himself in as the new interim president of Paraguay. The military *putsch* had been short and sharp, well planned and well executed. Although the official death toll was reported as 31, diplomatic observers and medical sources put the real figure much higher, possibly between 150 and 250, most of them members of the Presidential Escort Regiment. The day of San Blas (3 February) is a national holiday in Paraguay. As the inhabitants of Asunción surveyed the scenes of destruction with a mixture of disbelief and euphoria, the realisation began to dawn that the regime of General Alfredo Stroessner, for long considered indestructible by most of its citizens, had been brought down overnight. Stroessner had ruled the country for 34 years, 8 months and 29 days—longer than any other president in the history of Paraguay. Yet he had been overthrown in a swift and bloody *putsch* by none other than the man who had been his main military *confidant* throughout most of his presidency, and to whom he is even related by marriage. After a few days under house arrest at Rodríguez's military barracks in Loma Pyta, Stroessner was granted temporary political asylum in Brazil. At 3.50 P.M. on 5 February, as Paraguayan television showed live coverage of the plane taking him and his eldest son, Air Force Colonel Gustavo Stroessner into exile, it was clear to viewers that a major chapter in Paraguayan history had come to an end. The ousting of Stroessner led to intense speculation in the international media that Paraguay would soon join the broad trend towards democratic rule that has characterised the recent political history of the Southern Cone. General Rodríguez heightened this speculation in radio communiqués to the nation during and after the coup, when he stated that the rebels had acted in order to initiate a process of democratisation, to restore respect for human rights and in defence of the Catholic Church. Much more revealing however was the fact that he prefaced these noble objectives by two others—that the rebels had acted in defence of the dignity of the armed forces and for the full and total unification of the Colorado Party. Observers familiar with the political history of Paraguay over the past 50 years listened to these latter objectives with foreboding. For unlike the overthrow of Somoza in Nicaragua or of Marcos in the Philippines, Alfredo Stroessner was not ousted as a result of a popular uprising. Despite growing social discontent in the preceding months, the popular sectors played no part whatsoever in the events surrounding the 2 February coup. An understanding of the reasons for the coup therefore requires an examination of the complex relationship between the armed forces and the Colorado Party which has played such an important role in the political history of Paraguay over the past 50 years. This relationship, which both predates the Stroessner dictatorship, and which accounts in large part for the longevity of his regime, also provides the fundamental reasons for its eventual collapse. At the same time this relationship defines the parameters for the future political development of Paraguay over the medium term.

On 1 May 1989, exactly three months after deposing Stroessner, General Andrés Rodríguez was elected president of Paraguay as the official candidate of the Colorado Party. His convincing election victory reinforced the fact that the reputation of both the Colorado Party and the armed forces had emerged largely unscathed from their long association with the Stroessner regime. Rodríguez received 73 per cent of the presidential vote, while the Colorado Party won 69 per cent of the vote for senators and deputies in Congress. The Partido Liberal Radical Auténtico, which was not officially recognised during the *stronato*, was the only opposition party to register a substantial vote. Its presidential candidate Domingo Laíno received 21 per cent of the vote, while its candidates won 20 per cent in the elections to Congress. However, the remaining opposition parties fared badly. The other members of the Acuerdo Nacional polled surprisingly low votes. The Febrerista Party scored only 1.1 per cent, while the Christian Democrat Party performed even worse, at 0.7 per cent of the presidential vote. The three factions of the Liberal Party (Partido Liberal Radical, Partido Liberal and Partido Liberal Radical Unido) which had collaborated as a "loyal opposition" in Congress during the *stronato*, received 0.9 per cent, 0.4 per cent and 0.2 per cent respectively of the presidential vote. The enduring and preponderant strength of the Colorado Party and its willingness to endorse a military candidate as its presidential candidate in succession to Stroessner raises interesting questions in connection with the wider debate on democratisation of military regimes in Latin America. Although one writer has suggested that Paraguay was beginning to display features of "bureaucratic-authoritarianism" in the 1980s, [Guillermo] O'Donnell's classification of the Stroessner regime as "traditional" is more generally accepted, and aptly characterised by what he calls "predatory sultanism" (O'Donnell 1986a). However, in his comprehensive study of the transition from authoritarian rule, O'Donnell has suggested that such "traditional" regimes are more likely to experience a "revolutionary" transition than the "non-revolutionary" transition more characteristic of bureaucratic-authoritarian regimes. Yet the surprisingly smooth demise of the Stroessner regime would seem to lend little support to this hypothesis in the case of Paraguay. The social forces and political institutions that broadly supported the defunct Stroessner regime are not in disarray. Despite the ousting of the *militantes*, on balance the Colorado Party has been strengthened by the decision of the long-standing dissident faction, MOPOCO [Movimiento Popular Colorado], to abandon the Acuerdo Nacional and return to the Colorado fold. The composition of the new Junta de Gobierno of the party which nominated Rodríguez as its presidential candidate reflects the strong coalition established between the dominant *democrático* and MIC [Movimiento de Integración Colorado] factions and other minority factions such as MAC [Movimiento de Autenticidad Colorado], MOPOCO and the *éticos*. This re-unification of the Colorado Party, which was actively promoted by General Rodríguez, bears a striking similarity to the *re-encuentro* (re-union) of 27 October 1955 when Stroessner at-tracted back dissident groups such as the *guionistas* to the Colorado fold in order to isolate the *democráticos* whom he had overthrown a year earlier. Furthermore, the Paraguayan experience may indeed prove to contradict O'Donnell's bold assertion that in Latin America there is "no such case of a reasonably successful, self-confident and electorally supported authoritar-ian regime entering into transition" (O'Donnell 1986a: 13). Yet in his election campaign, Rodríguez confidently and successfully co-opted the rhetoric of the opposition—concern for democracy, social justice and human rights—to his own advantage, while projecting a "popular" image completely at variance with his previous role as the main military *confidant* of Stroessner. The nature of the electoral pact reveals the enormous imbalance in power between the regime and the opposition. All of the opposition parties (with the exception of the MDP [Movimiento Democrático Popular]) agreed to participate in the elections in exchange for official recognition and unre-stricted freedom of political activity. In return they dropped their demands for a postponement of the election in order to allow time for reorganisation after years of illegality and for a new electoral register to be drawn up. Simi-larly their demand for a reform of the autocratic features of the electoral law whereby the majority party is guaranteed two-thirds of the seats in Con-gress (Art. 8) and coalitions are prohibited (Art. 14) was quietly shelved. The coup which removed President Alfredo Stroessner from office was carried out with the prime intention of re-establishing the harmonious relationship between the armed forces and the Colorado Party which has dominated the political system of Paraguay since 1946, and which had been seriously disturbed in recent years by the activities of the *militantes*. As this article has attempted to demonstrate, virtually all factions of the Colorado Party are wedded to a corporativist political philosophy constructed on the basis of a strong historical identification of the Colorado Party with the national interest. At the same time, the armed forces have been prepared to support this arrangement, in exchange for wide-ranging institutional and personal privilege. The authoritarian political culture, to which this close relation-ship between the armed forces and the Colorado Party has given rise, is unlikely to be dismantled to any significant extent by the new Colorado government of General Rodríguez.

It is by no means certain that the liberalisation introduced by General Rodríguez indicates that a transitional process is underway in Paraguay. Yet if such a process does emerge, it may well provide that example, all too rare in the Southern Cone, of a "transition initiated from above by authoritar-ian incumbents with sufficient cohesion and resources to dictate the emerging rules of the game" (O'Donnell 1986b: 39). Whether the resurrection of the deeply buried civil society of Paraguay is capable of propelling such a *dictablanda* towards a democratic society remains problematic.

Works Cited

O'Donnell, G. 1986a. "Introduction to the Latin American Cases." In *Transitions from Authoritarian Rule: Prospects for Democracy*, ed. G. O'Donnell, P. C. Schmitter, and L. Whitehead. Baltimore, Md.: Johns Hopkins University Press.

———. 1986b. "Tentative Conclusions about Uncertain Democracies." In *Transitions from Authoritarian Rule: Prospects for Democracy*, ed. G. O'Donnell, P. C. Schmitter, and L. Whitehead. Baltimore, Md.: Johns Hopkins University Press.

My Deepest Respects to the Colorado Party

Helio Vera

This article was written on the eve of the presidential elections of 2008, which ended sixty-one years of Colorado Party control of the executive. By the time that the article was written, Fernando Lugo, the candidate of the opposition Alliance for Change, was ahead in the polls, and the Colorado Party itself divided. However, it was far from clear just what the election results would bring. Helio Vera (1946–2008) was a journalist and writer who specialized in social commentary, and was renowned for his perceptive but humorous critique of the character and ways of Paraguayans. The article is a scathing attack on the betrayal of the ideals upon which the Colorado Party was founded and of the achievements of its founding members. After sixty-one years in power through dictatorship and democracy, he argues that it had lost its way and had stagnated in a quagmire of corruption, greed, and lust for power.

How could one fail to feel respect for the Colorado Party? It was the political force that, with the few resources available, threw itself into building a reasonably modern country out of the ruins of a nation devastated by war.

To this aim, General Caballero lent his name and his prestige. He had already left the presidency, but he had the wisdom to call upon the most outstanding political personalities of the period, including José Decoud, Benjamín Aceval, Angel Para, Blas Garay, and Fulgencio R. Moreno, just to mention a few names off the top of my head. As we all know, Caballero was no intellectual but he did not need to be; he simply surrounded himself by those who really were.

Influenced by the predominant liberal vision of state and society, the party strove to build the foundations of an educational system capable of developing the youth of Paraguay. National primary schools, high schools, and the National University appeared thanks to the initiative of its members. Professors from Spain were employed to teach in them, and the Generación del 900, the most brilliant literary movement in our history, emerged from their demanding classes. And, strikingly, the members of the party came principally from humble backgrounds, almost always from the countryside or from families devastated by the Triple Alliance War.

Throughout the first half of the twentieth century and even in the first few years of the second, the embers of these venerable flames still glowed, personified in intellectual figures such as Pedro P. Peña, Natalicio González, Victor Morínigo, Vasconcellos, Mario Halley Mora, Osvaldo Chávez, and Edgar Ynsfrán. Meanwhile, a number of hardened and austere political figures continued this party pedigree during the stormy years following the 1947 civil war: Eulogio Estigarribia, Bernardino Gorostiaga, Tomás Romero Pereira, Juan Manuel Frutos, Federico Chávez, just to name a few that come to mind.

I wonder what became of this Colorado Party. I really do not know. All I see now is a complex bureaucratic machine, whose maintenance costs are increasingly expensive; so much so that were it not for its symbiotic relationship with the state, neither would make it through another day. If this state/party hybrid still has an ideology, it is doubtless known only to a privileged few who spend their time revising its dusty pages in some remote suburb of Asunción. If it does have anything resembling a political program or even a model of state governance capable of delivering security, freedom, and welfare for its entire population, then it remains a mystery as profound as the Holy Trinity itself.

But let us humbly accept that it may have such a program, even though we see no trace of it. It is a question of faith.

The Colorado Party has been reduced to nothing more than an overcrowded public sector employment agency. At the same time is has also become a kind of football club that lives off primitive emotions, fueled by the rhythms of a joyful polka and the waving of bright red flags. The polka always concludes to enthusiastic applause and the color is reproduced in a sea of red shirts and handkerchiefs. I should make it clear that I have nothing against either the polka or the color red, except when the latter makes a mockery of some poor soul forced to squeeze his ample midriff into a huge red shirt, giving him the appearance of a huge mollusk. Even here, my objections are merely aesthetic rather than political.

But we do not ask for any more of the party because there is no more. There is no program of government, no ideas. There is not even any trace of ideology (even though a while back they declared themselves Humanist Socialists), because for this there would need to be a class-based society. In Paraguay, there are no classes, only opposite poles: the misery of those living in extreme poverty contrasting with the opulence of the new rich. Nor are there statesmen, nor intellectuals. Even technocrats are only admitted to the party as *tembiguai*,[1] with no possibility of applying their knowledge for the common good of their fellow citizens.

Who are responsible for this situation? Simply, a group of career politicians who see power as the quickest and easiest route to becoming tycoons. They are armed with three rows of giant teeth top and bottom; teeth so powerful that they would make a *Tyrannosaurus rex* green with envy.

How many of them are there? Perhaps twenty, thirty at the most. Instead of a philosophy about the role of the state, or a political ideology, they simply offer us a series of empty, clichéd phrases, which are void of all substance. Their mental bankruptcy is so shocking that after four years in government they were unable to even stutter their way through a proposal for constitutional reform, even though it was designed to cover up their desperate attempts to hang onto power, and all the benefits such power carries with it. What else would we expect from them?

Instead of conviction, they have only greed; in place of reason they have only gluttony. Incapable of actually convincing anyone through political argument, they build consensus through grotesque bribes, which are as discreet as a blazing fire. They have done this, and continue to do so, in such a clumsy manner that nowadays anyone from outside the party who actually supports their policies only does so because they have received something, asked for something or have been promised something. Let us not kid ourselves.

I would be delighted if one of the many friends I have who call themselves Colorados could show me that everything I have said is false. It would be good news indeed for the country if I were wrong.

Asunción, April 11, 2008

Note

1. *Tembiguai* is a highly derogatory word in Guaraní—used behind people's backs—to denote someone who is exploited. The suggestion here is that the technocrats think they can influence the party, but in fact are being used and exploited by the party to give a false veneer of modernity. [Eds.]

The Characteristics of Oviedismo

Milda Rivarola

The figure of the former general Lino Oviedo has dominated the transition since 1989, on a number of occasions threatening to overthrow the incumbent government, while at the same time gaining significant popular support. Widely suspected of links with regional mafias, illicit business dealings, and a highly authoritarian political project, Oviedo has shown remarkable political resilience, undermining the arguments of those who have consistently underestimated his popularity or acumen and dismissed him as a spent force, a clown, or an irrelevance.

A mere colonel in the February 1989 coup, when he was credited with personally capturing Alfredo Stroessner, he rose rapidly through the ranks to become head of the army in the 1990s. His role in a coup attempt in 1996 led to his dismissal from the armed forces. He entered politics and was arrested in 1998 on charges of sedition, just when he was the clear favorite to win the presidential elections of that year. Released from prison by his former running-mate, the incoming president Raúl Cubas, in March 1999 he was accused of being behind the assassination of his archenemy, Vice President Luís María Argaña, and a further attempted coup, which was only rebuffed by thousands of prodemocracy demonstrators involved in violent street battles outside Congress over a period of three days (the heroic marzo paraguayo). *Fleeing into exile, he returned to Paraguay to serve out his prison sentence, only to be released in 2007 by President Nicanor Duarte in an unsuccessful attempt to undermine the candidacy of Fernando Lugo in the upcoming 2008 presidential elections. However, Oviedo came a surprising third in the elections with 24 percent of the vote, confounding his critics and making his Unión Nacional de Colorados Eticos (UNACE) a powerful party in Congress.*

To a large extent, the Oviedo phenomenon reflects the failure of a transition process that has been elite-led and has failed to improve the condition of the poor or reduce inequality. Many poorer Paraguayans, who find themselves excluded from the benefits of democracy, have been attracted by Oviedo's charisma, his self-portrayal as a man of the people, and his promises of a better future. The following unpublished report by Milda Rivarola, one of Paraguay's foremost political analysts, captures the powerful personality cult that Oviedo has built up around himself, and that, judging by the 2008 elections, continues to capture the imagination of many Paraguayans.

The existence of *oviedismo* is inseparable from the personality of Lino Oviedo, which combines various elements—authoritarian, military, Colorado, and *caudillo*. He presented himself to the public as a "messiah," chosen to save the nation, with whom the Paraguayan people, with their needs and hopes, could identify; the leader predestined to liberate them of their woes. And as a messianic leader, or populist *caudillo* (the term initially used to define him), he secured adherents and a loyalty verging on religious fanaticism.

This characteristic evolved over the period from the founding of UNACE (1996) to the inauguration of the Presidency of Raúl Cubas (August 1998). The image of "the chosen one" is evident in his election propaganda, which defines him as "the greatest hope of the people," "the undisputed flag-bearer of the poor," "the great laborer," "the force behind the unfulfilled proclamation of 1989," "the synthesis of the fusion of the people and the army, as in the historic moments of 1811, 1932 and 1989," who "will create the explosion in terms of national economic development."

In the writings of his followers he has been compared with De Gaulle and Perón, and described as the "most revered hero of the liberating coup." Even Luís María Argaña would have feared "his pride, his dignity, his energy, his combative spirit, that valiant and disinterested will." He was "the man of destiny" who returned after April 1996. A leader of such powerful magic "that every Colorado—as if bewitched—managed to create in their minds their own particular Oviedo: the revolutionary Oviedo, the great laborer, the protector of tradition and unity, the great progressive, the democrat . . . the austere military man, the cultured wise man . . . the great Colorado patriot."

An anthem of his movement, widely distributed at *oviedista* meetings, sanctified him in an almost childlike way: "The good Colorado extols Lino as the Savior," and "General Lino Oviedo, the torch that will illuminate the path of Paraguay."

The celebration of his birthday on September 23 was surrounded by ostentation and obsequiousness, reminiscent of the praise heaped on Stroessner, with paid adverts in newspapers, replete with the signatures of leaders of public employees' unions, and the use of official vehicles for transporting guests to the party and any necessary repairing of roads to do so.

An article by employees of the Ministry of Public Health and Social Welfare published on Oviedo's birthday in 1998 declared "Great men, statesmen, appear only very rarely. The Paraguayan people are blessed to count among their citizens one prominent man . . . a man of arms, loyal to his fatherland, the indisputable bearer of the nationalist and agrarian doctrine of Bernardino Caballero, Division General Lino Cesar Oviedo Silva."

Just as he was accustomed to do during previous administrations, Oviedo continued to claim government projects, such as the future construction of a new bridge over the River Paraná, as if they were his own initiatives. In the Cabinet he had the support of enthusiastic propagandists, who openly compared him with divinity. The minister of agriculture exclaimed, "I have God in Heaven and Lino Oviedo on Earth," while attributing to him "ten out of ten for intelligence, managerial ability and a range of virtues; he is a philosopher; comparable to Bolívar."

Oviedo prided himself—with good reason—on his absolute control of his movement. When the possibility of his prohibition from standing in the primaries for the presidency of the Colorado Party was being mooted, he stated, "Another candidate may well win, but only if I say that he will be the successful candidate."

The distribution in 1997 of 100,000 UNACE booklets bearing photos of Oviedo and the pope had already opened the way for later abuse of religious symbols by this messianic leader. Such reiterated allusions offended the Catholic clergy, and the bishops who compared him to Hitler in 1997 and later criticized him indirectly in statements about "the despots who would have our people believe that they are the Messiah" and the "populist *caudillos* who lie to the people" during the celebrations of the Immaculate Conception in December 1998.

Oviedo continued to promote this messianic image a few weeks later, when he compared himself to Jesus while a guest of honor at a graduation ceremony in the town of Coronel Oviedo. And in the same way that young conscripts who finished their service between 1994 and 1995 went home with little flags and insignia bearing his name, so medals inscribed "A souvenir from General Oviedo" were given out to state high school graduates by the vice minister of Culture at the end of 1998.

The cult of the figure of Oviedo was nourished in particular by the women of the UNACE movement. During the 1997–98 electoral campaign, women were the main callers to local radio stations, and one of his followers even exclaimed that "if Lino Oviedo tells us to throw ourselves in the river, then we'll all throw ourselves in the river." When they heard about Sentence 84 of April 1998 [sentencing him to prison for his alleged role in the 1996 coup attempt], several women fainted in the UNACE offices, and during a violent meeting on December 10 that year, a young man read aloud, without any embarrassment, a poem in which he likened Oviedo to "an illuminated messenger" and "a superman."

Political and parliamentary leaders have often highlighted the messianic character of his political project: the vice president of the Senate labeled the state envisaged by *oviedismo* as "a typical dictatorial, messianic scheme," and in his end-of-year address, the president of the Colorado Party also denounced the "messianic authoritarianism" of Oviedo. This characterization of followers of Oviedo as "messianists, coup plotters, and authoritarians" was repeated in later statements by mainstream Colorado leaders at the end of January 1999.

The self-perception of Lino Oviedo as the undisputed leader of the government and the country survived the assassination of Luís María Argaña. The controversy of Wednesday, March 24, should be remembered, the day when, contradicting President Cubas, who claimed he had ordered Oviedo's arrest, Lino Oviedo claimed he had presented himself voluntarily at Police Headquarters, solely in order to "clarify his legal position."

In Homage to the Victims
of Ycuá Bolaños

Luis Irala

On Sunday, August 1, 2004, a fire broke out in the Ycuá Bolaños supermarket in Trinidad, a neighborhood of Asunción. The three-story building was crowded with weekend shoppers, many of them families. The fire began in a grill located in the shop's food hall, which had a duct that had been improperly constructed and poorly maintained. The fire then spread unnoticed between the building's false ceiling and roof, causing the release of flammable gases. The shock wave created by the resulting explosion broke outside windows in the bakery section, sucking in oxygen, and enabling the fire to rapidly spread to the rest of the store. As the building turned into an inferno, flames entered the central air conditioning system, causing its nitrogen coolant to explode. The fire then spread downward to the underground car park, where one car exploded, setting off another shockwave that brought the ground floor crashing into the basement, and cutting off lower-level escape routes. Dozens died in their cars. Surviving witnesses told of the panic as people rushed screaming toward the exits in complete darkness and enveloped in thick smoke.

As well as poor maintenance, the tragedy was caused by the inexplicable absence of both a fire detection system and adequate emergency exits. But perhaps most shocking of all, survivors reported that when they finally reached the doors, they found them locked. Following company procedures, security guards had locked the emergency exits to prevent people leaving without paying for their goods. In the aftermath of the tragedy, piled around the locked exits were found many bodies of those who had died from crushing, asphyxiation, and burns.

The fire burned for seven hours and left a toll of 396 dead, nearly half of whom were children. Over 500 people were seriously injured, many suffering horrendous injuries including loss of limbs, loss of sight, and severe burns. Over 200 children were orphaned.

After a prolonged campaign for justice led by the Association of Victims, in February 2008 three men were found guilty of negligent homicide. Juan Pío Paiva, presi-

dent of the supermarket company, received a sentence of twelve years in prison. His son, Víctor Daniel Paiva, who was present at the start of the fire, was sentenced to ten years. Security guard Daniel Areco, who closed the doors, received a five-year sentence. The following piece is a powerful, moving, and poetic homage to the victims.

How different everything is now.

The streets of Asunción are gloomy and lonely, as if everything has stopped for a moment, waiting to wake up from this nightmare.

The silence is unsettling, deafening, and the air we breathe is infused with agony.

The burning faces have taken possession of the wind and bring us the suffering of their death.

In the heavy silence can be heard only the cries of our friends, of our neighbors, of the grandmother carrying presents, of the trolley boy, of the grocer, of our families, of our brothers and sisters, all pleading for just one second more in which to save themselves from the fury of the deadly flames.

Whole families were at the supermarket one Sunday; buying delicious food for a family lunch or celebration; mothers and fathers carrying home what they had earned with the sweat of their brow; children choosing colored pencils to finish their homework; mothers choosing the best vegetables for their children; children dreaming of toys. There were dreams, there were plans, there were lives.

They say that you can still hear them:

Mamá, why did they shut the doors?

Please! We aren't stealing anything; we can't breathe, we're getting burned!

Careful! Don't tread on the little girl!

Open the doors! My children are waiting for me!

Open the doors! My family is inside!

Papá? Mamá? What's happening?

Run!

Don't die, grandpa!

Please open the doors!

Cries that echo in our ears. Cries that never let us forget the day that they locked the doors on life. More than 300 bodies imprisoned in a luxurious, modern death trap; a trap of colors, of the smell of fresh bread; a burning cauldron with air conditioning, a miserable temple for the faithful and naive. We were with them, we tried to defend them, we tried to help them breathe; we threw rocks at the building, we broke windows, we tore open holes in the walls. But the death trap was too strong and the fire betrayed us.

Today:

there are empty desks at work,

empty seats at nursery,

hugs from mothers are missing,

there are no words of advice from grandparents,

no one is there to rock the hammock,

there is an empty plate at the dinner table,

a song is missing,

the football team is·a man short.

We are missing all those that fell in the trap.

Whole families faced the flames, clinging to each other. Others faced them absolutely alone. Old people, young people, children, all coming together in one cry that made the earth tremble, rising above it, giving voice to the pain, the despair and the impotence.

OPEN THE DOORS!

And the doors of Heaven opened.

Where Are They?

Alberto Rodas

Alberto Rodas (1964–) was one of the principal figures of the New Paraguayan Song movement, which became a vehicle for anti-Stroessner sentiment among the young in the mid- to late 1980s. A gifted songwriter, he produced some of the most moving, rousing, and popular songs of the time and was a constant presence in the folk music concerts and festivals that attracted and mobilized political opposition to the dictatorship. "Where Are They?" (¿Dónde están?) appeared on the album Utópico *in 1989, released just after the fall of the Stroessner regime. It became an instant hit, sung at rallies, demonstrations, and festivals, and covered by other singers. It captured the emotions of the time and highlighted the tragedy of the "Disappeared," forcing the issue onto the political agenda when many were too nervous of a return of authoritarianism to demand justice.*

Most recently the song was sung at rallies for the victims of Ycuá Bolaños supermarket fire and at the first concert in Paraguay by the renowned Cuban singer-songwriter Silvio Rodríguez, in 2009. It remains perhaps the most emblematic and well-known musical portrayal of the abuse of human rights under the dictatorship.

Where are they? ask the pamphlets
Where are they? insist our memories
Where are the crickets by the roadside?
Where are they? Where can they have gone?

Where are those iconic figures?
Where are they, from here and everywhere?
Where are the signposts on the path?
Where are those *compañeros*?

They have gone to a place where they can no longer die
They are sown in the earth,
And their bones have become stars
That shine in the night sky,
In the light of the people.

Where are they? implore the doves
Where are they? demands the sunrise
Where are they, with their heads held high?
Where are the Disappeared?

The Ayoreo People

Mateo Sobode Chiquenoi

The Ayoreo people inhabit a wide expanse of the northeastern Chaco. Historically they have been among the most resistant of all indigenous peoples in Paraguay to interference by outsiders. As a result, they acquired a notorious reputation as the most "uncivilized" and "barbaric" of all Chaco Indians. Efforts since the 1950s by Catholic missionaries of the Salesian order to evangelize among them failed, and attempts by Protestant missionaries of the New Tribes Mission to domesticate them using controversial, often extremely violent, techniques provoked an international outcry in the 1980s. The Ayoreo have their own traditional forms of organization and in the last decade they have created new political organizations to defend their interests when dealing with nonindigenous society.

In this extract, Mateo Sobode Chiquenoi, a former president of the Unión de Nativos Ayoreo de Paraguay (UNAP), condemns the destruction of their way of life and the usurpation of their lands, and highlights the desperate need to defend the rights of the "uncontacted" or isolated Ayoreo, whose lives are threatened by incursions from cattle ranchers and oil companies.

Our territory, the territory of the Ayoreo people, stretches across the entire northern Chaco, from Paraguay to Bolivia. We, the Ayoreo people, as is the way of our culture, lived in different local groups that each had their own leaders, and that moved within their own areas. Each of the groups knew their territory. Ayoreo territory is the sum of all of the territories where the different local groups lived. Our territory, Eami, is a living being that shelters us and which is illuminated when we are present. We express ourselves through our territory, and our history is etched in every stream, in every waterhole, on the trees, in the forest clearings, and on the salt flats. Our territory, Eami, also expresses itself through our history, because the Ayoreo people and our territory are a single being.

But sadly, up until now, the Paraguayan government seems to be unaware of where we lived, where we came from, and where our uncontacted brothers and sisters continue to live today. Uprooting us from our territory, they ignore who we really are. We can locate on a map the territories and areas where we the Ayoreo people used to live, and where the uncontacted Ayoreo continue to live. It is like a map of Paraguay, but it is an Ayoreo map. On the white men's maps, no one has ever mentioned the Ayoreo territories. It is as if they had erased our history, as if the Ayoreo people had never been there, and as if no Ayoreo continued to live there.

The white men say that we merely claim that these are our territories, that there is no way of knowing if they are ours. Or they say that these were Ayoreo territories, but they stress that they "were," and that now the situation is different because there are new owners, or because they are national parks. We cannot show a land title, but there in our territory there are still signs of our presence from the past and from today, which prove that it is our territory. For example, there in our territory are our huts, our paths, our crops planted in the forest and the holes carved in the trees from where we harvested the honey. The white men can see them with their own eyes; these are our property documents. And in addition, we have the living memory of our history; as soon as we come near our territory, it comes alive. Our elders continue to tell our children and our grandchildren where we lived, where we came from, and how we communicated with our Eami. For us, our territory is suffering, but it is still alive, even now, in this moment.

History of the Ayoreo People in the Last Fifty Years

We Ayoreo are like the trunk of a tree that used to grow in the Chaco. But the missionaries came and took our territory from us. That was like cutting down the life of our people. Our people are that tree that was cut down and is dying. But the wind had already carried off the seed of that tree, and in the sandy soil of the northern Chaco the seed grew into a new tree with branches and new fruit. That tree is our people in the forest, and the new generations born among us.

It was the missionaries who made it impossible for us to continue living in our territory. Beginning in the late 1950s, Mennonite missionaries, evangelical missionaries from the United States, and Catholic missionaries moved all of the Ayoreo off the lands where we used to live. It was as if the missionaries used their evangelization to clear the territory that belonged to the Ayoreo people. That made it easy for the cattle ranchers to buy up almost all of our land, and a few powerful white men took over our territory just like that. They say there are no longer any Ayoreo living there. Today they continue to sell our territory over and over again even though our uncontacted Ayoreo brothers and sisters are still living there. They are still illuminating our Eami. Eami is our mother. Eami is our forest.

The missionaries wanted to do away with all of Ayoreo culture and our beliefs. The missionaries wanted the Ayoreo to accept their God, the God of the white men, Even today the Mennonite missionaries and the missionaries from the United States continue to pursue this goal, but we think it is a bad idea, because believing in their God means we must feel ashamed of speaking our language and being the way that we Ayoreo are. They prohibited our songs and our vision of the world. They say that all we need is to believe in their God, and that we do not need our territory, but they do not realize that emptying out our territory meant emptying out our very way of being. They still think that they are the masters of the Ayoreo, they want to tell us what to do and how to live.

The missionaries continue pressuring us saying that we have to go out and look for our brothers and sisters in the forest who are living in sin because they do not know their God. They also say that they have the right to live a better life and enjoy everything that the white people have to offer them. But now we know what the white people offer us. Why should they leave the forest to come and live in poverty and in fear of being themselves? We are repeatedly calling on the government authorities to stop allowing the ongoing manhunt against our uncontacted brothers and sisters who are living in their own territory and their own culture. We do not want their culture, our culture to die.

Isolated Ayoreo Groups

There are still Ayoreo who shun all contact with the outside world. They live in the territories where all of us used to live. You white people call them isolated indigenous peoples or groups. They have maintained the same way of life that they have always followed, which is our traditional culture. Since 2005, the Union of Ayoreo Natives of Paraguay has been working for the protection of our uncontacted Ayoreo brothers and sisters, with the support of Iniciativa Amotocodie, which has been active as an institution since 2002, protecting the territory used by our brothers and sisters in the forest.

We know that there are at least six uncontacted groups of Ayoreo living in Paraguay, One of these groups is the Ayoreo-Totobiegosode. Three or four of the groups are in the southern part of the Ayoreo territory. The other three groups are in the north, in areas bordering on Bolivia, living on both sides of the border. One is in the area of Médanos del Chaco (Chaco

Dunes) National Park, another is in the area north of Defensores del Chaco National Park, between Agua Dulce and Palmar de las Islas, and the last for which we have confirmed data is in the area of Chovoreca; this is a large group, with more than twenty-five members. We have no doubt that they are Ayoreo, because they move within our territory and the signs that they leave show that they are Ayoreo. In addition, with the beginning of our monitoring work, the elders have begun to share their memories about the groups or families who stayed in the forest because they did not want to go and live with the white people.

These groups are in great danger. Ever larger areas of forest are being cleared for cattle ranching throughout the northern Chaco. Those responsible are Brazilians, Dutch, Uruguayans, Germans, Mennonites, and also Paraguayans who are buying up all of our territory, with no consideration whatsoever for the lives of our brothers and sisters in the forest. Another serious problem that we are very concerned about is all of the lines that are being cut in the forest in the area of Gabino Mendoza, by white men looking for oil. Evidence of the presence of our people is constantly turning up in this area.

In order for our uncontacted Ayoreo brothers and sisters to live peacefully in the areas they inhabit, there are laws, regulations, and international agreements which protect isolated indigenous peoples. These groups have the right to legal ownership of the territories where they are living. The right to self-determination of our people in the forest should also be respected. And in order to ensure that they are left in peace, the laws must be enforced, for example, the prohibition to enter or work in these areas, and to sell the land where they are living.

They are not interested in living with any missionaries or white people. All they want is to live in their own habitat, with the gods who are known only to the Ayoreo and they have the right to decide how they want to live. If they want to come out they will come out, but in the meantime they must not be pressured. They have their way of life in harmony with the forest. The forest, Eami, gives them what they need and protects them, and they take care of the forest. Before the white men came, we Ayoreo lived in our territory without changing the face of our mother, the forest, Eami. We are deeply concerned about what could happen to our people in the forest. We do not want them to suffer what we went through, dying like flies because of contact with the outside world, living without freedom and without respect, living in poverty.

Loss and Destruction of the Ayoreo Territory

Our most serious concern today is when we see how the cattle ranchers are destroying our whole territory. Every day we see them changing the face of our forest, of the forest we know. The cattle ranchers with their land use plans, and the government that gives them the necessary environmental permits, do not consult with the Ayoreo. Nor do they think about our brothers and sisters who are still living in the forest. If they cut down the whole forest and all of the trees, what will happen to the Ayoreo who are still living there? Where will they find their food, for example, the honey they find inside the tree trunks, and the wild animals that eat the roots of certain plants? If those plants are no longer there, they will die. All of the other animals will die too, and the people will die. They will die of thirst, because everything is being cut down and burned. Every day we watch with great sadness how the white men are destroying the forest, and along with it, how they are destroying our future.

Recovery of the Territory and of the Ayoreo People's Future

We need to recover and to protect our territory. We want it to be protected for our brothers and sisters who still live in Eami and we want to recover it for the Ayoreo elders who were taken away from it and are still alive, and also for the future generations. We, the Ayoreo people, suffered a great injustice when they moved us from our territories and took away everything that was ours. Now our territories have strange names and signs that say they are not ours. The Paraguayan government authorities must realize that now is the time to do justice and to give back what was taken from us. In this way they will give us back the possibility to have a future and to continue to grow like Ayoreo, not like the white people who want to have too much and end up destroying everything. We can see that if they continue destroying our Eami, no one will be able to live in the Chaco anymore, neither we Ayoreo nor the white people.

We see our territory that has been turned into national parks, without anyone ever asking us if we wanted this. We see that the white people are not even able to take care of the parks. In the meantime, they say that they are afraid of the indigenous people because we are going to loot the parks, but nobody comes to us to ask how we would like to and be able to take care of them. The recovery of the territories that were stolen from us means that we, the Ayoreo, will once again have access to the foodstuffs that we know and are familiar with and that give us strength. Our people will recover their strength. Our Eami, together with the Ayoreo people, will also recover and be filled with our aliveness. Without our territory it is difficult to continue being Ayoreo. We want development, too, but a development that will allow us to grow within our own way of life, our culture, within our Eami.

Today, the Ayoreo elders, our traditional leaders, weary of living among the white people, have begun again to teach our youth about our way of life, our beliefs, our ways of eating, growing food, and moving through the forest. And the Ayoreo youth are learning how to live in accordance with our identity, which will grow and become stronger living on our territory. Today there is a strong desire awakening in our people, led by these traditional leaders who want to go back to their territories with all the members of their groups. Among them are the Tiegosode, the Atetadiegosode, and the Garaigosode.

What is happening now reminds us of a shaman who had a vision more than 150 years ago, before we Ayoreo were taken from our territory:

> I see our people; our people are walking with their hands covering their eyes. They come to where the white people are, and when they open their eyes, they no longer recognize themselves as Ayoreo. The children begin to play the white people's games. Our people do what the king of the white people tells them to do. After two generations, the Ayoreo will want to go back and live in their grandparents' territory.

So Much Exoticism Can Be Deceptive

Alfredo Boccia

During the run-up to the April 2008 presidential election, many Paraguayans saw Fernando Lugo, the former bishop, as a contender likely to herald in significant economic and social change in the country. Alfredo Boccia, a medical doctor and one of Paraguay's most influential journalists, was one of the few observers to mark a note of caution, as in this wry piece. Nevertheless, he highlights the historical significance of the first appearance of programmatic debate in a presidential election campaign.

We have become interesting to the foreign press. The international spotlight has fallen on us for the first time, because to them what is happening here appears exotic. It's not everywhere that among the front runners for the presidency are a woman (for the first time), a political novice who was until recently a bishop, and a former coup-conspiring general who was behind bars until just a few months ago. If you add to the mix the fact that a party that has been in office longer than any other on the face of the earth is in danger of losing its grip on power, then you have all the ingredients for an irresistibly exotic concoction. And of course, the foreign press draws its hasty conclusions.

And indeed, they may well uncover other exotic elements. Modern history provides few examples of political parties that have offered unconditional support to personalist and seemingly interminable dictators, but that did not fall from power when the dictator was overthrown. Or that carried on winning elections, albeit with different rules of the game. Our foreign observers may also discover a kind of democracy that nobody is able to define. They used to call it a "transition to democracy," assuming that alternation between parties—something unknown so far in Paraguay—would be the ultimate test of whether the transition had actually ended. But as this has not happened yet—and the idea of a "transition" that lasts two decades seems a little ridiculous—so the idea of democracy continues to languish in a sea of poverty and corruption.

The fact that we are a little exotic does not mean that something extraordinary is about to happen. We should warn our foreign visitors that we are not witnessing the end of an era. Not simply because the Colorado Party cannot be discounted as the favorite to win these elections, but rather because, even if it does lose, there are no signs of the kind of structural changes in the political or social order over the short term that could substantially alter the Paraguay that we know today.

On the other hand, we have made some progress. No one is worried any more about the possibility of some strong military strongman kicking over the institutional table—something that only someone who has no understanding of our suffocating militaristic past could believe is unimportant. It also seems unlikely that there will be any political violence. There may be electoral fraud, but this time round it would have unimaginable political costs. So, yes, exotic, but certainly not the same as before.

Without wishing to exaggerate, we have also become more modern. We even have an electoral campaign with a mild flavoring of ideological debate, something that has never happened before. The candidates are debating issues in front of TV cameras, in public halls, universities, professional gatherings and even on CNN, whereas before we had elections with hardly any debate at all. Thanks to Lugo, parties on the left have gained a newfound electoral strength, whereas before they were just names on the electoral list that no one voted for. Moreover, thanks to an adroit move by Lugo, the question of hydroelectric sovereignty has appeared for the first time as an electoral issue, whereas before nobody even mentioned it. And in this election the PLRA (Liberal Party), which was previously always content to play second fiddle to the Colorado Party, is no longer part of the traditional two-party electoral carve-up.

So do come along and have a look, foreign friends. To tell you the truth, we are not so exotic after all. It's just our folkloric Paraguayan politics in all its splendor. For us there is only one issue to resolve. Will our collective discontent prevail over our fear of change? Are we writing yet another chapter in our history of national masochism or opening up a new page of uncertainty? That's the real question. All the rest is just electoral decoration.

Inaugural Presidential Speech

Fernando Lugo Méndez

On April 20, 2008, Fernando Lugo was elected president of Paraguay, at the head of the Patriotic Alliance for Change (APC). His election was greeted in disbelief by many Paraguayans who had known no other government than that of the Colorado Party. Indeed his election marked a watershed in Paraguay's difficult transition for a number of reasons. First, his election ended sixty-one years of continuous rule by the Colorado Party, through periods of civil war, dictatorship, and democracy. Second, his inauguration in August marked the first peaceful transfer of political power in the history of Paraguay. Third, Lugo, a former bishop and supporter of liberation theology, came to power on a radical electoral platform of far-reaching social, judicial, and land reforms, aimed at fighting Paraguay's unacceptable levels of inequality, poverty, corruption, and social marginalization.

His election speech on August 15, 2008, took place during a period of extremely high support for the new president (over 90 percent according to some polls) and widespread euphoria that, as he promised, Paraguay was about to enter a "new dawn" of social justice, democracy, and freedom. In his speech Lugo is clearly aware that change will be slow and difficult, although perhaps even he did not realize just how difficult it would prove to be.

Thank you, brothers and sisters, my countrymen; thank you presidents, the prince of Asturias, vice presidents, and dignitaries for being here today to plant with us the seeds of a new vision for Paraguay.

In every atom of our being today resides a burning desire: to rebuild the dream of José Gaspar Rodríguez de Francia, based on the ideas of solidarity, social equity, and our collective identity. In Paraguay it is our desire to re-kindle the message of Carlos Antonio López and Francisco Solano López, to bring our nation together in order to develop our human, productive, and strategic potential. We need to recover the values of those governments, which acted with honesty and austerity, and those men, who were an ex-ample of supreme sacrifice for the nation.

On April 20, when together we succeeded in bringing change to Para-

Fernando Lugo (born 1951) was the first former Catholic bishop to be elected as a head of state, when he won the Paraguayan presidential elections in 2008. Photographer unknown. Source: Office of the President, Paraguay.

guay, we made a commitment to the men and women who have struggled throughout our history. Today they implore us not to waste this opportunity, not to fall by the wayside, but to place our dreams on the high altar of hope.

Today brings an end to an exclusionary Paraguay, to a secretive Paraguay, to a Paraguay notorious for corruption. Today marks the beginning of a new chapter in the history of a Paraguay where leaders and citizens alike will deal firmly with those who steal, those who obscure transparency, and with enclaves of those few feudal leaders—relics of a strange and long-vanished country—who still survive.

It is our hope that Rafael Barrett, with his *Paraguayan Suffering* and Augusto Roa Bastos with his "island surrounded by land" can now rest in the knowledge that we have redeemed the past; that Juan, Maria, Felipe, and Roberto have decided this day to close the pages on an unreal and deceitful Paraguay and awaken instead the true, historic Paraguay, unstoppable on its path towards the new dawn of long-delayed happiness. We hope that artists like Elvio Romero who sang to the world of our history of stolen dignity, can now rest assured that, in his words, I am here "with those on my path; with the just, the poor, the hunted, the rebel"—that "from somewhere has emerged their voice through mine."

Compatriots:

Today we begin the difficult part of our task: collective leadership, the banner of our campaign. Collective leadership means overthrowing the *caudillismo* that undermines the very foundations of social cohesion in Paraguay. A process of development based on a sustainable economy and social equity implies laying solid foundations during the five years of my presidency.

We dream of a Paraguay based on social justice, where there will never again be such extremes of inequality that turn people against each other; inequality that produces inordinate luxury alongside hunger. In the words of Josué de Souza, I refuse to live in a country "where some cannot sleep for fear, while others cannot sleep for hunger."

Our reply will be to fight the causes of structural poverty, to create the conditions for the state to offer structural solutions for the most vulnerable sectors. Social responsibility will no longer be just a cosmetic discourse based on minor achievements; instead it will become the principal stage on which the state will interact with key social groups and with business to create a new social pact. This pact will imply proactively changing attitudes and, most importantly, allowing those who today see a society divided into "them" and "us" to recover the vision of a shared future.

We want a Paraguay in which everyone can grow.

It was within this framework that a small group of men and women, from diverse political and social backgrounds committed themselves to the political project known as the Patriotic Alliance for Change, which in less than a year changed sixty years of history.

This alliance has listened to the people and from that exchange of ideas a commitment arose to gain greater socioeconomic benefits from the energy projects currently shared with our sister nations, Brazil and Argentina. In the light of this mandate we will meet our partners in an effort to transform "national causes" into "binational causes" based on objectivity, solidarity, and awareness of a shared future.

Our project believes in integration; it believes in the poetry of nations without walls; it believes in the idea of constructive rather than oppressive frontiers. We welcome and support all efforts towards integration—those planned or already in existence—that consider ordinary people as their direct beneficiaries.

We will never forget Salvador Allende and his young supporters, demanding that "much sooner rather than later the great avenues will open and free men will walk along them towards a better society." Today these great avenues are open and vibrant because they are made not with asphalt, but with the dreams of the founders of our Great Nation.

The state that we promise to build corresponds precisely to the wishes of the people, expressed in the elections of April 20. Our first act will be to improve the institutional capability of our government offices, including their values, their missions, their efficiency, their transparency, and the public-spiritedness and accountability of our civil servants. This is vital: corrupt institutions do not exist without the civil servants that corrupt them.

We will do away with the secretive nature of the state. We will oblige our institutions to open their books and to improve the skills of those that work in them, under the eyes of a new, watchful leadership

A sign of these new times will be austerity. We will put special emphasis on accountability in public finances, to eliminate the eternal squandering of resources by the rich few while the vast majority, the country at large, lacks basic resources.

We will encourage the armed forces to play the most dignified role they have ever had, in a time of peace, and to be the allies and companions of the people. The covert operations of the past designed to sustain odious regimes are now behind us. This government proposes that the armed forces should walk side by side with the people on the path to development. No longer will a soldier instill fear, but rather trust.

We will put our greatest efforts into eliminating the stereotype of "liberated or no-go zones" in areas such as San Pedro or the riverside neighborhoods of Asunción. We know that the vast majority of the people who live there are as honest and as hard-working as in other areas of the country. Our government will not victimize anyone for being poor.

Conservation of what remains of our natural forests and environmental issues in general will be a major concern of this government. Key issues such as the Guaraní Aquifer, the wetlands, and, in particular, drinking water will be central to our strategic planning. Regional incentives to this end will receive our wholehearted support.

Indigenous people, Paraguayans, will be the foremost owners of the future of our natural resources, which will be for them to enjoy and even exploit for rational production. Indigenous peoples await the call to regain ownership of their lands. From today onward these lands will not only be culturally sacred, but will be protected under law. No white man who trades in indigenous lands, or who humiliates or victimizes the people there, will enjoy the impunity of the past. Crimes against indigenous persons will no longer remain beyond the reach of the law.

We will work tirelessly to achieve better living conditions for peasants and for the landless. Built into the program of the government that takes office today is the pledge to rid ourselves of social tensions rooted in inequality.

We will be drawing up plans in the areas of health and education to eradicate social exclusion. I would like to emphasize that the greatest social and political investment of this government will be reflected in a single, simple figure: that of a healthy, well-educated child. What aim could be more auspicious than one that sows the seeds of the future?

The Cabinet of our government, comprising the ministries and secretariats, will support this aim of structural renewal. We will not allow anyone to die of hunger as a consequence of our approach, nor will we eternalize poverty with purely charitable gestures.

Today when this man of faith, this committed layman before you, was crossing the city, he saw once again something that fills us with sadness and shame: street children. Their faces demand social visibility, understanding, and solidarity.

And I asked myself, how long will it take to find a solution to this situation? It would be neither serious nor wise to try to establish a timeframe for dealing with a kind of inequality that forces people to risk all kinds of danger for a couple of coins a day. I do not know how long it will take. I do not know if we will manage to overcome the demon of poverty that condemns them. But take note of this: that as with the indigenous peoples, children in poverty will be able to count not only on the support of relevant government institutions, but also on the personal concern of your president.

Compatriots:

Paraguay will not change on August 16. It will begin to change, very slowly, the day—the moment—that you join those who will be present in the first hundred days on the streets, diagnosing, taking action and evaluating.

In your hands you hold a brick with which to build our new Paraguay. Join us, regardless of your political party. Political affiliation is no longer an obstacle to working with the government.

Thank you to all the authors of change. Thank you to the patriots of April 20. Thank you to those who refuse to stop believing!

Paraguay is waking up.

Long live Paraguay!

First Person: Margarita Mbywangi

Margarita Mbywangi, as told to Jude Webber

Margarita Mbywangi was named minister of indigenous affairs in the incoming government of President Lugo in August 2008. She was also appointed as head of the National Indigenous Institute, charged with working on policy and distributing funding for programs for the native peoples of Paraguay. Mbywangi was the first indigenous person to hold a cabinet-level position in the history of the country. She belongs to the Ache people of eastern Paraguay, whose population was decimated by manhunts before and during the Stroessner dictatorship. This interview with a Financial Times *journalist reveals her personal tragedy.*

My name is Margarita Mbywangi. The Paraguayans called me Margarita but Mbywangi is my real name—it means a kind of rodent in my native language, Aché. I'm 47 and I was born in the jungle in the Department of Canindeyú in eastern Paraguay, the seventh of eight children. My parents were hunters. People went around naked and we only slept in a hut if it rained. When I was three my father was bitten by a snake and died. My mother was pregnant at the time, and it was hard because if you're a widow there's no one to get meat for you.

When I was five, I was captured by some Paraguayans and they sold me to the family where I grew up. I had been playing and I was hiding but they found me, and I remember crying a lot. The Paraguayans used to come with guns on horses and we knew we had to be careful, but that day they caught us by surprise.

I lived with the people who captured me for a while before they sold me for 5,000 guaraníes ($1 in today's money), which was a lot then. I called the lady who bought me "Mum," but I cleaned the house and looked after the grandchildren. They were ranchers and had ten children—I called them my brothers and sisters. None of them worked, they studied. I wore their hand-me-downs but I never had any presents and no one ever showed me love. I was a servant.

One of my "sisters" was a teacher and she got me into school. I got as far as fifth grade in primary, but I couldn't continue because you had to present a birth certificate and I didn't have one. But I thank God I was able to learn Spanish.

After some years, we moved close to Ciudad del Este, Paraguay's second-biggest city, but I had no friends. I decided to escape when I was sixteen. The first time I tried, I had no money—I didn't know I needed it for the bus. I got a job in a bar, but one of my "brothers" was a truck driver, and he saw me there and told his grandmother. She came with the police and they threatened to arrest me. So I went back. But I ran away again, and moved to Ciudad del Este to work as a domestic. I asked a priest to help me find my village and after two years he traced some people. When I went there, one of my real brothers recognised me. I was twenty.

I could no longer speak Aché. People from my community are very fun-loving but I thought they were laughing at me. By then, they wore clothes and lived in huts, sleeping around a fire. But there were no blankets. It was tough. I asked myself why I had come back; I became an alcoholic.

But I learned my language. I did a nursing course. Now I am the cacique, or chief, of the forty families in my community, which is called Kuetuvy. Before last year's elections, leaders of the Tekojoja movement that backed President Fernando Lugo asked me to run for the Senate. I didn't win, but the president asked me to be indigenous affairs minister. I consider myself a leader but I think politics is dirty, and it was hard being in an office all day. I left the post in December. Now I'm working for an association of Aché communities and also with Tekojoja. I still have two years of secondary school to finish.

After I went back to my community, I got married but my husband beat me and I left him when our son was two. I got married again and had another son and a daughter—my children are 27, 16 and 14. I have two grandchildren but I never found my real mother. My children live in my community—my husband doesn't want to come to the capital, Asunción, where I'm employed, and I miss them. But this work gives me strength to give to others what I never had: love and a family.

Lessons on Paternity from Lugo

Clyde Soto

In April 2009, just under a year after the electoral victory of President Lugo, a scandal regarding his alleged paternity of a young child rocked the country. The case involved his relationship, while still a bishop, with a young, impoverished parishioner, Viviana Carrillo. Following significant pressure and the threat of DNA testing, Lugo finally confessed that Guillermo Armindo was indeed his son and that he would henceforth support him and his mother. However, this revelation was followed over the next three years by three further accusations of paternity and abandonment, one of which he recognized, and two that he contested.

The accusations against Lugo did not significantly alter his political standing, and were widely seen as "amorous adventures" rather than abandonment of responsibilities, reflecting prevailing machista *attitudes toward women and gender relations in Paraguay. However, it did lead to criticism for a number of reasons. First, during the electoral campaign, he had used his position as a former bishop to portray himself as a man of God, as more trustworthy than traditional politicians. Second—a point that was not picked up in the mainstream Paraguayan press—he had abandoned at least one, probably more children and their mothers, who were living in poverty and could not easily support themselves. As Clyde Soto, a leading sociologist and one of the few writers to criticize Lugo on these grounds, points out, Lugo's behavior was not simply personal but also political. It reflected traditional male behavior in terms of both gender and power, and while his fathering of children out of wedlock may have been acceptable (except for the fact that he was a bishop), his denial of the consequences and his abandonment of his children and their mothers were clearly not.*

Exactly one year on from the general elections that elevated Fernando Lugo to the presidency, and a little more than eight months since the beginning of his mandate, the much-talked about and recently confirmed presidential paternity has threatened the already weak standing of the government. With no truce or let up in sight, today another accusation has exploded in the press; a young woman living in poverty has claimed that one of her children was also fathered by Lugo. Events will reveal the truth behind this new case soon enough—and more cases may well appear.

Despite the fact that much has been said on this issue in both the national and international media, and that the impact it may have is not yet apparent, it is nevertheless important to analyse various issues related to these presidential paternity suits that seem to bring together several key elements pertaining to the survival of patriarchal culture—and perhaps some signs of its possible breakdown.

The Threat to Patriarchal Paternity

In Paraguay it is quite commonplace for paternity to be irresponsible, denied, and of little consequence for the man involved. There may be many legacies in our history as a people that have contributed to the lamentable practice among men that leaves women as the sole carers of their children (such as the abusive *mestizaje* practised by the Spanish colonizers or the near extermination of our men during the Triple Alliance War). But without seeking to go into the possible causes, what is clear is that in Paraguay it is normal for men not only to not worry about their offspring, but in fact to consider them as a "trophy of war" that they need not even have to look after. Many politicians, presidents, and even church leaders have displayed a tendency to think and act in this way. Examples abound and, in Paraguay at least, they are well known. Just recently a priest said in Guaraní, by way of an excuse for his own previously denied paternity, "Oikóntema voi aga" ("These things just happen"), summing up in a few words the traditional (but hopefully not majority) attitude on this issue.

Thus Lugo's paternity, exposed by an apparently unexpected accusation, and only confirmed as the pressure of scandal grew, fits neatly into the great Paraguayan patriarchal tradition. What is interesting here is that it teaches us a glaringly obvious lesson: today women have the means at their disposal to stop this from happening, whether it involves the president of the Republic or a representative of the hierarchy of the Catholic Church. This is the lesson that the mother of this child has shown us, and it goes beyond the unfathomable intricacies that might have surrounded the accusation that landed on the desk of a judge in Encarnación. It is certainly not the first case, and it will not be the last, but the circumstances that surround it make it an especially good example. If women learn from this case, it will represent an important step toward the exercise of rights in Paraguay. If men also learn from it, so much the better.

Mechanisms for the protection of the rights of children and of women have evolved over years of struggle on the part of many organizations. But the mechanisms are not always well known, and even when they are, they are not always made use of because of many obstacles, in particular poverty and lack of legal protection. In Paraguay it is still common for the powerful to use all manner of devices to deny the rights of the most vulnerable members of society.

DNA at the Service of a Break with the Past

Until recently it was almost utopian for women to attempt to prove the paternity of their children if it was denied by the father. Today, thanks to science, this is no longer the case. We will never know what Lugo would have done if the threat of DNA testing had not been hovering overhead as a foolproof means of revealing his role in the birth of the little boy he has now recognized publicly as his son. He had previously had ample time and opportunity to recognize his paternity without causing scandal: he had received dispensation from the Vatican, he had won the election, and he had been in power for a year. . . . Or perhaps he dreamt of waiting to be free of all responsibilities before recognizing his child, waiting until his mandate came to an end. In any case, there can be no justification for refusing to recognize a child, and to do so simply responds to archaic and harmful moral double standards.

Paternity: A Private Issue?

A feminist slogan that has taken root in the history of our struggle declares that "the personal is political." The Lugo case reopens this debate. We have heard countless times that "this concerns the president's private life." That is simply not the case, or at least feminists have struggled for years to make sure it is no longer so. Paternal irresponsibility with respect to children forces women to take full responsibility for the reproduction of the human race. For many women, this implies sacrifice, economic dependence, and poverty. The stereotypical, ideological portrayal of maternity as unavoidable destiny and sacrifice is the basis of a reality which has as its flipside an interpretation of paternity based on chance and denial, of a prize with no strings attached.

The survival of this traditional attitude is not simply a private matter. Feminists have long maintained that the struggle over these issues is part of a public debate, and should be translated into policies that promote change directed toward joint responsibility for pregnancy and childcare between a man and a woman. For this to happen, we have designed ways (already in place in Paraguay) of obliging men who have previously avoided responsibility to accept and assume it. Moreover, children now have the right to an identity. We have moved on from the idea of the recognition of children as some kind of gracious concession to the idea of the rights of children.

So the paternity of Lugo is, apart from the intimate details, a public issue; not only because he is the protagonist, but because of the context of the case.

Ecclesiastical Contradictions

The Lugo affair casts a dim light on a church that already carries on its shoulders numerous accusations of sexual abuse and violations of its strict sexual guidelines. It is a blow that has even led the Catholic hierarchy in Paraguay to ask for forgiveness for its sins. But is collective forgiveness enough in this case? Would it not be better instead to revise unachievable and irrational mandates relating to human sexuality, a force so powerful that virtually no institution or rule can contain it?

In the end Lugo is a victim of irrational rules that mean the only way out is through lies and double standards. He has found that it is better to erase and conceal the facts than to accept the reproductive consequences of his sexuality. And he does so in a society that at times seems more prepared to accept such behavior in ignorance than to make decisive changes in its own ways of thinking and acting.

The president himself has been simultaneously both representative and leader of an institution whose own rules he has not been able to abide by. Furthermore his churchman's halo probably helped him to his current position as head of state. It is understandable for a man not to be able to live up to an oath of chastity; but it is hypocritical in the extreme for an entire society to continue to put up with moralistic rulings that the very representatives of the institution dictating them cannot obey.

We need a *mea culpa*, not for the "sins" of one person, or even of several, but for the mistake of allowing such inhuman precepts to go unchallenged for so long.

The Power behind the Throne

Patriarchal tradition allows for and glorifies emotional and sexual relations in which men enjoy far greater power than women. It is not by chance that "a good catch" for a woman often comes in the form of a wealthier, wiser, taller, and older man. And transgressions tend to be costly. So the Lugo case is not only a textbook example of how the normative image works, but it could also be showing us its darker side: the power of men at the service of their sexuality, even to the extent of being abusive.

For the moment we do not know if the allegation of the boy's mother that the relationship began when she was sixteen is true. If it is, then we have a case in which power associated with position, age, and authority was clearly used to seduce.

As we approach the first anniversary of the election of April 20, 2008, there is no doubt that it would have been better to have been analysing other issues—or even celebrating. Recent events, however, prevent us from doing so.

Itaipú: A Historic Achievement That Will Need to Be Closely Monitored

Ricardo Canese

During his 2008 electoral campaign, Fernando Lugo repeatedly promised to rene-gotiate the Itaipú Treaty, under which Paraguay sells most of its 50 percent share of the energy from the largest hydroelectric generating plant in the world to Brazil. Lugo repeatedly denounced "Brazilian colonialism" and vowed to take the matter to the International Court of Justice if Brazil refused to renegotiate the unequal terms of the treaty. This was the first time that a major Paraguayan politician had ever made such a threat, and his promise captured the mood of the population. As the campaign progressed, all other candidates were forced to reposition themselves behind the call for renegotiation. As a result a national political consensus soon emerged inside Paraguay on the issue.

The Itaipú hydro plant, jointly owned by Paraguay and Brazil, is the world's largest, with an installed capacity of 14,000 megawatts, generating around 92 mil-lion megawatt hours in 2011. Under the terms of the Itaipú Treaty, signed in secret in 1973 between the military dictatorships that ruled in both countries at the time, Paraguay must "cede" the unused portion of its 50 percent energy share to Brazil. Sales to third-party countries are prohibited under the fifty-year treaty, which ex-pires in 2023. Paraguay currently uses only 7 million megawatt hours per year and must cede its remaining 38 million megawatt hours to the Brazilian state electricity corporation, Eletrobras, at cost price. The sale price of Paraguayan energy from Itaipú is totally delinked from the soaring world price and the arrangement is of enormous economic benefit to Brazil.

The gigantic Itaipú hydro-electric plant is crucial for the Brazilian economy, providing 19 percent of all its electricity consumption in 2009. For over three de-cades the Brazilian government has adroitly paid off the Paraguayan political and economic elite in order to maintain this lucrative arrangement. Prior to the 2008 election, Brazilian foreign minister Celso Amorim said that no renegotiation could take place before 2023. However, at a private meeting on July 25, 2009, the Brazilian president Luiz Inacio Lula Da Silva and Fernando Lugo signed a thirty-one-point

Together with Nepal, Paraguay has one of the highest hydroelectric power potentials per capita in the world. The Itaipú hydroelectric plant on the River Paraná is jointly owned by Paraguay and Brazil. Constructed between 1973 and 1984, it has an installed capacity of 14,000 megawatts, the second largest in the world after the Three Gorges Project in the People's Republic of China. Photograph by Daniel Snege, Itaipú Binacional 2007. Used by permission of Itaipú Binacional.

letter of intent on Itaipú and related issues, which was finally approved by the Brazilian Senate in May 2011.

Ricardo Canese is Paraguay's foremost expert on Itaipú. Author of several books and many articles denouncing the terms of the 1973 treaty, in this article Canese reflects on the significance of the July 2009 agreement, in which he played a major role as chief technical advisor to President Lugo in the negotiations with Brazil.

Anyone who says that the July 25, 2009, agreement meets all the objectives that Paraguay has been fighting for over Itaipú is entirely mistaken. We are still a long way from that—as far away as Panama was in 1977 when Presidents Torrijos and Carter signed the historic agreement for the canal, full sovereignty over which only became a reality for Panama twenty-two years later, in 1999. But anyone who says that we did not make any progress on July 25 is equally mistaken. The progress made (not the final objective, which remains to be attained) was historic. To describe it in such terms is not to engage in hyperbole, but simply to highlight the magnitude of what has been agreed.

It does indeed represent a real change of direction, thirty-six long years after the Itaipú Treaty was signed in 1973. From an obliging, almost groveling, posture, we have advanced to one that insists on what Paraguay has always demanded. It is not simply that we have demanded change but that we have actually forced Brazil to the negotiating table, something that many people said would be impossible before the treaty expires in 2023. To oblige a more powerful country than your own to negotiate is no easy task. For over a century Argentina has been trying to get the United Kingdom to negotiate over sovereignty of the Malvinas (Falklands Islands) and has still not succeeded. Bolivia has been trying to do the same with Chile over its access to the sea, and neither has it succeeded after more than a century.

This was indeed a historic achievement—as was the Torrijos-Carter agreement—not only because Paraguay forced Brazil to the negotiating table, but also because the July 25, 2009, agreement clearly addresses Paraguay's six-point agenda—hydroelectric sovereignty, the concept of a fair price, a procedure for the revision of debt, parity in management, the principle of oversight and transparency, and completion of outstanding works. On each and every one of these six Paraguayan demands there has been a significant advance through the agreement. Insofar as this short article allows the space to do so, I will look at each of them in detail.

First, Brazil has accepted that it is feasible for Paraguay to sell its energy to third-party countries within the next fourteen years. While it is true that we still insist that this principle should come into force immediately, we must recognize that every step toward recovering our sovereignty is difficult. If proof of this were needed, we need only look at Argentina and Bolivia, neither of which has yet recovered its sovereignty, as mentioned above; or Panama, where the process took twenty-two years. At the same time, Brazil has agreed to press forward on regional integration of energy markets. This will undoubtedly strengthen the principle of energy sovereignty, since such integration is based on freely undertaken energy sales that are in the interests of all parties.

Second, Brazil has accepted that Paraguay may sell its energy surplus directly on the Brazilian market, without limitations. This is tantamount to meeting our demand for a "fair price," a price for our energy which reflects its value on the open market. This has already been accepted in principle, and meetings are under way to ensure that the resulting fair price benefits the sole proprietor of our Itaipú hydroelectric energy—the Paraguayan people.

So how much could Paraguay earn by selling its energy directly onto the Brazilian market? According to the current volume of exports and prices in the Brazilian market, the earnings for Paraguay would be around US$700m per year. But when the energy can be sold to third countries, this would be considerably greater, approximately US$1,000m per year.

In addition to achieving a realistic (market) price, a principle which Brazil has now accepted, and which will involve a gradual process of implementation, Paraguay has also achieved a tripling in the compensation paid by Brazil for the cession of energy, from US$120m to US$360m per year. This figure is a "baseline" value, guaranteeing that Paraguay will receive a minimum payment even if market prices were to fall below it, something that has occurred in all kinds of markets, and frequently in the energy market. This tripling of the baseline, or minimum, payment that Paraguay will receive once the Brazilian Congress approves the letter of intent already unanimously approved by the Paraguayan Congress, should in no way be considered "peanuts." It bears repeating that the "baseline" is *not* the fair price itself; the latter concept refers, first of all, to the market price in Brazil, and subsequently to that in third-party countries as indicated above.

Third, for the first time in thirty-six years, Brazil will allow our national auditor general to audit the binational debt on Itaipú. At the same time, Brazil has committed itself to examining the company's balance sheets, thereby demonstrating its political will to revise the amount of that debt in the event that our National Audit Office should find evidence meriting such action—something we believe will indeed be the case.

Finally, the July 25 agreement has also enabled progress on the three other (less contentious) demands. Since July there has been genuine parity in the management of Itaipú: Brazil is no longer the sole decision maker on matters of energy and finance. Furthermore, full regulation and transparency has been agreed, reflected in the auditor general's analysis of various points of expenditure on Itaipú. Finally, outstanding work on infrastructure is at last going ahead with some speed, in particular the substation on the right (Paraguayan) side of the dam, and the tendering process for the construction of a 500 kilovolt transmission line from Itaipú to Greater Asunción at no cost to Paraguay.

To sum up, then, Itaipú has indeed "changed direction." Our hydroelectric sovereignty has been recognized, even though it will take fourteen years to achieve. This is not an excessively long time if we compare it with the Argentine case of the Malvinas, the Bolivian demand for access to the sea and the Panama Canal. We will bring to bear all our political weight (Itaipú is, after all, a national cause transcending party differences) to ensure that the Brazilian Congress approves the letter of intent to enable a tripling of remuneration. This seems achievable with President Lula of Brazil himself committed to a change of direction in Paraguayan-Brazilian relations. In all probability, by 2011 (the timetable makes any earlier date unlikely) we will be able to sell Paraguayan energy from Itaipú to Brazil for the greater benefit of the Paraguayan people and so begin the process that will lead to us receiving a genuinely fair price for the excess energy we cannot use in our own country.

We call upon all organizations in civil society to support the National Audit Office's historic task of auditing the debt of Itaipú Binacional. On the results of this audit will depend whether we all have either cheaper electricity, or, at least, greater financial benefits in the form of a debt revised to legitimate levels. The active participation of our people will be the best guarantee that the historic advance made on July 25, 2009, will culminate in the achievement of each and all of our six demands: hydroelectric sovereignty, a fair price, legitimate debt, parity in management, regulation and transparency, and completion of outstanding works.

A Fine Woman

Andrés Colmán Gutiérrez

Paraguay is still a very machista *society, where discrimination against women often comes as second nature to men from all walks of life. This is true also within sections of the peasant farmer movement, which although challenging many inequalities in Paraguayan society, has made limited progress in overcoming gender stereotyping. This short article, written by Andrés Colmán, one of Paraguay's best known journalists, draws attention in a humorous manner to the hypocrisy of those grassroots leaders who, despite their flowery rhetoric of social change, retain authoritarian and sexist attitudes that manifest themselves in their day-to-day political behavior.*

Francisca's hands rise and fall over the mortar with computer precision, in the ancient and fascinating ritual of grinding corn. A pestle in each hand, two long poles that rise in the air and drop at even intervals into the hole dug into the trunk of the *timbó* tree, thumping and crushing the grains of corn, producing a deep steady rhythm, primeval music approaching the perfection of a symphony.

Francisca is almost seventy and has the geography of pain etched on her face. Looking at her there, in the patio of her tiny shack in the hamlet of Zanja Corá, crushing corn in the old mortar and using the primitive technique she learnt from her grandparents, I ask myself time and again how is it possible that such a simple daily act can take on a dimension of magic.

Minutes before, I had been recording an interview with Críspulo Sandoval, leader of a neighborhood committee of small farmers, sitting in the shade of some trees with a fresh pitcher of *tereré.* The man was speaking to me in Guaraní about the deep crisis facing the Paraguayan countryside; he was starting to describe the valiant and heroic struggle of the peasant farmers when he sensed that the dull thud of the pounding was interrupting his train of thought.

"Stop that pounding, would you!" he shouted to the old woman angrily, and in an arrogant tone.

In the late 1990s a small armed movement, the Ejército del Pueblo Paraguayo (EPP), appeared in the impoverished northern departments of Concepción and San Pedro. Like many political organizations in the country, it draws its inspiration from the national heroes of the past. Here, in a rare photo found after a military operation, a recruit poses in front of its flag, which shows Francisco Solano López on horseback. The image is of poor quality because it was taken from a captured cellphone; however, it remains one of the only images of an active EPP member. Photographer unknown. Source: Public Prosecutor's Office.

I told him not to get upset and to let her get on with her work; the noise did not affect my recording and in any case the woman was probably doing something important.

"Don't worry," he replied, "It's just woman's work."

The derogatory comment about the old lady's hard work annoyed me intensely. My limited and evasive feminist consciousness rose up in me from some hidden corner, and I decided to take the arrogant peasant leader up on it: I asked him whether he could grind corn as skilfully as Francisca.

The man smiled uncomfortably and asked me if I was joking. I told him I was serious, that I wanted to learn how to do it myself and was keen for him, surely an expert in all the work of the countryside, to teach me. He couldn't resist the challenge. He got up and walked determinedly toward the mortar.

Francisca looked at us in silence, with an expression of passive incredulity. With a flamboyant gesture, Críspulo got hold of the two huge pestles, one in each hand, and set about doing the best he could.

It was a miserable failure. The pestle blows rained down in all directions, without style or rhythm, grains of corn flying into the air and scattering on the ground to the delight of the hens. He tried for several minutes, until one of the pestles almost crushed his right hand. Then he invented a silly excuse and declared the demonstration at an end.

I gave back the pestles to Francisca with a triumphant smile. She said nothing. She simply put some more grains of corn into the mortar, raised her hands in the air and resumed the regular dull thumping as though she had been doing it for centuries.

Back under the trees, I tried to go on with the interview with Críspulo, but it was going to be difficult now. His voice had lost its arrogance, and what he was saying had lost all importance.

Ciudad del Este's Deadly Trade Route

Jude Webber

Smuggling has become such an integral feature of the Paraguayan economy that accurate calculation of the size of foreign trade has been rendered virtually impossible. Referred to by Stroessner as "the price of peace," it continues to provide a major source of illicit income and wealth for members of the political and business elite as well as senior figures in the public administration. Large-scale contraband trade originally focused on whisky and cigarettes, which arrived in Paraguay "in transit" and was smuggled out again in light planes to Argentina and Brazil. However, since the early 1990s there has been a notable increase in a range of illicit activities linked to smuggling, including arms trafficking, money laundering, and drug trafficking. Paraguay is a major conduit for Colombian cocaine and the largest producer and exporter of marijuana in South America. However, smuggling involves not just the rich and powerful. Small-scale contrabando hormiga ("ant smuggling") is carried out by poor people who carry consignments of basic foodstuffs (vegetable oil, flour, sugar) and light consumer goods (clothing, toiletries) across the Paraguay and Paraná rivers. Timber, agricultural produce (especially cattle and soybean) and locally manufactured cigarettes are also smuggled to Brazil to avoid tax and customs duties, while a reverse flow of consumer durables (particularly stolen vehicles and white goods) cross into Paraguay from Brazil. As this extract from a Financial Times investigation shows, the border city of Ciudad del Este has become the focal point of the contraband trade, which has blossomed to include counterfeit DVDs, IT equipment, electronic goods, and small arms; a city where one can purchase almost anything—for the right price.

Adelin has a big smile and no shame. His monthly shopping trip from Brazil to Paraguay's Ciudad del Este complete, he saunters back across the Friendship Bridge. Carrying three plastic bags packed with a DVD player, a stereo, a cordless telephone and a few smaller items, he looks like any Brazilian tourist toting home a few bargains for his relatives from the shoppers' paradise next door.

"Oh, this isn't for my family," he says. "It's to sell." His haul cost him 800 reais, or about $447—only a little more than the $300 monthly duty-free limit imposed by Brazil in a bid to crack down on trafficking from the contraband capital of Latin America. But Adelin can't resist spilling the beans: "I spent another $11,200 today—I bought digital cameras, perfume, makeup. They'll bring it to my hotel tonight," he says, pleased with his boldness, although he draws the line at having his photo taken.

Adelin is one of the army of petty smugglers known by their Brazilian name *sacoleiros*, or bag-carriers. Until recently, people such as Adelin would have been even more brazen, and busier too, bustling over the border in greater numbers and lugging bigger bags. Since it opened in 1965, the Friendship Bridge has become one of South America's most well-worn informal trade routes. A few years ago, its footway would have been chock-a-block with porters ferrying boxes of goods destined for resale in Brazil at a handsome mark-up. Similarly, the traffic heading to Foz do Iguaçú, on the Brazilian side, would have been clogged with vans piled high with crates of consumer goods, making their way past border officials busy turning a blind eye.

Now, though, Brazil has clamped down on contraband in an effort to get a grip on the billions of dollars in tax revenue that are being lost to evasion and piracy. Trade liberalisation has also eroded the competitive advantage Paraguay enjoyed in the legal sale of consumer goods that it imports cheaply wholesale, taxes lightly and then sells retail (a situation taken advantage of by the smugglers, who then spirit the goods across the border, evading higher Brazilian taxes). Paraguay, too, has stepped up efforts to boost taxes and clean up its image by bringing the town's merchants into the formal economy.

At the Brazilian end of the Friendship Bridge, a large green flag flutters over the border crossing at the entry to Foz. But on the Ciudad del Este side, advertising hoardings announce that you're stepping into Paraguay, and visitors pass the gleaming white façade of a new shopping centre and casino even before they arrive at customs (where there are, anyway, no checkpoints or passport controls). A small flag in Paraguay's red, white and blue colours flies from a tower a few hundred yards away, but it looks like an afterthought. Multilingual messages to consume are everywhere.

The "City of the East" is some 200 miles east of Paraguay's capital, Asunción, and it reeks of money. It was hacked out of the jungle 50 years ago when the country needed an eastern outpost to link it to Brazil, and lies in the "Tri-Border Area" where Brazil, Argentina and Paraguay meet, near the gigantic Iguazú Falls. Now, its cramped downtown is full of shopping centres, some patrolled by rifle-toting security guards, with computers, watches, cameras and toys on sale.

On the streets, row after row of stalls display everything from fake sunglasses, bootleg DVDs and rip-off trainers to blankets, children's clothes and imported tools. Hawkers mill around trying to press gaudy Chinese-made trinkets on to passers-by or, if you prefer, fake watches, fake perfumes, fake Viagra. There is a big trade in Chinese-made goods that are finished in Paraguay and embellished with false logos.

Money-changers with fat leather wallets sit in the shade, sipping Paraguay's ubiquitous chilled herbal drink, tereré. Brazilian, US and Paraguayan currencies circulate as seamlessly as the languages that fill the air, among them Paraguay's native Guaraní and the Arabic of its thousands of Lebanese immigrants. The place looks and feels shifty, a city of hustlers, a mix of nationalities including Chinese, Korean and Indian, and it throbs with the buzz of motorbikes ferrying people in and out over the bridge.

But many observers—not least the city's counter-terrorist and anti-narcotics officials—believe that even as the volume of contraband consumer goods is squeezed, a growing trade in less visible but more lucrative drugs and arms smuggling is where the real money is being made. Fear of the crime bosses operating out of the city is palpable.

Small wonder, then, that Ciudad del Este is regarded as one of the seediest and most suspicious border crossings in the continent. And its illicit activities show scant signs of disappearing, even though Fernando Lugo, the country's president, made cleaning up the corruption and crime with which Paraguay is so associated a key pledge when he took office in 2008.

The city's raison d'être is smuggling; legitimate trade was eclipsed long ago. Huge planeloads of goods are flown legally into the city's tiny airport from Asia, paying Paraguay's rock-bottom import duties. Taxes—including port taxes and sales tax—on computers and electrical goods, which make up 65 per cent of the goods on sale, can be as low as 3.5 per cent.

Ten to 15 years ago, total sales in Ciudad del Este—including the retail resale of imported goods—were worth $15bn–$20bn a year but that fell gradually to about $3bn by 2003. It hovered around those levels until the 2008–09 global financial crisis, says Nelson Amarilla, industry and trade secretary in the Alto Paraná departmental government, which includes Ciudad del Este. He reckons the crisis, exacerbated by currency fluctuations, slashed total sales in the city to between $1bn and $1.5bn, but said that sales had recovered to pre-crisis levels of around $3bn. "We're expecting a good 2010 for Ciudad del Este," he says.

Though the volume of electronic goods smuggled over the border and resold illegally has fallen, the cargoes men such as Adelin are likely to be biking or carrying across the bridge are often easier to conceal. And, says Andrew Nickson, a Reader in Latin American studies at the University of Birmingham, less can well mean more because items such as MP4 players and pen drives have high resale values. "You don't see the same degree of movement, but that doesn't necessarily mean the value [of contraband] has declined drastically," he says.

Paraguayans rise early. The city of 280,000 inhabitants is alive before dawn, so by mid-morning, Ciudad del Este's shopping centres are crammed with men piling electronic goods, toys, perfumes and watches into cardboard boxes. As the business day draws to a close around 3pm, the air is filled with the screech of fat rolls of sticky tape being unfurled to secure hundreds of goods-crammed boxes ordered for illegal delivery to Brazil. Once every inch of the boxes has been waterproofed with tape and secured for the voyage ahead, teams of youths hoist them into the trucks and off they rumble, bound for the river. No one bats an eyelid.

A brief boat trip is all it takes to see where the contraband goes next. Steps carved into the banks of the River Paraná are easy to spot; so too the clusters of wooden rowing boats. Even in broad daylight, bare-chested men, some of them pretending to fish, lounge beside the plastic-clad boxes piled up on the rocks for loading. These clandestine ports operate in full view of the Friendship Bridge, where Paraguay's police, customs and navy are on duty all day.

In the space of a 10-minute ride downriver you can spot ports like these every couple of hundred yards, although it is upriver, just beyond the bridge, in the shanty town of San Rafael, where some of the biggest and most dangerous ports operate. The owner of the boat I take down-river, a member of a fishing club, refuses to go near San Rafael for fear of reprisals. "These people have eyes everywhere. They're very, very dangerous," he says.

María Adelaida Vázquez is one of Ciudad del Este's two anti-narcotics prosecutors. Her work makes chasing down tax-dodging MP3-smugglers look like a piece of cake. Paraguay is one of the world's top marijuana producers and its pot is prized for its strength. Colombian cocaine and crack is also flown into the Paraguayan border town of Pedro Juan Caballero, north of Ciudad del Este, or arrives overland from Bolivia, and is transited through the city to Brazil, where it can command double the price.

"We know for sure that cocaine moves millions of dollars," says Vázquez. She believes that some drugs traffickers are running their narcotics rings from the city's Paraná Country Club, a fiercely guarded ultra-chic housing development overlooking the river. Many of the "Country's" mansions have their own heliports. She believes that drugs are packed in among other contraband and ferried across the river from the club. She is certain that arms, too, are smuggled across.

"Who's monitoring this? Nobody! You could get anything through, even an elephant," says Vázquez. There are only eight government anti-narcotics special agents and two anti-drugs prosecutors in the entire Alto Paraná department—and the prosecutors don't even have vehicles. The special agents have just one. "It seems like the state isn't really bothered about cracking down on drugs trafficking," she says.

But she's not giving up. Last September, she oversaw the arrest of two Brazilians suspected of supplying drugs and arms to the infamous Comando Vermelho gang, which funnels them to Rio de Janeiro's crime-ridden favelas. In January this year, she impounded three light aircraft allegedly used by drugs traffickers to fly marijuana into Argentina.

Vázquez is critical of the country's navy (although landlocked, Paraguay does have one); one of whose commanders has an office right down on the river bank. But if you expected to see detailed charts of the river on his wall, perhaps plotting the likely locations of the scores or even hundreds of clandestine ports believed to dot the area, you would be disappointed. Instead, there is a large map of the world.

Vázquez accuses the navy of looking the other way when it comes to the smugglers' ports operating under its nose. "The navy is conscious of all this and there's a reason why," she says. "This is not simple omission. We're almost certain they're part of the corruption."

Ciudad del Este's anti-contraband prosecutor, Humberti Rosetti, also has nothing but criticism for the main crime-fighting authorities. "The police, the navy and the customs are all giving protection to the people running the clandestine ports," he says. Young and cool, with black, slicked-back hair and a revolver lying casually on his desk, Rosetti looks as if he could have stepped off the film set of Miami Vice, parts of which were filmed in Ciudad del Este in 2005.

Rosetti says that port bosses are frequently tipped off about raids on the shanty towns of San Rafael and nearby Remansito. By the time his team arrives, all the merchandise has been spirited out of sight. Or, when he asks for police support, "they're suddenly not available and they switch their cellphones off. It's impossible." It's also dangerous. "It's like in the films—there are clashes. I've been shot at and have had to fire back."

But corruption among officials is a fact of life in this part of the world, and Rosetti knows who he blames. "If contraband exists, it's because both Paraguay and Brazil have porous frontiers and authorities," he says.

Ciudad del Este is widely considered the "lungs" of Paraguay, breathing life into the economy of one of the region's poorest countries and accounting for about a fifth of the nation's total tax income. But amid the global economic crisis, merchants such as Charrif Hammoud say the city has been undergoing a gradual transformation over the past few years, with businesses increasingly emerging from the shadowy informal sector by paying taxes and workers' contributions (although the city's mayor, Sandra McLeod de Zacarías, says last year's tax revenues have roughly halved since 2008 and officials say recovery is still slow).

The next step is legislation proposed by Paraguay and signed into law by Brazil's President Luiz Inácio Lula da Silva that will, in effect, transform the *sacoleiros* into micro-businessmen by levying an import tax at a rate expected to be 25 per cent. (The law is not yet in force, however, as certain regulatory issues have still to be defined.) The aim is to give them an incentive to operate legally without incurring charges higher than their existing transport costs, thus reducing evasion and cutting crime to "acceptable levels," says Nelson Amarilla.

Turning Ciudad del Este legal will not wipe out its competitive advantage, says Amarilla. Although its electronic goods vendors are finding it harder to compete with increasingly cheap, Brazilian-made computers, he believes the city will retain a niche as a place to buy the latest high-tech items. "The danger of Ciudad del Este disappearing as a centre for shopping is still far off," he predicts.

Some visible changes are under way. A new tourist police has slashed the number of robberies perpetrated on bus passengers travelling from Brazil on shopping trips, and a new customs command is being built at the end of the bridge. But revolutionising ingrained attitudes towards what is legal and acceptable will take far longer. Despite its ambitious pledges, Paraguay's government has had little impact so far in stamping out the culture of graft. In Ciudad del Este, pliable journalists are still bribed by corrupt officials while uncooperative ones are cold-shouldered. The city still appears to run on well-greased wheels, challenging McLeod de Zacarías' assertion that the city is "winning the war to change our image."

Rosetti, the prosecutor, is sanguine. "We're not going to get rid of all this. We just have to try to reduce it," he shrugs. "We can't expect to eliminate drugs and contraband. It's impossible."

The Challenge of Conserving a Natural Chaco Habitat in the Face of Severe Deforestation Pressure and Human Development Needs

Alberto Yanosky

From the 1970s the immigration of Brazilian commercial farmers producing soybean for export led to massive deforestation of the Atlantic forest in the eastern region of Paraguay. By the new millennium this had caused major ecological damage and exacerbated the problem of landlessness and rural poverty as small farm holdings were increasingly squeezed out by large-scale commercial agribusiness. By contrast, until recently the semiarid western Chaco region, comprising 60 percent of the national territory but only 2 percent of the national population, had for centuries been largely protected by its relative isolation. However, as Alberto Yanosky, one of the leading campaigners seeking to protect the rich biodiversity of the Chaco, reports here, by the bicentenary in 2011 the Chaco was also under serious threat from an escalation in deforestation by Brazilian cattle companies.

Paraguay is ecologically unique. It is located at the juncture of six ecoregions: the Atlantic Forest, the Humid Chaco, the Chaco Woodland or Dry Chaco, the Pantanal, the Southern Grasslands, and the Cerrado. To the east of the River Paraguay are the remnants of the Alto Paraná Atlantic Forest, an ecozone that contains many endemic subtropical tree species, as well as tropical and Cerrado and Pampas species. To the west of the river vast alluvial plains support the Chaco Woodland, the habitat for numerous other rare and endangered tree and animal species.

Rapid deforestation is the major threat to Paraguay's rich biodiversity. As has been reported by a number of international organizations, the country has experienced a severe reduction in forest cover over the last several decades. In 1973, 73.4 percent of the Atlantic Forest region was covered by for-

The Swiss-born naturalist Moisés Bertoni (1857–1927) settled in Paraguay in 1887. He established a scientific research station at Puerto Bertoni, an isolated spot on the upper reaches of the River Paraná, where he set up his own printing press. He was the first director of the School of Agriculture (1897) and founded the National Agricultural Society (1903). With 524 publications to his name, he became the foremost authority on the flora, fauna, climate, folklore, and medicinal herbs of Paraguay and the father figure of the country's environmental movement. Source: website of Fundación Moisés Bertoni, Paraguay.

est. This had fallen to 40.7 percent by 1989 and to just 24.9 percent by 2000. According to Guyra Paraguay and wwf-Paraguay, by 2010 only around 10 percent remained. Two competing deforestation processes contributed to this rapid loss, the first driven by settlers and the second by large private landowners. During the period 1989–2000, 80 percent of deforested areas were cleared by private landowners and 20 percent by settlers.

The establishment of "protected areas" succeeded in slowing down the rate of deforestation within the areas designated, although not on the land surrounding them: the average percentage forest loss in the five kilometers immediately outside the boundaries of Paraguay's major protected forested areas was 39 percent over the period 1989–2000, a situation that left the protected areas isolated in ecological "islands" critical to the preservation of species endemic, or limited, to the Atlantic Forest region.

Despite the seriousness of the situation, an encouraging reversal of the trend has occurred since 2004 following a series of measures taken by the Government of Paraguay in collaboration with NGOs. These measures included the adoption of a national environmental policy prioritizing the conservation of natural resources; the 2004 Zero Deforestation Law, and the strengthening of the Environmental Protection Agency (SEAM). The deforestation rate was significantly lower in 2005 and 2006. Among other things, the Zero Deforestation Law prohibited any change in land use in forested areas in eastern Paraguay. However, although it aimed to force government institutions to provide incentives for forest protection, it was not implemented effectively. According to Guyra Paraguay, deforestation in the Atlantic Forest from 2006 to 2008 was still 55,000 hectares, due in part to government land reform programs that distributed small plots of forest for conversion to farmland: holdings of less than 20 hectares are not subject to the new law.

Massive deforestation and the loss of biodiversity are chiefly the result of, on the one hand past government policy and a legal system that have actually provided *incentives* for deforestation, and on the other of the absence of measures preventing increased land clearance for logging, livestock production, and large-scale mechanized soybean farming. The situation has been exacerbated by weak enforcement of existing laws, a lack of coordination in planning at national and local levels, and the negative impact of inadequate political and economic policies with regard to the stock of natural resources. Deforestation is also leading to soil erosion, loss of soil fertility, and a decrease in the quantity and quality of water resources, thus constraining the livelihoods and economic productivity of farmers in the region. Both deforestation and land degradation have been reduced throughout eastern Paraguay over the last decade, but are still happening at an alarming rate.

Until very recently, the Chaco, and in particular the Western Chaco, represented one of the last undisturbed wilderness areas in Latin America. However, the current minimum estimated rate of deforestation is around 200,000 to 300,000 hectares per year (2005–9). Land clearance for ranching is now at rates often exceeding 1,000 hectares per day. By mid-2009, 19.1 percent of the whole Chaco region had already been converted to pasture, and further licenses for forest clearance had been issued to landowners. A recent analysis of economic drivers indicates the very strong likelihood that all suitable land (i.e., land not located within national or private protected areas or reserved for indigenous communities) will have been turned over to cattle production by 2025.

Such a phenomenal rate and scale of land use change carries major environmental consequences. The Dry Chaco currently supports several "important bird areas" (IBAs) in addition to officially protected land areas. Since bird populations reflect wider ecological health, these IBAs are recognized as international key biodiversity areas. In further recognition of its global importance, a significant area of the Chaco has also been given the title Biosphere Reserve of the Great Chaco, with privately owned land forming buffer and transition zones.

Many of the unique features of this extensive, dry, homogenous environment are a result of its size. Any reduction, be it through habitat loss, degradation or fragmentation, jeopardizes the entire ecosystem and its diversity. The Dry Chaco is fragile, with real long-term risks following from the clearance of the natural vegetation. Loss of soil fertility and increased salinity, for example, lead to forms of desertification that are already becoming evident at a local level. It is conservatively estimated that the level of deforestation predicted for the Dry Chaco will result in emissions of around 60 million metric tons of carbon dioxide. This process is already well advanced in the southwestern Dry Chaco.

Environmental issues translate into a threat to the future of indigenous communities, whose cultural and natural heritage is being lost. The Chaco provides the habitat for one of the last indigenous groups still avoiding contact with outsiders, the Ayoreo. Areas inhabited by this people coincide with those containing some of the greatest wealth of biodiversity and surface and subterranean fresh water sources. If these cultural and biological corridors are not kept free from deforestation, the traditional habitat and the biodiversity associated with Ayoreo territory will be reduced to that contained within the national parks, which themselves lack financial sustainability and sufficient human resources.

The dramatic clearance of the Dry Chaco has prompted widespread concern both in Paraguay and among the international community. A series of moratoria on clearance have been proposed, but represent only temporary solutions. The general trend, one which is driven by powerful economic forces, is inexorable, but, depending on the responses adopted, the endpoint will be more or less environmentally stressful. The ultimate aim is to produce a land use pattern that is an optimal balance between environmental and economic concerns, to the long-term benefit of all.

To date, responses have been principally legislative. The most effective, especially when backed by an efficient monitoring system, is the legal requirement to set aside and protect 25 percent of all forested land on a given landholding during conversion to cattle ranching. The selection of the forest so retained is left to the rancher, and results in various configurations, for example, single blocks, geometric strips, and patches that contribute to stock management. Adopting this measure at the level of individual properties is a clear gain, but it misses the opportunity for coordination at the landscape scale, something which could vastly increase environmental benefit without added cost to the ranch owner.

Despite the often confrontational tone of the debate on deforestation, it must be recognized that ranchers are not indifferent to environmental issues. A proposed increase in the set-aside to 40 percent was rescinded under industry pressure, perhaps indicating the limitations on regulation, but the 25 percent legal requirement is now adhered to scrupulously, and indeed often imaginatively. Furthermore, members of the ranching community are key cooperators in conserving IBAS on their properties, while others have expressed interest in the potential for using carbon credits to maintain more extensive natural cover on their holdings. This raises the possibility of a conservation strategy that makes greater use of such incentives in combination with legislation.

Meanwhile, however, it must also be noted that management funding is insufficient for the areas that have already been designated as protected. This is most noticeable in the national system of protected areas. To be credible, any initiative aimed at decelerating deforestation on private land must be mirrored by improvements in the management of land already conserved. A blanket prohibition on land use change in the Chaco is not supported by Guyra Paraguay, the leading biodiversity NGO in Paraguay. Their monitoring has shown that each time an announcement of a particular prohibition, regulation, or moratorium on the Chaco has been made, the rate of deforestation has escalated. This suggests that the 2004 Zero Deforestation Law for the Atlantic Forest may not be applicable to the Chaco.

Without proper controls, progress toward a sustainable development of the Chaco is impossible. The concerns of opposing views on the way forward have fed into a national debate; this debate must secure sustainable development and devise control and monitoring systems to reduce the rate of deforestation of the Paraguayan Chaco. Current levels of economic exploitation without adequate control are inadmissible if the future of the Paraguayan Chaco, and thereby of the South American Great Chaco, are to be ensured. Clearly, Paraguay must develop economically, and there is enormous potential in the Chaco for food production—especially beef—for the global market, but it is a matter of urgency that sustainable development is supported by a combination of agriculture and conservation of critical areas. Guyra Paraguay has invested significant resources in generating fortnightly updates on land use changes in the South American Great Chaco, and shares its information with state authorities and citizens throughout the media, enabling a broad debate on the future among a number of interested organizations and groups. The fact that Guyra Paraguay tracks change does not mean that forest clearance is illegal, however. Current regulation is only the reflection of existing public policy and state action in the Chaco, and these are not sufficient to underpin sustainable development—by which we mean economic growth, improved quality of life, job creation and higher income for the entire population of the Chaco in parallel with protection of the native forest that provides the basis for the traditional life of indigenous communities and for the rich biodiversity of the region.

There is a pressing need to elaborate an ecoregional vision in which proposed land developments are analyzed case by case, and to increase the rate of set-aside, especially in areas of biocultural importance. There is a need to immediately implement attractive incentives for forest conservation and private investment in the Chaco, with a corresponding strengthening of monitoring mechanisms. There is also an urgent need to clearly define procedures that ensure the active participation of forest owners in providing benefits and environmental services for carbon markets, and payment into these for environmental services rendered. The importance of the protection and control of remaining forest cover, particularly in bioculturally sensitive areas, cannot be overemphasized. The rescheduling of the 2001 Act for Payment for Environmental Services (PES) to compensate for the environmental debt of landowners in the Eastern Region may be directed toward the Chaco territory. This would focus efforts on the Chaco rather than on the replanting of the stripped Atlantic Forest in eastern Paraguay—plantations grow quickly, but cannot replace lost biodiversity. The conservation of forests must be a government priority: the state bodies charged with it, and with achieving the sustainable use of those forests, must be given the resources necessary to do their job properly. During the period of change, as new measures are implemented, existing legislation must be applied strictly.

VII

What Does It Mean to Be Paraguayan?

Paraguayan national identity has been shaped by a number of factors rooted in its history. As a colony, Paraguay rapidly found itself subject to commercial and political isolation from the rest of the Spanish Empire, as well as shaped by the strength of Guaraní identity and language, which rapidly became part of a distinct mestizo culture. This gave rise to a strong sense of difference and of "otherness" that explains its firm resistance to Brazilian expansionism and Argentinian efforts to incorporate its small northern neighbor following independence. This in turn also helps explain its isolationist development model in the nationalist period (1814–70), with its emphasis on national sovereignty, independence, and self-sufficiency. Isolationism continued under Stroessner, as did the development of a strong nationalist discourse, based on revisionist and romanticized reflections on the nationalist period.

Yet since the end of the Triple Alliance War (1870) in which up to 90 percent of the adult male population died, Paraguay has also been the recipient of diverse waves of immigrants ranging from Germans and Italians, to Japanese and Koreans, to Slavs, Brazilians, and Mennonites—some fleeing poverty or repression, others attracted by the dream of creating utopian communities. This has created something of a melting pot, with most foreigners rapidly subsumed into the Paraguayan population, but also leaving a range of diverse cultural legacies, as reflected in language, food, literature, music, and many other areas of cultural expression. With a tiny indigenous population, Paraguay remains overwhelmingly mestizo, a true mixture of peoples and cultures.

Given this, it is striking that despite repeated efforts to enforce Spanish as the national language, Guaraní remains spoken by the majority of the population, far outstripping Spanish in terms of usage. Spanish may be the language of official communication, but Guaraní is very much the language of the people, especially in rural areas. And as the language of Paraguayans, it remains a central component of national identity.

Yet surprisingly, these tensions between isolationism and immigration, nationalism and diversity, or Guaraní and Spanish, have not prevented the development of a strong sense of national identity. As becomes clear in this section, Paraguayan identity finds expression in a wide and constantly evolving range of concepts, ideas, and experiences that are rooted in its past and its people, and which substantially distinguish Paraguay from her neighbors.

History, Identity, and *Paraguayidad*

Peter Lambert

Despite the predominance of Guaraní language and the image of Paraguay as hav-
ing a powerful indigenous influence, Paraguayans are the result of conquest and,
over the past 150 years, waves of colonization. Like other countries, most notably the
United States, this led especially in the twentieth century to the rise of a dominant
nationalist discourse in an attempt to pin down what paraguayidad *or "Paraguay-*
aness" was. Of course, there is no answer, only observations. Most Paraguayans
speak Guaraní, yet there is no significant remaining Guaraní population or culture
(there are only about 100,000 indigenous Paraguayans); Paraguay is characterized
by isolation but also by immigration; and Paraguayans may talk of the raza guaraní, *but Paraguay is a true melting pot, where foreigners of all colors and origins are*
rapidly absorbed and become Paraguayans. This extract touches upon some of the
major influences in the construction of a sense of national identity.

A Paraguayan sociologist once suggested to me that there was no *ser nacio-*
nal, no national identity, nothing that bound Paraguayans together, other
than the coincidence of common place of birth. Nationalism, she said, had
been reduced to wearing the national football shirt, waving the national
flag at political demonstrations, or just populist rhetoric used by politicians
in place of any ideology.

On the face of it, such an analysis may appear to have a reasonable basis.
Paraguay in many ways is a nation characterized by division: rural and urban, rich and poor, Spanish and Guaraní, while Paraguayans are the result
of an almost endless series of waves of immigration that make the idea of
a deep-rooted Paraguayan identity highly debatable. Indeed, Paraguay, like
many nations, is perhaps as much divided along grounds of language, race,
class, and gender as it is united.

And yet, there exists an undeniably strong sense of common identity
among Paraguayans, based not on any aggressive sense of nationalism
or racial superiority but rather on a common view of the world that has
arisen from certain defining influences and experiences that have shaped

Paraguayan history and culture, and led to a very definite, popular sense of shared identity, of *ñandé reko*.

History and Nationalism

The search for a fixed national identity is not new, and runs through much of the writing, academic or not, on Paraguayan history. Yet although opinions abound, the absence of major objective works on the history of Paraguay is striking, and is a reflection of a deep lack of consensus regarding fundamental historical events. This makes the themes of history (and hence identity) an extraordinarily contested field—or minefield as some would put it. Helio Vera, a prominent Paraguayan writer, once remarked that in Paraguay "the past does not exist as history but as legend. . . . We do not have historians but troubadours, emotional singers of epic tales, tear-jerking guitar-playing poets of the past."[1] The writing (and rewriting) of history by such "troubadours" of national identity, and the confusion between myth and reality, history and fable, are a long established tradition.

From 1870 until the Chaco War, the idea of the nation had been dominated by the liberal positivist version of national identity, espoused by writers such as Cecilio Báez. This interpretation, regarded by its detractors as the "official" view imposed by the victors of the Triple Alliance War (1864–70), maintained that colonial rule had been replaced by republican despotism under the dictators Francia and the Lópezes. A highly centralized authoritarian state had frustrated the liberal ideas of liberty, free trade, and international integration and Paraguay, it was argued, had become the "China of the Americas"—closed, authoritarian, and characterized by a lack of scientific, cultural, and political enlightenment.

This version was challenged in the first decades of the twentieth century by a revisionist interpretation, developed by a group of writers among the so-called Generación del 900. Through an intentionally rousing and poetic literature, writers such as Juan E. O'Leary (1879–1968), J. Natalicio González (1896–1966), and Manuel Domínguez (1869–1935) attacked the dominant liberal discourse and created a new historical narrative, which sought to restore a sense of pride, identity and direction to a nation devastated by war.

This new nationalism was based on a number of disputed but emotionally powerful tenets, which turned the liberal version on its head. The nationalist period (1814–70) was reinterpreted not as one of authoritarian despotism, but of independent development, progress, and prosperity—a veritable "golden age," led by the "father" of the nation, the dictator Dr. Francia (who ruled 1814–1840) and the "builder of the nation," his successor,

Carlos Antonio López. Most strikingly, Francisco Solano López (ruled 1862–70), was transformed from his previous vilification as an evil (and perhaps mad) tyrant who had led Paraguay to disaster in the Triple Alliance War, to the personification of the nation, the essence of *paraguayidad*. Parallel to this, the catastrophe of the Triple Alliance War was transformed into heroic defense and inevitable but glorious defeat, complete with landscapes (the ruins of Humaitá), symbols (the tragic battlefields of Acosta Ñu), and heroes (Caballero, Díaz, and of course, Francisco Solano López).

Nationalist writers also developed the idea of the *raza guaraní*, a founding myth of common ancestry and of common ethnic community. Paraguayans, it was argued, were the result of the mix of Spanish and Guaraní, the enlightened European and the noble savage, the "warrior farmer." This formed the basis for the claim of a unique and distinctive nation in terms of history, culture, land and race.

With the Febrerista revolution of 1936, this glorified narrative of the Paraguayan nation became part of the official government discourse. Most important, following the Civil War of 1947, it provided the ideological foundations of the Colorado Party and the subsequent dictatorship of General Alfredo Stroessner. These deep and emotionally charged differences in the basic interpretation of Paraguay's past remain alive today.

The Ties That Bind

So if the official nationalist discourse is contested (or at least seen by many as too closely associated with the Stroessner dictatorship for comfort) and Paraguay remains divided in its interpretation of history and identity, what is left? What remains are perhaps the "real" elements of national identity— the historical, cultural and social influences that have molded Paraguay as a nation, creating a strong shared experience among the population. It is these shared experiences that arguably provide more fertile ground for understanding what lies at the root of any concept of national identity, and to which we now turn.

The Myth of the Raza Guaraní

Before examining the factors that may bind Paraguayans, it is important to address the myth of the *raza guaraní* not only in terms of the above-mentioned nationalist construct, but also the false image presented (often by foreign journalists) of Paraguay as a country with a large indigenous (Guaraní) population. In fact, Paraguay's indigenous population is today very small (less than 2 percent of the population) and it is not Guaraní (which is more a linguistic than cultural or racial term). Even when the Spanish arrived, Guaraní-speaking groups were only present in parts of the east, while an array of very different groups (in terms of language and culture) dominated other areas.

Instead, Paraguay is largely mestizo. This is a result of a colonial policy (or necessity) encouraging intermarriage, or at least interbreeding, and equally importantly the successful, innovative, and unique effort by Dr. Francia to destroy the power of the Spanish (and hence the white ruling class) following independence, by obliging white Spaniards to marry mestizos or indigenous people. Any remaining concept of a Paraguayan "race" was further diluted by the annihilation of the Triple Alliance War which decimated the adult male population, and led to a sustained period of repopulation fueled partly by immigration. Many Paraguayans may passionately believe themselves to be part of a Guaraní "race," but genetically any "Guaraní blood" is likely to be very thinly dispersed in modern Paraguay. As Bartomeu Melià has argued, "Given the historic and social reality of Paraguay and the fusion of such diverse ethnic elements—above all European—the concept of race has no meaning at all. The so-called Guaraní race is in no way a defining element of our national being."[2]

If it is not race, then what does define Paraguay in terms of identity? There are perhaps five factors that have influenced Paraguay's historical development and identity through shared national experience: isolation, war, land, immigration, and language.

Geography and Isolation

Landlocked, far from major commercial trading routes, with none of the gold, silver, or other natural resources coveted in much of the rest of Latin America, Paraguay languished as a backwater during most of the colonial period. As Buenos Aires, Lima, Montevideo, and Santiago grew, so Asunción was neglected, cut off from the west by the vast inhospitable Chaco semidesert and from the sea by Brazil and Buenos Aires, which controlled its only trade route, the River Paraná. This isolation was intensified by Dr. Francia who, under threat of annexation from both Argentina and Brazil and wisely distrustful of British intentions, placed strict controls on international trade and contact. Self-imposed isolation, autarkic development, and authoritarianism added to the reality and the perception of Paraguay as an isolated, mainly Guaraní-speaking oddity, the "island surrounded by land," which remained outside the dominant liberal development model.

That was until the catastrophe of the Triple Alliance War brought it back into line.

However, isolation did not stop in 1870, but continued to be a recurrent theme in Paraguayan history, exaggerating concepts of difference and at times used for political convenience. The highly successful policy of "benign isolation," as Fernando Masi has termed it, was adopted by the Stroessner dictatorship as a means of continuing constructive relations with key partners (most notably the United States), while allowing Paraguay to keep out of the international limelight and avoid political condemnation for human rights abuses. Out of sight, out of mind. Paraguay returned to its position as the oft forgotten land, a fruitful source of fiction, rumor, and fable. Such isolation had a huge cultural impact, creating a more inward-looking society and fostering a stronger sense of shared cultural norms and identity.

Power and Warfare

Isolation has been exacerbated by the intimately related factor of geopolitics. While until recently Paraguay was effectively isolated from Bolivia due to the inhospitable nature of the Chaco, its history has been dominated by the overbearing presence of its two other neighbors, Brazil and Argentina. Even today, Paraguay's population of seven million is dwarfed by Brazil's population of 192 million. And the harsh realities of politics have reflected this imbalance in power, resources, and population, in many ways, ranging from the almost perpetual postcolonial fear of Argentinian or Brazilian annexation, to the historical issue of gaining permission from Buenos Aires to have access to the sea, to Paraguay's present efforts to rectify what it sees as the scandalously unfair financial terms of the 1973 treaty concerning the binational Itaipú hydroelectric project with Brazil. A history of living between two regional giants has shaped a certain shared perception of the world and Paraguay's place within it.

This perception has been further affected by the experience of essentially defensive international wars with all of its neighbors. Indeed, from independence Paraguay found its very existence threatened by its neighbors. It defended itself successfully against General Belgrano's "army of liberation" sent from Buenos Aires in 1811. It also went to war with Bolivia in the brutal and tragic Chaco War (1932–35) against what it saw as a creeping Bolivian invasion of disputed territory. However, it could do little against the combined forces of Brazil, Argentina, and Uruguay in the infamous Triple Alliance War (1864–70). Whether one believes this to be a heroic defense by the entire Paraguayan nation (women and children included) against an international alliance that sought to destroy Paraguay's development model, or the result of the exaggerated political ambitions of an arrogant dictator, Francisco Solano López, the very real fear of imminent destruction and possible elimination as a sovereign people led Paraguayans to fight to the bitter end. The magnitude of the destruction was extraordinary; as well as losing 25 percent of its territory to Brazil and Argentina (including the Iguazú Falls) it also lost over 60 percent of its population. Such sacrifice and devastation scarred the collective memory, while the shared suffering and the collective sense of irreparable injustice proved fertile ground for a strong sense of national identity, solidarity, and difference.

Immigration

If the concept of the *raza guaraní* is highly questionable in genetic terms, (however much it is "felt" or referred to by many Paraguayans), what is the ethnic composition of Paraguay? To a great extent Paraguay is a country of immigrants. Isolationism did not stop waves of immigration, most notably from Europe, but also from neighboring countries. Paradoxically, many immigrants were attracted by the very image of Paraguay as an isolated backwater, of starting afresh in "the land without evil," an image that inspired attempts to set up a multitude of new colonies, some idealistic (Nueva Australia), some religious (the Mennonites who developed areas of the Chaco), and some more sinister (Nueva Germania). Either way, Paraguay was seen from the outside as a new Eden, an untouched paradise, the land for new beginnings.

This is relevant to the question of identity for two reasons: first, it reflects the openness of Paraguayans (who are famously welcoming) to foreigners, dispelling any myth of xenophobia resulting from isolation. Racism toward foreigners is almost nonexistent and contrasts markedly to such problems in Western Europe (although the recent expansion of soya production and the related significant growth in the *brasiguayo* population are certainly increasing social tensions and undermining such tolerance). Second, the cultural impact of immigration is reflected in a multitude of ways: from the Spanish spoken in Paraguay, which has been nuanced by regional (Portuguese) as well as European (especially Italian) influences, to the flora (even the ubiquitous mango, Paraguayan jasmine, and sugarcane are essentially imports), to music (the harp, the polka), to popular cuisine (pasta, hamburgers, and rice) and much more. This might further undermine the notion of a "Guaraní" identity, but it should not be equated with any lack of national identity. In fact, quite the reverse is true.

Language

Given that immigration has played such an important role in the development of this former Spanish colony, and that indigenous peoples make up so
few of the population, it is perhaps striking to an outsider that the Guaraní
language is such a key defining characteristic. Despite three hundred years
of Spanish rule, Paraguay was almost entirely monolingual in Guaraní at
least until the beginning of the twentieth century. Even today, Spanish may
be the language of the political system, the mass media, the legal system,
and the public administration, but Guaraní is the preferred language of the
majority. Despite the historical bias toward Spanish in terms of the state
(including attempts to eradicate Guaraní), according to the 2002 census 59
percent of Paraguayans still feel more comfortable speaking in Guaraní, a
figure that rises to 83 percent in rural areas. Or put in another way, 88 percent of the population speaks Guaraní while only 50 percent speaks Spanish.
In a complex and confusing relationship, Spanish is clearly the "language of
power," but Guaraní is the "language of the people," spoken by the majority.

   This characteristic is one that affects Paraguayans' ways of seeing and
expressing the world around them and their place within it. Quite simply,
it contributes to a sense of uniqueness and *paraguayidad,* as well as a strong
sense of difference. Bilingualism (or more precisely in this case, diglossia)
creates the phenomenon of duality or dual personality, of different ways of
expressing and interacting. Moreover, there is a marked difference between
bilingualism in say French and Spanish, on the one hand, and Spanish (modern) and Guaraní (pre-Columbian) on the other. Paraguayans are therefore
tied to both pre-Columbian and modern roots, subject not just to linguistic,
but also to cultural duality. Strikingly, however, according to the 2002 census, about 6 percent of the population speaks only Spanish. That they are
excluded from much of Paraguayan cultural expression is unfortunate; that
they are generally the elites who dominate much of the world of business,
politics, and government is a telling reflection of the structures of power
still prevalent in Paraguay.

Land

The words "poverty" (*mboriahú*) and "land" (*yvy*) resonate in poetic and cultural terms far more in Guaraní than in Spanish. From colonial times, lack
of international trade, the absence of lucrative natural (especially mineral)
resources and economic mismanagement have meant that Paraguay has remained comparatively poor and underdeveloped—a feature that has often

been accepted and even romanticized in popular culture, from poetry to song. The reality, however, is that large pockets of wealth exist alongside widespread poverty; Paraguay, despite its own self-image, is not the poorest country in Latin America, but it does rank among the most unequal.

This inequality is exemplified in the issue of land. Until recently Paraguay was predominantly rural, a key characteristic in terms of cultural identity, with the land (*la tierra colorada*) seen as a key feature of *paraguayidad*. When populist presidential candidate Lino Oviedo said in 1997, "Jake jevy okape" (We will all once again sleep in the open air) he touched upon a deep-rooted desire to be in close contact and harmony with nature, to be at one with the land, and on a more popular level, be able to be on one's own land, sipping *terere*, swinging gently on a hammock in the shade of the mango tree. Acquisition of land has also traditionally been—and still is—a symbol of wealth and success, whether for politicians, the military, businessmen, or *contrabandistas*. Indeed, although Paraguay has often, quite accurately, been described as a "land without people and a people without land," in reference to the high levels of inequality, concentration of land, and landlessness, the shared aspiration to have one's own piece of land still very much forms part of the "Paraguayan dream."

Conclusion

In any country, the assertion of a fixed national identity is a construction, and very often—as in the case of revisionist writers in Paraguay such as Juan O'Leary and Natalicio González—a political construction, or at least a narrative that could later be used for political ends. It is usually exclusionary (toward the "other," whether political opposition, immigrant, or minority) and many would argue pertains to a romanticized ideal, based more on the need to unite a population in a shared vision, than to seek an objective interpretation of history.

Highly charged political nationalism may well be on the decline in Paraguay—and arguably it was never a true reflection of national identity. Instead, to gain any understanding of *paraguayidad* we need to focus on the specific historical and environmental influences and experiences—geographical isolation, warfare, poverty and inequality, land, language, and immigration—that have combined to shape the development of national culture and society and create a strong sense of shared identity. These influences have not only helped create deeply rooted, shared cultural references but also marked differences from others (principally from Argentinians). Paraguayans, like most other countries, may be divided in many ways and there may well be no *ser nacional.* However, this does not mean that there are not multiple identities and ways of being, which are tied together and enriched by shared experience and memory, creating a strong set of cultural bonds and references which are uniquely Paraguayan.

Note

1. Helio Vera, *En busca del hueso perdido* (Asunción: RP Ediciones, 1990), 131.
2. Bartomeu Melià, Una nación, dos culturas (Asunción: RP Ediciones & CEPAG, 1988), 59.

Change and Continuity in Paraguayan History—1811, 1911, 2011

Andrew Nickson

Paraguay has seen dramatic changes during the first two centuries of its existence as an independent nation. This essay, written in commemoration of the bicentenary, explores these changes—in demography, ethnic composition, land use, and economic profile. It also draws attention to some enduring features that are crucial to an understanding of Paraguayan society, namely the continued strength of the Guaraní language, the continued dependence on the export of primary products, and the continuation of an exclusionary system of governance.

Paraguay has changed out of all recognition in the two centuries since its independence in 1811 and yet some deep-rooted cultural features provide an enduring link with the past. Even the territory of what we define as "Paraguay" has altered considerably as a result of the country's involvement in two major wars. In 1811 the independence leaders of Paraguay had laid claim to significant areas of what is today Argentina and Brazil. Both of these powerful neighbors refused to even recognize Paraguayan independence until many decades later. By 1911 Paraguay's defeat in the Triple Alliance War (1865–70) had stripped it of roughly one-fifth of its prewar territory—land comprising part of the modern-day Province of Misiones, Argentina, and the State of Matto Grosso, Brazil. The simmering dispute between Paraguay and Bolivia concerning possession of the enormous Chaco region worsened over the subsequent decades and was finally resolved with Paraguayan victory over Bolivia in the Chaco War (1932–35). So by 2011 the definitive borders of the country had been established, giving it ownership of most of the Chaco Boreal, which now comprises 61 percent of the total area of the country.

Many of the dramatic changes in Paraguay's history have been driven by rapid population growth. On the eve of independence the estimated population in what is today Paraguay was no more than 110,000 and most people lived in small rural settlements within a fifty-kilometer radius of the capital, Asunción, which had a population of only 7,000. By 1911 the total population has risen to around 600,000, much less than would have been the case had the country not suffered the genocidal effects of the Triple Alliance War, which decimated the population. A recent major study calculated that the population fell from around 420,000–450,000 in 1864 to around 140,000–166,000 in 1870. This represents a loss of 60 to 69 percent of the prewar population, far higher even than previous estimates. Recuperation was slow until basic health care was finally extended into rural areas during the second half of the twentieth century. As a result, the population growth rate rocketed from the 1960s, nearly tripling in the forty years from 1972 (2.3m) to 2011 (6.7m).

The ethnic composition of the population has also altered considerably over the past two hundred years. On the eve of independence in 1811, around 11 percent of the population of the Province of Paraguay and 45 percent of the population of Asunción was black, comprising former slaves and their descendants who had escaped from servitude in Brazil. Today, the 8,000 African descendants in Paraguay are a tiny share of the total population, concentrated in Kamba Kua and Emboscada. At independence, indigenous peoples, at least 35 percent of the total population, were largely located in the Chaco and the dense forests of eastern Paraguay. Yet already by 1911 the expansion of the agricultural frontier had brought killing and disease, greatly reducing their numbers. It was not until the mid-1960s that the hunting of indigenous peoples by *mestizo* peons at the instigation of cattle ranchers was brought to an end. During the second half of the twentieth century, there was a slow but steady recuperation in the growth rate of the indigenous population. But by 2011, at around 100,000, they still accounted for only 1.7 percent of the national population.

The aftermath of the Triple Alliance War saw the inflow of a sizeable immigrant population from Western Europe, especially Spain and Italy. Although on a much reduced scale compared to that in neighboring Argentina and Brazil, by 1911 most urban centers had sizeable communities of first-generation European immigrants. The 1930s saw the arrival of new migratory flows—Mennonites, fleeing from Russia via China and Canada, followed by eastern Europeans from Poland and Ukraine in the 1940s and 1950s. Immigration of East Asian peoples started from Japan in the 1930s, followed by Koreans and Chinese in the 1960s and 1970s. But the most sizeable immigrant flow, beginning in the 1970s, came from neighboring Brazil, comprising the so-called *brasiguayos*, commercial soybean farmers of second-generation Germanic and Slavic extraction. So by 2011 Paraguay had become a far more ethnically heterogeneous and cosmopolitan country than it was in 1911, a phenomenon personified by thirty-one-year-old Yolanda Park, one of the country's top TV presenters, whose parents are Korean.

At independence, foreign trade was virtually confined to the export of *yerba mate* tea, hides, and tobacco. By 1911 there had been considerable diversification of exports, into cotton, sugar, tannin extract, timber, and corned beef, much of which was produced by a British company, Liebig's. During the second half of the twentieth century the agricultural economy underwent a radical transformation as virtually all of these crops and products were replaced by soybean and chilled or frozen meat produced by commercial farmers and modern cattle ranchers. In the process, the area under agricultural and intensive cattle production expanded rapidly, forcing a growing migration of underemployed school-leavers to urban areas and, more recently, into economic exile. By 2011, 810,000 young people, 48 percent of all those aged between fifteen and twenty-nine, were either unemployed or underemployed.

One striking feature of this evolution of the economy is that in 2011 Paraguay remained as reliant on the export of "primary products" as it had been in 1911 and 1811. Despite the massive 7,000 megawatts of electricity generating capacity from its joint ownership with Brazil of the Itaipú hydroelectric plant, Paraguay has not experienced any energy-intensive industrialization process in the period after 1980 when the first turbines came on stream.

The overreliance on agriculture and the associated expansion of the agricultural frontier has decimated the dense forest that once covered most of Paraguay. In 2011 less than 2 percent of the semitropical "Atlantic" forest that previously covered much of eastern Paraguay remained. In the decade up to 2011 an even more rapid process deforestation began to take place in the Chaco, at an average rate of 2,500 acres per day. In both parts of the country the destruction of the natural environment has been led by *brasiguayo* soybean farmers, encouraged by weak enforcement of Paraguay's environmental protection laws. As a result the visual landscape of the country has altered out of all recognition over the past two hundred years. This is most striking in the Departments of Alto Paraná and Itapúa, which extend to the Brazilian and Argentine borders respectively. In 1911, the indentured laborers who picked and carried yerba mate on their backs were called "miners" precisely because they used lamps to guide themselves through the dense forests. In 2011 this region of the country now resembled the flat plains of the Midwestern states of the United States.

While forest cover is fast disappearing, Paraguay's other great natural resource—the Paraguay-Paraná river system—is making a greater contribution to economic development. The tapping of the enormous hydro energy potential of the Paraná basin has led to the development of the Itaipú and Yacyretá hydroelectric plants with Brazil and Argentina respectively. Now that the Three Gorges hydro plant in the Peoples Republic of China is completed, Itaipú is, at 14,000 megawatts, the second largest hydro plant in the world. In the process of its construction, the majestic Guairá waterfalls, a hitherto emblematic feature of the country, visible yet inaccessible in 1911, disappeared under water when the Lake Itaipú dam was filled. A new canal and lock system around both hydro plants, together with extensive dredging, have greatly increased commercial transport on the Paraná and Paraguay Rivers, and by 2011 the bulk of Paraguay's soybean and other grain exports were transported on enormous barge convoys to the River Plate.

In spite of improvements in the delivery of basic health and education, the culture of the public administration system in 2011 continued to reflect the exclusionary nature of Paraguayan society inherited from the past. This was built on an extremely unequal system of land tenure, which remained little changed throughout most of the twentieth century. In the absence of a merit-based system of recruitment and promotion, patronage and nepotism continued to strongly influence the inner workings of ministries and public sector bodies. Although a targeted antipoverty program in the poorest departments of San Pedro and Caazapá got off the ground from 2006, public sector workers, especially in the judiciary, continued to display negative attitudes toward the poor majority that were surprisingly similar to views reported from a century earlier.

Efforts to bring the state closer to the citizen have been very slow in Paraguay. Even the basic parameters of citizenship were very slow to evolve. It was not until 1914, three years after the centenary of independence, that a law was passed extending the registration of births and deaths by the state, the *registro civil*, from Asunción to include the rest of the country. Although a semblance of local government already existed in 1911, with seventy-two municipalities, it was only in 1991 that municipal mayors were elected by citizens for the first time—prior to that they were all appointed by the president of the Republic. Judicial reform has been similarly slow and treatment of the rural poor by the judicial system remains grossly inadequate despite the construction of six brand new court buildings throughout the country during the 1990s. Legal redress for the poor remains an illusion as they continue to be at the mercy of unscrupulous lawyers, in a fashion also not dissimilar to one hundred years ago.

This continuity in the gross weaknesses of the public administration system is not surprising when viewed against the limited democratization that has characterized most of Paraguay's life as an independent nation. Despite the much vaunted "liberalism" prevalent in 1911, politics remained the preserve of a tiny majority, who settled their differences by coup and countercoup rather than appealing to the democratic wishes of the people. Numbers on the electoral register were tiny in relation to the size of the adult population. Recourse to the mass of the population was primarily for cannon fodder at times of armed conflict. In fact, throughout the century from 1911 to 2011 there were no fewer than twenty occasions on which the government changed as a result of a military-led coup, as well as countless more failed coups. It was not until President Lugo was elected to the presidency in 2008 that for the first time in Paraguayan history a political party replaced another in a democratic election.

It is noteworthy that Paraguayan culture has demonstrated great resilience in spite of enormous structural changes in the country over the past two centuries. Popular religiosity remains strong although the influence of the Catholic Church has diminished considerably. While in 1911 over 96 percent of the population were nominally Catholic, the actual presence of the church was already extremely limited in rural areas, and became increasingly dependent on foreign-born priests and nuns. By 2011 a growing presence, within rural and urban communities, of missionaries from the evangelical branch of the Protestant church, Mormons, and Jehovah Witnesses had reduced the proportion of nominal Catholics to little more than 50 percent of the population.

Culturally isolated for many decades before and during the Stroessner dictatorship, the "island surrounded by land" (as Augusto Roa Bastos once called Paraguay) opened rapidly to the outside world during the decade prior to the bicentenary under the influence of the global IT revolution. "Foreign" cultural influences have clearly gathered strength. *Cachaca* and *cumbia* have replaced the polka and the guarania as the preferred music and dance of young people. Yet unlike virtually anywhere else in Latin America, most people in Paraguay still speak an indigenous language—Guaraní. Indeed, the most striking example of the strength and identity of Paraguayan culture is this endurance of the national language in the everyday lives of Paraguayans. In 1811 all Paraguayans spoke Guaraní, and Paraguay remained almost completely monolingual in Guaraní at least until the beginning of the twentieth century. By 1911 less than 5 percent of the population, almost exclusively concentrated in Asunción, did not speak Guaraní.

Most significantly, there is little evidence of a decline in Guaraní usage despite the rapid rural-to-urban migration that has taken place since the

1980s. The 2002 census showed that Guaraní was still the favored language in Paraguay, preferred by 59 percent of households compared with 36 percent of households that preferred Spanish. A further 5 percent of households spoke other languages, mainly Portuguese, German, and Korean. In rural areas, Guaraní remained by far the predominant language, preferred by 83 percent of the population, and more households there spoke other languages (8.9 percent) than spoke Spanish (8.4 percent).

Yet the national language has endured in spite of the extreme hostility toward it shown by the Paraguayan elite and the state throughout almost all the nation's two-hundred-year history. In 1911 it was still officially prohibited to speak Guaraní in schools, a situation that did not really come to end until the 1960s. Even in 2011, the Paraguayan state, with rare exceptions, does not communicate with its citizens in the national language. Medical students at the Universidad Nacional are not required to pass an exam in Guaraní as part of their training, in the judicial system there is no provision for defendants to give evidence in Guaraní, and Guaraní still does not even figure on road traffic signs. This contradictory attitude toward Guaraní—at one and the same time praising it as "the embodiment of Paraguayan identity," while at the same time showing disdain for Guaraní speakers—is at the heart of the complex belief system that maintains an exclusionary style of development.

Many of the problems facing Paraguay can be traced to this exclusionary style of development that has characterized the country's history during the first two hundred years of its independent life—the limited nature of democracy, the gross inequalities in income and land tenure, the venality of many powerful politicians and administrators, and the disdainful attitude toward the poor and marginalized groups. Indeed, the challenge of the next century will be for Paraguay's leaders to break with this tradition and promote a genuinely inclusive style of development in which the poor majority is allowed to play a more important role in the economy. With the necessary political will and a massive investment in high quality public education, there is no reason why richly endowed Paraguay should not be able to provide a sustainable and decent standard of living to all of its citizens by 2111.

The Arcadian Tragedy

George Pendle

For many years George Pendle's little book Paraguay: A Riverside People *(1956) was the standard English-language introduction to the country. The first half gives a concise history of the country up to the beginning of the Stroessner era in 1954, while the second half describes the economy, with chapters on agriculture, transport, industry, foreign trade, and finance. Although written a long time ago, the enduring strength of the book is the reliability of its wide range of information, condensed into a short text. The conclusion, reproduced here, offers an interpretation of the perennial tension within Paraguay between the opposing forces of isolationism and cosmopolitanism.*

> Paraguay could have been a paradise.
> —James Preston, *Latin America*

Paraguay grew up in isolation, with its own language, legends, and customs. Because of its remoteness, communication with the outside world was always difficult and slow; and the isolation was aggravated by events. As has been shown, after the emancipation from Spain all international communication was prevented for long periods by the action of the nation's rulers and surrounding States. In a single century the Paraguayan people endured the "closed door" of Dr Francia's dictatorship, the blockade of the river by the Buenos Aires autocrat Rosas, enemy encirclement during the War of the Triple Alliance, and the rigid frontier control imposed by Solano López. Even since López's death the country has been virtually inaccessible for months at a time when, as the result of internal conflict, normal traffic has been interrupted.

Isolation is natural to this land and its people, and although the lack of easy and regular traffic with other regions has undoubtedly retarded economic and social development on modern Western lines, it has also been the direct cause of the persistence of an unusual homogeneity in the race and a remarkably strong national character, both of which are highly valued by most Paraguayans. It can even be argued that Paraguay has been more often weakened than strengthened by the opening of its frontiers. Wars, waged by this nation in isolation and against formidable opponents, have not destroyed it. But a serious threat to survival occurs when the door is open, for, as already explained, it is then that workers in their thousands, seeking higher wages, filter into the much larger and more prosperous neighboring States; cattle are smuggled over the border for better prices than they fetch at home; speculators contrive to place their assets outside the country; students, writers, and musicians are attracted away, wishing to participate in the wider culture of the cities of the Rio de la Plata. This human and material wastage to some extent offsets the benefits obtained from incoming foreigners, such as the aid received from the United States financial and technical missions which have come to the country since 1942. Indeed, some local isolationists deplore the degree to which in recent years Washington has been encouraged to intervene in the financial institutions of Paraguay and in defence matters. Before the signature of the treaty of "economic union" in 1953, the Argentines, who of course are opposed to the growth of United States influence in Asunción, retaliated by introducing commercial restrictions which, although economic in appearance, had political significance.

The tragedy of this natural Arcadia, therefore, is that it can neither live in idyllic solitude nor compete on equal terms with the great nations that surround it. The predicament recurs in every branch of life. Paraguayan literature, for example, has been gravely weakened by the fact that any writer who wishes to appeal to a public that is not merely parochial, must write in the Spanish language. The most authentic and successful Paraguayan literature—such as the poems and plays of Julio Correa (b. 1908) and some of the poetry of Manuel Ortiz Guerrero (1897–1933)[1]—is in Guarani, which is the language in which the people naturally express their emotions. "The Paraguayans love, hate, and fight in Guarani. In this tongue they shout on the football fields and whisper their declarations of love in the dark corners of the patios of their old colonial houses."[2] It is a rich language wherein a single word often combines both a noun and its attendant adjective, the subject and its quality. *Pyjhare* means not only "night" but also "infinity"; *purajhei* signifies simultaneously "song" and "the manner of uttering pretty things"; and *cuña* has the combined meaning of "woman" and "devil's tongue." Paraguay does not lack poets, and if none of them has yet attained international fame it is, perhaps, because, as Augusto Roa Bastos (b. 1918), himself one of the most talented of younger Paraguayan writers, has remarked, the Spanish version of their ideas and sentiments is a translation and therefore a betrayal. When they write poetry in Spanish they feel constrained, and their creative power is weakened. The same is true of prose fiction. Paraguay really has no novelists in Spanish, although Guarani folk-lore abounds in long narratives and stories. The explanation is doubtless that the Spanish language is inappropriate for expressing dialogue which was originally conceived in Guarani.[3]

It is only by means of music that the Paraguayans can communicate their emotions to the outside world: the languid Guaranias composed by Asunción Flores and the lilting polkas—played on harp and guitar—effectively convey the spirit of the people and the quality of their country to foreign audiences. Literature, split by bilingualism, cannot perform this function.[4]

Many Paraguayans would not agree that open frontiers are a mixed blessing or that any useful purpose would be served by the group of intellectuals who at the present time are trying to encourage the development of Guarani culture. They know that prosperity comes through trade with other lands. (Walter Wey has pointed out that no commercial firms in Asunción have Guarani names.) Professional men, industrialists, engineers, and progressive agriculturalists recognize the need for up-to-date equipment from abroad and foreign or foreign-trained teachers and technicians. United States loans and financial advice are welcomed by local politicians. Some military leaders owe their powerful position to the support of their colleagues in the Argentine army.

There is much to be said in favour of both schools of thought: the cosmopolitan, and the narrowly Guarani. On the one hand Paraguay desperately requires the assistance of the outside world; on the other hand the nation cannot afford the draining away of its human and material resources which occurs when communication is unimpeded. If political stability can be achieved by an enlightened, tolerant, and honourable Government; if the value of the currency can be sustained; and if the standard of living can be raised, then the emigration and the outflow of funds may cease. Unfortunately, however, thousands of the most able and public-spirited Paraguayans, whose services are needed at home for national reconstruction, are living in foreign countries, divorced from the Guarani heritage which should be their inspiration.

Dr and Mrs Service—whose *Tobati* was published after the appearance of the first edition of this book—are utterly pessimistic about Paraguay's future. They argue, in any case, that there is no such thing as a "Guarani culture" to preserve, because (in their opinion) Paraguay's culture is merely a variety of lower-class Hispanic culture—though these controversial authors do recognize of course that Guarani is the real Paraguayan language and that "Spanish is a language more or less artificially grafted on to Paraguayan life."[5] The Services explain the hopeless state of Paraguay, as an agricultural nation, in the following manner:

> The internal market for agricultural produce is very small, as there are no large cities and the percentage of non-agricultural population is the smallest in the [western] hemisphere, except for Haiti. The foreign market is almost non-existent, partly because the only egress is via the Argentine-dominated Paraguay River, where shipping costs are enormous. The cycle of sale of crops for cash, in order to invest in equipment or more land, in order to increase production for more profit, never received the necessary impetus to get it started and never can, until a sufficient market exists. . . . Piecemeal economic aid of the sort offered by loans and technical assistance programs sponsored by the United States of America may lead to improvements in parts of the economy or at least may benefit certain individuals. . . . But the nation itself does not have the means to maintain the improvements now initiated, much less to continue further development. . . . The agrarian bulk of the population in Paraguay will remain peasants until their produce can be sold in the external market or internally to a larger proportion of non-agriculturalists who are producing something else for the external market.[6]

Meanwhile, although Paraguay is not quite the paradise that it might have been, it is a land of character and great charm where every man can grow enough food for his own family and sing his melodious Guarani songs to his heart's content, without a thought for the Services' pronouncement that they are not Guarani at all.

Notes

The epigraph is from Preston E. James, *Latin America* (New York, Odyssey Press, 1950), 257.
1. Ortiz Guerrero died of leprosy.
2. Walter Wey, *La poesía paraguaya: Historia de una incógnita* (Montevideo: Biblioteca Alfar, 1951), 24.
3. These quotations are from a letter from Augusto Roa Bastos to the author.
4. One of the most successful books by a Paraguayan writing in Spanish is a collection of short stories on local subjects: Augusto Roa Bastos, *El trueno entre las hojas* (Buenos Aires: Losada, 1953).
5. Elman R. Service and Helen S. Service, *Tobati: Paraguayan Town* (Chicago: University of Chicago Press, 1954), 147.
6. Ibid., 295–97.

The Bicentenary of Paraguayan Independence and the Guaraní Language

Miguel Ángel Verón Gómez

Paraguay is the only country in Latin America where an indigenous language—Guaraní—is the language spoken by a majority of the population. Remarkably, Guaraní displayed a striking endurance in spite of two centuries of language repression. Even today, although recognized as an official language, the Paraguay state operates almost exclusively in Spanish, a fact that continues to have very negative consequences for governance and citizen participation, especially in rural areas. Knowledge of Guaraní is still not a formal requirement to enter the medical school, witness testimony in courts is not allowed in Guaraní, and there is virtually no signposting in Guaraní on highways or state ministries. The democratization process since 1989 has led to a revitalization of Guaraní, focused on efforts to introduce bilingual education in state schools. Here Miguel Ángel Verón, a leading campaigner pressing for the introduction of a comprehensive language policy, traces the long history of official subjugation of Guaraní, highlighting its close association with national identity.

Mba'éicha rupi oúta pytaguakuéra omboaparypy tetã guaranime, oikuaa'yre iñe'e ha imba'embyasy.

How can foreigners who know nothing of our language or our ways come here to enslave the Guaraní nation?
—Chief Lambaré

By Way of Introduction

In 2011 Paraguay will celebrate two hundred years of independence, just as Argentina celebrated its own independence in 2010. Aside from the festivities, this date is of profound importance in the life of our nation, and should provide us a moment of reflection, of self-analysis and of revision of all that we have done and not done over the last two centuries of independent existence. One of the revisions that we urgently ought to make is to our cultural and linguistic sovereignty.

Throughout the history of Paraguay, the most widely spoken language has been Guaraní. It is claimed that in 1811 close to 99 percent of the population spoke Guaraní, while Spanish was spoken by no more than 10 percent. Despite this, it is the colonial language that has—paradoxically—remained almost continuously the officially recognized language across the whole tumultuous period. Guaraní flourished under Dr. José Gaspar Rodríguez de Francia, but subsequent governments have, overtly or covertly, assumed an anti-Guaraní stance and sought to impose Spanish-speaking monolingualism.

There has always been a complicit and silent apathy toward the situation of Guaraní on the part of the authorities in Paraguay, but it has been the most widely spoken language since the *conquistadores* first arrived in the region. According to the 2002 census, 88 percent of the population spoke Guaraní, 67 percent spoke Spanish, 60 percent was bilingual, 27 percent was monolingual Guaraní, 7 percent monolingual Spanish, and 6 percent spoke other languages. Clearly the majority language is overwhelmingly Guaraní. If we move back in time the margin becomes even greater. In 1992, the year in which Guaraní became an official language on an equal footing with Spanish, monolingualism in Guaraní ran at 37 percent, and over 90 percent of the nation spoke it. Yet, despite it being our majority and emblematic language, the language which represents Paraguayan identity, Guaraní continues to be marginalized and discriminated against; its speakers have been flagrantly discriminated against on linguistic grounds for practically the whole of our two hundred years.

Fortunately Paraguay, like the most of Latin America, has experienced over the last few years a new linguistic awareness and has woken from a long period of lethargy, an awakening that has made us conscious of our centuries-old cultural and linguistic alienation. One of the most treacherous acts of theft committed against the men and women of Paraguay since the end of the Triple Alliance War—140 years ago—has been that of their Guaraní language: by undervaluing the language of the majority and of national cohesion, we negate ourselves as a society, and this has, over the long term, damaged our self-esteem and turned us into both an inward-looking and underconfident community—a sociocultural situation that in turn has a negative effect on the social and economic life of the nation.

Now, on the eve of the celebration of the bicentenary of independence and in the context of a rising impulse from civil society, there is a growing collective pressure for Guaraní to be revalued and reinstated alongside Spanish as the majority language of our nation.

The Historical Contribution of the Guaraní language: Guaraní during the Colonial Period

During the colonial period the only widespread language in Paraguay was Guaraní. The colonizer's language had a very limited remit. At first the Spanish attempted to impose their language, but they soon realized that such a policy was not viable, as the Guaraní-speaking indigenous people would never submit to a language that was not their own: Antonio de Nebrija's idea that language goes with empire did not apply in Paraguay, nor in several other Latin American countries. Occasionally the Spanish colonizers would even complain that things had got to the point where the language of the conquered was the norm and the language of the conqueror was marginalized.

Guaraní was the language usually employed in church: Roberto A. Romero describes how the Diocesan Synod of Asunción, meeting in October 1603 under the presidency of Brother Martin Ignacio de Loyola, bishop of the Rio de la Plata, resolved to adopt the Guaraní language for the teaching of Christian doctrine by virtue of its being the more precise language and the one generally spoken throughout the provinces; priests charged with such teaching were required to learn it. In the Jesuit reductions the only language, even for trade, was Guaraní, Spanish being virtually unknown. Félix de Azara declared, after visiting the reductions, that "no one there understood Spanish. All reading and writing was in Guaraní." Hernando Arias de Saavedra, the first *criollo* governor of Rio de la Plata and Paraguay, decreed in 1603 that all acts of his government be issued in both of the main languages of the region: Guaraní and Spanish.

Guaraní after Paraguayan Independence

All of the preliminaries to the treaty of emancipation of May 4–15, 1811, were conducted in Guaraní. The first resolutions of the Supreme Governing Junta were printed in bilingual Guaraní-Spanish format. However, it was during the government of Dr. José Gaspar Rodríguez de Francia—the principal force behind the struggle for independence, and president of the Republic of Paraguay from 1814 until his death in 1840—that Guaraní enjoyed its greatest expression. The national anthem was sung in Guaraní: "I do not want it in the language of the Spanish foreigner," insisted Dr. Francia, when shown at his request the proposed text of the anthem. "Write it in the people's language." His orders were followed, and the first Paraguayan national anthem, entitled "Tetã Purahéi" (Song to the Nation), was written entirely in Guaraní.

For the twenty-six years that Dr. Francia remained in office, Guaraní was the official language. The president spoke to the people in Guaraní, and oral official communications were issued in that language. The policy of the Karaí Guazú (Great Leader) should be understood as a response to the needs of the majority rather than to those of the minority Spanish and *criollo* oligarchy, and was aimed at guaranteeing national independence through internal growth. It was only during the government of Carlos Antonio López, Francia's successor, that discrimination against Guaraní took hold. López supported the dominance of Spanish, as it was this language that provided a link to the sister nations of Latin America, and to much of the world. His policy, however, gained little ground, as his son, Marshal Francisco Solano López, who succeeded him on his death in 1862, favored the use of Guaraní, especially during the war against the Triple Alliance that ravaged Paraguay from 1865 to 1870. The Marshal gave his speeches in Guaraní, the newspapers read in the trenches were printed in Guaraní or were bilingual, and popular poets sang in Guaraní.

The Destruction of Paraguay and the Exile of Guaraní

In 1870, at the end of the contemptible imperialist genocide, the assault on our national identity and on the Guaraní language, basis of social cohesion and popular resistance in Paraguay, began. To kill the Paraguayans, first you have to kill their cursed language, railed the victors. From being the standard language, used in every official and social sphere, Guaraní was forbidden as soon as the war ended. Irrefutable proof of a deliberate policy to exterminate Guaraní is to be found in the school system: on March 7, 1870, six days after the end of the war, a puppet government signed a decree prohibiting the use of the national language in schools, and so began the crimes against humanity suffered by Paraguayan boys and girls. Corporal and psychological punishments inflicted on the children for speaking in school the only language they knew included, among other things, slaps on the mouth, detention during recess, canings, insults, and name-calling. These insults and attacks endured by schoolchildren over more than a century have created a genuine social mutism, with serious effects on the collective self-confidence of the Paraguayan people.

From the catastrophe of 1870 onward, governments neglected Paraguayan identity and the majority language, and violated the human rights of its speakers continually. Only with the outbreak of another armed conflict in 1932 against neighboring Bolivia did we remember our national language— only to throw it once more into the dungeon of oblivion like a disposable object once it had served its purpose. The *criollo* oligarchy, in the pay of imperialist interests, knew—and knows—that Guaraní is the language of national resistance. Amazingly, Guaraní was the only official language during the Chaco War (1932–35); Spanish was displaced. One historic document is General Order No. 51 of 28 May 1933, in which the compulsory use of Guaraní for front line army telegraphic communications was established. Article 7 required that "communications shall be in Guaraní exclusively, and secrets encrypted." At the end of the "naked war," as this mutual butchery of the two poorest countries in Latin America has been termed, we Paraguayans put on our masks again and, as a country, resumed the old theatrics of prohibiting and discriminating against Guaraní and negating our identity. We have carried this hypocrisy along with us ever since, and brought it right up to the bicentenary of national independence.

In spite of very encouraging signs in the last few years, particularly since the new government took office in 2008, the Paraguayan state continues to function exclusively in Spanish. This fact makes it both absolutist and fundamentalist: it ignores and excludes directly and on cultural and linguistic grounds almost 30 percent of the population who speak only Guaraní, as well as the 60 percent who also speak Spanish but prefer to inhabit the two languages. Twenty-one years after the fall of the dictatorship and the start of the transition to democracy, Guaraní speakers are denied the fundamental right, for example, of having their identity card written in their own language. This is the document that identifies them as citizens. Until recently it was issued in Spanish and English and now only in Spanish, in spite of the insistence over some ten years on the part of civil society that it, and all similar documents, be issued in the two official languages.

Nevertheless, the positive signs should be acknowledged. In spite of the resistance from the pro-Spanish elite, bilingual education is in good health; civil servants are studying Guaraní, with the upper management of the civil service confident that its workforce will be bilingual within a few years.

The Ministry of Education and Culture (MEC) is increasingly open to discussion regarding how the bilingual education program might be improved. The Commission for the Commemoration of the Bicentenary of National Independence has embraced a focus on language within the celebrations of the two-hundredth anniversary of independence. And the Languages Act, a piece of legislation that several institutions and organizations have been drafting for more than five years, and which has the backing of the MEC and which will enforce the constitutional article in which Guaraní is established as the official language alongside Spanish, will almost certainly be passed later this year.

The Bicentenary and Cultural and Linguistic Sovereignty

The celebration of the bicentenary of national independence is the ideal opportunity to address Paraguay's cultural and linguistic sovereignty. The Languages Act will test the will of the political classes. It will signal the beginning of the standardization of the process of bilingualization of the state and the extension of the use of Guaraní with Spanish. It will also focus attention on the other languages spoken in our country, particularly among the indigenous population.

The construction of an inclusive, just and democratic Paraguay is not possible until social and political segregation on linguistic grounds is removed and we consolidate our identity as a nation. The time has come for Paraguayan men and women to take pride in the Guaraní land of their birth and to know and use Guaraní, the language that has been spoken here for thousands of years. The dictatorships and obscurantism that have blighted the nation, imposed by external interests abetted by local elites, have sought to extinguish national identity and the Guaraní language; now that the population is stirring from long inaction to broaden democracy and bring about sociopolitical change, better times lie ahead for Guaraní. As we organize movements to promote our sovereignty in the political, geographical, and energy sectors, we should also fight for the cultural and linguistic sovereignty of our nation.

People of African Descent in Paraguay: Invisibility, *Mestizaje*, and the Presentation of Our National History

Ignacio Telesca

Until very recently the history of Paraguay was written almost exclusively from the perspective of a tiny intellectual elite who were usually also important actors on the political scene. This writing of "history from above" has produced gross distortions in the understanding of how the Paraguayan nation has been formed over the years. A new generation of professional historians, working from archival sources and oral testimonies, is now beginning to challenge this approach. Foremost among them is Ignacio Telesca, professor of history at the Catholic University of Paraguay, who presents below a damning critique of the denial by traditional historians of Afro-Paraguayan heritage and the "air-brushing" of the very existence of Afro-Paraguay-ans and their contribution to Paraguayan history.

The first question for the Paraguayan historian should not be the personal qualities of Doctor Francia or the last words of Marshal López. The key issue is what it means to write history in a country where more than 50 percent of the population lives in poverty. To paraphrase Enrique Dussel in his dialogue with Karl Otto Apel, the historian must respond to the cry of the excluded, who throw in his face the question "What is the history of my hunger?"

This is the question that people of African descent in Paraguay are currently asking: What is my history? Without any doubt, it is a hidden history, just like that of the indigenous peoples. Let us begin by looking at the mestizo nature of our society. Today Paraguay defines itself as a mestizo country; from the academic world to the popular sectors, nobody has any difficulty in recognizing it as such. But what does this process of *mestizaje* actually mean? The response that springs to mind is that the mestizo is the product of the union between the Spanish and the indigenous. In characterizing this union, the view expressed by Efraím Cardozo in his *Paraguay Colonial* has become commonplace:

> Regarding the hardy Guaraníes, . . . it was not necessary only to conquer them by force of arms but also, and mainly, through the sweet but irresistible vigour of love . . . . The clerics closed their eyes, guns were placed on shields, and under the leadership, and indeed the example, of Irala, there began in Paraguay the most extraordinary campaign of reciprocal capture of two races through the vehicle of free and untrammeled love. . . . Everywhere there was the free and voluntary surrender of nubile women to the recent arrivals. (Buenos Aires: Ediciones Niza, 1959, 64)

Putting aside the view of various historians (a view not shared by all) that this was not free love but rather the mere sexual and economic exploitation of the female workforce, there is another point here that merits attention. The impression is given that through this union—or this rape—a new race was born, that of the "sons of the earth," the mestizo fruit that would give rise to the Paraguayan nation.

However, this reading of what actually happened is questionable. In the first place, immigration from the Iberian peninsula only occurred until 1571, after which more than two centuries would elapse before the Asunción shoreline would witness a new wave of immigrants from overseas. In other words, the continuing process of mestizaje did not take place between Spanish and mestizos but rather between the few mestizos and other indigenous peoples and people of African descent.

There is a further point that it is important to highlight; namely that these "sons of the earth" did not in fact regard themselves as mestizos, but rather saw themselves as Spanish. The category of mestizo did not even appear in population censuses. In choosing between their Spanish and indigenous forefathers, the "sons of the earth" decided to adopt one and reject the other. It is clear that this option formed part of a survival strategy: to be classed as an indigenous person implied living in a *pueblo de indios* (Indian reservation) and to be subject to the forced labor of the *encomienda* system. To be considered *pardo* [a mixture of white, black, and indigenous] signified paying a special levy or else to be protected by, and working for, a Spaniard.

In a society characterized by its remoteness from Lima, the center of power and capital of the Viceroyalty of Peru—its frontier situation producing perennial struggles against the Portuguese and indigenous groups that had not been subjugated, such poverty that the currency in circulation was yerba and tobacco, and a monolingual Guaraní-speaking population—it was not so difficult for an indigenous person to make the leap to becoming considered "Spanish."

Let us look at the figures. According to the 1761 census by Bishop de la Torre, 61 percent of the population of the Province of Paraguay was indigenous. By 1782, according to the census of Governor Melo de Portugal, this had dropped to 31 percent. Finally, by 1846, according to the census of Carlos Antonio López, the indigenous population represented only 0.5 percent of the population. During this period no genocide of indigenous peoples took place, nor was there any wave of immigration. So what had happened?

Between 1761 and 1782 the total population increased by 13.4 percent while the nonindigenous population rose by 99.9 percent. Between these two dates the expulsion of the Jesuits had taken place and the majority of the population of the Jesuit missions had abandoned their place of origin and joined the free peasantry who lived in the rest of the province (the population of the Jesuit missions having fallen from 46,563 in 1761 to 20,383 in 1782). This was made possible by the fact that the Indians were not part of the encomienda system, and that no particular interests were therefore threatened. The same occurred when the encomienda system disappeared at the end of the colonial period and the beginning of the independence period. The indigenous population that had previously been subject to the encomienda fled from the "pueblos de indios" and integrated with the local peasant population.

Does this add up to mestizaje? At first view it would seem more like a "Guaranization" of society, but contemporaries viewed the process as a "Hispanization" or "Paraguayization" of society. However, we must be careful in our interpretation: for them, this was not a process of mestizaje but one of "whitening": to be Spanish would be replaced by being Paraguayan, and both words were synonymous with being "white." To ratify this idea, let us see what the Paraguayan diplomat Gregorio Benítez said in 1889 in reference to Paraguay: "Called the China of the Americas, this is nothing other than Paraguay, a Christian people, *European by race, who speak the Spanish language.*"

The same process of invisibility took place among the population of African descent. If the history of the indigenous population of the Americas is tragic, then so is that of those whose history originated on the African continent, and who were brought to these lands as slaves. "But where are they?" many ask, while others say, "In Paraguay there are no blacks." Those seeking an explanation remind us that in 1820 the exiled Uruguayan general Gervasio Artigas had brought with him a large number of blacks, around 80 percent of his contingent. There are others who point a finger at black

Brazilian soldiers who left their descendants as the fruit of the sexual abuse committed during the Triple Alliance War.

However, the demographic data reveal something completely different. Well before the Triple Alliance War, and indeed even before the arrival of Artigas, descendants of Africans already represented a significant minority of the population. Toward the end of the colonial period, they made up around 11 percent of the total population of Paraguay, of whom two-thirds were free and one-third were slaves. These descendants were concentrated in urban areas. For example, they represented 54.7 percent of the population of Asunción in 1782. Furthermore, toward the middle of the nineteenth century, during the government of Carlos Antonio López, 4 percent of the population were still slaves. Slavery was not abolished until the 1870 constitution.

Of course this presence of people of African origin was constantly denied. I have already mentioned the observation of the diplomat Gregorio Benítez. Years later, when celebrating the centenary of independence, Arsenio López Decoud had no qualms in affirming that "a perfect ethnic homogeneity exists among us: our skin is not darkened by black inheritance" (*Álbum Gráfico de la República del Paraguay* [Buenos Aires: Compañía Argentina de Fósforos, 1912], 8).

Just like the indigenous population, the population of African descent was obliged to adopt strategies to avoid suffering discrimination for being pardo. Let us begin with those who suffered in slavery. Male slaves sought unions with free women so that their descendants would cease to be slaves. Meanwhile, female slaves were condemned to see their descendants suffer the same stigma as themselves because slavery was transmitted through the female line.

The free pardo, meanwhile, continued to be subject to discrimination in the form of a tax on his skin colour unless he was "protected." That is to say, if the pardo did not have sufficient means to pay the tax, he would have to work for a Spaniard who would assume responsibility for it. But this was tantamount to a hidden form of slavery. In addition, there was a whole variety of legal and social discriminations.

Obviously, such a population would do everything in its power to cease being considered pardo and instead to be considered first as Spanish and then, after 1811, as Paraguayan. Strategies for achieving this "classificational leap" were various. In the National Archive of Asunción there is an act of 1757 in which the following is recorded with regard to the attire of mulattoes:

The attorney general arrived with a petition stating that because male and female blacks and mulattoes dressed in silk, with stripes of gold and silver in their garments, and the mulattoes used silver spurs and bridles, there was no longer any distinction between them and the Spanish gentry at public events . . . and, the matter having been discussed, it was agreed that the said blacks and mulattoes should only be permitted to dress in clothing of Castilian wool, decently and without belts and stripes of gold and silver, and that nor should they be permitted to use silver spurs or bridles, to which the governor replied that he would issue an edict to ensure observance of this. (National archive of Asunción, Historical Section, Vol. 125–1, folio no. 273. Act of the Cabildo of 3 March 1757)

This act sheds light on a minority, the pardo population, who wanted to position themselves on equal terms with the rest of society and struggled to avoid being stigmatized and discriminated against, seeking rather to integrate with the rest of the population. (It is worth mentioning that not all pardos, nor indeed the rest of society, dressed in silk or used golden stripes.)

In the same act we find evidence of a second strategy used by descendants of Africans: the use of churches. In Asunción there was one church, San Blas, that was specially reserved for the pardos and indigenous peoples. The rest of the churches were for the exclusive use of Spanish. However, the members of the *cabildo* (town council) complained that the blacks and mulattoes did not confine themselves to their own church for baptisms and marriages, but also used the "Spanish" churches.

A third and final method used to achieve the change of category from pardo to Spanish (with the accompanying status attributions) was through the militia. Toward the end of the eighteenth century the provincial militias were reorganized and the "companies of pardos" were faced with the problem of fewer and fewer recruits. The commanders of the four pardo companies in existence complained to the authorities

that such companies have been exhausted of individuals, through the extraction or separation of these soldiers, because of those who, forgetting their classification, have joined in the Spanish militias, as well as because of the lack of the legal means to place obligations on the various free pardos, who have been exonerated from all duty and granted full liberty and leisure, and who are useful to neither God nor the King (National Archive of Asunción, Historical Section, Vol. 166–6, dated 10 September 1796).

What is noteworthy is not just that the pardos wanted to escape being considered as such by joining the Spanish companies, but that the Spanish companies actually accepted them without any fuss. The same could be said in the case of the churches—if the pardos could use churches other than San Blas, it was because no obstacles were placed in their way. That is to say, when attempting to understand the strategies used by both descendants of Africans and indigenous peoples to cease being considered as such, we must also reflect on the kind of society in which these strategies were being effected.

In this regard, Ildefonso Bermejo, one of the foreigners brought to Paraguay by Francisco Solano López, left an interesting account of the 1857 meeting of the National Congress to reelect President Carlos Antonio López. He comments that among the deputies he saw no blacks but "that I did see a large number of mulattoes" (*Episodios de la vida privada, política y social de la República del Paraguay* [Asunción: Quell y Carron, 1913], 167). We must not forget that to be eligible for a parliamentary seat one had to be a property owner—in other words, the Congress was the Paraguayan elite in session. It goes without saying that while Bermejo alone saw "mulattoes," the rest of society, and in fact the deputies themselves, saw only "Paraguayans." Once again, clearly we are talking about a society that did not see itself as multicultural, but one where, on the contrary, all differences were subsumed within being "Paraguayan," which was understood to mean "white."

The same occurs today. We still suffer from a colonized viewpoint that prevents us from recognizing difference. For the great majority of Paraguayans the person of African descent simply does not exist and the indigenous person is someone who lives in an indigenous community. For example, if a member of the Mbya tribe leaves his community and goes to live in a town or city he will be immediately regarded by the rest of society as "Paraguayan." The same happens with the descendants of Africans. We know that the town of Emboscada was created in 1740 as a place exclusively for free pardos, that Paraguarí was a slave ranch belonging to the Jesuits, that Areguá was a slave ranch run by the Mercedario Order, and that Tavapy, today known as San Roque González, was a slave ranch belonging to the Dominicans. But, with rare exceptions, neither the people living there nor the wider society recognizes the African origins of these places. It is only recently that the inhabitants of Kamba Kua, in Fernando de la Mora, have begun to retrace their roots and assume their African identity.

Yet we must not deceive ourselves. The task of reestablishing such identities belongs to the whole of society. It is not simply a question of obliging the communities with origins in Africa themselves to recover their identity, but also of getting the wider society to recognize that being Paraguayan is not synonymous with being white, and that to be a mestizo is to fundamentally assume one's indigenous, one's African, and also, but to a lesser extent, one's European, ancestry. At the same time, it is a question of recognizing that the history of Paraguay has also been constructed on discrimination and the exclusion of the majority of the population. A more just and socially inclusive society implies recognition of multiculturalism. This should not be from a pseudo "national culture" angle that simply gives space to alternatives, to the other, to the African, and to the indigenous, but rather one that discovers that the African and the different indigenous peoples that exist or existed in our territory represent an integral part of the "Paraguayan."

So in response to that key question "What is my history?," posed by the person of African descent, our reply should be that, although historiography may have ignored it, "Your history is also our history."

Authoritarian Ideology: Final Comments

Guido Rodríguez Alcalá

Paraguay remains deeply divided over the legacy of its nineteenth-century history. While for many the three leaders of the postindependence nationalist period (1814– 70) were responsible for securing the independence, security, and economic development of the nation (at least until the catastrophe of the Triple Alliance War), others view the period primarily as one of tyranny and despotism accompanied by isolationism and oppression. Although the latter view dominated the period from 1870 to 1930, the rise of nationalism led to a revisionist interpretation of the nationalist period that became dominant in the second half of the twentieth century, especially during the dictatorship of Alfredo Stroessner.

In Ideología autoritaria *(Authoritarian ideology), Guido Rodríguez Alcalá argues that to glorify the nationalist period is to mistakenly justify an authoritarian tradition that has dominated Paraguayan political history and has been manipulated by a series of rulers to justify dictatorship, oppression, and the denial of political rights and civil freedoms in the name of the national interest. Written during the Stroessner dictatorship,* Ideología autoritaria *represents a thinly veiled attack on the construction and use of nationalism by the Colorado Party and the Stroessner regime and their celebration and continuation of the tradition of "centralized bureaucratic authoritarianism." The book and the views expressed in the debate remain as contested and divisive today as when it was published in 1987.*

At an international level there is what might be called a kind of populism directed toward the "most underdeveloped" (so to speak) countries. It is not acceptable to talk about Paraguay pejoratively—or even to give the impression of doing so—if one does not want to risk falling into the prejudice of Sarmiento, where all things local equate to barbarism and all that is imported, civilization—including tailcoats, top hats, and all the paraphernalia of European fashion which, when Latin Americans tried to imitate it during the Sarmiento years, was the cause of so much hilarity in Europe. The claim, attributed to Sarmiento, that Paraguayans ought to be killed in the womb, an atrocity committed by the occupying armies in Paraguay during the Triple Alliance War, has led many Latin American, European, and U.S. historians to see Francisco López and his two predecessors as great rulers. Nothing could be further from the truth.

An (overly) favorable judgment of Paraguay and its glorious past is not dangerous if it is simply an error of analysis, but it certainly is when it is used for the purposes of political manipulation. I refer to the cult of Francia and López that forms part of the official ideology of modern Paraguay, and which would have us believe that Marshal López is a leader to be obeyed blindly and voluntarily (the textbooks attempt to inculcate primary school children with the idea that they should be prepared to sacrifice themselves as willingly for the nation as the child martyrs of Acosta Ñu). Carlos Antonio López is portrayed as the benevolent grandfather, the paternal figure who watches over us, while Dr. Francia is presented as the sole founder of the Paraguayan nation. In both cases, the individual *is* the nation; to criticize their political actions is to be anti-Paraguayan. This is more than merely a historical misjudgment, as found in Eduardo Galeano's writing on Paraguay. The mystical halo that surrounds the figures of these three autocrats sets them above and beyond any historical judgment, and converts them into potential tools for political manipulation. In schools one hears things like "We must love Don Carlos; we must not speak badly of our heroes; we must obey as the Marshal's soldiers obeyed." The individual's capacity for critical thinking is nullified from an early age, and children are taught to accept authoritarianism, and are subjected to indoctrination techniques on a par with Hitler's.

This transformation of history into myth (a typical feature of fascism) became widespread with the growth of authoritarian political movements in the 1930s (contemporaries of Francia and López were not *francistas* or *lopistas*: the apotheosis came later). *Febrerismo* became unfortunately wedded to the cult of the Marshal, at the same time that it implemented the agrarian reform program that put an end to the *encomienda* system still in existence on some rural farms.

However, we should not be too harsh on the Febrerista revolution. The confusion of Right and Left is typically Latin American, and can plainly be seen in the popular movements centering on Gertulio Vargas, Juan Domingo Perón, and Natalicio González. It is not so much Right versus Left; there is also the influence of Keynes. The combination of Keynesianism with socialist and fascist ideas became commonplace as the politics of laissez faire were abandoned and the state (or government) began to actively intervene in the economy. In Paraguay, interventionism has a long tradition, beginning under colonialism: the economy was not free (nor were its subjects), and the king decided how, when and where goods were to be bought and sold. It is not that the economy took precedence over politics, as occurred in Europe and the United States from the Industrial Revolution or before, but that politics conditioned the economy, even though it did not determine it.

Such is the Spanish tradition from which the centralized bureaucratic authoritarianism of Francia and López was born, a tradition which managed to survive the Liberal period, and which regained prominence after the tyranny of Morínigo, whose own brand of nationalism was as authentic as the beautiful locks of Mme. Lynch, a woman who had her French hairdresser shot for suggesting that she wore a wig. Morínigo may well have been a nationalist and an anti-imperialist, but his nationalism and anti-imperialism had the blessing of the U.S. Embassy, which always sees dictatorship as the best solution for "those countries south of the Rio Grande." If López was seduced by Europeanization, then Morínigo was seduced by modernization: the horrible modern buildings constructed under the General are the equivalent of the Marshal's neoclassical buildings. The López opera house is as lacking in authenticity as Morínigo's development projects. Nevertheless, it should be said, in defense of the intelligence of these two politicians, that they supported many nationalists who performed byzantine feats of intellectual contortion with the "contemporary relevance of the political values of López." But the values of López and Francia were no more than the rationalization of an authoritarian political praxis. These values and this praxis were recycled in the rise of totalitarian movements (as well as in some ideologically vague popular movements). Official propaganda promoted and simplified them in the process, simplifying intellectual activity in general to the point where the "ideology of Dr. Francia" attained the status of a core subject in the Paraguayan university system. Indeed, Liberals, Christian Democrats, socialists, and right-wing thinkers in general all form part of the chorus in praise of authoritarianism.

With the Help of Doña Petrona
We Make an Incursion into Folk Cuisine

Helio Vera

The idea of paraguayidad, *of what a Paraguayan is, remains highly contested albeit at an emotional rather than factual level. Paraguayans (often very European-looking Paraguayans) often refer to the alleged shared roots of Paraguayans in the Raza Guaraní as a defining element of their national identity. However, given the combined effects of miscegenation, the destruction caused by the Triple Alliance War, and the repeated waves of immigration, there is very little factual basis to this idea of shared indigenous blood. In the following extract from his* En busca del hueso perdido—*one of the best-selling books ever in Paraguay—the renowned Paraguayan sociologist Helio Vera (1946–2008) addresses the issues of race in a typically controversial yet humorous way.*

Every year on October 12 in Paraguay we religiously observe the "Day of the Race." There are ceremonies in schools, songs, flowers, flags, and speeches. And the Spanish ambassador is usually present. The unleashing of emotions is on behalf of a very highly populated group: the "American race." But what "race" are we talking about? An anthropologist would certainly be pushed to answer this thorny question if put on the spot. And it would be nigh on impossible for him to pinpoint October 12 as the date of the appearance of a new race on Earth.

What is today called Paraguay was inhabited during the pre-Columbian period by a number of "races"—if we can call them that—who were very different from each other and often engaged in furious wars of mutual annihilation. Even today, there are no less than seventeen ethnic groups in Paraguay that can be subdivided into five entirely different linguistic groups. A Mbya-Apytere from Caaguazú has about as much in common with a Maká from the Chaco, as a desert Arab would have with an Eskimo freezing inside his igloo. As for the Guaraníes, who live mostly in the eastern region, they were only united in terms of language and a few cultural features. Ethnically, they did not correspond precisely to any overarching commonality.

Bartomeu Melià has no hesitation in declaring that "given the historical and social reality in Paraguay, and the fusion of such diverse ethnic elements—above all European—the concept of race has no meaning at all. The so-called Guaraní race is in no way a defining feature of our national being."[1]

Doña Petrona's Recipe

So what are we, ethnically speaking? Everything and nothing. If we wished to create a recipe with which to "make" a Paraguayan, we might propose the following: put in six measures of indigenousness, mainly Guaraní from the central region, but not forgetting a little Payaguá, Guayakí, Guaikuru, Tobá, Moro, or Chamacoco. Stir in two parts Andalucian and Extremeño and a little Basque. Add a pinch of English, German, and Italian, as well as North African or Jewish of unknown origin. Don't forget a generous drizzle of black African.

Be patient and wait a couple of centuries, before adding equal measures of Italian and German. Wait a little longer and sprinkle some Arab, French, Croat, Serb, Montenegrin, Polish, Russian, and Ukrainian. Stir well. Don't rush, as you will also need to add some Armenian, Scandinavian, and Irish. Pause and breathe deeply; then rest. However, do not be tempted to think you have finished, because, before removing the cake from the oven, you will still need to add equally generous portions of Japanese, Chinese, and Korean. Leave the mixture in a *bain marie.*

Don't worry if some of the ingredients do not seem to go well with others. You must be patient: only time will allow you to return to the oven and take out the final result.

Note

1. Bartomeu Melià, *Una nación, dos culturas* (Asunción: RP Ediciones & CEPAG, 1988), 59.

Enough of the Triple Alliance!

Jorge Rubiani

The signing of the Mercosur Treaty in 1991 was a historic act that promised to bring the four signatories—Argentina, Brazil, Paraguay, and Uruguay—closer together in primarily economic, but also cultural and political, terms. In a new era of regional cooperation it held the prospect of a reduction in tensions (especially between the two regional powers, Brazil and Argentina) and growing interdependence and cooperation. Twenty years on, Mercosur has found itself stagnating, unable to push through key policies to deepen regional integration in political or socioeconomic terms. In Paraguay, the poorest and most underdeveloped member of Mercosur, this has led to increasing disillusionment and frustration with the other three members, who have failed to provide the aid, investment, support, and solidarity that Paraguay had hoped for in 1991—and who have actively blocked such measures. To many Paraguayans, the lack of solidarity, the broken promises, and the deafness to Paraguayan requests and demands were not new or unexpected, but were merely a continuation of a historical relationship dating back to the Triple Alliance War.

The following article is strident in its tone, but reflects a growing resentment in Paraguay toward what is perceived as the arrogance of both Argentina and Brazil, and their failure to address or even speak of the injustices of the past. It also reflects both the strength of nationalist sentiment and the presence of past grievances when interpreting current events.

Rights cannot be enjoyed by any nation or society without the prior condition of justice. And in this lies the root cause of the asymmetry in relations between Paraguay and her more powerful Mercosur partners, Brazil and Argentina. It has ever been thus, since the beginning. Treaty or no treaty, it is as though the agreement that brands all our misfortunes, the Secret Treaty of the Triple Alliance, and the subsequent war, still applied. Indeed it would appear that the assumptions in that treaty remain intact for two of the three signatories, while Paraguay still carries with it the status of "the defeated nation." This is because one fundamental issue is routinely omitted from discussions aimed to establish blame or motives for that war.

That is, that the survival of Paraguay as an autonomous independent nation was gravely threatened by the virtual annihilation of its population, by the postwar occupation of its territory, and by the enormous burden of debt that plagued its future. And that, apart from attributing responsibility to the government of Francisco Solano López, the allies did not honor a single one of the arguments they originally used to justify the war. When it was over, our country was left without peace, and without the "civilization and liberty" they had promised.

Paraguay not only suffered defeat—the risk inherent in any armed confrontation—but the added ruthless pillaging of its scarce assets. Not only the annihilation of its male population, young and old, but the massacre of its civilian population verging on genocide. Yet the governments of Brazil and Argentina have never voiced a word in admission of guilt or in apology, and never expressed compassion, solidarity, or even sympathy for the difficulties that have marked our existence since those terrible events.

Argentinians often wonder why Paraguayans are generally more hostile toward them than we are toward the Brazilians. The answer tends to be couched in irony that conceals the true reasons for the anger our brothers in the River Plate perceive. There could in fact be many underlying reasons, but many of the woes occasioned by the aggression that Paraguay was historically subject to from the Portuguese—subsequently the Brazilians—could easily have been spared us by the Argentinians . . . and they chose not to act.

Perhaps they might have recalled that it was Paraguay that provided a barricade to hold back Portuguese expansion from Buenos Aires for centuries. Perhaps they should have placed themselves "on the side of the Republics of La Plata," as Bartolomé Mitre suggested in 1865; or they might have recalled our common origins and history and the numerous episodes of Paraguayan support for Argentina in her first tentative steps. But they put their relationship with Brazil first. Then as now. Although the River Paraguay draws our allegiances southward, the Argentinians could have offered Paraguay more than its nominal protection—which, true, they always did—and avoided for us the endless impositions that made existence in our country so difficult, and even drove us from it in search of a better life. And that, simply, is how it has been, ever since Phillip III signed the infamous Royal Decree of December 16, 1616, and left us landlocked, smothered, at the mercy of those who kept the key to our access to the world hanging from their belt.

With Brazil it has been different—although the same. "No diplomacy in the business of war," wrote Pedro II to his foreign minister in 1867. That has been the constant in relations with Paraguay: strong-arm diplomacy and strong, armed forces deployed along the "constantly movable frontiers" with which to harass the weak Spanish province of the time. And to complete an impeccable picture of imperialism, they adopted the policy of plunder, *uti possidettis*—annexing of conquered territory—to compound all the treaties signed and ignored, the gifts and the bribes, the bombardments and ultimatums. To be exact—and honest—Paisandú, Montevideo, and Asunción. The attitude is summed up in a single statement: "The empire does not have permanent friends, nor permanent enemies. It has permanent interests." Reading history over their shoulders, it is clear that these interests justified anything and everything: secret missions, secret treaties, secret archives. A court that secretly fled its own capital in 1808 to save its skin would not think twice in other less-than-ethical matters when it came to securing exclusive benefit or advantage. An obsession with secrecy—or the conviction that it was more viable at the time to go against the grain of decency or morals.

And unfortunately for Paraguay in its dealings with Brazil, there were still more "conflicting interests" in the aftermath of the war of 1870: the bribing of our authorities, the financing of coups d'état, overthrowing or "electing" our presidents and vetoing candidates, the imposition of treaties, the financing of certain organs of the Press (*La Libertad* in 1893) and the closure of others (1903). It may be that these are the secrets that President Lula wishes to keep hidden now. But Paraguayans know them only too well—we have had to live with the consequences. And, important as they are, they are not the only ones that constitutional, socialist Brazil, with its democracy and solidarity, should recognize and make public as part of its responsibility to history.

The same reasons apply to Argentina, guilty of the same cruelty and obscurantism, and which must now help forge a new alliance in the region; a genuine, productive, dignified alliance that recognizes the contribution and the rights of Paraguay from the very beginnings of all our nations. They must finally accept that our ineffective past governments were the consequence of the failure of Argentinian and Brazilian policy—a perennially overlooked explanation. That the idea of a "pendular" relationship did not come from Paraguay but arose because Brazil and Argentina used Paraguay in their mutual political maneuverings. That with troubles of its own, Paraguay had no need for pendulums, pulleys, or treaties which have in any case been continually broken right back to independence. That to go on suffering, Paraguay did not need a common market: it would have been sufficient simply to dismantle the obstacles to trade put in place by Argentina since the days of the "One Port" policy.

It is time Brazil and Argentina understood that Paraguay's hardship and geopolitical and structural problems are the real cause of "asymmetries" in Mercosur. Just as they have acknowledged the bravery of our soldiers in the past, they need now to acknowledge our demands for recognition of the unnecessary suffering inflicted on the Paraguayan people. They need to acknowledge their theft of our land, the occupation of our sovereign territory, the pillaging of property, the rape of defenseless women, and their political intervention in every one of our postwar governments.

None of these things, however, is comparable to the deaths of thousands of innocent women, adolescents and children as "collateral damage" in the conflict. This constitutes a crime against humanity, a loss of human life from which Paraguay would never recover. What do other countries do under similar circumstances? They demand an admission of guilt, and compensation from the murderers. In order to achieve this, governments take action and make demands through argument, prestige and legitimacy, first before their neighbors and then before the international community, making full use of appropriate fora and the media. This should become our domestic national cause, especially now in light of plans to commemorate the bicentenary of independence, when Paraguay became the first South American Republic on October 12, 1813.

Meanwhile, perhaps we need a presidential decree like the one issued by Dr. José Gaspar Rodríguez de Francia. Toward the end of the 1820s, struggling for recognition of Paraguay's independence, he ordered that these words be embroidered on all national flags: *Long live the Republic of Paraguay. Independence or death!*

Tereré as a Social Bond

Derlis Benítez Alvarenga

Together with the harp and ñandutí lace, the drink known as tereré is one of the icons of Paraguayan culture. Few Paraguayans, either inside or outside the country, are to be found without their gourd (mate), their flask (termo), and metal straw (bombilla) filled with yerba mate. In this extract, Derlis Benítez analyzes this profound national attachment to tereré, which clearly represents more than just a drink.

Tereré is deeply embedded in our way of being, not because it *makes* us what we are but because we *are* what we are when we drink it. Tereré has come to be a kind of symbol, a sort of mythological pivot around which the essence of our cultural identity has evolved. Unfortunately, in today's world, where those who hold power tend to standardize all things in order to influence as many people as possible, tereré constitutes an obstacle; hence the accusations made against it. The standardizers have no time for different ways of life. What others have or produce is not "good": only those who live as they themselves can be "good," "developed," "civilized." It is a deeply unfortunate fact that our politicians, intellectuals, and businessmen subscribe to and follow the guidance of these standardizers in spite of the fact that their attitude is detrimental to our cultural identity. It is inadmissible that we should want to be like those who are "not us," in other words, like them. That would be tantamount to a violation of our own cultural heritage and of the identity of our own people. So we must stand firm and strive to recuperate lost space in the name of securing diversity. If not, the world will become increasingly standardized and depersonalized. Just as an individual who loses his identity becomes unhappy, entire peoples run the risk of such anguish. Paraguayans have no reason to wish to be like non-Paraguayans by merely aping the so-called prototypical human being that the foreign standardizers offer in their movies and propaganda. Paraguayans must not relinquish tereré. They must not lose that informal space where they are able to express themselves and share their world, their reality, and their

El Terere

Bombilla

Guampa

Yerba mate

Menta'i

Eucalipto

Tereré—the national drink of Paraguay. Photograph by Joseph Samuel Nickson, Birmingham, England. Used by permission of the photographer.

hopes. To Paraguayans, tereré is similar to what "spare time" is to a philosopher: it allows them to reflect, clarify ideas, seek solutions, etc. Today more than ever, in this highly technological world, its pace determined by the pace of machines, a relentless pace that leaves no time for conversation, sharing, love, crying, or laughter, we humans must question a mechanical way of life, and free ourselves from its enslavement. Human beings should be the masters of machines, of space, of time, and of progress in the sciences, and not the other way round.

Paraguayans, and all Latin Americans who have not completely abandoned their indigenous heritage, have a naturally contemplative temperament. They know how to live in harmony with the environment, and actively seek close contact with friends and family. They have an enormous capacity for informal gatherings and for easy conversation. They shun verbosity and long-windedness, activism for its own sake, extreme formality, noisiness, and superficiality. For this reason, through tereré Paraguayans almost unconsciously seek an opportunity for relaxed, cordial, and informal community, free from superiorities, social artifice, protocol, and anything else that might undermine authenticity and originality in the human relation. We see examples of it daily in every corner of the nation, in town and country.

More than fulfilling a biological need, the drinking of tereré fulfils a clear sociocultural purpose. At a certain time of day, a group of companions will arrive religiously at the meeting place, not just to drink tereré, but to meet and spend time with friends, free from the formalities and routine of studies and of other demands on their attention. Anyone arriving from outside, and carrying the weight of a cultural inheritance very distinct from our own, will not—it is immediately evident—understand what is going on. Their assessment of the behavior they see will be according to the parameters of their own cultural values, so distant from ours. Which is why, for them, the drinking of tereré might seem a waste of time, or even a nonsense; they may associate it with an unwillingness to work or study, as our standardized compatriots so often do.

Tereré as a Return to Roots

Tereré never tastes better than when it is weaving round a circle of hands to the sweet sound of our mother tongue—in the literal sense of the word—Guaraní, a language that, far from being weakened, continues to gain strength in the educational sector and in the national consciousness. Until recently, there were some Paraguayans who did not want to speak Guaraní because they thought that to do so would be to lower themselves. This fitted perfectly with the wishes of the standardizers, or *conquistadores*, whose own aim was precisely that. But those of us who continued to speak Guaraní with pride in spite of the difficulties were the ones who wanted to vindicate our mothers' language without implying for a moment that this constituted a rejection of that of our fathers. We have not renounced our mothers as, sadly, some have done. On the contrary, we have defended her, we love her and we speak to her in her own sweet Guaraní language.

It is no surprise that tereré tastes best when drunk in a group conversing openly and intimately in Guaraní. From time to time one hears it said that "when we speak in Guaraní it's as if we're more ourselves." This is quite true. Guaraní is the language of the home, of affection, of the primary re-lationships within the family, among children and among friends. All the popular sayings, the slang, the *ne'enga*, and the nicknames are created in Guaraní. "When we're drinking tereré and making jokes, Spanish doesn't feel right, or sound right—it's a time when the whole atmosphere is Guar-aní." All of this happens because through tereré the originality and idiosyn-crasy of Paraguayans are brought to the fore. They feel free to speak as they wish and to be who they are, without the censures imposed by frameworks copied from other realities or societies different from their own. Tereré becomes the means by which we return to the source of our cultural identity. It is a sort of return to our roots.

It is like coming back home to our dear old village after a long time away, to a place full of good memories, old friends, and family we have missed; a place of familiar landscapes and cherished childhood memories. Tereré refreshes the well-trodden and the familiar; it is as if it brings to life the seeds of identity sown long ago, nurturing and strengthening it to face the challenge of an uncertain future. It is like rich fertilizer that coaxes the root to grow vigorous and luxuriant, ensuring good fruit and abundant shade for the generations who will find shelter there and eat from the same branches.

The whole internal world of *lo mitá paraguayo* blooms—revives and renews itself—eloquently in the round of tereré that enables this cultural world to survive and flourish. Tereré affords the space necessary for spontaneous and informal togetherness, eliminating all barriers of protocol and formalities in a place where the official language is precisely the language of "the boys"—Guaraní. The language of "the boys" is built on official language of the round of tereré. It is in this context that one must look for the value, importance, and usefulness of tereré.

With regard to the expression *Shall we drink tereré?*, it is more than a simple invitation to drink tereré. It talks to us of its communal dimension, namely that of sharing. This lies close to a central concern of this book. We must recognize that tereré, seen from the viewpoint of other cultures, is little more than an exotic drink. But we who see it and feel it inside us know, even if we cannot explain its real significance in words, that it is something more than that. When giving an opinion, either negative or positive, about tereré, one must bear in mind a complex of underlying cultural factors if the opinion is to be coherent. Tereré cannot be evaluated without reference to the context that surrounds it, that is to say, it should not be reduced simply to its external appearance: in every cultural context, external signs reflect subtle meanings and profound internal spiritual experience. An image or a cultural symbol can occupy a small space and can easily be measured, but its symbolism can span cosmic spheres, and escape all modern attempts at measurement. This is the case with tereré. Although the objects involved are simple and visible, in its cultural usage in Paraguay its meaning and content transcend the world of the visible and are lost in the world of the spiritual-experiential.

Tereré as a Commitment to Paraguayanness

By *paraguayidad*, we understand everything that identifies the cultural world of the Paraguayans: what makes them what they are, and at the same time, what distinguishes them from others. We may ask ourselves—What is it that identifies Paraguayans? What is it that forms the essence of what they are? The reply appears simple: what identifies them and what forms the essence of what they are, is their culture. But the implications of this reply are complex and nuanced, that is to say, they are a question of culture. I have already noted that culture is neither simple nor easily defined. It involves the whole of human life and cannot be reduced to a simple definition. The underestimation and ridiculing of this complexity has led to disastrous and cruel violations of cultures across the millennia that have led not only to the shedding of blood and tears, but to terrible genocides that have still not been acknowledged.

The identification of tereré with paraguayidad is far-reaching and profound, but its most important facet is the time that it gives Paraguayans. Time to commune with themselves, time to sit and think, without which it is difficult to decide the road to follow; time to spend in conversation with friends—to accompany and be accompanied. Time to simply "be" which avoids being limited to *doing*, and to doing things; time for recreation, for philosophy, theology, poetry, music, art, imagination, love, friendship, and contemplation. The time for tereré has arrived.

Tereré has penetrated deep into the cultural world of Paraguayans. It has put down deep roots, to become a luxuriant tree that offers them, and all those associated with them, cool shade for rest and abundant fruit for refreshment. Tereré promotes catchphrases and popular sayings, the famous *ne'enga*; it has inspired poems and songs. It has been a driving force of our Guaraní language, in which resides the greater part of our cultural world and which itself offers refuge from external subjugation. Few realize that thanks to Guaraní, the *teko paraguai* (the Paraguayan way of life) remains firmly established along our frontiers. Even though trade, finance and even language are being influenced by external pressures, Paraguayans still feel and think in Guaraní. The vast majority of those living on the frontier with Brazil speak Portuguese, which influences their Spanish, and hence when speaking Spanish they mix it with Portuguese. However, Portuguese has no influence whatsoever on Guaraní. Hence, when speaking Guaraní, the frontier dweller does so without mixing in any Portuguese. This makes Guaraní an invincible barrier against cultural invasion, because it protects the content of the language, that is to say, the cultural world that it encapsulates, the cosmovision and idiosyncrasy of our people. Guaraní is sweet, profound, and robust, and wherever it takes root it is difficult to eradicate. For that reason Guaraní survives in large parts of Argentina, especially around Corrientes and Misiones, enlivening both music and poetry. Although some may not believe it, Guaraní is one of the greatest treasures our country possesses. Together with tereré, it has served as a source of refuge and of survival in moments of persecution and strife. Guaraní confirms our identity, and has simultaneously become the vehicle for protest against all that threatens that identity.

We live in a fast-changing world, at a pace that could prove to be a double-edged sword. We are on the brink of the third millennium, when humanity will either savor or suffer the fruits of its own actions. In the coming millennium humankind will realize that machines, however sophisticated and beautiful, will always be merely machines, and never a key to happiness, as many assume. We must not forget that human beings can choose to live either in freedom or as slaves. To allow oneself to be carried on the winds and tides of fashion simply leads to the absence of any need to think for oneself or to be creative or original, or to be the protagonist of one's own history. Instead one becomes a passive spectator.

Paraguayidad should be promoted everywhere, in all areas of national life (government, education, religion, the arts) so that Paraguayans can become the protagonists of their own history rather than bystanders as outsiders determine our history. This is all the more necessary when those outsiders seek paraguayidad in name only—not in our way of being and our lifestyle. A different way of being and lifestyle precludes them from easily monopolizing control and influence. For the powerful with a thirst for world domination, things are much easier if we all live the same way and speak the same language. That would enable them to exercise absolute power, with unforeseeable consequences. Uncritical standardization is the aim of ambitious imperialists. It enables them selfishly to be the main protagonists in world history. Only a thinking people, one that, based on its cultural identity, commits itself to its destiny, is capable of opposing and triumphing against those who seek to manipulate and exploit their plans for a standardized planet. Drivers of the standardizing approach dismiss tereré and seek to demean it, all the while offering substitutes for "modern times," and using mass advertising campaigns to exalt them as drinks of the future—or of modernity—rather than of Indians and peasants. But a thoughtful people will ensure that tereré emerges victorious against "crazycolas": Paraguayanness against the uniform standardizers.

Tereré and Solidarity

In spite of everything, in tereré we find reflected the formidably generous spirit of Paraguayans, who always share what they have with others, and especially with the needy. That spirit has been gradually eroded by the spirit of capitalism—calculating, egotistical, self-seeking, and competitive. The drinking of tereré can also be attacked and eroded because it does not respond to the capitalist ideal. In tereré there is a sharing from start to finish; during the round everyone shares the same yerba mate, the same straw, the same gourd, the same water, the same medicinal herbs, the same subject of conversation. Tereré unites, and shares its taste, from hand to hand to the end. There is a lesson in this. It is a model for the joining of hands, interlinked hands of solidarity, capable of restoring happiness to the sad, curing the infirm, clothing the destitute, giving food to the hungry.

Contrary to what the present-day materialist world preaches, our parents and grand-parents taught us that sharing the little that we have and lending a helping hand to others neither demeans nor prejudices us; rather it enriches and ennobles the human being, since to be human is in essence to "be-with-others" and to "be-for-others." Those who close themselves off from others are egotists, and sever themselves from their own development as human beings. They may have everything that they want in terms of material possessions, but they will not have what really makes a human being happy—openness, caring, confidence, and the happiness of others.

The Status of Women

Riordan Roett and Richard Scott Sacks

As a result of the decimation of the male population during the Triple Alliance War (1864–70), in the early decades of the Liberal period there was a marked predominance of women in the labor force. The establishment of female-headed households, a cultural tradition that persists to the present day, dates from the period following that catastrophic war. But despite this quasi-matriarchal economic structure, women retain a subordinate role in society, suffering widespread discrimination in a society heavily dominated by machista *cultural values. It was only in 1961, following international pressure, that legislation was passed granting women the right to vote, the right to be elected to political office, and the right to join together and organize themselves within political parties. Furthermore, with the dictatorship acting as an obstacle to the emergence of women's rights and organizations, it was not until the beginning of the 1990s that campaigns for gender equality before the law came to public attention. Despite recent gains in terms of greater equality, much of what Roett and Sacks observed in 1980 remains highly relevant today.*

Though it is changing, Paraguay is still a conservative, male-dominated society. Paraguayan women were among the last in the Western world to vote in elections, a right they gained as recently as 1963. Although changes to the civil code in recent years have given women protection in the division of marital property in the event of separation, divorce is still not a legal option in Paraguay. Yet broken marriages are common (women headed 18 percent of all households in 1982). The women's movement as such is still embryonic. Paraguayan society frowns on women who demand things for themselves, branding them as "egoists" who have lost their femininity. This is not to say that Paraguayan women are marching in the streets demanding equal treatment or equal opportunity. Even politically active women are likely to fulfill their traditional roles within their families.

Public health statistics for women are troubling. High maternal mortality rates (469 per 100,000 live births in 1980) imply that women are not receiving the pre- or postnatal care that they need. Although abortion is a significant social issue in other Latin American countries (such as Brazil, where it is legal), it is still illegal in Paraguay. In general, although many women have jobs outside the home, they tend to earn less money than men. One reason is that women tend not to hold well-paying salaried positions as often as men; rather, they are apt to be independently employed in small businesses or as maids or laundresses. Men outnumber women in the labor market (four to one), where women have only a 20 percent participation rate. Working women earned less than the minimum wage on average in 1986, and salaries for women in the private sector totaled less than half of male salaries.

Women in Paraguay play important roles within the family and within the economy but have almost no power to influence public decision making on the local or national level. In other words, their political power is next to nil. Although a few women have seats in the Congress, women almost never hold positions of civil authority; a female mayor or judge is an extreme rarity in Paraguay. On the other hand, the economic role of women in Paraguay is very important, especially in the countryside. The economic contribution of Paraguayan women has always been crucial to society; the 1864–1870 holocaust of the Triple Alliance War, after which very few men were left alive, furnishes only one example.

Rural women in Paraguay perform all domestic work and most of the field work as well. They cook, collect firewood, tend the hearth, and raise the children. If a woman accompanies her husband on a trip, she carries their goods in a great basket on her head or back. Women also spin, weave, and dye cloth, and carry water. With the exception of clearing land, ploughing, and planting manioc, women do all the agricultural work as well, performing such tasks as planting, weeding (whether with hoe or machete), harvesting, and gathering wild fruits. Little wonder, perhaps, that feminist spokeswomen in Paraguay claim that peasant women are "raised to be servants."

The arrival of the Spaniards in 1537 and their "alliance" with the Guaraní tribes were disasters of the first magnitude for women. Overnight, women were transformed into concubines, field hands, and procreators—a chattel that could be bought, sold, traded, or even wagered in a game of cards. Women were valued only for the economic work and sexual services they could perform. Although some Spaniards doubtless felt genuine love for their multiple consorts, in general they did not exactly regard these Indian women as fully human. Often they thought nothing of cohabiting with sisters or with a mother and her daughters, which the Guaraní considered even more incestuous than the Spaniards did. Sometimes the *encomendero* would not permit a woman to nurse her own child because he required her services as a wet nurse. The colonial system killed more Indians than it produced *mestizos*; the Guaraní population took centuries to regain the level it had attained before the conquest.

Desperate in their new situation, as Paraguay "was being converted into a concentration camp of physically violated . . . prostituted women," these Indian women resorted to suicide and murdering their children. As exploitation increased and the initial "friendship" between the races waned, the Spaniards resorted to kidnapping women from Indian villages. The frequent Indian revolts against Spanish authority (there were at least 23 rebellions between 1537 and 1660) were the direct result of these raids.

Little changed regarding the condition of women for centuries after the conquest. The first female feminist thinkers and writers appeared in Paraguay after 1900, as part of the general cultural enlightenment that accompanied the first Liberal governments. During the 1980s, feminist circles in Asunción rediscovered the frankly feminist doctoral dissertation of Serafina Dávalos, Paraguay's first female lawyer. Entitled "Humanism," the 1907 dissertation analyzed the position of women in the lower, middle, and upper classes and proposed radical changes in the law to allow a massive incorporation of women into civil society.

The Chaco War offered women an opportunity for organizing independent groups, as much to help nurse the wounded as to help organize public administration. Because most of the leaders of these groups were mothers, daughters, or wives of Liberal party politicians, many were exiled and their groups disbanded after the February Revolution of 1936. But this "feminist boom" continued under Febrerista auspices as Maria Casati, an Italian woman with anarcho-syndicalist tendencies, organized the Feminine Union of Paraguay and founded a newsletter.

By the late 1940s, Colorado and Liberal politicians were promising women absolute legal equality before the law, although not much was actually being done. By 1951, the League for Women's Rights (La Liga pro Derechos de la Mujer) was formed to struggle for equal rights. A 1954 law finally established a framework of legal rights for unmarried women and widows, but changed little about the status of married women. Organizing for women's rights stagnated under Stroessner, as did all organizing activity not directly controlled by the Colorado party. Current and future opportunities for women will improve to the degree that Paraguay liberalizes in the post-Stroessner era. Nonetheless, in their struggle to break free of the roles that many societies have traditionally assigned to women, Paraguayan feminists identify their biggest enemy as the Roman Catholic church.

An upsurge in women's organizing activities, especially in Asunción, accompanied the general increase in social unrest that followed the abrupt end of the Itaipú boom. Groups of female writers and intellectuals began to study the social condition of women in Paraguay. Female journalists played a key role, publicizing the activities of various women's groups. By 1986, the women writers and intellectuals had helped prepare society for the beginnings of a public discussion of women's issues. One women's group that appeared at this time—Women for Democracy (Mujeres por la democracia)—became an important actor in the struggle against Stroessner. The group was largely organized by middle- and upper-class wives of politicians who were interested in politics and were tired of being *pastelitos*[1]—tired of having to cook for and organize the social functions of their husbands. Not overtly feminist, Mujeres por la democracia nonetheless helped advance the cause of all women in Paraguay by demonstrating the success of a women's group that was willing to struggle for social goals. A variety of women's groups have since emerged (many of them in Asunción), from associations of female lawyers to the Association of Rural Women (Coordinación de las mujeres campesinas). Nonetheless, no large, fully constituted, nationwide movement of women exists today in Paraguay.

Note

1. A *pastelito* is a little pastry or sweet.

Self-Portrait

Bernarda

Self-Portraits, *published in 1984, was a ground-breaking book. Comprising a series of interviews with poor, mainly rural women, it documented the daily hardship that so many of them suffered, bringing their lives into the bookshops of Asunción and the living rooms of the educated middle class. The interviews reflect the day-to-day lives of such women and they are striking for their matter-of-fact tone. Without seeking to be sensationalist, sentimental, or campaigning, they constitute an extraordinarily powerful critique of issues such as poverty, gender relations, inequality, domestic violence, and lack of access to education, healthcare, and sanitation, all of which today still constitute a reality for many Paraguayan women. Indeed, for many rural women, little has changed in the decades since this book was first published. The book also reflects the sense of resignation among many poor women who see little way out of their situation. As one of the contributors, Petrona, states, "I'm speaking because if what I say is published, people will know what life is like for a girl like me, that we have no other destiny in life than to work and look after children."*

The following interview with Bernarda gives a fascinating insight into her existence. Despite the grinding poverty in which she struggles to bring up children, she sees herself as comparatively fortunate, with a "good" husband and a small business and able to educate her children.

I got married ten years ago when I was nineteen. It's a good age to get married and have children. Francisco and I could have tied the knot sooner, but we wanted to save up before, so we waited three years from when we first met. I met Francisco here in Amambay-ty, at a party. He was a "foreigner"— he came from Tobatí. We stayed here because I can't leave my family; I'm the eldest daughter so I've got family responsibilities. When we met, he told me straight away that he wanted to marry me. He asked my father for my hand and then we started saving; he'd bring me the money and I'd save it to buy our own plot of land.

I worked as well, but women's work isn't paid. I'm a seamstress but I didn't have the time, because I was always looking after my little brothers and sisters and sewing for them. Sewing takes me a long time because I still don't have a machine. I'm one of nine brothers and sisters in all. I was responsible for looking after the others because I was the eldest. I always tried to give them what I never had: a childhood. Childhood? Mine was just work, work, and work. I didn't have time to play. My toys were my brothers and sisters that were born every year. From the time I could sit down I remember having a baby in my lap. I've worked since I was born, then I got married and carried on working, and now I'm working more and more because at the moment Francisco is out of work and I've got to shoulder everything.

I was born just over there, in that straw and adobe hut, where my mother and father and my brothers and sisters still live. Their youngest is eight, the same age as my little boy. My parents have always lived there. When they got together, my grandmother gave them about two hectares and the house. They lived together without getting married for a long time, but when Francisco and I started to go out together, they felt a little ashamed and so they got married. We girls were becoming *señoritas* and since we are very Catholic they didn't want to set a bad example. They wanted us to get married in the church rather than just hook up with someone, because there's no commitment in that, and they were worried that we might end up just going from one man to the next, and that's no good. If you're married it's different. I'm not like the other women round here that get together with a man, then split up and end up with kids with different fathers.

My family are good people and my parents never separated. They brought us up as Christians. My dad still works, doing odd jobs, because they still have kids in school. We all finished primary school. At the moment, my father's planting potatoes, corn, manioc, peanuts, and beans, but that's not enough to survive on. The school wants more things all the time like uniforms, books, and pinafores and new shoes for parades; it's expensive nowadays, going to school.

Our main way of earning money used to be growing cotton, but cotton's no use nowadays if you're poor. Maybe it's good business if you've got a lot of land, but not if you've only got two hectares. My dad always ends up losing money. If he breaks even he's happy. Around here Señor Pérez, the company middleman, he lends money, gives us pesticides and fertilizer, but then he ends up with the cotton crop and everyone still owes him money. This year the cotton failed because the seed that the Ministry of Agriculture gave us was useless—all wet. So in the end, all that work was for nothing.

Francisco and I built the shop out of brick. Now, with the crisis, the shop's our lifeline, because at least we have food. I get up at four o'clock in the morning, I make *pasteles*[1] and then if they sell, I can buy meat and make soup. If they don't, we just have pasteles for lunch. While I'm frying them, my youngest, the two-year-old, tends to wake up and I have to give him breakfast. Then the eldest gets up and has his breakfast and starts work; he feeds the pigs and the chickens—I've got more than a dozen; they always come in handy when I have to buy tools or medicine. Then he goes off to school. If I have a big order for pasteles, sometimes I keep him at home so he can deliver them. I also make them to sell at parties. Here we work from the minute we're born, always working; it seems that if you are poor, even when things start to go well, there's always something round the corner that crops up.

It's terrible that all the men around here have to go off to look for work. There's one man who owns almost the whole town, and all the good land is his. He exploits everyone. Francisco worked for him for a few years, but for every 100 lines he picked, we had to give him 40, and even if the crop was poor we still had to pay him. He doesn't lift a finger. We don't know the man ourselves. We always have to settle up with the foreman. We have to buy everything, even the fertilizer. They don't do anything. It's no way to make a living. So Francisco went with my brother to look for work in Santaní, but he came back after a while with nothing, just dirty clothes for me to wash. That foreman has got no shame. He tries to take advantage of us women—he even abused the daughter of one of our neighbors. He tried it on with me but I told him to get lost. That's another reason Francisco doesn't want to work there anymore.

If my parents hadn't had so many kids, I could probably have been a good seamstress, because I look at magazines and make new designs. I make all the clothes and the school uniforms for my little brothers and sisters too. I always say that next year I am going to buy a sewing machine.

People ask me why I haven't got more kids. I don't want to be like my parents, because being the eldest daughter it was so hard for me. I remember my mamá being pregnant all the time. I'm not complaining because I was happy to look after my little brothers and sisters. But there are nine of us and I remember I always wanted to play, to study more, and how I cried when I finished sixth grade because I wanted to carry on studying—even sewing. But I knew I wasn't going to be able to because I had to bring up my brothers and sisters. I can remember always having the youngest on my hip, and carrying water, washing clothes, taking food to my dad where he was working, feeding the pigs and chickens, and collecting firewood.

The thing I find hardest about this life is that our husbands have to go away to find work in other places and it's not because there's a lack of land; there is a lot of good land around here; next to us there's a rancher who's so mean he won't even pay to put in an electricity line because he's already got generators he can switch on when his friends come from Asunción; and the rest of the time they just use candles.

Toward the south there is another big property where Francisco used to work. If they'd allowed us to we'd have been able to work it peacefully. But now someone's bought it. It's people from Asunción rather than peasants who have land these days.

My husband's away at the moment, working in Alberdi. There aren't any men here, only women and children. My sister-in-law Mary, who's got six children, is on her own too because her partner is working in Alto Paraná and she has to get by on her own with the six kids. The eldest is nine and he helps her collect coco seeds. Sometimes they go to Caacupé to sells herbs. That's why he still hasn't got beyond first grade at school.

I get on really well with my husband. He's a good man; he doesn't drink, doesn't gamble, and doesn't hit me. We struggle along together although there's never enough money, which is why I don't want any more kids. What would I do on my own with another child?

When I go to the market or to Caacupé or Eusebio Ayala my eldest looks after his little brothers and sisters, but even so, I try to make sure he doesn't miss school. But then he never has his notebook. Homework? No, the teacher knows how poor we are and that in our house we are struggling just to survive. She's very good and doesn't insist the kids wear shoes like the other teacher in the third grade used to—although that one never got her way, because we don't wear shoes even when it's cold, and even less with socks to go to school every day. How could we buy notebooks for homework when we've hardly got enough to eat every day? He's got the textbook; I've covered it so his brother will be able to use it, even though they say next year they're going to change the curriculum and they won't be using it any more. Everything's harder these days. When I was at school they gave us a glass of soya milk, because we hadn't had any breakfast or just had watery *cocido*;[2] it didn't taste very nice. Despite everything, I was a good student—I could have gone on to college. But I'm resigned to my fate; how was I ever going to go to college if I had to look after so many brothers and sisters, and had so many responsibilities at home?

Nowadays I get up at four in the morning, clean the house, make pasteles, and while they're cooking I open the shop. I sell biscuits for breakfast and yerba for cocido. This shop has saved me. The suppliers for the bread rolls, sugar, and yerba all pass by, and some stop for breakfast, which I make for them because I have the fire going from when I get up. I really want a wood-burning stove, those Brazilian ones that have hot water all day, but for now I just cook on the floor on four bricks. That hurts my back but I don't want one of those burners that they hang on the wall that the ministry supplies because in winter we all keep warm by the fire in the middle of the kitchen. And if Francisco's here, he and I talk about things and drink mate, before the kids wake up.

The men that do stay around drink a lot. I think they're bitter about always being broke. Then they go home and hit their wives and girlfriends. I can't stand them—and I tell them that to their faces. The whole town respects me because they see how hard I work to support my family. And if anyone tries anything at night, I've got my knife.

It took a lot of work for us to get a brick house. One room is the shop and the other is for sleeping. I sleep in the double bed and my eldest boy in the little one over there. The other children still sleep in the hammock in the same room. What I need now is a proper brick kitchen, but that would cost a lot and I want it to be big like the one I've got made of adobe, because I keep all the coco seeds, tobacco, and bananas in there to exchange for yerba, sugar, pasta, and meat. I used to sell meat but now people don't eat it because it's so expensive. We live on rice and pasta, although in our house we do sometimes have meat because I can get it cheap, and Francisco doesn't take all the money and throw it away like other husbands do—letting their wives work and then taking the food from their children's mouths so they can spend it on drink.

This straw corridor is cool. This is what you called the social area, but for me this is where I serve coffee and food to people. I've got five coffee plants that I planted myself. I pick the coffee, toast it, and grind it. Why is it so sweet? So the visitors don't think we are being mean with the sugar. There is more sugar here if you want.

I like the garden a lot. I've planted roses and resedás.[3] Around here all the houses have flowers, even the poorest. No matter how poor people are, they always want to have a clean house full of flowers. It just takes up a lot of your time.

My father is a good man, like I said. He is an example for us all. There are us five sisters and my mum, but more than anyone it was my dad who made sure we had everything we needed, and we got a basic education. And he didn't have any children with other women—he didn't have the time for playing around with women for one thing, since he always worked from dawn to dusk. Life was easier in those days. There was plenty of land, a lot of it abandoned because no one wanted it. It's only recently, about six or seven years ago, that this man Torales came to say that he owned the whole community, that he had all the land titles and we had to pay him. My father never had a land title in his life, but he always worked on the land and raised us. He doesn't have a problem now because they've told him he's worked the land for more than forty years, but the land is so poor you have to plough it two or three times and he's not so strong any more, even though my two brothers help him. He doesn't have any machinery; he just picks up the hand plough and goes along with my brothers turning over the earth. But the land is exhausted. There's not enough of it and there's no chance of getting any more.

We've been here a long time, like everyone else in Amambay-ty. My grandparents farmed the land here. It's a shame my father can't read or write; he can only just sign his name. But he's looked after us all. Well, I help him now, and because I'm working, Francisco buys the school uniforms for his children.

Bernarda (29), Amambay-ty, August 1984

Notes

1. Pasteles (literally cakes) are savory rolls made from flour, cheese, milk, and eggs and then fried.
2. Cocido is a hot tea made from toasted yerba mate.
3. Resedá is a flower found in the Paraguayan countryside, which is now very rare.

María and the Serpent

Pepa Kostianovsky

On February 14, 2007, a poor woman called María Estela Lima arrived at the studios of Radio Aquidabán in Concepción with an incredible story. She recounted that her husband, Carlos Gutiérrez, a farm hand in Puerto Colón in the Chaco, had been eaten by a giant kuriju (boa constrictor). The story attracted massive public interest and María became an overnight celebrity. But gradually doubts arose about the veracity of her account. Two weeks later, her husband turned up fit and well and she was forced to confess that she had invented the story in order to obtain help. She was then subjected to intense criticism by the media, which had been fooled by her story. This fictionalized account of the incident, which is far more sympathetic to María's plight, is written by Pepa Kostianovsky, one of Paraguay's leading contemporary journalists.

The floods had cut off the hut that served as an outpost for the Karajá cattle ranch in the far north. When she could gather the necessary strength, María picked up her newly born baby and the toddler, told the oldest child to hold on to her skirt, and without any baggage—because she did not have any—got into the tiny boat, settled her children down, and summoned up the energy to row to the higher land. From there she walked and walked, guided only by her instinct.

She could not remember how long ago it was that, when still a girl, she had walked in the opposite direction with the man who found her wandering in the market, frightened and all alone. She had fled from the house where her mother worked as a kitchen maid until one afternoon when she had been hit and taken to the police station after the lady of the house accused her mother of stealing her gold rosary beads.

Hidden among the branches of the large mango tree, María had seen what happened, the two men on horses fading into the distance with her mother dragged between them, her hands tied by rope to a saddle. When the neighbors left, the girl took the chance to run away before anyone blamed her for what had happened. By nightfall, and dead tired, she slumped down, resting her head against a front door.

Basilio noticed her fear and hunger straight away. He sat down under the shadow of the door where she had placed her desperation and, without saying anything, opened the greasy paper in which he kept two pasties and some warm *mandioca*. Captivated by the aroma of coriander and fried oil, she could not take her eyes away from the tasty feast. With a clear and pleasant smile, the man invited her to share his meal. She accepted the invitation and savored it slowly, hoping that it would never end. Then he got up, and made a gesture to her with his head. Without any question, she followed him and mounted the back of his horse.

The journey was long but she wanted to go far away. When they arrived at the hut, he asked her name and invited her to wash in the river. From time to time, the man left early and returned at night. He brought oil, kerosene, yerba, noodles, cigars, and rum. When the first child was born, he also brought a piece of white cloth. It was raining on the morning that he left for good. She saw the flood level rising as her belly swelled for the third time. She had begun to feel the first birth pains but had fallen asleep and dreamt of a large snake. It was only then that she knew that Basilio would not return and that they also had to leave.

The hand of fate guided her back to the town. She recognized the market square and her former fear returned. She walked fast and sought refuge by the side of the church. Together, the four of them looked like a sleeping child born with multiple arms, legs, and heads. The fat ruddy-faced priest woke them up and ordered the young altar boys to take them to the kitchen. The children dared not to touch the cups of sugary milk, the pieces of *chipa*, the bunch of yellow bananas, and the *dulce de guayaba* that was as dark as mud; they only realized that a banquet was on offer when their mother encouraged them, starting to eat herself as she breast-fed the youngest. The priest waited until they had finished the breakfast before asking any questions. Fear took hold of her again and she told him that her name was María, María Lima. When she came to talk about the man, she said that he had been eaten by an enormous snake, which had swallowed him whole.

The news traveled fast, first to Concepción and then to the whole country. The next day, the newspapers in Asunción printed the story on their front page—of how a cattle-ranch hand had been eaten alive by a kuriju. Some said that this was impossible, that in that part of the country there were no snakes of such a size. Others argued that the floods could have brought it down from the northern marshlands; that climate change was responsible for creating such monstrous creatures; that it was punishment for crimes against nature; and that it was the fault of the governments that had ignored the cutting down of the forests; or punishment from God for abandoning the Christian faith; or that it was even a biblical prophecy.

The skeptics insisted that the woman was mad, that she was hallucinating. A diligent public prosecutor insinuated that it would be dangerous to leave the children with her. There was even a journalist who accused her of being a "traitor to the motherland," because her crazy story—together with genuine and repugnant tropical fevers—would dissuade tourists and foreign investors. Someone suggested timidly that what she really needed was help. But nobody took up the matter. The politicians were too busy. The public and private welfare bodies had their hands full with the outbreak of dengue fever and the floods. The press decided that the news had run its course. And even those who first believed the story let doubt take over in their minds for fear of appearing foolish. The owners of the cattle ranch took advantage of the confusing facts supplied by María in order to drop any investigation into the disappearance of the ranchhand, from whose family they had never received any formal notification. So they washed their hands of the whole affair

The four poor souls remained forgotten in a room of the vicarage. The priest knew that it was only a temporary solution. But he relied on his faith. God would provide, he said, in the full knowledge that if his gift did not arrive, at least they would be protected by oblivion. María looked at the two young ones wedged against her body, switched the baby to the other breast and, as she did so, removed the gold rosary beads from among her rags.

Erico

Jorge Barraza

Soccer is the most popular sport in Paraguay and, as in other Latin American countries, borders on a national obsession. It has been played at club level since it was introduced by British contract workers on the Paraguay Central Railway in the early 1900s. Despite a thriving club structure, it is the national team, the Albirroja ("the red-and-whites") that evokes the greatest passion. Of all the soccer-playing nations in South America, only Uruguay has a smaller population and only Bolivia is poorer in economic terms. Yet Paraguay has a strikingly impressive record, having reached the World Cup finals in four competitions in a row, in 1998, 2002, 2006, and 2010, and defeating on the way some of the world's best teams, including Brazil (with a national population thirty times greater) and Argentina. There is no easy explanation as to why a small nation should be among South America's most successful teams. Some point to the Paraguayan team's tactics of highly disciplined, almost unbreakable defense and rapid counterattack; others put it down to the fighting spirit and strong sense of unity of the perpetual underdog facing seemingly insurmountable odds. Either way, soccer seems to reflect history.

Ironically, Paraguay's greatest player never actually played a competitive game for the national team. Arsenio Erico (1915–77) was a member of the Paraguayan Red Cross team that traveled to Buenos Aires during the Chaco War to raise funds for medical supplies in 1933 and 1934. His outstanding skills were spotted by the Argentinian team Independiente and he was immediately offered a contract. Erico went on to play for Independiente for the next thirteen years, scoring an extraordinary 293 goals in just 325 games—still a record for the club and the Argentinian first division. He was the top scorer in the league in 1937, 1938, and 1939, notching up 47 goals in just 34 matches in 1937. In 1938 he was offered a lucrative contract to play for Argentina in the World Cup finals, an offer he politely declined out of loyalty to Paraguay, even though he would never get the chance to play a competitive match for the Albirroja. Powerful and fast, but with a velvet touch, huge leap, and astounding ball control, he become the greatest striker in Argentinian league history, and one of the most revered players of all time.

There are many eulogies to Erico, but perhaps the greatest comes from Alfredo Di

Stefano, widely regarded as one of the greatest players of all time. In this interview from 2007, Di Stefano talks of the elegance, the humility, and the skills of the Golden Paraguayan, who was his personal inspiration.

Alfredo Di Stefano: "I wanted to wear the number 9 shirt, just like my hero, Arsenio"

Alfredo Di Stefano forms part of the select group of the greatest soccer players in history. Although the younger generations agree that he could never be relegated below fourth place in the all-time rankings, that he is in the same category as Pelé, Maradona, and Cruyff, many older observers, especially Europeans, vote the mythical "Di" the most complete player of all-time. The number one. But the mythical Alfredo Di Stefano himself chose as his idol and greatest influence the humble Guaraní striker.

Anyone who approaches Di Stefano for an interview does so under the advice that the first reaction of the honorary president of Real Madrid will be a growl—hardly a sign of welcome. But they will also have been advised that those eighty-one years of prickliness and apparent impoliteness soon dissolve to reveal a soccer-playing soul with a love for nostalgia. Even more so if he hears the magic words:

"No, Alfredo, we don't want to ask you about Argentina's defeat against Brazil. We want you to tell us about Erico."

"Ah, Erico, Erico. The Paraguayan. An incredible man."

"Is it true that he was your childhood hero?"

"Absolutely. I wanted to wear the number nine shirt, just like my hero, Arsenio. I played for River, which always had great center forwards, but I admired Arsenio because he was a master goalscorer, a dancer, a genius for headers and back-heels. Erico didn't run; he glided. He was so elegant. He was different from the great goal scorers of his time, like Masantonio, Perdernera, or Bernabé. Erico was acrobatic, and moved like a dancer when he ran. He was so skilful with his feet, he could out-jump everyone, and he could place the ball in the net like the gods."

"Why was he your hero?"

"Because he played with such style, because he could jump so high for headers, because he was just absolutely amazing. He was my hero because he scored goals and I've always liked players who know how to put the ball in the net. I'll never forget when I was in the youth team, I did an interview and I said I really admired Erico. A few days before, I'd gone with Perdernera to see him at a shop he'd opened that sold Paraguayan fabrics. I'd gone along just because I was a young kid. Then one day a while afterward I was waiting for the bus in Barrancas de Belgrano after a training session at River, and he came up to thank me for what I'd said in the interview. I couldn't believe that Erico had thanked me, or even spoken to me, a kid from the youth team. In those days young players always addressed the stars formally—I always called them 'Sir.' But there we were chatting together."

"As a goal scorer yourself, what did you learn from watching Erico?"

"He was the quintissential goal scorer. I was different—I played all over the pitch. The aim of a striker is to shoot; if it goes in, it's a goal. At River I played up front, because if I went back my teammates would send me forward again, but later in Colombia and Spain, I played all over the pitch. Erico wasn't like that; he was always near the goal. All the same, one thing I did copy was to back-heel a lot. The Paraguayan did it all the time. And me too—at River they tried to fine me for doing so many back-heels."

"Did you see him after he retired?"

"No, because I was already in Europe. But I was very happy when I went to see a match at the national stadium in Paraguay and I saw that one of the stands was named after him. He was a very caring person. And a very principled one too. I remember when he won a car as the Cigarillos 43 Prize,[1] he accepted it, then immediately sold it and shared out the money."

During the 1966 World Cup in London, Alfredo Di Stefano met Carlos Barciella, a close friend of Erico. The Real Madrid star sent his regards to the "Golden Paraguayan" in a short note: "Through your friend Barciella, please accept a special greeting from London. I would like to take the opportunity to reiterate my admiration for you as a footballer, and say how well I remember your afternoons of glory. As a mere imitator of yours, it is an honor to be able to write these lines to you. Yours affectionately, Alfredo."

They only faced each other on the pitch twice, both times in 1946 when "the German" was on loan to Huracán and Arsenio was in his last year at Independiente. The first of these was on June 30 in Avellaneda and Independiente ("the Reds") won 4–3. It was a festival of goals, a worthy homage to two greats who devoted their lives to scoring them. Di Stefano, then just starting his career, scored twice and leveled the score at 3–3 after sixty-three minutes. But one minute later, Erico scored the winning goal, the last of his 293 in Argentina.

Destiny, wise and patient, had long awaited the moment for such glory to be handed on.

Note

1. Cigarillos 43 was a brand of cigarettes. The "Cigarrillos 43 Prize" was awarded to any player who scored forty-three goals in a season.

Recipe for Chipa Guazú

Doña Aída

Paraguayan cuisine is highly distinctive and plays an important role in national identity and culture. One of the main ingredients used is corn. Chipa guazú is a popular traditional dish, quick and easy to make, and certainly worth trying. This recipe is courtesy of Doña Aída.

Ingredients

- 1 kilo of sweet corn, or better, corn from the cob
- 2 medium onions
- 6 eggs
- 45 milliliters of vegetable oil
- 300 grams of cheese (Variety depends on taste but best to use mainly hard cheese, such as Cheddar. Including about 50g of mozzarella also works very well.)
- 240 milliliters of milk
- A pinch of salt to taste

Preparation

Cut the onions into small pieces and fry gently in the oil, until transparent. Rinse the corn well and then liquidize with the milk and eggs. Grate and/or cut the cheese and add to the mixture, along with the onion. Add a pinch of salt to taste.

Pour into a greased dish and place in a preheated oven. Cook at 200 degrees Centigrade for approximately 35–40 minutes, until the top of the chipa guazú turns golden brown. Delicious served hot or cold.

The National Anthem in Guaraní:
Tetã Purahéi Guasu

Félix de Guarania

On August 15, 2008, during the inauguration of Fernando Lugo Méndez, the incoming president, Paraguayans stood for the customary rendition of the national anthem. However, instead of the expected official version in Spanish, accompanied by a military band, the renowned singer and social activist Ricardo Flecha walked to the front of the stage and sang a version of the national anthem in Guaraní. This act was of huge symbolic importance. It was the first time that the anthem had been sung in Guaraní at an official event of this kind. In effect the new president was recognizing that Paraguay was a multicultural and pluriethnic nation and that Guaraní and not Spanish was the preferred language of the majority of the population. Despite coming under pressure not to make what was considered by some to be a highly controversial decision, Lugo insisted, arguing that this was just the symbolic beginning of the "new dawn" that he promised for Paraguay.

Ñapu'ã tetã rayhupára	Rise up, those who love your country
Peteîcha oñondivepa	All together as one
Yvate ñane mbojeroviáva	Let us raise the flag that represents us,
Ao veve ñande yvy ra'anga	the symbol of our land
Mba'apo ñeha'ãme maymáva	Let us all work together
Paraguái jahupi jerovia	and place our faith in Paraguay.
Ára ha pyhare taipo'áva	Day or night, we will strive
Tekove tavayguápe guarã	to make a better life for our people.
Tetã'ỹrõ vokói ñamanóne	Until death takes us from our land
Peteîchaondive Paraguay	All together for Paraguay,
Torypápe opa ára jaikóne	where life will be in harmony
Jejopy ñande yvýpe ndaijái	and oppression will have no place.

Epilogue: The Impeachment
of President Fernando Lugo

On June 21, 2012, the Paraguayan Chamber of Deputies voted 76–1 to initiate the impeachment of President Fernando Lugo on the grounds of "poor performance of functions" (*mal desempeño de sus funciones*). The following day, after the briefest of debates, the Senate voted 39-4 to confirm the decision, thus bringing to a premature end an administration that had initiated the first democratic change of power in the country's history, promising a "new dawn" based on social and political reform in favor of the poor. Lugo reluctantly resigned, and his vice president, Federico Franco, of the Partido Liberal Radical Auténtico (PLRA), who had long disagreed with the president's reformist policies, was sworn in for the remaining fourteen months of the presidential term of office.

Lugo had begun his presidency in August 2008 on a strong wave of popular support, promising long-overdue reforms and an end to institutionalized corruption. Indeed, his early approval ratings reached almost 90 percent. However, crucially his policies did not have the support of a majority in Congress: his electoral victory was dependent on an alliance with the center-right PLRA, many of whose members opposed key elements of his reform program; the Colorado Party, despite losing the 2008 presidential elections, remained the largest political party in terms of seats in both houses of Congress, as well as on departmental and municipal councils; and his reform program (especially land and tax reform) was vehemently opposed by powerful rural lobby groups with strong representation in Congress.

Unsurprisingly therefore, Lugo's period in office was characterized by political instability, crisis, and conflict with Congress. Despite some significant achievements, most notably in the renegotiation of aspects of the 1973 Itaipú Treaty with Brazil and free access to basic health care, his ambitious reform program failed to materialize. On the three areas identified as his reform priorities—land, taxation, and the judiciary—his administration failed to make any significant progress, as the opposition majority in Congress proved highly adept at blocking or delaying executive initiatives. By 2012 his popularity had plummeted, principally as a result of his inability to implement promised reforms, but also because of his personal behavior (namely paternity scandals, both alleged and proven).

The impeachment process was based on five charges, which were striking for their lack of any reference to serious malpractice. There was no accusation of corruption, theft, abuse of human rights, violation of the constitution, or breach of the presidential code. Instead, the charges were based on five counts of "poor performance," chief among which was that he had been unable to address growing insecurity. In particular, he was deemed to have been responsible for instigating and facilitating land invasions in the area of Curuguaty, where eleven peasants and six policemen were killed in a shoot-out during a botched police operation on June 15, 2012, to clear landless peasants. The tragedy was the worst single incident of political violence for decades. It occurred on a two thousand–hectare property at Campos Morombí, which had been spuriously obtained during the Stroessner era by a corrupt businessman and former Colorado senator, Blas Riquelme, under the guise of "land reform." In the immediate aftermath of the killings, Lugo was accused of negligence, ineptitude, and incapacity to act decisively.

The impeachment process itself was widely criticized. Despite official assurances that the process was constitutional, no evidence was presented at the impeachment trial. In fact the formal accusation document even stated that this was not necessary because the facts were "common knowledge." Lugo was given just twenty-four hours to prepare his defense and less than two hours to present it to Senate. On all of these counts, the process violated Article 17 of the 1992 constitution, which protects the rights of the accused to see the charges, challenge the evidence, and be given the necessary time to prepare an adequate defense. Due process fell by the wayside as Congress rushed through the "express" impeachment.

In many ways, this was a coup waiting to happen. Lugo had already survived various attempts by the Colorado opposition to impeach him on spurious charges, as well as a long-standing campaign by the media to undermine his credibility, including alarmist accusations of seeking to create an "extremist" political movement through alleged links to radical peasant organizations, links to the Ejército del Pueblo Paraguayo (EPP) guerrilla movement, and even of designs to emulate President Hugo Chávez of Venezuela. The impeachment therefore involved more than just maneuvering for power in Asunción. The vehemence of opposition to a center-left president whose policies were more social democratic than revolutionary and who actually achieved very little, reflected key fault lines in the democratization process in Paraguay.

The impeachment of Lugo shows that it remains extremely difficult to address Paraguay's highly unequal system of landownership, which has become increasingly concentrated as a result of the recent rapid expansion of commercial agriculture (especially soybean and cattle ranching). This is partly due to the lobbying of two powerful economic interest groups, both of which exert a strong influence inside Congress: the Rural Association of Paraguay (representing mainly large cattle ranchers) and the Paraguayan Soybean Association (representing fifty thousand *brasiguayo* commercial farmers who control most of Paraguay's huge soybean production). However, an equally important factor is that access to power and wealth in Paraguay is synonymous with access to land; almost all members of Congress are also members of Paraguay's tiny landowning elite, with titles held either directly or in the names of friends and family, and are hence opposed to any reform project that would adversely affect their personal interests. In fact Lugo was even unable to kick-start a land reform project by confiscating and redistributing the so-called *tierras malhabidas*. These are the eight million hectares of state-owned land, equivalent to one-third of the cultivated area of the country, that were illegally transferred in the form of large tracts (typically two thousand hectares and above) to political cronies, military supporters, and family friends during the Stroessner dictatorship and the subsequent two decades of Colorado rule (and even into Lugo's own administration), under the cynical guise of "land reform."

This elite hostility to genuine land reform is matched by their hostility to tax reform, the absence of which helps maintain Paraguay's extreme income inequality. Although Paraguay is now the world's fourth largest exporter of soybean, throughout Lugo's period in office Congress repeatedly opposed a tax on unprocessed cereal exports and maintained the tax on commercial agriculture at derisory levels. But even more significantly, Congress repeatedly postponed legislation to introduce personal income tax, which would affect only the top 5 percent of the population, even though it would be levied at an extremely low rate and with virtually all personal expenses tax-deductible.

The issues of land and taxation in turn reflect deeper problems with democratization in Paraguay. For the past two decades Congress has had extremely low levels of popular legitimacy and citizen trust because it is understandably seen as representing and defending the interests of a tiny economic and political elite. Furthermore, politics is widely seen as highly clientelistic and self-interested, with the major parties constantly maneuvering for political advantage and overwhelmingly motivated by the desire to regain or retain political power (in terms of capture of the state, public posts, and financial resources) rather than any wider concern for the national interest.

As Lugo's reform efforts floundered, tensions rose in rural areas in the form of land occupations and evictions, as well as demonstrations by both landowners and peasants, and ensuing violence. Alarmed by growing "security issues" in rural areas and Lugo's plans for reform, Congress decided to act. The impeachment of Lugo sent a clear message that the elite would simply not tolerate a challenge to Paraguay's exclusionary and corrupt pattern of landownership.

The impeachment itself rapidly became a regional affair with far-reaching consequences. Criticism of the process came from across the political spectrum, from Chile and Colombia to Venezuela and Bolivia. International condemnation of the "parliamentary coup" led to a refusal to recognize the new government, and then international isolation as Paraguay was suspended from both UNASUR, the South American regional political bloc, and more significantly from MERCOSUR, until presidential elections in 2013. In an unexpected twist, MERCOSUR partners took advantage of Paraguay's suspension to approve Venezuela's membership, which had previously been blocked by the Paraguayan Senate.

Within days, regional condemnation produced an extraordinary upsurge of nationalism, as the media, politicians, and elite lobby groups talked of foreign aggression, ignorance, and a lack of respect for the nation's sovereignty, and even of a "Bolivarian Triple Alliance," in which Venezuela replaced Great Britain as the perfidious "fourth ally." The Stroessner-era nationalist discourse of anticommunism, insidious foreign influence, and "legionaries" (fourth columnists) underwent a striking resurgence, drowning out the protests over the impeachment process.

Lugo declared that his impeachment was effectively a coup d'état that fractured the fragile democratic process in Paraguay. This may or may not prove to be true, but it certainly represented a blow to the popular legitimacy of Paraguay's democratic institutions and processes, and led to widespread international condemnation and regional isolation. Above all, the extraordinary events of June 2012 underlined serious weaknesses in Paraguay's democracy: the weakness of the rule of law, the limits of political competition, and the commitment of entrenched and conservative political elites in Congress to preserving the country's grossly unequal distribution of land, income, and wealth.

In 2008 Lugo had been elected on a wave of optimism that political and social change was indeed possible. His impeachment after nearly four years of conflict reflected just how difficult such change continues to be in Paraguay.

Suggestions for Further Reading

There is growing interest in Paraguay among scholarly writers and journalists. If you are interested in a more in-depth understanding of the country, here is a list of books that are not cited directly in extracts that we chose for the *Reader*. However, some of them contain outstanding analysis and are well worth reading for both general and specific information. We have not listed articles, academic or otherwise, or chapters from edited books, simply due to the overwhelming number available. If one exists, we list the English translation of books first published in Spanish, although we encourage readers to consult the original if possible.

General

Hanratty, Dennis, and Sandra Meditz, eds. *Paraguay: A Country Study*. Washington: Library of Congress, Federal Research Division, 1990.

Hebblethwaite, Margaret. *Paraguay*. Chalfont St. Peter, England: Bradt Travel Guides, 2010.

Medina, Ricardo, ed. *Enciclopedia del Paraguay*. 2 vols. Barcelona: Océano, 2000.

Mora, Frank, and Jerry Cooney. *Paraguay and the United States: Distant Allies*. Athens: University of Georgia Press, 2007.

Munro, Robert, ed. *Paraguay 200 Years of Independence in the Heart of South America*. Oxford: Whap Production, 2010.

Nickson, R. Andrew. *Historical Dictionary of Paraguay*. Metuchen, N.J.: Scarecrow Press, 1993.

———. *Paraguay*. World Bibliographical Series, vol. 84. Oxford: Clio Press, 1999.

Roett, Riordan, and Richard Scott Sacks. *Paraguay: The Personalist Legacy*. Boulder, Colo.: Westview Press, 1991.

Telesca, Ignacio, ed. *Historia del Paraguay*. Asunción: Taurus and Santillana, 2010.

Warren, Harris Gaylord. *Paraguay: An Informal History*. Westport, Conn.: Greenwood Press, 1982.

Websites

http://www.abc.com.py. *ABC Color*, Paraguay's largest-circulation daily newspaper, with numerous links and a free archive.

http://www.uhora.com.py. *Ultima Hora*, Paraguay's second largest-circulation daily newspaper.

http://www.presidencia.gov.py. The Presidential Office, with links to government ministries and autonomous state agencies.

http://www.tsje.gov.py. The electoral commission, with data on national, departmental and municipal elections results from 1989 onward as well as political authorities, including all previous presidents.

http://www.dgeec.gov.py. The General Office of Surveys, Statistics and Censi, with up-to-date and easy access to a wide range of data on population, employment, and poverty, including an annual household survey.

http://www.senatur.gov.py. The National Tourism Office, with free email newsletter.

http://ea.com.py. Virtual news magazine with critical analysis on economic and social affairs.

http://www.cadep.org.py. The Centre for Analysis and Dissemination of the Paraguayan Economy, the country's prime economic think tank.

http://www.ateneoguarani.edu.py. The Athenium for Guaraní Language and Culture, the prime center for the study of Guaraní.

http://www.codehupy.org. The Coordinating Committee for Human Rights in Paraguay is a group that includes over twenty-five social organizations and NGOs that work in the field of human rights. Its annual report provides an excellent analysis of human rights in a wide variety of areas.

Part I. The Birth of Paraguay

Caraman, Philip. *The Lost Paradise: An Account of the Jesuits in Paraguay, 1607–1768.* London: Sidgwick and Jackson, 1975.

Ganson, Barbara. *The Guaraní under Spanish Rule in Río de la Plata.* Stanford, Calif.: Stanford University Press, 2003.

Gott, Richard. *The Land without Evil: Utopian Journeys across the South American Watershed.* London: Verso, 1993.

Kahle, Gunter. *Orígenes y fundamentos de la conciencia nacional paraguaya.* Asunción: Instituto Cultural Paraguayo-Alemán, 2005.

Kleinpenning, Jan. *Paraguay, 1515–1870: A Thematic Geography of Its Development.* 2 vols. Madrid: Iberoamericana, 2003.

Susnik, Branislava, and Miguel Chase-Sardi. *Los indios del Paraguay.* Madrid: Colecciones MAPFRE, 1995.

Part II. The Nationalist Experiment

Burton, Richard. *Letters from the Battlefields of Paraguay.* London: Tinsley Brothers, 1870.

Centurión, Juan Crisóstomo. *Memorias o reminiscencias históricas sobre la Guerra del Paraguay.* 4 vols. Asunción: El Lector, 1987.

Doratioto, Francisco. *Maldita guerra: Nueva historia de la Guerra del Paraguay.* Buenos Aires: Emecé Editores, 2004.

Irala Burgos, Adriano. *La ideología política del Doctor Francia*. Asunción: Ediciones Carlos Schauman Editora, 1988.

Lillis, Michael, and Ronan Fanning. *The Lives of Eliza Lynch: Scandal and Courage*. Dublin: Gill and Macmillan, 2009.

Phelps, Gilbert. *Tragedy of Paraguay*. London: Charles Knight, 1975.

Plá, Josefina. *The British in Paraguay*. Richmond, England: Richmond Publishing, 1976.

Potthast-Jutkeit, Barbara. *"Paraíso de Mahoma" o "país de mujeres"?: El rol de la mujer en la sociedad paraguaya del siglo XIX*. Asunción: Instituto Cultural Paraguayo-Alemán, 1996.

Rivarola Matto, Juan Bautista. *Diagonal de sangre: La historia y sus alternativas en la Guerra del Paraguay*. Asunción: Ediciones NAPA, 1986.

Roa Bastos, Augusto. *I, the Supreme*. New York: Alfred A. Knopf, 1986. (Translated by Helen Lane).

Robertson, John Parish, and William Parish Robertson. *Letters on Paraguay: Comprising an Account of a Four Years' Residence in That Republic, under the Government of the Dictator Francia*. New York: AMS Press, 1974. 3 vols. Reprint of original published in London by John Murray (1838–39).

Rubiani, Jorge. *Verdades y mentiras sobre la Guerra de la Triple Alianza*. Asunción: Grafitec, 2007.

Whigham, Thomas. *The Paraguayan War: Causes and Early Conduct*. Lincoln: University of Nebraska Press, 2002.

Williams, John Hoyt. *The Rise and Fall of the Paraguayan Republic, 1800–1870*. Austin, Texas: Institute of Latin American Studies, 1979.

Part III. A Slow Recovery

Carrón, Juan, María Monte, Anselmo Ayala, and Salvadora Giménez. *El régimen liberal: 1870–1930*. Asunción: Arandura Editorial, 2004.

Kleinpenning, Jan. *Rural Paraguay, 1870–1963*. Madrid: Iberoamericana, 2009.

Lewis, Paul. *Political Parties and Generations in Paraguay's Liberal Era, 1869–1940*. Chapel Hill: University of North Carolina Press, 1993.

MacIntyre, Ben. *Forgotten Fatherland: The Search for Elisabeth Nietzsche*. London: Macmillan, 1992.

Rivarola, Milda. *Obreros, utopias y revoluciones: La formación de las clases trabajadoras en el Paraguay liberal (1870–1931)*. Asunción: Centro de Documentación y Estudios, 1993.

Warren, Harris Gaylord. *Paraguay and the Triple Alliance: the Post-War Decade, 1869–1878*. Austin: University of Texas Press, 1978.

———. *Rebirth of the Paraguayan Republic: The First Colorado Era, 1878–1904*. Pittsburgh, Penn.: University of Pittsburgh Press, 1985.

Part IV. From the Chaco War to the Civil War

English, Adrian. *The Green Hell: A Concise History of the Chaco War between Bolivia and Paraguay, 1932–35*. Stroud, England: History Press, 2007.

Farcau, Bruce. *The Chaco War: Bolivia and Paraguay, 1932–1935.* Westport, Conn.: Praeger, 1996.

Ferreira Pérez, Saturnino. *Proceso político del Paraguay, 1936–1949.* 4 vols. Asunción: El Lector, 1987–89.

González Delvalle, Alcibiades. *El drama del 47.* Asunción: Editorial Histórica, 1988.

Grow, Michael. *The Good Neighbor Policy and Authoritarianism in Paraguay: United States Economic Expansion and Great Power Rivalry in Latin America During World War Two.* Lawrence: Regents Press of Kansas, 1981.

Seiferheld, Alfredo. *Economía y petróleo durante la guerra del Chaco.* Asunción: El Lector, 1983.

Zook, David. *The Conduct of the Chaco War.* Newark, N.J.: Bookman, 1960.

Part V. Dictatorship and Resistance

Arditi, Benjamín. *Adiós a Stroessner: La reconstrucción de la política en el Paraguay.* Asunción: CDE/RP Ediciones, 1992.

Arditi, Benjamín, and José Carlos Rodríguez. *La sociedad a pesar del estado.* Asunción: El Lector, 1987.

Blanch, José María. *El precio de la paz.* Asunción: Centro de Estudios Paraguayos "Antonio Guasch" (CEPAG), 1991.

Boccia, Alfredo, Myrian González, and Rosa Palau. *Es mi informe: Los archivos secretos de la policia de Stroessner.* 4th ed. Asunción: Centro de Documentación y Estudios, 1994.

Costa, José María, and Oscar Ayala. *Operación Gedeón: Los secretos de un golpe frustrado.* Asunción: Editorial Don Bosco, 1996.

Farina, Bernardo Neri. *El Ultimo Supremo: La crónica de Alfredo Stroessner.* Asunción: El Lector, 2003.

Flores, Elena, ed. *Jornadas por la democracia en el Paraguay.* Madrid: Partido Socialista Obrero Español, 1987.

Lachi, Marcelo, ed. *Insurgentes: La resistencia armada a la dictadura de Stroessner.* Asunción: Universidad del Norte, 2004.

Masi, Fernando. *Stroessner: La extincción de un modelo político en Paraguay.* Asunción: Ñanduti Vive/Intercontinental Editora, 1989.

Münzel, Mark. *The Aché Indians: Genocide in Paraguay.* Copenhagen: International Working Group for Indigenous Affairs, 1973.

Nickson, Andrew. *Paraguay: Power Game.* London: Latin America Bureau, 1980.

Painter, James. *Paraguay in the 1970s: Continuity and Change in the Political Process.* London: Institute of Latin American Studies, University of London, 1983.

Stephansky, Ben, and Robert Alexander. *Report of the Commission of Enquiry into Human Rights in Paraguay.* New York: International League for Human Rights, 1976.

Treherne, Cristina. *The Guerrilla War of the Paraguayan Communist Party.* Portsmouth, England: Prensa Libre, 1982.

Part VI. A Transition in Search of Democracy

Abente, Diego. *Paraguay en transición*. Caracas: Editorial Nueva Sociedad, 1992.

Berry, Albert, et al. *Losing Ground in the Employment Challenge: The Case of Paraguay*. New Brunswick, N.J.: Transaction Publishers, 2010.

Fogel, Ramón, and Marcial Riquelme. *Enclave Sojero: Merma de soberanía y pobreza*. Asunción: Centro de Estudios Rurales Interdisciplinarios, 2005.

Lambert, Peter, and Andrew Nickson, eds. *The Transition to Democracy in Paraguay*. Basingstoke, England: Macmillan, 1997.

Miranda, Aníbal. *Dossier Paraguay: Los dueños de grandes fortunas*. Asunción: Miranda y Asociados, 2000.

O'Shaughnessy, Hugh. *The Priest of Paraguay: Fernando Lugo and the Making of a Nation*. London: Zed Books, 2009.

Riquelme, Marcial. *Negotiating Democratic Corridors in Paraguay*. Pittsburgh: Latin American Studies Association (LASA), University of Pittsburgh, 1994.

Turner, Brian. *Community Politics and Peasant-State Relations in Paraguay*. Lanham, Md.: University Press of America, 1993.

Part VII. What Does It Mean to Be Paraguayan?

Bareiro, Line, and Clyde Soto. *Vencer la adversidad: Historia de mujeres líderes*. Asunción: Secretaría de la Mujer, 1999.

Cadogan, León. *León Cadogan: Extranjero, campesino y científico*. Asunción: Universidad Católica, 1990.

Clastres, Pierre. *Chronicle of the Guayaki Indians*. London: Faber and Faber, 1998.

Escobar, Ticio. *The Curse of the Nemur: In Search of the Art, Myth and Ritual of the Ishir*. Pittsburgh: University of Pittsburgh Press, 2007.

———. *Una interpretación de las artes visuales en el Paraguay*. 2 vols. Asunción: Centro Cultural Paraguayo-Americano, 1982–84.

Hay, James Diego. *Tobatí: Tradición y cambio en un pueblo paraguayo*. Asunción: CERI, 1999.

Hill, Kim, and A. Magdalena Hurtado. *Ache Life History: The Ecology and Demography of a Foraging People*. Piscataway, N.J.: Transaction Publishers, 1996.

Melià, Bartomeu. *El Paraguay inventado*. Asunción: Centro de Estudios Paraguayos "Antonio Guasch," 1997.

Méndez-Faith, Teresa. *Narrativa paraguaya de ayer y hoy*. 2 vols. Asunción: Intercontinental Editora, 1999.

Stover, Richard. *Six Silver Moonbeams: The Life and Times of Agustín Barrios Mangoré*. Clovis, Calif.: Querico Publications, 1992.

Velilla de Aquino, Josefina. *Tembi'u paraguai*. Asunción: Instituto de Arte Culinaria, 1981.

Vera, Helio. *El país de la sopa dura: Tratado de Paraguayología 11*. Asunción: Servilibro, 2010.

Vera, Saro. *El paraguayo: Un hombre fuera de su mundo*. Asunción: El Lector, 1997.

Acknowledgment of Copyright and Sources

Part I. The Birth of Paraguay

"The Foundation of Human Speech," anonymous, from *Ayvu Rapyta: Textos míticos de los Mybá-Guaraní del Guairá*, edited by León Cadogan (São Paulo, Brazil; Faculdade de Filosofia, Ciéncias e Letras, Boletim no. 227, Antropologia no. 5, 1959), 13–28. Used by permission of the Fundación León Cadogan.

"Contact, Servitude, and Resistance," by Branislava Susnik, from *El rol de los indígenas en la formación y en la vivencia del Paraguay* (Asunción: Instituto Paraguayo de Estudios Nacionales, 1982), 68–89 (abridged). Used by permission of the Fundación La Piedad.

"Spanish-Guaraní Relations in Early Colonial Paraguay," by Elman R. Service, from *Spanish-Guaraní Relations in Early Colonial Paraguay* (Westport, Conn.: Greenwood Press, 1971), 92–97. Reprint of original (Museum of Anthropology, University of Michigan, Anthropological Papers, no. 9, 1954).

"The Land-without-Evil," by Hélène Clastres, from *The Land-without-Evil: Tupí-Guaraní Prophetism* (Chicago: University of Illinois Press, 1995), 59–64 (abridged). © Hélène Clastres. Used by permission of the author.

"The Republic of Plato and the Guaraní," by José Manuel Peramás, from *La República de Platón y los Guaraníes* (Buenos Aires: Emecé Editores, 1946), 45–106 (abridged).

"A Vanished Arcadia," by R. B. Cunninghame Graham, from *A Vanished Arcadia: Being Some Account of the Jesuits in Paraguay, 1607–1767* (London: Century, 1901), 73–85 (abridged).

"The Revolt of the Comuneros," by Adalberto López, *The Colonial History of Paraguay: The Revolt of the Comuneros, 1721–1735* (New Brunswick, N.J.: Transaction Books, 2005), 133–47 (abridged). © 2005 by Transaction Publishers. Reprinted by permission of the publisher.

Part II. The Nationalist Experiment

"A Report on Paraguay in the London Press of 1824," anonymous, first published in the *Morning Chronicle* (London), August 23, 1824.

"A Nation Held Hostage," by Justo Prieto, from *Paraguay, la provincia gigante de las Indias* (Asunción: Archivo del Liberalismo, 1988), 142–48 (abridged). Used by permission of Alex Prieto de Martínez.

"In Defense of Doctor Francia," by Richard Alan White, from *Paraguay's Autonomous Revolution, 1810–1840* (Albuquerque: University of New Mexico Press, 1978), 2–8.

Reprinted by permission of the University of New Mexico Press and Richard Alan White.

"Autonomy, Authoritarianism, and Development," by Thomas Whigham, written exclusively for *The Paraguay Reader.*

"The Treaty of the Triple Alliance," by Carlos Castro, J. Octaviano de Almeida, and Rufino de Elizalde, from *Independence or Death!: The Story of the Paraguayan War,* by C. J. Kolinski (Gainesville: University of Florida Press, 1965), Appendix 2, 219–22. Reprinted with permission of the University of Florida Press.

"I Die with My Country!," by Thomas Whigham, written exclusively for *The Paraguay Reader.*

"A Chronicle of War," by Leandro Pineda, from "Crónicas de una guerra," in *Testimonios de la Guerra Grande,* vol. 1, edited by Rubén Bareiro Saguier and Carlos Villagra Marsal (Asunción: ABC Color/Servilibro, 2007), 33–45 (abridged).

"The Lomas Valentinas Note," by Francisco Solano López, from *Independence or Death!: The Story of the Paraguayan War,* by C. J. Kolinski (Gainesville: University of Florida Press, 1965), Appendix 3, 222–23. According to the original, "this informal translation of the major portion of the text of the note is based on the texts contained in George Thompson, *The War in Paraguay,* pp. 301–3; and Arturo Bray, *Solano López,* pp. 370–72." Reprinted with permission of the University of Florida Press.

"Memoirs of the Paraguayan War," by Gaspar Centurión, previously published as "Recuerdos de la guerra en Paraguay" in *Testimonios de la Guerra Grande,* edited by Rubén Bareiro Saguier and Carlos Villalgra Marsal, Colección Imaginación y Memorias del Paraguay, vol. 2 (Asunción: ABC Color/Servilibro, 2007), 15–29 (abridged).

"The Women of Piribebuy," by Juan O'Leary, previously published as "Las mujeres de Piribebuy" in *El libro de los héroes,* edited by Rubén Bareiro Saguier and Carlos Villagra Marsal (Asunción: ABC Color/Servilibro, 2007), 113–17.

"The Death of López at Cerro Corá," by Silvestre Aveiro, previously published as "Cerro Corá" in *Testimonios de la Guerra Grande,* vol. 1, edited by Rubén Bareiro Saguier and Carlos Villagra Marsal (Asunción: ABC Color/Servilibro, 2007), 65–74 (abridged).

"Sufferings of a French Lady in Paraguay," by Dorotea Duprat de Lasserre, from *Sufferings of a French Lady in Paraguay* (Buenos Aires: Standard Office, 1870), 23–31 (abridged).

"Declaration and Protest," by Eliza Lynch, from *The Lives of Eliza Lynch: Scandal and Courage,* by Michael Lillis and Ronan Fanning (Dublin: Gill and Macmillan, 2009), appendix 208–43 (abridged). Used by permission of Gill and Macmillan and Michael Lillis.

"The Psychology of López," by William Stewart, from *Historia del Paraguay,* unpublished paper, Miami University, n.d., 11–12, 17–20 (abridged).

Part III. A Slow Recovery

"Paraguayan Society in the Postwar Decade," from *Paraguay and the Triple Alliance: The Postwar Decade, 1869–1878,* by Harris Gaylord Warren, with the assistance of Katherine F. Warren (Austin: Institute of Latin American Studies, University of Texas,

1978), 149–56, copyright © 1978. By permission of the University of Texas Press (published here in abridged form).

"The 'Lincolnshire Farmers' in Paraguay," by Annie Elizabeth Kennett, available online at http://www.argbrit.org/pioneers/LincolnfarmersB.htm (abridged). Used by permission of Jeremy Howat and Barbara Johnson.

"My Pilgrimage to Caacupé," by Norman O. Brown, previously published in *The Wide World Magazine* (1900): 324–28 (abridged).

"What It Is Like to Work in the Yerba Plantations," by Rafael Barrett, from *El dolor paraguayo* (Caracas: Biblioteca Ayacucho, 1978), 121–32 (abridged).

"The Treatment of Tree Fellers and Timber Workers," by Reinaldo López Fretes, from *Lo que he visto en el Alto Paraguay* (Asunción: Imprenta Nacional, 1946), 25–30.

"The Golden Age (Without a Nickel)," by Helio Vera, from *En busca del hueso perdido* (Asunción: RP Ediciones, 1990), 131–42 (abridged). Used by permission of Angeles Vera.

"The Causes of Poverty in Paraguay," by Teodosio González, from *Infortunios del Paraguay* (Buenos Aires: Talleres Gráficos L. J. Rosso, 1931), 95–103 (abridged).

"The Mennonites Arrive in the Chaco," by Walter Quiring, previously published as "The Canadian Mennonite Immigration into the Paraguayan Chaco, 1926–1927" in *The Mennonite Quarterly Review* 8, no. 1 (1934), 32–42 (abridged). Used by permission of *The Mennonite Quarterly Review*.

"The Paraguayan Character," by Juan Sinforiano Bogarín, from *Mis apuntes: Memorias de Monseñor Juan Sinforiano Bogarín* (Asunción: CIDSEP, Universidad Católica, 2001), 96–102. Used by permission of CIDSEP.

"The Paraguayan People and Their Natural Tendencies," by J. Natalicio González, from *El Paraguay eterno* (Asunción: Cuadernos Republicanos, 1935), 45–56 (abridged).

"Cultural Exile," by Agustín Barrios, from *El inalcanzable Agustín Barrios Mangoré*, by Carlos Salcedo Centurión (Asunción: Congreso de la Nación, Centro Cultural de la República EL CABILDO, 2007), 127–28. Used by permission of Carlos Salcedo Centurión.

"Profession of Faith," by Agustín Barrios, from *Mangoré: Vida y obra de Agustín Barrios*, by S. Godoy and L. Szarán (Asunción: Don Bosco, 1982), 82. Used by permission of Luis Szarán.

"A New National Ideology," by Oscar Creydt, Obdulio Barthe, Anibal Codas, et al. (Asunción: La Colmena, 1929), 59–66 (abridged).

Part IV. From the Chaco War to the Civil War

"Capturing Volunteers," by Carlos Federico Reyes, from *Mis memorias y mi mundo de mitaí churí* (Capiatá: Alamo SA, 1996), 103–5. Used by permission of Mercedes Reyes.

"The Battle of Boquerón," by Alfredo Seiferheld, from *La guerra del Chaco* (Asunción: Servilibro/ABC Color, 2007), 77–87 (abridged). Used by permission of Bibi Yurrita.

"Memoirs of a Man from Concepción," by Carlos María Sienra Bonzi, as told to Roberto Sienra Zavala, from *Memorias de un concepcionero*, by Roberto Sienra Zavala (Concepción: [n.p.], 2006), 85–159 (abridged). Used by permission of Roberto Sienra Zavala.

"A Visit to Villa Hayes Military Hospital Number 16," by Reginald Thompson, from *Land of Tomorrow* (London: Duckworth, 1936), 143–46.

"Scenes of Thirst," by Hugo Rodríguez Alcalá, from *Estampas de la guerra a medio siglo* (Asunción: Cromos SRL, 1985), 41–42. Used by permission of Hugo L. Rodríguez Alcalá.

"A Handful of Earth," by Hérib Campos Cervera, from *Poesías completas y otros textos* (Asunción: El Lector, 1996), 89–93. Used by permission of Rodrigo Campos Cervera.

"Proclamation of the Febrerista Revolution," by F. W. Smith and Camilo Recalde, from *The Politics of Exile: Paraguay's Febrerista Party*, by Paul H. Lewis (Chapel Hill: University of North Carolina Press), 41–45. Copyright © 1968 by the University of North Carolina Press. Used by permission of the publisher. www.uncpress.unc.edu.

"How Beautiful Is Your Voice," by Ernesto Unruh and Hannes Kalisch, from *Wie schoen ist deine Stimme* (Ya'alve-Saanga: Nengvaanemkeskama Nempayvaam Enlhet, forthcoming), chapters 51, 55, 64, and 75 (abridged). Used by permission of Hannes Kalisch.

"The Revolution of 1947," by Carlos María Sienra Bonzi, as told to Roberto Sienra Zavala, from *Memorias de un concepcionero*, by Roberto Sienra Zavala (Concepción: [n.p.], 2006), 205–37 (abridged). Used by permission of Roberto Sienra Zavala.

"A Half Hour in My Childhood," by Eva Bichsel (abridged). © Eva Bichsel. Used by permission of the author.

Part V. Dictatorship and Resistance

"Toward a Weberian Characterization of the Stroessner Regime," by Marcial Riquelme, previously published as "Towards a Weberian Characterization of the Stroessner Régime in Paraguay, 1954–1989" in *European Review of Latin American and Caribbean Studies/Revista Europea de Estudios Latinoamericanos y del Caribe* (a publication of CEDLA), vol. 57 (December 1994), 29–51 (abridged). Used by permission of CEDLA.

"The Revolutionary Spirit of the Colorado Party," by Luís María Argaña, from *Historia de las ideas políticas en el Paraguay* (Asunción: El Foro, 1983), 145–49. Used by permission of the Argaña family.

"The Tragedy of Fram," by Jorge Rubiani, previously published as "La tragedia de Fram" in *ABC Color* [Asunción], April 4–6, 2006 (abridged). Used by permission of the author.

"Be Careful, Dictator," by Elvio Romero, from *Poesías completas* (Asunción: RP Ediciones, 1990), 286–87. Used by permission of Élida Lucía Vallejos.

"The Worm inside the Lotus Blossom," by Graham Greene, from "The Worm inside the Lotus Blossom," *Daily Telegraph Magazine*, January 3, 1969 (abridged). Used by permission of David Higham Associates.

"A Short History of the Northern Ache People," by Kim Hill, written exclusively for *The Paraguay Reader*.

"The Testimony of Saturnina Almada," from *Testimonios de víctimas de la dictadura stronista* (Asunción: CIPAE, 2003), 42–61 (abridged). Used by permission of CIPAE.

"An Interview with Corsino Coronel," from *Kokueguara Rembiasa (Experiencias campesinas): Ligas Agrarias Cristianas, 1960–1980*, vol. 3, *Misiones y Paraguarí*, by the Comisión Nacional de Rescate y Difusión de la Historia Campesina (Asunción: Centro de Estudios Paraguayos "Antonio Guasch," 1992), 28–32. Used by permission of CEPAG.

"Apocalypse," by Alfredo Boccia, from *La década inconclusa: Historia real de la OPM* (Asunción: El Lector, 1998), 143–58 (abridged). Used by permission of the author.

"My Farewell Speech," by Carmen de Lara Castro, previously published as "Congresswoman Pleads for Freedom in Paraguay," *Latinamerica Press* [Lima], February 2, 1978, 3–4, 8 (abridged). Used by permission of Jorge Lara Castro.

"The Death of Somoza," by Claribel Alegría and Darwin Flakoll, from *Death of Somoza* (Willimantic, Conn.: Curbstone Press, 1996), 132–35 (abridged). Used by permission of Claribel Alegría.

"My Vote Is for the People," by Alcibíades González Delvalle, from *Mi voto por el pueblo y otros comentarios* (Asunción: Editorial Histórica, 1988), 156–58. Used by permission of the author.

"Paraguay's Terror Archive," by Andrew Nickson, previously published as "Paraguay's Archivo del Terror," in *Latin American Research Review* 30, no. 1 (January 1995): 125–29 (abridged). Used by permission of LARR/LASA.

"'A Hundred and Eight' and a Burned Body: The Story Not Told by the Truth and Justice Commission," by Anselmo Ramos, previously published as "La historia no contada por Verdad y Justicia: 108 y un quemado" in *Edición Digital de Noticias Somos Paraguay*, August 30, 2008. Used by permission of the author.

"The Final Report of the Truth and Justice Commission," by Andrés D. Ramírez, from *Derechos humanos en Paraguay 2008*, by the Coordinating Committee of Human Rights in Paraguay (Asunción: CODEHUPY, 2009), 756–83 (abridged). Used by permission of the author.

"Alfredo Stroessner: Revisiting the General," by Isabel Hilton, previously published as "The General," in *Granta*, no. 31 (Spring 1990): 11–83 (abridged). Used by permission of the author.

Part VI. A Transition in Search of Democracy

"We Have Left Our Barracks," by Andrés Rodríguez. Communiqué broadcast on multiple radio stations, February 3, 1989.

"Reestablishing the Status Quo," by Andrew Nickson, previously published as "The Overthrow of the Stroessner Regime: Re-Establishing the Status Quo" in *Bulletin of Latin American Research*, vol. 8, no. 2 (1989): 185–209 (abridged). Used by permission of John Wiley and Sons Limited.

"My Deepest Respects to the Colorado Party," by Helio Vera, previously published as "Mis respetos al Partido Colorado" online at http://www.larueda.com.py/hv042 .htm. Used by permission of Angeles Vera.

"The Characteristics of Oviedismo," by Milda Rivarola, previously published as "Las características del oviedismo: Caudillo populista, líder mesiánico" in *Investigación del asesinato del Vicepresidente Constitucional de la República del Paraguay*, unpublished report, October 1999, 5–8 (abridged).

"In Homage to the Victims of Ycuá Bolaños," by Luis Irala, previously published as "En Homenaje a las víctimas de Ycuá Bolaños," online at http://ycuanuncamas .org/www/index.php?option=com_content&task=view&id=74&Itemid=40. Used by permission of the Organizaciones de Víctimas de la Masacre de Ykuá Bolaños.

"Where Are They?," by Alberto Rodas, from the album *Utópico* (Blue Caps Label, 1990). Used by permission of the author.

"The Ayoreo People," by Mateo Sobode Chiquenoi, from *The Case of the Ayoreo*, by the Unión de Nativos Ayoreo de Paraguay (Asunción: IWGIA, 2010), 4–36 (abridged). Used by permission of the author.

"So Much Exoticism Can Be Deceptive," by Alfredo Boccia, previously published as "Tanto exotismo los lleva al engaño" on his *Ultima Hora* Blog, April 5, 2008, online at http://blogs.ultimahora.com/post.php?idBlogPost=737&idBlogger=50&t= tanto-exotismo-los-lleva-al-enga%C3%B1o-&_pagi_pg=4. Used by permission of the author.

"Inaugural Presidential Speech," by Fernando Lugo Méndez (abridged). Public broadcast transmission, August 15, 2008.

"First Person: Margarita Mbywangi," by Margarita Mbywangi, as told to Jude Webber, previously published in the *Financial Times* (London), July 4, 2009. © The Financial Times Limited 2009. All Rights Reserved. Used by permission of The Financial Times Limited.

"Lessons on Paternity from Lugo," by Clyde Soto, previously published as "Lecciones sobre paternidad de Lugo" in *La Micrófona*, no. 13, April 20, 2009 (Asunción: Centro de Documentación y Estudios) (abridged). Used by permission of the author.

"Itaipú: A Historic Achievement That Will Need to Be Closely Monitored," by Ricardo Canese, previously published as "Itaipú—un histórico avance que require seguimiento" in *ABC Color* [Asunción], January 3, 2010. Used by permission of the author.

"A Fine Woman," by Andrés Colmán Gutiérrez, previously published as "Kuña Guápa" in *Ultima Hora* [Asunción], November 25, 2006. Used by permission of the author.

"Ciudad del Este's Deadly Trade Route," by Jude Webber, previously published in the *Financial Times* [London], March 13, 2010 (abridged). © The Financial Times Limited 2010. All Rights Reserved. Used by permission of The Financial Times Limited. Andrew Nickson and Peter Lambert are solely responsible for providing this abridged version of the original article and The Financial Times Limited does not accept any liability for the accuracy or quality of the abridged version.

"The Challenge of Conserving a Natural Chaco Habitat in the Face of Severe Deforestation Pressure and Human Development Needs," by Alberto Yanosky, written exclusively for *The Paraguay Reader*.

Part VII. What Does It Mean to Be Paraguayan?

"History, Identity, and *Paraguayidad*," by Peter Lambert, previously published in *Paraguay 200 Years of Independence in the Heart of South America*, edited by Robert Munro (Oxford: Whap Production, 2010), 15–22 (abridged). Used by permission of Robert Munro.

"Change and Continuity in Paraguayan history—1811, 1911, 2011," by Andrew Nickson, previously published in *Paraguay 200 Years of Independence in the Heart of South Amer-*

ica, edited by Robert Munro (Oxford: Whap Production, 2010), 87–92 (abridged). Used by permission of Robert Munro.

"The Arcadian Tragedy," by George Pendle, from *Paraguay: A Riverside People* (London: Royal Institute of International Affairs, 1954), 92–94. Reprinted by permission of Chatham House.

"The Bicentenary of Paraguayan Independence and the Guaraní Language," by Miguel Ángel Verón Gómez, previously published as "El bicentenario de la independencia paraguaya y la lengua guaraní" in *Dossier Paraguay* (Buenos Aires: Instituto de Estudios de América Latina y el Caribe, Facultad de Ciencias Sociales, Universidad de Buenos Aires, May 2010), 19–23. Used by permission of the author.

"People of African Descent in Paraguay," by Ignacio Telesca, previously published as "Afrodescendientes en el Paraguay: Invisibilidad, mestizaje y la narración de la historia nacional" in *Estudios Paraguayos* 25, nos. 1–2 (2007): 77–87 (abridged). Used by permission of the author.

"Authoritarian Ideology: Final Comments," by Guido Rodríguez Alcalá, from *Ideología autoritaria* (Asunción: RP Ediciones, 1987), 120–23 (abridged). Used by permission of the author.

"With the Help of Doña Petrona We Make an Incursion into Folk Cuisine," by Helio Vera, from *En busca del hueso perdido* (Asunción: RP Ediciones, 1990), 69–70 and 81–83 (abridged). Used by permission of Angeles Vera.

"Enough of the Triple Alliance!" by Jorge Rubiani, previously published as "¡Basta de Triple Alianza!" online at http://www.paraguaymipais.com.ar/opinion/2010/08/%C2%A1basta-de-triple-alianza/. Used by permission of the author.

"Tereré as a Social Bond," by Derlis Benítez Alvarenga, from *El tereré: Algo más que una bebida* (Asunción: El Lector, 1997), 76–95 (abridged). Used by permission of the author.

"The Status of Women," by Riordan Roett and Richard Scott Sacks, from *Paraguay: The Personalist Legacy* (Boulder, Colo.: Westview, 1991), 96–99. Used by permission of the authors.

"Self-Portrait," by Bernarda, from *Pintadas por sí mismas: Historia de diez vidas*, edited by Marylin Godoy Ziogas, Olga Caballero Aquino, and Manuelita Escobar de Peña (Asunción, Intercontinental Editora, 1987), 91–101 (abridged). Used by permission of Olga Caballero Aquino.

"María and the Serpent," by Pepa Kostianovsky, from her *ABC Color* Blog, July 31, 2008, online at http://abctv.com.py/blogs/post/461/maria-kuriju. Used by permission of the author.

"Erico," by Jorge Barraza, previously published as "Alfredo Di Stefano: Yo quería ser número nueve como mi ídolo, como el gran Arsenio Erico" in *Erico para siempre* (Asunción: El Lector, 2010). Used by permission of the author.

"Recipe for Chipa Guazú," by Doña Aída.

"The National Anthem in Guaraní," by Félix de Guarania, performed as "Tetã Purahéi Guasu" at the inauguration of President Lugo, August 2008. Used by permission of Mercedes Giménez.

Every reasonable effort has been made to obtain permission. We invite copyright holders to inform us of any oversights.

Index

Peter Lambert is a senior lecturer in Spanish and Latin American studies in the Department of Politics, Languages and International Studies at the University of Bath. He is the editor (with Gian Luca Gardini) of *Latin American Foreign Policies: Between Ideology and Pragmatism* (2011); (with Will Fowler) of *Political Violence and the Construction of National Identity in Latin America* (2006); and (with Andrew Nickson) of *Transition to Democracy in Paraguay* (1997).

Andrew Nickson is the honorary reader in public management and Latin American studies at the University of Birmingham. He is the author of *Local Government in Latin America* (1995); the *Historical Dictionary of Paraguay* (1993); and *Paraguay* (1987). He is the editor (with Peter Lambert) of *The Transition to Democracy in Paraguay* (1997).

Library of Congress Cataloging-in-Publication Data
The Paraguay reader : history, culture, politics /
Peter Lambert and Andrew Nickson, eds.
p. cm.—(The Latin America readers) (The world readers)
Includes bibliographical references and index.
ISBN 978-0-8223-5249-5 (cloth : alk. paper)
ISBN 978-0-8223-5268-6 (pbk. : alk. paper)
1. Paraguay—History. 2. Paraguay—Civilization. 3. Paraguay—Social life and customs. 4. Indians of South America—Paraguay. I. Lambert, Peter. II. Nickson, R. Andrew. III. Series: Latin America readers. IV. Series: World readers.
F2668.P255 2013
989.2—dc23
2012034780